Friends for Life

Other books by the same author

Advertising by Charities (editor)
Charity Annual Reports
*Relationship Fundraising: a Donor-based Approach to the
   Business of Raising Money*

Friends for Life

Relationship Fundraising in Practice

KEN BURNETT

The White Lion Press Limited London
in association with
The International Fund Raising Group London

Published by
The White Lion Press Limited
White Lion Court
7 Garrett Street
London EC1Y 0TY

In association with
The International Fund Raising Group
295 Kennington Road
London SE11 4QE

First printed 1996

Printed and bound in the United Kingdom by
H Charlesworth & Co Ltd, Huddersfield

Contents

Part III: What's next?

Acknowledgements

At first I had no intention of writing this or any other sequel to my 1992 publication, *Relationship Fundraising*. So this list of acknowledgements should start with a word or two for the sceptics and the doubters who, after reading that book, pressed me to go on and prove that the ideas I had put forward would actually work in practice. They may have done me a service, but it's been a painful one.

I do owe a debt of gratitude to many people who have helped me in preparing this book. Lists tend to be boring for everyone except those who are in them, so I hope the following people – who have all either taught me a lot or helped me significantly in forming my views on donor development – will all enjoy this hugely: Harold Sumption, Rich Fox, Per Stenbeck, Bernard Ross, Tony Elischer, David Ford, Stephen Lee, Harvey McKinnon, Redmond Mullin, Pegg Nadler, Judy Nichols, John Rodd, Tom Smith, Steve Thomas and Jennie Thompson.

All who contributed so generously with case material deserve thanks for their openness, frankness and willingness to spend time telling their stories and reviewing the relevant drafts of the manuscript. They include Sandra Byrd, Gwen Chapman, Angela Cluff and her colleagues at the NSPCC, Marion Cooper, Stewart Crocker, John Durham, Rich Fox (again), Sanchi Heesom, Karl Holweger, Darren Instrall, Vickie Kemp, Roger Lawson, David Love, Judith McNeill, Tom McSorley, Tony Manwaring, Annie Moreton, Valerie Morton, Hilary Partridge, Giles Pegram, Simon Pell, Jackie Petras, Frank Smith, Lawrence Stroud, Ian Ventham, Daryl Upsall and colleagues Minnie Landin, Jasna Sonne and Sarah Woodward from Greenpeace International and numerous others throughout the Greenpeace world, David Watson and Ana White. Thanks too are due to the many donors who have provided their views, as donor quotes.

I have quoted from several valuable publications, particularly *Designs for Fundraising* by Harold J (Si) Seymour (McGraw-Hill), *Understanding Organizations* (Penguin) and various other works by Professor Charles B Handy, *Total Customer Satisfaction* by Jacques Horovitz and Michele Jurgens Panak (Financial Times/Pitman), *Influence* by Robert Cialdini (Quill Books), *The One-to-One Future* by Don Peppers and Martha Rogers (Piatkus Publishers), *Relationship Marketing* by Regis McKenna (Addison-Wesley), *Made in America* (Minerva) by Bill Bryson, and everything else I can find that he's written, and the US journal *The Chronicle of Philanthropy*. These were a great help and I am very grateful to them all.

Ian Ventham and Giles Pegram should be singled out for particularly grateful praise for their additional efforts in reading the draft manuscript, correcting all my errors and oversights and then writing their superb foreword. I know it was very hard work. That they undertook their tasks without murmur or complaint, at least to me, shows their great commitment to the voluntary sector.

Readers might be forgiven for raising an eyebrow at the number of times the North London firm of Burnett Associates is mentioned as the direct marketing agency of some of the charities featured in the case histories. The less charitable might conclude that this entire book is merely a piece of naked self-promotion for me and my agency.

Well I certainly didn't do it to get rich from book sales so I have to admit a degree of self-interest here. But I have tried to keep this to a minimum and I freely confess that there are other agencies every bit as dedicated to donor development as we are. In Britain there are several I could mention by name, but it's my book so I'm not going to.

Readers of George Smith's book *Asking Properly: the Art of Creative Fundraising* may notice more than just a touch of consensus between us when comparing some of his conclusions in that book with some of mine. This is not merely coincidence, but neither is it plagiarism. We do work together. We have developed legacy and committed giving campaigns together for various organisations around the world. We were also writing our respective manuscripts at approximately the same time. And we agree. Innocent the overlap certainly is, and it is also minimal. I can recommend anyone to get a hold of his excellent and entertaining book. There isn't anything better anywhere on creativity in fundraising.

I am very fortunate that my colleagues at Burnett Associates are tolerant and understanding enough to have allowed me the time and space to abandon real work for weeks at a time to wrestle with this book. Their competence and willingness to shoulder extra work are sometimes unacknowledged by me, but never unappreciated. Individually and collectively they all contributed hugely to this book, as many of the case histories will show. There are now too many to mention individually here, but I wish to say thanks in particular to Fay Buller and Celia Cole for managing the production process so smoothly, and to Jackie Fowler, Ernst Goetschi, Derek Humphries, Rachel Kempster, Richard Berry, Patricia Collins, Jackie Donnellan, Kate Mazur (for her spelling), Marc Nohr and George Smith, all of whom helped me a lot.

Derek, Marc and Jackie contributed great chunks of the writing, which made my life much easier and happier. Marc and Derek also acted as referees, marking the manuscript and suggesting areas for improvement.

The cover design is the work of Roy Williams and Lawrence Bradbury. I have worked with Roy for 22 years now and have often benefited from his brilliance. The hands on the cover this time belong to Cath Parrott and Roy Williams. The text and illustration pages were designed and laid out by Jane Fricker and Ernest Muller. They had the Herculean task of assembling all the text into pages, and could easily have complained more than they did. As editor in chief Marie Burnett worked harder than anyone to make this book excellent. Its quality of

production and professional appearance are more of a
credit to her than me.

It took me a long time to put this book together and
often I felt like giving up. That I didn't is largely due to the
unfailing support and encouragement of my wife, Marie.
And also of course to my mum and dad, who taught me
that if you believe something is right you should stick with
it, come what may.

This book is dedicated to all who gave so selflessly of
their time, commitment and professionalism. Thanks.

Ken Burnett
Kermarquer
France
September 1996

Foreword

What is relationship fundraising, has it made a difference, and where are we now? Over to two self-confessed exponents – Ian Ventham and Giles Pegram.

GP: So, Ken Burnett has asked us to write a joint foreword for this new book of his...

IV: What on earth is a joint foreword?

GP: Joint views? Differing views? I don't know. He's said it's entirely up to us. So what did you think of the book?

IV: Well, it really clarifies the fact that relationship fundraising is a philosophy, not a science.

GP: When *Relationship Fundraising* first came out, the concept was seen as wonderful manna from heaven and in many cases was almost applied mechanically, without thinking. And the whole point is that it *shouldn't* be mechanical. It's got to be a way of life, that leads to a way of dealing individually with particular donors and their relationship with the charity.

IV: We talk sometimes about 'donors' as if they were a species in the zoo, to be prodded and admired. But, of course, they're all very different people with different views, and I suspect they'd be horrified if they knew books had been written about their behaviour!

One of the common misconceptions many people had with *Relationship Fundraising* was that they assumed it to mean that every one of your donors, whether you have 250 or 250,000 of them, had to have a deep and meaningful relationship with the charity. So we should all put huge resources into developing those relationships. Whereas in fact, many of our donors actually have a very distant relationship with the charity – and that's what they want.

Some donors *will* want a deep meaningful relationship, and we should nurture them that way. But others will not. Half the time, I suspect they've forgotten they're actually donors at all. And that's fine, if that's what they want. We can do a bit to nurture the relationship, but actually we should bear in mind that they want to remain distant, and respect that.

GP: I have an elderly aunt and I send her a postcard once a year from my holiday. She sends me a nice present at Christmas, and I send her a really well-worded thank you letter. And that relationship suits us both perfectly. If I were to try to push that relationship, I think she'd feel smothered.

IV: And you'd destroy it.

GP: Absolutely.

IV: Also, of course, it's got to be cost-effective, hasn't it? At a certain level, the value of the relationship is such that you can't afford to put vast resources into developing it. So it's a gentle, nurturing process rather than a huge resource-led one

GP: And ultimately, relationship fundraising is only a means to an end. It's a means to help us, as fundraisers, raise more money in the longer term. It isn't something we do for its own sake because it's a nice idea, because it makes us feel warmer. We do it because in the long term it's going to maximise the lifetime value we get from the donor.

IV: But that also highlights the dilemma that we all

constantly face. While we can aspire to relationship building in the longer term, we can all be blown off course by the urgent need to raise short-term cash.

GP: Yes: I think that I'm a relationship fundraiser – and yet, as you pointed out, it's still just theory in a sense, because our trustees want to see quarterly or yearly results. So we say we want to build relationships, but what we really want to do is produce as much cash as possible this year...

IV: ...and somehow develop relationships in the longer term as well.

One will always work against the other. You need courage to take the long view: how do you fight off the need for short-term gain? How do you fight off the trustees' need to see that you're still at the top of the league?

GP: I can see another book coming – *Relationship Fundraising for Trustees.* But I think you're right. Until trustees understand the difference between long- and short-term relationships, then we can only play at it...

IV: So has relationship fundraising made a difference, then?

GP: I can certainly pinpoint actual significant donations we've received in the last few years that I'm certain would not have come in unless we'd been using the philosophy expounded in *Relationship Fundraising.*

IV: Yes: back in the eighties we had a huge burst of enthusiasm for adopting commercial direct marketing techniques in the fundraising sector. It took us a long time to realise that they must be tempered with a quite distinct charitable flavour. I think Ken's first book did a lot to help that change in thinking.

GP: His book was *about* that change in thinking – and that's why, when people talk about relationship fundraising as a fashion, I don't agree. It's not a process, it is a way of life that debunks technique. It sees techniques solely as serving your relationship with your donor.

IV: ...and not an end in itself. Thanks to Ken's book the formulaic approach – you know, 'we can send our donors 12 mailings a year' – is now out of the window. But what do you think the new book adds?

GP: *Relationship Fundraising* was very concerned with principles. It was a bit like hearing Bernard Ross talk – or George Smith – you feel good at the end of it but you can't actually remember what it is you're supposed to do!

Whereas the great thing about *this* book, is that it is absolutely rooted in real experience, and full of practical examples. As I read it, I was constantly thinking, 'that's me'. So I think this book is more helpful because the reader will come away with a list of more things he or she can actually do tomorrow...

IV: ...rather than just hypothetical notions. Yes, I agree. I think Ken is exemplifying the issues he raised in *Relationship Fundraising*, with some particularly good examples from a variety of very different causes.

GP: And it's not just 'the NSPCC did 1, 2, 3 and became donor-led' – you get it warts and all, with all the personalities and the difficulties explained.

By showing how other people have done it – what's worked, what hasn't – this book will help people not just to have ideas, but to have an approach that they can apply to their own organisation.

IV: And I do think it's important that the ideas expounded in *Relationship Fundraising* have got to actually permeate right through your organisation. Even if your job is driving a van for the charity, you're actually a visible part of the charity and therefore you have a part to play in relationship building.

I'll give you an example. We had a couple of mechanics who were off duty one working day but happened to be wearing their RNLI overalls. They were seen repairing a car all day and we got a complaint about it – that our staff were wasting RNLI time and resources. They weren't, but they'd been identified as RNLI and somebody went away quite miffed that their donation was being wasted.

GP: So your relationship fundraising is only as good as your weakest staff having a bad day.

IV: So what are we saying?

GP: I think we've said it.

IV: It's a philosophy, not a science. It's an evolutionary process. It's got to be donor-led, so the relationship may be very distant – if that's what the donor wants. Or very close – if that's what the donor wants. It's not an intensely meaningful relationship with every donor all the time.

We're beginning to espouse relationship fundraising, and it's beginning to permeate our organisations. But we're deflected from the philosophy by short-term, cash-driven needs; by people who don't perceive themselves as part of the fundraising process and therefore don't embrace the philosophy; and by misinterpretation of the philosophy.

But that doesn't invalidate the philosophy at all; far from it. It's something we should endeavour to take right into the heart of our organisations. And in 10 years' time we'll be even better at it.

GP: Also it isn't a philosophy that Ken invented. It's been around for a very long time and Ken happened to be in the right place to write the right book at the right time. Now, having put relationship fundraising on the map, he's gone through the case histories and come up with good and not so good examples in a really helpful way.

IV: I have to say that even since reading the manuscript, I've implemented one change in my organisation; something from *Friends for Life* struck a chord and I changed a particular procedure the next day.

GP: Well, it's been very interesting talking to you, but what on earth are we going to do about the foreword for this book?

IV: Leave it to somebody else to write.

London
August 1996

Ian Ventham is head of fundraising and direct marketing at the Royal National Lifeboat Institution, Poole, Dorset.
Giles Pegram is deputy director and director of appeals at the National Society for the Prevention of Cruelty to Children, London EC2.

Introduction

Death of a salesman

 Our earth is degenerate in these latter days. Bribery and corruption are common. Children no longer obey their parents. Everyone wants to write a book... The end of the world is evidently approaching.

On a stone slab carved in Assyria
in the year 2800 BC

Fundraising at the turn of the twentieth century is clearly a business undergoing rapid and substantial change. Despite its claim to be the second oldest profession – fundraising is mentioned in the Bible and there are records of professional fundraisers (and fundraising improprieties) going back to the Middle Ages – fundraising's emergence as a modern commercial activity is very recent. Most of its important developments have occurred in rapid succession within the last two decades or so.

Dramatic changes are still the norm in fundraising and the pace of change seems likely to be maintained for the foreseeable future.

If the 1980s were the decade when mass marketing first made its gigantic impact on fundraising, then the 1990s are likely to be recalled as the decade of donor and supporter relationships. It is not, I believe, that the second directly replaced the first, rather that in the 1990s professional fundraisers became more actively aware that their business is uniquely long term and that with few exceptions they were not in the business of making a quick sale. I say uniquely because I am unaware of any other business sector where it is necessary to wait until after one's best customers have died before benefiting from (and sometimes even knowing of) their most substantial transaction. But it is so with fundraising. Although most of their *real* customers only become so comparatively late in life, the benefits of a fundraiser's care and service will very often take the rest of the customer's lifetime – and beyond – to be realised.

So fundraising is definitely not the business of the quick sell. In recent years the more far-sighted of fundraisers have increasingly emphasised the long-term nature of their business when preparing their marketing strategies, as the realisation has grown that strong, mutually beneficial relationships are the foundations of their business.

My book *Relationship Fundraising: a Donor-based Approach to the Business of Raising Money* unashamedly capitalised on this increasingly obvious trend. The book was the expression of concern I was feeling at the time that professional fundraising was in danger of losing its way amid mass-marketing techniques that were anathema to the majority of real donors; that hard-sell fundraisers risked losing the feel-good factor on which good fundraising so depends. It was also my attempt to set down some of the main components of developing effective long-term relationships with that unusual and very special group of people we know as donors. Although illustrated by brief examples and anecdotes, it is essentially a book concerned with the theory – or rather with the philosophy or attitude – that lies behind what I suspect is *every* fundraiser's approach to relationship fundraising. I didn't invent it. I just decided that it was time someone wrote about it, and that it might as well be me.

Rather than set out to create a new theology, *Relationship Fundraising* merely tried to illustrate and predict the practical benefits that would follow if a certain approach were to be adopted.

It only partly succeeded. While it has undoubtedly built up quite a following, one or two readers somewhat missed the point and others have expressed some misgivings about the central idea.

For many fundraisers the idea of building relationships with vague, long-term objectives seemed much more comfortable and attractive than the hectic commercial world of target-driven sales campaigns. They mistakenly perceived relationship fundraising as a fashionable soft option. That wasn't what I had in mind. The book also left a number of others wondering if relationship fundraising was not a rather cosy and possibly expensive self-indulgence and whether or not it could have direct and quantifiable financial benefits when put into practice.

So *Friends for Life: Relationship Fundraising in Practice* is my attempt to provide an answer to the question, 'does relationship fundraising work?' This may be trying to quantify the unquantifiable and so may be doomed from the outset. I have never pretended relationship fundraising is easy and I know it is not cheap or quick, but my experience is increasingly leading me to believe what I instinctively felt from the beginning: that in most situations relationship fundraising pays off. This book doesn't prove that conclusively, so you must form your own opinion. I hope that it will at least make fundraisers think about the consequences of developing donor relationships and that those who are practising what they believe to be relationship fundraising will document their performance so that further evidence may be provided at a later date. There is much yet to learn.

This book is deliberately a sequel. Writing a second book on the same subject is rather like having a second baby, or, as Oscar Wilde believed, like entering into a second marriage (which Wilde described as a triumph of hope over experience). I know from young Charlie Burnett that second children are a delight, but I wouldn't blame any mother who after her first experience of childbirth declared: 'never, ever again'. It's a sentiment felt, perhaps less emphatically but no less deeply, by writers of books on heavyweight subjects like relationship fundraising. But time has a way of fooling the memory and hope usually does triumph over experience. No book is easy to write but I have found this one especially difficult, perhaps because the questions that confronted me have no easy answers.

Experience teaches everyone

In order for it to be different from and independent of the first, this sequel sets out to introduce the reader to practical examples of relationship fundraising. Consequently, it is dominated by real case histories and people other than me do most of the talking.

The case histories are deliberately detailed. It's my experience that fundraisers don't just want to know the essentials of a case, they want to know what it felt like, what was behind the thinking, what distinguishes and flavours the case. So I don't apologise for what some will consider gratuitous colour and non-essential verbiage.

They are also deliberately unstructured. If you don't find any one of them interesting, or relevant then you can easily jump along to the next.

I have included among the case histories shorter examples from the United States and one from Canada. I am sure there are at least as many innovative instances of relationship fundraising to be found there as anywhere. These cases however are generally more concise, not because they are any less noteworthy but because they are not part of my personal experience so I couldn't easily embroider them as I have the others. I am sorry not to be able to include cases from continental Europe and other parts of the world. That there are many I am sure.

As to the style of writing, I apologise to my American friends, collaborators and readers for my decision to stick mainly to English English throughout this book. I am a recent convert to the contribution American English has made to international linguistic colour, so I am well aware it is far more than just a corrupted version of the original. But this book is published in London, so English English is what you get.

All of the people I interviewed for this book agreed to be open, honest and candid about their thinking, methods, results and experiences and I am grateful to them for their candour as well as their time.

I am a great believer in trying to learn from mistakes as my experience is that failure is often at least as good a teacher as success. In Ithaca, New York State in the USA, a museum of failures has been started, The New Product Showcase and Learning Center, which under one roof houses thousands of exhibits of failed products and ideas that bombed. Curiously at a time when more conventional museums are having difficulty in charging even a few dollars' admission, this monument to failure charges $1,500 just for entry and is reporting a roaring trade. Why? Because commercial enterprises are becoming increasingly aware that they can learn at least as much from a product that failed as they can from one that succeeded.

The heart of this philosophy

Other than acknowledging my indebtedness to the many people who have helped in the preparation of this book, my original inclination was to pass directly on to those case histories, but I can't do that without some explanation of the background to relationship fundraising and the approach that lies at the heart of it.

I have also chosen to use this sequel to update some of the thinking I expressed in *Relationship Fundraising* and to add comment on some new areas that now, to me, seem important. I'll forgive any readers who feel they've had enough theory and want to skip straight to the practical examples, the case histories.

On page 48 of *Relationship Fundraising* I defined the concept as follows:

> Relationship fundraising is an approach to the marketing of a cause that centres not around raising money but on developing to its full potential the unique and special relationship that exists between a charity and its supporter. Whatever strategies and techniques are employed to boost funds, the overriding consideration in relationship fundraising is to care for and develop that special bond and not to do anything that might damage or jeopardise it. In relationship fundraising every activity of the organisation is therefore geared towards making donors feel important, valued and considered. In this way relationship fundraising will ensure more funds per donor in the long term.

Long-winded, isn't it? Unfortunately I haven't come up with a more concise definition since and, worse still, I want to enlarge a little on this description because I think many other qualities and attributes are needed if relationship fundraising is to work really well. At its best, a commitment to relationship fundraising goes hand in hand with that other essential of fundraising, commitment to the cause.

People who think deeply and care deeply about what they do evolve a complex philosophy about their work, particularly when that work is the promotion of a cause in which they believe passionately. That philosophy will be more powerful than logic and will be heavily interlaced with emotion. Most fundraising offices are emotional places in which to work. This is good because employees find it impossible to be indifferent and, as any fundraising director knows, the essence of successful fundraising is that belief in, passion for and commitment to the cause must be ingrained without exception throughout the fundraising department. Indeed, they should be ingrained throughout the whole organisation.

It follows that any fundraiser not wholly committed to the cause should be weeded out.

An emerging controversy

Concerns expressed about the basic concepts of relationship fundraising have mainly been variations on a few consistent themes: it's too costly, it's unrealistic, donors might not want a relationship and so forth.

I think these are all valid views and I try to remind the worried people who propound them that I don't necessarily subscribe to a contrary view to theirs just because, some time ago, I wrote a book about the subject. Opinions can change. And anyway, even if they have read my book the chances are that their memory of what's in it isn't infallible.

My opinions have modified and I hope matured in some areas over the past few years, but I have no worries about relationship fundraising's meaning and practicality. My advice to those who do would be: by all means take the subject seriously but please don't get carried away. Relationship fundraising is not a panacea. It is simply a donor-based approach to fundraising. There are several other approaches and in some circumstances these may work better, or more quickly, or more surely. Or they may not.

A hotbed of consent

When I wrote *Relationship Fundraising* in 1992 I had quite modest aims for the book. I hoped that at least 50 people would buy a copy – the 50 people I wanted to be clients of my company, the London-based advertising and marketing agency Burnett Associates, during the next 10 years or so. I justified this selfish motive by thinking that I deserved some benefit, as writing that book was quite hard work.

In the event *Relationship Fundraising* sold rather better than I had expected. It is now in its third printing, has sold in at least 35 countries and seems to have enjoyed generally favourable comment.

Certainly it seems to have spawned some debate and that can only be a good thing. At ICFM's* 1995 National

*The Institute of Charity Fundraising Managers, the equivalent organisation in the UK to America's National Society of Fund Raising Executives.

Fundraisers' Convention, in Birmingham, a fringe meeting was devoted to discussing relationship fundraising. Despite its absence from the official programme, this event was even better attended than many of the other sessions.

I stood at the back listening with some amusement as various speakers wrestled with their interpretations of the concept and how its application as originally expounded had been used or misused. Sometimes I found it hard to recognise what was being discussed. Defence of the concept vastly outweighed the criticisms, however, and several misunderstandings were amicably cleared up. If the organisers had anticipated a hotbed of dissent they would have been disappointed for there have been fewer more consentient and trouble-free gatherings. In the end I confessed that I believed relationship fundraising was not an exact science, that many people's thinking, including my own, had moved on since 1992 and that if anyone, anywhere, had any right to be heartily sick of the wretched and overused phrase it was me.

So I have very little time for those who regard relationship fundraising as a theology, or as a finite thing, or who believe there is a right or a wrong way to do it, whatever 'it' might be.

Relationship fundraising is at best an attitude of mind. Whether you call it donor care, or supporter loyalty, or donor development, or just common sense it all comes down to the same thing – a donor-based approach to the business of raising money.

That, by the way, was the subtitle to this book's predecessor. Perhaps I should have concentrated on the subtitle and left out the title – which I obviously borrowed from the then-fashionable concept of relationship marketing.

Of course, I wasn't alone in spotting this emerging fad. I fantasise that similar tomes have been produced: *Relationship Banking*, *Relationship Taxidermy*, *Relationship Dentistry*, *Relationship Counselling*, and so forth.

Seriously though, relationship banking is a far from novel

or obscure concept. Christopher Parkes, writing in the British financial daily the *Financial Times*, in December 1995, took pains to contrast the American and the German responses to a long-term international decline in the banking industry.

The American approach to the decline was to cut costs and streamline by reducing training and 'down-sizing'. The *California Management Review* was quoted as alleging US commercial banks had 'shifted away from customer cultivation towards an emphasis on customer acquisition'. In the process, Parkes said, the banks had lost contact with their most important source of marketing information – their customers.

The cunning Germans meanwhile had discovered relationship banking and, apparently, this focus had helped banking maintain a stable share of the financial services market despite all sorts of predatory threats and other nasties.

And while US banks were facing a variety of staff problems, including all their good bods being poached by outside firms, German staff turnover had fallen to seven per cent.

Won't buy? You're fired

Obviously we fundraisers must exercise great caution when attempting to learn from our more affluent brothers and sisters in more 'commercial' trade. Consider for example what the London *Times* reported in September 1995 as 'the latest idea in marketing' – sacking customers who don't generate enough profits. Some banks (them again) and stores in the United States (where else?) have apparently been writing to unprofitable customers telling them that their accounts are being closed.

This makes some sense, and may even be the logical flipside to true relationship marketing, ie a mutually beneficial relationship. 'It's as much about who you don't want a relationship with as who you do', asserts Professor Adrian Payne, a relationship marketing expert at the UK's Cranfield School of Management.

Fundraisers however would be wise to think twice before taking overt action on this advice. I am not such an enthusiast for relationship fundraising that I have stopped believing that *every* gift, however small, is important and valuable to our cause (and worth saying a sincere 'thanks' for).

Welcome change

Thankfully, fundraising is changing all the time. The not-for-profit sector continues to grow and to improve. The human values and relationships that underpin fundraising may be unchanging, but new techniques, technologies and ideas are enabling us to continuously rethink the ways in which we communicate with donors and so improve how we promote what we do. It is a time for great invention. We want change, and constantly. There's no guarantee that what worked last month will work as well in the next. We can never say that what worked fabulously for one organisation will not be a dismal failure for another.

That's why the field of fundraising is so varied and exciting now. And why concepts such as relationship fundraising are worth revisiting and challenging from time to time.

But some fundraisers at that meeting in Birmingham back in 1995 did seem to have taken it all very literally. Several were worried that some donors might not want a relationship with them. Others were, rightly, anxious that fundraisers might abuse the relationship, so should donors be protected, and how? And anyway was it really possible to have any kind of deep and meaningful relationship with hundreds of thousands of donors through the post?

These concerns seem to centre around the words I chose to describe the concept. 'Relationship fundraising' has become a fashionable piece of jargon. It could just as easily have been called a variety of other names, such as those mentioned on page 8. But I don't think 'donor care', or 'supporter loyalty', or 'donor development' would have sold as well.

So why this sequel?

This book does not set out to be the definitive guide to relationship fundraising. I would find that quite impossible. Although the phrase is now widely used, people often mean different things when they use it and if one person's idea is different from another's that doesn't mean it is either better or worse.

So there are no 'right or wrong ways' in this book. There is no attempt to state what is good or bad relationship fundraising. Nor are any of the examples in this book intended to present the only, or even the best, way to put relationship fundraising into practice. They are merely the experiences and observations of some of those who have tried to be donor-oriented and are included here simply to explain how others have fared. And just because an organisation is featured here describing one aspect of its fundraising doesn't mean it is a paragon of relationship fundraising in all – or even in any other – aspects.

In fundraising, as long as you have a firm grasp of the fundamentals, it pays to be flexible and to constantly modify your approach. I hope this new book will clarify and expand upon some of my earlier concepts and that some of the ideas and experiences described here will contribute to the neverending and very valuable process of change and take it forward.

Other people's money

At the end of the day, relationship fundraising is all about money. Other people's money. Lots of it. Ever increasing amounts of it. Doing lots and lots of good.

In the opening sequence of the film *Other People's Money* (Warner Bros, 1991) the predatory financier Garfield, played by Danny De Vito, explains why he loves money so much.

> It doesn't care whether I'm good or not. It doesn't care whether I snore or not, it doesn't care which god I pray to. There are only three things in this world with that kind of unconditional acceptance – dogs, doughnuts* and money. Only money is better. Because money doesn't make you fat and it doesn't poop all over the living-room floor.

There's only one thing Garfield likes better than his money and that is, inevitably, other people's money.

But De Vito's Garfield is obviously dangerously deranged. He cares more about money than about the things it can buy. The only good he wants to do is for himself. For him money is not a means to an end, it is an end in itself. And he doesn't care who gets upset in his remorseless drive to get hold of it.

Although he was pretty good at making money, Garfield would have been a rotten relationship fundraiser.

Every fundraiser knows that fundraising is not just about raising money. It's about meeting needs, it's about work that needs doing, it's about ideals, it's about passionate conviction and being a catalyst for change – change for the better. For fundraisers money is simply a means to a variety of important and socially justifiable ends. It is a barometer of success, a convenient and convertible way of measuring and translating achievement.

In fundraising, as in financing, no goods change hands. In fundraising no direct benefits are offered, or if they are, their value in exchange is almost always just a fraction of their apparent costs. Any benefits a fundraiser gives are more as an encouragement than a reason to give. Fundraisers don't sell. They influence, facilitate, or inspire a voluntary gift. They prompt giving, or they help donors to plan their giving. The strategies and the tactics they deploy

*Garfield is addicted to doughnuts.

may be every bit as complex and cunning as the machinations of financiers like Garfield, or as wheedling and persuasive as the best professional salesperson, but the essential difference is that to be successful they require the willing and voluntary compliance of their prospects. Fundraising nowadays is not a business for quick hits and one-off hoodwinking. To be viable in the late 1990s fundraisers need that willing compliance over a very long period of time. To be really successful we need sustained and enthusiastic commitment from donors. Fundraisers today increasingly realise this and are becoming increasingly skilled at generating it.

But fundraising success is still measured in money. In the final analysis, it is about money. And relationship fundraising is no exception.

Relationship fundraising is about other people's money. Lots and lots of it, freely and gladly given. Coming again and again, growing ever more generous and doing rather a lot of good along the way, for the receiver, for the giver and for the causes they both believe in so passionately.

But if relationship fundraising doesn't lead to more of other people's money, lots more of other people's money, then I'll be the first to accept that it just doesn't work.

That's what this book is about.

Part I:
Fundamentals
of relationship
fundraising

Brilliant return of service

Keeping the customer satisfied

I have a fixation about donor service mainly because in our business it is so important and because in my experience fundraisers everywhere are generally rather bad at it. I'm sorry to have to say this, but it is true. It's not that most fundraisers don't know what they should do, it's just that so often they don't seem to even think about it. I am convinced that this is a costly and debilitating oversight and I am dedicated to seeing it change.

The giving of a charitable gift is a voluntary and sacrificial action. Because of this, we fundraisers have the best of all reasons for ensuring we are as encouraging as possible to donors, particularly at the start of the relationship.

Relationship fundraising may be a little over-ambitious for many of today's fundraisers for their donor development practices are still in the fundraising Dark Ages. If the objective of donor development is to create friends for life by building a close and mutually satisfying relationship, these fundraisers – and they include some of the largest and best-known charities and not-for-profits in Britain, the USA and elsewhere – have not yet got to the stage of saying 'hello' properly. The customer-service culture in charities today, if it exists at all, is at its best inconsistent and at its worst depressing, unhelpful and off-putting.

The truth is that our donors are much more likely to experience good, efficient, planned, friendly customer service at the hands of their bank, or their favourite airline, or their petrol company, even their local McDonald's, than they are likely to experience at the hands of their favourite charity.

If you think this judgement is a little harsh, here is a simple test you can do yourself from the comfort of your own home or office to find out how fundraisers normally communicate with their donors.

I call them road tests. The term, I think, comes from motoring magazines who periodically take car manufacturers' products on the road and put them through a carefully structured and rigorous series of tests. The resulting write-up gives the enthusiastic motoring public an unbiased evaluation of the chosen model's performance in a comprehensive range of real-life situations, while providing the magazine's publisher with a cheap and easy source of editorial.

What works for motor cars can be, and is, also applied to a whole range of other products from washing machines and hair dryers to compact discs and computer games. For some reason they are still referred to as road tests. For years a variety of popular journals have road-tested all sorts of things and some magazines – such as the Consumers Association's *Which?* – devote almost all their editorial to them. *Popular Woodworking* magazine will road-test glues, varnishes and jigsaw blades, while *Direct Response* magazine has road-tested mailing houses, telephone answering services and suppliers' response times.

It was this latter activity that gave me the idea. My road tests are perhaps somewhat less rigorous and scientific than the original variety but they are no less instructive and can be great fun. I first used the road test in the early 1980s to test how charities responded to a request for their annual report. The results were appalling (*see* my book *Charity Annual Reports*, page 7, Directory of Social Change, London, 1987).

Making people up

Here I have to make a confession. I have a habit of inventing donors. Readers who have read *Relationship Fundraising* may remember the donor profiles that appear at the end of each chapter. Someone once asked me why, when preparing these donor profiles, I hadn't included a photograph of each of the donors that I'd featured there.

I had to admit that I couldn't because these people don't exist.

However, I did seek to justify myself by saying that I do know a lot of real donors who are very like my imaginary creations. And there's no law against inventing donors. They are an essential part of the road test.

So for that initial test, some 42 of the major British charities received a phone call from an apparently typical potential customer – a woman 'supporter' requesting a copy of the organisation's annual report and explaining rather convincingly why she wanted it.

Many of those who answered the phone appeared unaware of what an annual report is, and few gave the impression of having been trained to deal with such a request. Several passed the buck to someone else. Some organisations appeared to resent the call. Others asked the caller to pay for the report first. Most simply appeared uninterested. Indifference, real or imagined, is invariably the greatest enemy of customer service.

Many of those who promised to post a copy didn't do so. Most had no covering letter. What follow-up there was, without exception, was poor and inconsistent.

And when the annual reports did arrive they were generally of such low quality that my tester claimed 'most were fit only for the waste-paper bin'.

I later used the results of this experience to demonstrate to fundraisers the price of failure to make good use of their annual report and the opportunity this presented to produce a good one and ensure its efficient and effective deployment.

The effect was startling. Fundraisers everywhere rushed to improve their annual reports, perhaps partly due to the increasing professionalism that was occurring anyway throughout fundraising in the 1980s and partly because Britain's Institute of Chartered Accountants was offering the annual charities accounts award – with a cash prize of £1,000. But also, I suspect, because they didn't want me or my likes to hold their annual report up before their peers as a fine example of how *not* to do it.

Flushed with this evidence of the effectiveness of fundraising road tests, I turned my attentions to donor relationship building by post (better known to most readers as fundraising by direct mail).

The analogy in the spam

In a recent fundraising seminar on the subject of customer service I indulged myself by showing my audience a clip from the *Monty Python* television series. This was the famous spam sketch – or rather the infamous spam sketch.

In this seminar I claimed that the *Monty Python* spam sketch is in fact an analogy, a metaphor for donor service in this modern age. If you don't remember this vintage piece of television and can't borrow it from anyone then I will attempt the near impossible and try to describe it. If you do, or if you can, then skip the next few paragraphs.

The spam sketch takes place in a sordid but typically

British café – perhaps 'caff' is more appropriate. (I'll leave out the bits about the Vikings, the chicken and the Hungarian because they will just complicate matters.) A run-down, seedy waitress is reciting her menu to some newly arrived customers, a middle-aged couple. The trouble is, everything on the menu consists of varying quantities of spam (a block of processed meat popular in Britain in the days of post-war austerity). On informing the woman she can't have anything without spam, the waitress eventually condescends that she can have spam, spam, spam, chips, egg and spam 'because that hasn't got a lot of spam in it'.

'But I don't like spam', wails the woman, to totally indifferent and apparently deaf ears. Her husband chips in to point out that he loves spam and explains that he's having spam, spam, spam, spam, spam, baked beans and spam and he'll have her spam too if she'll just stop making a fuss.

It is an extreme example of the strangeness of British humour as well as the British public's seemingly endless tolerance of rudeness and poor service – and I accept that it loses something in the telling. But the *Monty Python* spam sketch does make some valuable points that should not be overlooked by fundraisers.

The spam sketch shows clearly that customers – or, in our case, donors – are often noisy, inconsiderate and unruly. They behave strangely. They have weird and outlandish tastes. They shout. They sometimes just won't do what they're told. Obviously, sometimes, they simply don't know what's good for them.

At other times, like the husband in the spam sketch, they can be the exact opposite. They can be extremely amenable. Really rather nice, likeable, helpful and easy to deal with.

But the waitress, or cook, or whatever she is, treats everybody the same: with equal contempt and equal aggression.

In the café in this sketch, any behaviour is forgiveable as long as you like spam. But the crucial thing to realise is that despite the gloomy surroundings, despite the greasy, dismal decor and the dire, dreadful waitress, the punters will probably come back again and again to this awful place for just one reason – they really like spam.

In my analogy, of course, the middle-aged customers are obviously the donors, the waitress is the fundraiser and the dismal greasy café is the typical British charity.

But there is also the *analogy in the spam*.

Whereas the dreary café can tempt its customers to come back again and again with the lure of spam, we fundraisers can offer no such inducement.

Anyway, enough of *Monty Python*. Personally, I love spam and I am also very fond of charities and of fundraisers, and I'm more than a little anxious about how badly we sometimes treat our customers – our donors.

Enter Myles Barnett and friends

For years I have collected examples of the great and the gruesome in fundraising direct mail. From time to time I find something that really works. Occasionally I even come across something that moves me. At times I have seen examples of truly excellent communications from fundraisers, fundraising communications so good that I have thought 'I wish I had done that'. But most of what comes my way is mechanical and dull – definitely not worth collecting. These mailings are the products of followers of a formula who are doing little more than going through the motions of providing the mass of their recipients with a letter, a leaflet and a reply form, inhabited by some pictures and lots of words that say a great deal but convey very little.

Every now and again, of course, one comes across a real stonker, a turkey, the fundraising piece that is so bad, so off target, so inept that it is comic-tragic – and well worth saving on slide for the next fundraising seminar.

Such examples, which sadly for me but happily for most donors are becoming increasingly rare, have included

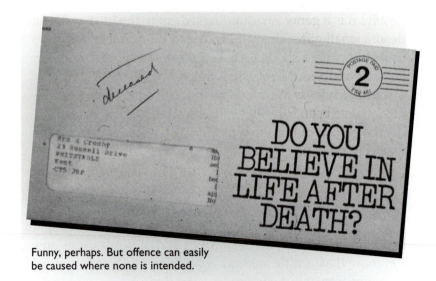

Funny, perhaps. But offence can easily
be caused where none is intended.

amusing misspellings, grotesque gimmickry, insensitive
salutation, berserk overuse of computer identification
numbers, multiple mailings of supposedly personal
invitations and lots of other sins, including the classic legacy
mailing with the strident message 'do you believe in life
after death?' emblazoned across its front that had been
returned marked 'deceased' alongside the recipient's
address. (I have on slide a French fundraising mailing that
allocates its recipient a computer code 42 digits long. Yet
eight digits provide more than enough opportunity to
allocate an individual number to every living soul in France.
Ten numbers would cover everyone in the world nearly
twice – so why 42? The French taxman is even worse. He
gives me 46.)

Funny, of course, but also irritating and insulting to
donors and ultimately counter-productive. But most
communications of this type (except those from the taxman)
are examples of unsolicited mail and generally can be
discarded. They represent only one facet of how charities
communicate with their donors.

To find out more about some of the other facets, please
meet Myles K Barnett of Finsbury Park, North London.

Myles is a generous chap. A few years ago he decided to send a small gift – £5 – to 50 of the top fundraising charities in Britain with a short, friendly letter requesting some information about their work. Now you will realise this was a set-up. Myles is me, and vice versa. But he could just as easily have been Mr or Mrs Typical Donor.

The results of this philanthropy were startling. Myles started to receive quite a lot of postal communications

Myles is clearly a donor with potential.

Myles K Barnett
9 Somerfield Road
London N4 2JN

October 1993

To XYZ Charity

Dear Sirs

Please find enclosed a small donation of £5.00 to help you in your important work.

I would be grateful to know more about your organisation and hope to be able to help you again in the future.

Yours faithfully

Myles K Barnett

from Britain's leading fundraisers. A trickle at first that within weeks had grown to a flood. In fact Myles had never been so popular. Myles's brief existence was solely for this test, yet two and a half years later he was still getting more mail than me. In just a couple of months, Myles's postbag filled a large cardboard box.

Since sending that letter, Myles has collected enough mail to fill several waste-paper baskets. He has been written to by finance directors, appeals officers, donations secretaries, chairmen, and even computers. One letter sent to Myles was actually signed by the general administrative secretary, fundraising/direct marketing. Pretty important people, these fundraisers.

Within a few months Myles had already received seven appeals from one major charity, who shall remain nameless.

Only the lonely

Undoubtedly Myles's benevolent gesture towards Britain's biggest fundraisers resulted in his receiving some interesting communications. He found himself confronted by a bewildering array of opportunities – invitations to flag days, questionnaires, preprinted receipts, receipts with appeals, appeals and more appeals, loads of newsletters, catalogues, annual reviews, annual reports, brochures, leaflets and more leaflets. He was even sent one leaflet explaining how to cross the road with a guide dog. In all, a confusing plethora.

If you are lonely, or don't get out much, sending a fiver to the top 50 charities might be just what you need. Otherwise it could be a bit of a pain.

The volume and variety of Myles's mail reflected the scale and diversity of a clearly flourishing voluntary sector, or at least the larger players within it. But Myles got quite a few things he hadn't expected, including being addressed by several charities as if he were female. His own fault, perhaps, as Myles is, apparently, an ambiguous name. But that doesn't explain why one leading child-care organisation addressed him first as Mr and later, without any reference to poor Myles, changed his sex, to Ms. Many charities played safe and left gender out of their salutations while others wrote to 'Dear Sir/Madam' and gave Myles the chance to choose.

He was also awarded strings of computer numbers before and after his name by nearly all his new friends, received some communications so pale he felt tempted to send another fiver asking that it be spent on a new typewriter ribbon, and he got lots of form letters and endless numbers of appeals. One charity seemed a trifle over the top when it wrote 'I appreciate your unwavering help'. Even more so was the message on the envelope of another that read 'You held my hand when my husband was dying'. Myles had, after all, just once given them each £5.

Rascals

Three charities subsequently sent Myles appeals even though they hadn't been on the top 50 list. They might otherwise have got away with it had Myles existed in any form prior to his creation – like Frankenstein's monster – solely for the purpose of road-testing Britain's biggest (but not necessarily best) fundraising organisations.

These three rascal fundraisers could have acquired Myles's name by only one means – reciprocal mailings, list exchanges with some organisation or organisations in the top 50, but not one committed to direct mail fair play and the code of practice that decrees donors should first be given the chance to opt out of reciprocal mailings. No such offer was made to Myles in those early months.

All was not gloom, however. Myles did receive some individually personalised and very donor-friendly responses properly acknowledging his gift and sending him the information he required.

But consider a little more closely how the top charities in Britain serviced this direct approach from the good Myles –

a legacy prospect if ever there was one.

■ Six of the top 50 never acknowledged his gift at all. Perhaps it went astray?

■ Of the 44 who replied, 21 per cent took more than one month to do so.

■ Three charities wrote to Myles who were not in the original 50.

■ Four got his name and address details wrong.

■ 48 per cent sent a preprinted letter or receipt.

■ Most charities offered no introductory materials but instead immediately put Myles on their appeals 'conveyor belt'.

■ Not one sent a special welcome pack or planned welcome letter.

■ 16 did not send the information Myles had asked for.

Now let's be fair...

This was a few years ago and I have told the story of Myles in public a few times since. I do believe that in some areas things have definitely improved. Which is good.

After all, giving really matters to donors. Donors, as I have said, are nice people and they really don't expect much in return for their gift.

But they do expect us to be nice, too.

People really care about the causes they support. It really matters to them, even to those who affect not to care very much. And small donors care just as much as big donors. All gifts are important – to the donor, at least. Donors, justifiably, like to feel good about their gifts and their giving. And who can blame them?

But as Myles Barnett showed, some charities – in Britain at least – sometimes don't seem to treat the gifts or the givers with the same interest or respect that donors would surely think they deserve.

Exit Myles

In the meantime Myles had become quite famous in fundraising circles and whenever database operatives congregrated whispers were raised against him.

I suspect that some decided to eliminate him altogether from their records – fair enough – while others marked him down for special treatment so they might shine the next time Ken was invited to address a forum of fundraisers. So I decided that Myles had outlived his purpose and did away with him myself. And, just to be awkward, changed address.

In his place meet Mrs Ellie R Kempster of Aylesbury, Buckinghamshire – equally generous and just as interested to know more about the work of the same group of charities. The only distinctions were a slightly differently worded letter, the gender of its author (a better legacy prospect perhaps?) and the passage of nearly two years.

As many of Britain's top 50 fundraisers had been well exposed to the sorry tale of Myles Barnett's experiences during the intervening period it is perhaps not surprising that Ellie fared better. But, it has to be said, only slightly better.

Still six out of the top 50 didn't bother to respond at all. And it wasn't the same six. Average response times were quicker, but only marginally so. Fewer extraneous leaflets were sent, but not many. There was no sign of illicit reciprocals. Some letters were welcoming and there were fewer spelling and gender errors. But the avalanche of direct mail continued with equal force and volume.

Were Myles and Ellie victims of the big charity machines? Are small charities in Britain more donor-friendly? Or is it just head offices that are heartless and unfeeling about their donors? Are regional offices more personal, and more caring?

Is it any better elsewhere? Fundraisers in Britain have a tradition of looking to the United States for guidance and inspiration. How, I wondered, do fundraisers treat their donors in America, the home of customer service, the land of the welcoming smile and 'have a nice day'?

Well as luck would have it, late in 1994 I was invited by the American Public Broadcasting Services (PBS) in Washington to undertake some research on this very subject among the 375 assorted television and radio stations that form America's public television network.

PBS is the TV channel in America that doesn't have any commercials but instead depends on fundraising.

That research I did for America's public broadcasters led to my being invited by the database marketing office of the Smithsonian Institution, the world's largest group of museums and art galleries, to test customer-friendliness among their 32 museums and other institutions, again in the United States.

Here was my chance to test donor service among leading fundraisers from across the Atlantic. I got so excited I rushed to invent two more fictitious donors, Rebecca Brown and Agnes Holliday, to go with me.

These tests gave me a unique opportunity to find out just how well donors are looked after in the USA, and I learned a lot. It was also rather fun to have a chance to tell our American friends how to do things for a change.

Meet Rebecca...

Rebecca is from Venice, California and on page 29 is the letter that she sent with a token gift of $5 to 35 different PBS stations across the American nation, selected at random.

Despite receiving this rather charming letter with its small but nonetheless useful token gift, almost half of the stations Rebecca wrote to *didn't reply at all*. Presumably, 17 stations took the money and left Rebecca and her questions unanswered. Of those who did reply, about half waited

c/o Richard Brown
1047 Superba Avenue
Venice
California 90291

20 July 1994

Dear Friends

I miss you.

I used to live in Fort Wayne. I must tell you how
much I enjoy your station, and how much I miss it
now - not just because my eyesight isn't what it
was so I spend most of the day listening to the
radio, but because I'm stuck out here with my son
and his wife and will be for the next few months
at least, until my husband's estate is settled.

Please send me some information about your work,
if you have any.

I can only send you a small donation at present,
although I have given some in the past. When the
estate is settled I may be able to send more.

Yours truly

R Brown
Rebecca Brown

Rebecca's delightful letter and one of the more friendly, and inexpensive, responses.

July 29, 1994

Dear Mrs Brown,

Thank you for your note and your donation to
public broadcasting. We hope you are enjoying
your stay in California, and that you'll soon
be able to return to Buffalo. In the enclosed
issue of ON Air, you'll find information on
upcoming events on Channel 17. Perhaps you
will be able to find these programs on your
local public broadcasting station.

Wishing you the best,

The Membership Office

carol   *May*   *Dana*   *Wendie*   *Sue*

three weeks or more to respond.

Rebecca was subjected to many responses fit only for the waste-paper bin.

■ She got tiny unreadable standard receipts.

■ Letters that misspelled her name and street address.

■ Anonymous leaflets stuffed in anonymous envelopes.

■ She got circulars and preprinted acknowledgement cards.

■ She got lots of what could only be called junk mail.

And, worryingly, several fundraisers thought it all right to just clip their business card to a recent programme guide and bung that in an envelope.

Not very good. However to compensate for this, Rebecca got quite a few nice, straightforward friendly responses, both typed and handwritten. Several stations sent simple personal letters, accompanied by a programme guide or a leaflet and a reply envelope.

...and Agnes

Mrs Agnes M Holliday is from Anapolis, Maryland on the other side of the USA from Rebecca.

Agnes had recently been widowed and was wondering what she could do in her remaining years to uphold her late husband's principles and values, and spend his not inconsiderable sums of money...

The letter Agnes sent to some of her husband's favourite institutions – to 30 museums under the auspices of the Smithsonian Institution – was, perhaps unsurprisingly, rather similar to Rebecca's

It was a lovely, touching letter and full of clues. We really tried to make it easy for them.

I was a bit worried that we had made her a little too nice, and a little too believable. When I read her letter I really

Who could refuse
such a charming
request?

1547 Shipsview Road
Annapolis, MD 21401
January 20, 1995

Anacostia Museum
1901 Fort Place, SE
Washington, DC 20560

Dear Friends:

I hope you can help me.

My husband was a great admirer of your organization. He died
last March and in his memory I would like to support some of
those organizations that he believed in, so I am sending this
letter to you and also to a few other organizations like yours.
Do you have any information that explains how I can do this? Do
I have to become a member?

I would really be grateful for any relevant information you can
send. But please don't send me anything with very small print.
My eyesight now isn't what it was and I hate struggling with
small print.

I enclose a few dollars to cover the cost of this. When my
husband's estate is settled I may be able to send more.

Yours truly,

Agnes Holliday

Agnes Holliday (Mrs.)

wanted to reply to her myself.

But,

■ Of the 30 valid addresses Agnes wrote to, just 14 – fewer than half – bothered to respond to her letter.

■ Of those 14 most took three or four weeks, or more, to get their response in the post.

■ Several failed totally to pick up on what Agnes had actually asked for and sent entirely different information according to some pre-set agenda of their own. Agnes, I'm sure, would have been as bewildered as I was.

■ Several of the respondents failed to acknowledge Agnes's token donation, causing poor Agnes to wonder if it had ever been received.

■ Two of the respondents actually returned Agnes's thoughtful contribution of $5 towards postage costs. The reason given was that such information as they were enclosing was free. (In fairness Agnes had volunteered her $5 for a particular purpose but I'm not sure if returning a gift gives the right signal to a potential donor.)

■ Only one letter in all 14 responses actually used large type. Yet it's easily done these days – just select 12 point or above on your word processor.

■ Agnes received several silly standard letters and forms.

■ She got horrible peeling labels and computer digits.

■ And she got letters from the wrong people writing about the wrong things and demonstrating numerous missed opportunities.

There were several very good responses too, of course. And a lot of useful lessons emerged for the Smithsonian Institution.

I am sure that, like me, you will have been surprised to see from these examples so many instances of unfeeling lack of care, even contempt, for the customer, for the donor, in America – where supposedly the customer is king.

Great expectations

This should be seen as a warning for fundraisers everywhere. I have since done several similar donor-service road tests in Canada and Britain and now feel sure that my original concerns about the absence of a culture of customer service in fundraising are well founded. The problem is universal, and we ignore it at our peril.

I think I should subject you to one more road test that further proves and expands this point. So now please meet Mrs Camilla Cole, last and favourite of my four imaginary donors. And this time we're back in Britain. In Fanshaw Street, London N1 to be exact.

For the purposes of this specific experiment, Camilla had three tasks.

■ She wanted to test the top 20 fundraising organisations in Britain to update Myles's experience and try them with a somewhat larger donation – £15. (These experiments, by the way, have cost Burnett Associates a small fortune.)

■ Camilla also wanted to test the regional offices, or branches of some of the larger charities.

■ She wanted to try some much smaller charities to see if there really is truth in the saying that small is beautiful.

There were slight variations in the letters for each group, but essentially they were the same. Each bore a striking similarity to the letter Agnes had sent to the Smithsonian Institution.

So how was this friendly missive received? First, the leading British fundraisers.

Of the 20 charities mailed three responded within the first week, seven responded in the second and three in the third. Five of the big charities took four weeks or more to respond and two, 10 per cent, didn't respond at all – not even to a letter as promising as this. One non-respondent actually sent an appeal 11 weeks later.

Ten of the letters to the top 20 included Camilla's phone number. Only one telephoned her. She wasn't in but her answering machine was on. She also received a friendly follow-up letter a few days later. I was rather pleased to see it came from my old friends ActionAid.

Just five of the 20 enlarged the typeface of their letters to take account of Camilla's failing eyesight. But only three of these were able to enclose printed material in large print. Two of those didn't have anything prepared but were thoughtful enough to simply enlarge their material on their photocopier. Now Camilla had asked for this small consideration quite specifically but presumably *75 per cent of the top fundraising charities in Britain* thought this simple kindness just wasn't worth their while...

What of Camilla's request for information?

Fifteen of the 18 who responded fulfilled this request quite well, although a lot of the material wasn't very welcoming. Little of what was sent had been specially designed for this task. There were no specifically designed welcome packs – not one. Most had used other material adapted for the purpose. Many seemed to have sent whatever was nearest to hand.

Two simply sent annual reports. One just sent a preprinted receipt.

Now, by comparison, how did the regional offices of the large charities fare?

Only one of the 10 regional offices to receive Camilla's lovely letter failed to respond. Of course, that is one too many and the same percentage failure as the head offices: 10 per cent. Five responded within the first week and the other four had all responded within three – not too bad.

But only two of the nine enlarged the letter text and only one enlarged the accompanying materials. All the rest of the information sent would have been *very* difficult for Camilla to read. Most of the material sent was dull. One regional office wrote to say that Camilla's letter was being passed to head office to deal with. This was the same head office who, having received a £15 donation, volunteered to poor Camilla that they were and I quote –'putting your name and address on our computer so you can receive mail shots in future...' Lucky Camilla!

Some regional offices, however, did much better than their central counterparts and for a smaller donation too. Certainly, there appears from this small test to be little co-ordination of policy between regions and head office

Is small beautiful?

How did the smaller charities do?

I would have expected them to be more donor-friendly – and Camilla found they were. But why? Big charities have no less reason to look after their supporters. They may have a larger task, but they also have correspondingly larger resources.

All the smaller charities responded, although half of them took between four and five weeks. Four of them enlarged the letter type – which means six ignored poor Camilla's request. Only one enlarged the printed material.

But most did answer Camilla's direct request for more information, and did so fully, pleasantly and well, if not particularly promptly. Their information was also much more interesting, which is strange.

Not conclusive proof, perhaps, but a sign that small is indeed beautiful. Maybe some of the big charities have something to learn from the wee guys after all.

Generally, must try harder

As I mentioned, we also carried out a similar test in Canada, where we inflicted the charming and very generous Mrs

Dora Smith on 75 of Canada's leading fundraisers. I won't go into detail, but suffice it to say that, despite Canada reputedly having the most generous individual donors in the world, only 15 out of the 75 responded well.

Although there were some variations between the tests, the following summarises what we found.

■ At least 10 per cent of fundraising organisations won't even acknowledge a letter like those sent by Camilla and the others, let alone attempt in some way to realise its potential. In some cases the percentage of non-responders approached 50 per cent.

■ Almost half of those that do respond will take more than three weeks to do so.

■ Many of these acknowledgements that take so long to arrive will be nothing more than preprinted receipts or standard unpersonalised letters. Quite a few will just send further appeals.

■ Most of the printed materials sent in response to this kind of request will be irrelevant, or so dull, or badly produced they will be fit only for the waster-paper basket.

■ The majority of those who do respond will fail to pick up on one or more, or all, of the questions asked.

■ As few as one in 10 will respond to a direct request for large print from a partially sighted donor, even though type size in letters can be increased simply on a word processor and printed materials can be easily enlarged on a photocopier.

■ With one or two exceptions, regional offices are no different from their head offices and often show little or no co-ordination or evidence of common policy towards donor enquiries.

■ Small charities are usually somewhat better at customer service than big charities.

■ Some of the responses to this kind of enquiry – perhaps as few as three or four out of every hundred – will be brilliant. Many others will be quick, relevant and appropriate. However, thoughtless, mass-produced, dispiriting and off-putting responses will outnumber good responses by about four to one.

I was saddened by these experiences. Relationship fundraising may well be more difficult if you have an ancient and cumbersome database but that is no excuse for the absence of basic policies of thank you, welcome, donor development and upgrade.

But things are changing, and changing fast. Even as I write, many charities are reviewing their policies for donor service and communication.

It is now clear that what I call machine marketing – the indiscriminate use of computer numbers, gimmicks, the conveyor-belt approach to donor communications, and so on – is on the way out. Fundraisers now realise they have a different culture from the culture of mass marketing. They know it is important to understand the difference, for that informs the way we communicate.

We are different from the sellers of directly marketed commercial products and that difference should be clear when we communicate with our donors and potential supporters.

Marketing for a better world

A glance at the daily television news will tell you that we live in a lousy world. Over the last decade or so, the general public has finally begun to realise that our politicians are not going to change that.

During this time they have begun to appreciate that campaigning social action organisations frequently can, and frequently do, bring about real change – Amnesty, Greenpeace, Oxfam, and hundreds of others.

The organisations fundraisers work for.

So clearly we shouldn't be talking to our supporters and potential supporters as if they are merely fodder for our marketing machines, as if what we promote is no more important than the *Reader's Digest*, or time-share apartments, or the latest development in cotton/Lycra underwear. We shouldn't be wrapping up our offers, propositions, submissions and promotions as if we were selling magazine subscriptions, or trying to get people to shift to a different brand of toothpaste.

Fundraisers today need a different kind of marketing. Proven, technically efficient marketing of course, but marketing invaded and taken over by the culture of fundraising rather than the other way around. Marketing designed to help us to open a relationship rather than to close a sale.

We need real communications. Communications that matter, about subjects that matter.

We also need a basic level of donor service that will make all who come into contact with us feel welcome and valued. Anyone who interacts with us should be left with the impression that we are at least polite and efficient. But we could go further. We could be an example to other industry sectors. I think we fundraisers should strive to be the standard bearer in customer service. We should practise only *world-class* donor service, and thus set an example that others will wish to follow.

Meet Bertie Wooster

What does it mean to offer world-class donor service, and how will it pay?

Before I introduce you to the concept of world-class service, there's someone else I'd like you to meet. He is one of literature's most endearing characters, P G Wodehouse's superb creation Bertie Wooster. You probably know him quite well already.

Bertie Wooster was very lovable but a complete fop – an idle, empty-headed, upper-class twit. Yet, in his otherwise useless and disorganised existence, Bertie Wooster did just one thing right. It was a small act, but its effect and its implications were to be colossal. They were so transformational for young Bertram that this one simple act more than compensated for all his other shortcomings, and metamorphosed young Bertie from a shiftless, work-shy, scatterbrained gadfly into a supremely glittering, competent and satisfied human being.

What was it? What single act of uncharacteristic brilliance so fundamentally changed the young Bertie?

Simply this: he recruited Jeeves. And thereafter, whatever scrapes life might throw at him, Bertie Wooster was always able to sail through triumphantly.

Exit disarray, enter Jeeves

Jeeves too seemed fulfilled by the partnership and passed his years apparently contentedly maintaining the illusion that he was the servant and the young toff the master, rather than the reality, which was much more the other way around. Perhaps he derived his satisfaction from the thrill of being *really* in control. As for Bertie's multitude of friends and family, they found the whole strange arrangement absolutely top-hole. All sorts of folk constantly enquired of Bertie in terms of 'Where did you find that spiffing man?' And advised, 'Bertie, dear boy, whatever else you do, hang on to old Jeeves!'

It was an eminently satisfactory situation all round.

What on earth has all this got to do with fundraising?

Well I heard this analogy from a delightful and impressive woman called Jacquelyn Petras who teaches customer service in California. She used the example of Wooster's personnel selection skills to emphasise the importance of recruiting *the right person* for customer service. I had found myself in her workshop almost by accident. It happened to be just across the hall from mine, where I had just given a really rather depressing and exhausting portrayal of the devastatingly low standards of customer service then being experienced by many donors in North America. We were both, Jacquelyn and I, guest speakers at the PBS annual convention. I, of course, was there to report on the experiences of Rebecca Brown, whom you will remember I introduced you to a few pages ago.

Jackie Petras was there because she firmly believes in the benefits of customer service for all types of business. She absolutely rejects any notion that fundraisers are different, or should compromise, or that somehow they will be excused when they provide slipshod or inadequate service.

Is it really too much for a donor to expect prompt and efficient service? Obviously not. In fact, we fundraisers have the best of all reasons to give our customers the most impressive service they are likely to get anywhere. Because they don't have to buy our product. We don't have anything like spam to keep our customers coming back for more. If they want to they can so easily go elsewhere.

Jackie encouraged PBS fundraisers to reassess the service they provide to their donors as a matter of course, through a series of anecdotes that all revolved around personal experiences – a brilliant example of putting oneself in the customer's shoes. Her stories included the hotel receptionist who gave up his own room to accommodate an over-booked couple and the woman who cancelled a series of extremely expensive eye operations, because the car park attendant wouldn't allow her to park without paying the $5 parking fee in cash, which this particular billionaire didn't have.

Not everyone can, or even should, provide truly world-class donor service, but we can all aspire to it. I don't have a formal definition of world-class service, but I guess it means wholehearted commitment to a level of customer service that is just as good as it can be. Service that puts the customer – the donor – first, not the fundraiser, the administrator, or the organisation.

Here are a few practical hints if you wish to avoid being caught out by any of my various imaginary donors in future. More importantly, I hope they will help you to introduce *world-class* donor service to your organisation. I call these the 10 keys to donor service.

■ Be committed. You have to *believe* in donor service. You have to want to do it. If you are not committed to giving your donors the very best service and the very best impression you possibly can then move over and give the job to someone who is.

■ Be properly resourced. You can't do donor service on the cheap. It needs adequate staff and appropriate materials. So budget for it. If it is well managed, donor service will pay for itself many times over.

■ Be consistent. Donors and supporters should know what to expect and be able to rely on it.

■ Be quick. Don't let your donors wait, wondering what's happening. A prompt response is a response from someone who cares. The opposite is also true. Programme in response times for different types of donor request. If you can't respond immediately, or within hours, at least you can get a letter sent within two days. And get your staff to always try to improve targets.

■ Be appropriate. Tailor your responses to your donors. Use the clues in their correspondence to determine the right type and level of response for each individual.

■ Be personal. Use your donor service strategy to build relationships. Use your database to record personal information for future use. People, universally, like to be noticed, they like to be remembered. People like people who are nice to them.

■ Be known. It pays to advertise. So put your hotline numbers and contact addresses on all your publications.

And show your people. Give them names and faces. People relate to people.

■ Be meticulous. Keep good records. Always do what you say you will. Live up to your, and your organisation's, ideals.

■ Be there. The best time for supporters to contact you is usually between six and nine in the evening. So your supporter services people can't go home then. In fact, it may pay you to offer a 24-hour service. Whatever, you should let your donors decide.

■ Be open. If something has gone wrong, or if you can't deliver as promised, admit it. Your supporters will love you for it because you have shown you care, because you are honest and trustworthy.

Looking for clues

In all my road tests the very best example of relationship fundraising I received came in response to Rebecca Brown and her letter to 35 public television stations.

In the second paragraph of her letter Rebecca says, 'I must tell you how much I enjoy your station and how much I miss it now, not just because my eyesight isn't what it used to be...'

If that isn't a clue I don't know what is.

The best response to Rebecca's letter wasn't a letter at all. It was an audio tape personally recorded for Rebecca by Diana Scheuerman, director of development at Channel 8, WDCN in Nashville, Tennessee.

Its effectiveness wasn't so much in what she said but in the way that she said it. Sadly I can't give a copy away with this book, you'll just have to use your imagination. Or, if you prefer, think about what *you* might say in a specially recorded message for an interested potential donor such as Rebecca.

The best response
Rebecca received wasn't
a letter at all.

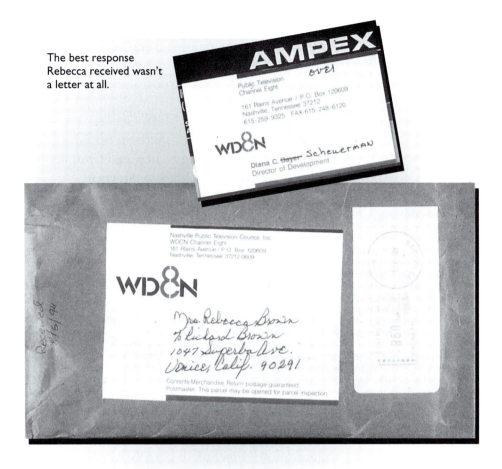

If, like Rebecca, I had been looking for a public
broadcasting station to leave a substantial legacy to I know
which one I'd have chosen.

Many donors are in contact with a lot of charities, just like
Rebecca. The truth of customer service in the charity world
today is that many charities are not very good at it, so good
service – *world-class* service – really stands out.

And believe me, it gets its own rewards. It pays.

So be nice to your donors.

...and beware.

Your next customer who enquires about, say, monthly
giving may not be *quite* what he or she seems. Your next

apparently innocent request for an annual report from Miss Mabel Appelbe of the 'Bide a While' retirement home in Pittenweem, Fife may have another purpose entirely. Or perhaps you may find yourself subject to an apparently irrational but vitriolic complaint from Major General Ferdinand Le Drogo of Kermarquer, in southern Brittany. Or you may receive a surprisingly strong legacy lead from Ms Olive Sowerby of Jock of the Bushveldt Bungalows in Mpumalangu, Cape Town, in which she mentions her darling and beloved Ern, who might be her son, her husband, her lover – or her cat.

Who knows? The fact is you never really know, so it pays to play safe and to treat all your customers to the same standard of service – world-class service.

Meet Bumé McPoot*

Bumé McPoot is another fictitious character sent to haunt the purveyors of junk mail, perhaps the most ambitious of them all. His story has little to do with donor development, but it is brief and it illustrates quite well both the delights and the dangers of road-testing your own and your competitors' organisations. I include it here merely to encourage you to submit your work regularly, but carefully, to cunningly contrived and undetectable road tests and to use the information thus gleaned to improve your response and service to your donors.

Bumé McPoot started life as plain Timothy Moore Esquire, an occasional contributor to the British daily newspaper *The Independent*. Tired of conforming to the dull limitations imposed by our modern society, plain Mr Moore one day responded to an innocuous enough request for his name and address by inserting the name Hattytown before his street name and number. A small thrill followed when mail arrived thus addressed, the kind of thrill reserved only for those who have successfully cheated the system. Timothy Moore was hooked.

*Abridged from an article that appeared in *The Independent*, London, UK, 13 November 1992.

Other deceptions followed. An idle passing interest quickly became an obsession. Soon Mr Moore was writing to direct marketing firms as Lord Perris of Spoon, signing himself to insurance companies as Dr Moore of the Old Piggery, and awarding himself an array of impressive honours and awards when communicating with film processing concerns.

The disguise of Wing Commander Bilston Wilson DFC was popular for a time, and his *alter ego* was keenly amused to find how often this aristocratic name was sold on to other direct marketers. In time Lady Eleanor of Aquitaine moved into Hattytown, as did figurine fanatic Kurt Large, Nintendo freak Kenneth Bed Warmer (who filled in his occupation variously as apprentice bow re-hairer and copper's nark) and Brahmin Tony, who occupied the attentions of Time Life Books for several months thereby causing them to consume a small acreage of renewable softwood solely on his account.

Eventually Hattytown became a little overcrowded and its original occupant found the range and complexity of promotional mail rather hard to keep up with. A variety of postal salespeople then learned of their quarry's demise in bizarre bowling accidents, peasant insurrections and falling satellite disasters.

But the mail kept coming. Then the phone started ringing. One day Tim's (or Kurt's, Brahmin's, Kenneth's, or whoever's) girlfriend was trapped by junk mail wedged behind the front door as she opened it.

Then a 'lifestyle' questionnaire arrived. The chance of creating a proper well-rounded character proved impossible to resist.

So enter the vastly rich, quite ancient renter of fleet vehicles whose favourite pastime is yachting and whose favourite snack food is melamine-faced chipboard – Mr Bumé McPoot.

At first the flood of offers and invitations to Mr McPoot was amusing. Then it became distinctly embarrassing. Bumé was enticed to buy everything from replica hearing aids to screwdriver sets. Then he was warned not to let funeral expenses be a burden on his grieving wife, Bootsy, and the younger McPoots.

The crunch came when Bumé, a keen golfer, was offered an all-expenses-paid weekend as the guest of a Scottish time-share establishment. When the plane tickets and vouchers arrived McPoot was trapped. There was no way out. So, with girlfriend, he went.

Embarrassed by his unlikely choice of name and the difficulty of maintaining a rather obviously fake Scottish accent, McPoot was hastily explained to the receptionist on arrival as an unfortunate misspelling – could happen to anyone – of an ancient Dutch Malaysian surname, Maroot.

Unfortunately one of the hotel's staff was herself of Dutch descent and had grown up in the Far East. Besides, the figure presenting himself as Bumé McPoot was at least 30 years younger than he should have been. The tale of Tim Moore's decline into paranoia as his recently created persona disintegrated around him is sobering but I will spare readers the details, save to advise that when in disguise it is best not to pay hotel bills by credit card.

So as the exposed Bumé Maroot fled back to safety south of the border his creator decided never again to yield to the temptation not to accord direct mail the seriousness it so obviously needs and deserves. Perhaps there's a message for Myles Barnett here? And for Rebecca, Agnes, Dora and Camilla... and for me, too.

As a postscript to all this, Timothy Moore is now convinced Bumé McPoot is immortal. Only recently he received a mailshot from the Worldwide Fund for Nature. Beneath a huge picture of a tiger was the catchline 'Fear or fascination? What's your reaction, Mr McPoot?'

Such antics of course are irreverent and irresponsible. They do, I suppose, waste both time and money. But they fulfil a very important function. They keep an otherwise naturally irresponsible industry on its toes.

Getting ahead...
and staying there

Relationship marketing is not just about delivering superior customer service, however important that might be. Relationship marketing is about forecasting the potential future value of a customer and taking whatever steps are necessary to enhance it profitably.

Graeme McCorkell
Direct Response magazine

If donor service among fundraising organisations is even half as bad as my donor-friendliness road tests appear to indicate, then in some areas of fundraising things have got to change substantially – and quickly. It doesn't take a genius to identify that a more donor-based approach might just be a tad more appropriate in today's competitive and complex market-place.

Three key concepts, I think, are useful here. Two of them – being donor-led and the 90-degree shift – are phrases coined by my friend and source of much inspiration Giles Pegram of the NSPCC and they are almost synonymous. The third, the concept of being 15 minutes ahead, has a more dubious provenance, but is no less appropriate for relationship fundraisers.

Donor-led or donor-leading? What it means to put the customer first

At first the term donor-led might appear to be yet more jargon, just a synonym for donor care, or supporter loyalty, or even relationship fundraising. But the concept of being donor-led is a good one because it imposes a great discipline on fundraisers. When you are donor-led you can no longer do just what you or your organisation wants to do. You have to also do what your donors want you to do. That means taking a new look at such tried and trusted concepts as revenue targets, how issues are presented, mailing frequency, organisational structures, job titles – even the very concept of marketing itself. In other words, fundraisers should go to work in the morning thinking about the donors they are building relationships with, not the techniques they are responsible for organising.

Being donor-led obviously doesn't mean you subordinate the organisation's values, mission and interests to those of the donor. You can assume that the donor's interests, if correctly channelled and managed, will closely match those of your cause.

To be donor-led you have to make the 90-degree shift and put yourself in your donor's shoes, to get under her skin, to see things through her eyes. Now this sounds a bit invasive and physically rather difficult, and it is. Being donor-led requires more than just a sound understanding of your donors. You have to think as a donor and to react as a donor would. It will be easier, perhaps, if you actually *are* a donor (now *there's* an idea for the serious fundraiser to ponder).

Close your eyes and try it for a while. Think of one of your donors and try to shrug off for the moment your own personality and preferences, and take on his or hers. Try to think and act like he would, or she would. Get right inside her skin.

Now ask yourself, 'How would I like to be targeted? How would I react if I met the fundraiser who once signed his letter to me as general administrative secretary, fundraising/direct marketing? What would I feel if I saw my entry on the charity's database? Would I be taken in by the charity's most recent mail shot? Would I find the latest annual report credible, or even interesting?'

And so on. It can be quite an experience to do this and can lead to much sober reappraisal of practices and published material that have long been taken for granted. But it is a difficult thing to do consistently and over a long period of time. As Giles Pegram has found in his organisation, it is particularly difficult to ensure that others do it and do it well.

The real skill for the fundraiser, however, is to enable donors themselves to see and to believe that their interests, values and ambitions coincide exactly with the organisation's and so by helping the fundraiser achieve his or her goals donors also achieve their own desires. For the fundraiser this may involve a subtle mixture of being donor-led and donor-leading.

A supremely challenging task, of course, which to be successful will require all the diplomacy, skills and know-how of a professional fundraiser.

But then I never said it was easy...

To quote Giles Pegram, 'Even when we think we've done it, the whole notion of being donor-led is that there is always going to be more we can do. Once we have all got out of that mind-set of thinking about direct marketing, telefundraising, mail order, and so on and actually start thinking about the different groups of donors and how to build relationships with them, then the possibilities – and the opportunities – are endless. But we have to hold our nerve.'

As others see us

The 90-degree shift is a part of being donor-led. It is nothing more complicated than developing the ability to see things from your donor's point of view rather than (or in addition to) your own or your organisation's point of view. It is seeing your communications and even your role as a fundraiser through your donor's eyes.

In fundraising, the 90-degree shift inevitably leads to a rather different view of some fairly fundamental concepts. Take these two different job definitions that essentially have the same function. The example comes from Don Peppers and Martha Rogers' book *The One-to-One Future*.

> **The brand manager's task:** to persuade you and 26.7 million other faceless consumers to buy all the boxes of Frosted Flakes that Kellogg hopes to sell this coming quarter.
>
> **The customer service manager's task:** to figure out how to increase Kellogg's share of perhaps 1,800 or more boxes of dry cereal that you will buy in your lifetime.

It may amount to more or less the same thing, but the customer service manager is coming at it from a very different angle. That's the 90-degree shift. Fundraisers nowadays need to be customer service managers, not brand managers. The change is fundamentally important. Once you have made the 90-degree shift nothing will ever be the same again.

In the last chapter I showed that many fundraisers are still treating their donors very badly, as if they were nothing more than fodder for direct marketing machines – the 'churn and burn' school of fundraising, where fundraisers are only interested in the money coming in and not in the least interested in the people who are sending it.

I said that appropriate donor service was the exception not the rule and I showed, I hope, that those who are 15 minutes ahead in this area will achieve very significant advantage over their competitors.

So what does it mean to be 15 minutes ahead? And why should you want to be it?

FIFTEEN MINUTES AHEAD

Minds immeasurably superior to ours...

Alien concepts

We are – most of us – from a generation that was reared on stories, images and visions of invasions from outer space. *Star Wars*, *Star Trek*, *The War of the Worlds*, these tales of extraterrestrials always revolve around the notion of our space visitors being light years in advance of us, scientific streets ahead, with minds immeasurably superior to ours. Usually these superior beings then set about quelling we puny earthlings into submission with their fabulous heat-rays, stun-guns, phasers or similar death-dealing machines.

But the American comedian Woody Allen had a vision of a different kind of space invader. He foresaw invading aliens not as light years ahead, but just 15 minutes ahead.

These space beings, Woody Allen believed, would be 15 minutes ahead in *everything*. They'd always be first in the queue at the supermarket checkout, first to grab the last available drier at the launderette, first to predict the winner of the 3.30 at Epsom, or the World Series, or the Superbowl, or whatever. These infuriating extraterrestrials would always be in front, constantly pipping us at the post, thereby ensuring that whatever we may try to do they would always win. As a result of being 15 minutes ahead, total world domination would be easy.

Now there is a parallel here for fundraisers. It is increasingly difficult these days to get really significantly ahead of the field and almost impossible to be light years ahead. But you can still win, by being just 15 minutes ahead. If you can be just 15 minutes ahead of your competitors that's all that's necessary in these rapidly changing times to ensure all the success you could possibly wish.

So my advice to you is to be constantly on the lookout for ways to put you and your organisation 15 minutes ahead. One way you can do just that is by developing a proactive programme committed to delivering world-class donor service as described in the preceding chapter. Another is to develop a proactive strategy to annihilate your competition.

Who are our competitors?

Surprisingly it's not, principally, other charities, not-for-profits, educational institutions, arts groups, or political parties. Not really. Most donors rarely decide on a certain fixed amount they will spend on good causes and then shop around. Most of the reasons why people give (or don't give) are not logical at all but depend on emotional and psychological triggers. What most charities see as competition – other charities – in fact generally *increases* the size of the market because, up to a point, it helps create a climate and tradition of giving.

Donors, we have to accept, are promiscuous. They like to support several causes simultaneously, often without clear ties to any of them. While they will sometimes have great loyalty to certain organisations, they usually avoid any suggestion of exclusivity. Freedom and choice are important to most donors. They will resist being tied down. Quite right too. This is another example of how different our customers are from those of most retailers. With charitable giving it is rarely an 'either/or' choice. It is more likely to be a question of justifying additional expenditure, or generosity.

Purchases, on the other hand, are different. When donors buy a television they have to choose between Philips, Sony, Panasonic, or other companies. When they hire a car it's between Hertz or Avis, or maybe Budget. When they buy a car they also have to make a choice of one, or possibly two, from hundreds of competing brands. When they fly they have to choose between British Airways, Delta, Air France, or whoever, either by deciding which one goes most conveniently to their desired destinations or, now, by which one offers the best deals to frequent flyers on upgrades or air miles.

We can't offer inducements on the same scale as the big consumer organisations so we can't stimulate artificial choice, even if we wanted to. We don't have the philanthropical equivalent of spam to tempt the palates of our customers. But while we might have to accept that our donors are uncontrollably promiscuous we can still make ourselves so alluring, so irresistible that even if, for whatever reason, they stop supporting all their other charities the last relationship to suffer will be ours.

Of course, charities do compete with each other and, as more and more fundraisers become increasingly strident, this competition may become even less welcome as donors are forced to make difficult choices.

Donors generally prefer charities to co-operate rather than compete among themselves. So I think it will pay fundraisers not to appear competitive with other causes, but instead to focus on more serious and insidious threats from those competitors that fundraisers *really can* overcome.

Annihilate these competitors

The real competitors for charities are distrust, uncertainty, lack of comfort, fear of criticism, inconvenience, inertia and being put off. It's worth looking at these in a little detail and planning strategies to obliterate them.

Distrust

Charities have a poor image for efficiency and effectiveness. Why should donors trust you? They see horror stories in their media with depressingly predictable frequency. So fundraisers have to ask: 'what can we do to make sure donors will trust us?'

Uncertainty

Most donors have no clear plan for their charitable giving. They like to be sure that when they do give their gift will be honourably treated and their decision will be a right one. What have they got to go on? From the charity, most probably various promotional materials – sales material. In Britain at least, anyone selling anything will put 98 per cent of the public immediately on the defensive. So fundraisers have to ask, 'How can I avoid looking like a salesman? How can I give my donors confidence in me, my organisation and in what I'm asking them to do?'

Lack of comfort

Distrust and uncertainty can lead to a prospective donor feeling sufficiently uncomfortable to decide not to make a gift now. Many other factors can contribute to donor discomfort – not asking at the right time, asking for too much or too little, asking for the wrong thing. We almost invariably ask for money, yet only nine per cent of our donors' assets are in money and although money is often the most liquid of assets it is not always the easiest to dispose of.

An American fundraiser told me a story that, while somewhat incredible, illustrates the point. He had for some years been developing a relationship with an elderly couple and had them to the point where they were considering setting up a charitable remainder trust (a tax-efficient form of giving in the USA). While reviewing their general financial circumstances prior to this, the woman had mentioned, almost as a throw-away remark, that her husband, John, had $1.7 million in..., she named a particular type of stock, but explained her husband didn't like it. The fundraiser was staggered. This was a much bigger sum than he had been building up to and his prospect had overlooked it because *he didn't like* the stock.

Some time later my American friend left with a gift of $1.7 million for his charity that really had cost the donor very little because he hadn't wanted it.

Fear of criticism
Giving is an intensely personal thing. Even when decisions about giving are made in couples or in family groups, it is very private and it's not something most donors like to broadcast or even discuss with anyone, even their nearest and dearest. Sometimes their nearest and dearest are the *very last* people donors will want to discuss their giving with.

So reassurance is important for donors. They really need to believe in what they're doing and to feel it is a commendable thing, beyond reproach. If they detect even a hint of possible criticism, from any quarter, your gift will evaporate.

Some people enjoy condemning the generosity of others as a way of covering up their own guilt feelings. 'You must have more money than sense', they'll say. Or, 'There's one born every minute.' Most people are sensitive to being seen as a sucker. Some won't even want their bank to know. And if your donor gets too friendly with her bank manager (or solicitor or financial adviser) you could be in trouble if he, or she, feels her giving to your cause might be seen as anything less than a sound and sensible investment.

Inconvenience

All purchasing is inconvenient to some extent so we either have to get people really in the mood, or make things if not actually enjoyable then at least incredibly easy for them. As a gift to charity is the ultimate intangible product (no warehousing, packing, shipping, or insurance costs) delivery is relatively easy. We already all do most of the conventional things that make for easy collection of payment. But do we really go as far as we could to make it convenient? Some charities now are introducing 24-hour service lines that take credit card donations over the phone. Others don't even accept credit cards. Some charities are now offering no-quibble, money-back guarantees of satisfaction. Others would find the idea alarming. Some charities are prepared to accept gifts in any form, not necessarily money. Others consider reversionary legacies (where a charity has to wait before it can collect its gift) an inconvenience. Others still only thank donors who give above a certain level.

Saturday opening and piped music for visitors may yet be some way off – but not perhaps if our donors would find that convenient and comforting.

And if restaurants and petrol stations can offer hand-held swipe machines for credit or debit card payments, why can't the charity collector on any doorstep or street corner? (I've been pushing this idea for years since seeing these gadgets widely used in France. I don't know of any major charity who has taken it up, although some isolated instances have been reported, but the PR alone would be invaluable. Just think, you could hang a sign on each collector saying that all major credit cards are accepted. And each donation would be a minimum of £5.)

Inertia

In *Relationship Fundraising* I described inertia (not a word that translates very well, but a vitally important concept) as 'the most consistent human response to the really important things in life'. Put another way, 'oh yes, I really will do that sometime soon...', plus 101 similar evasive responses. In a world dominated by long lists of don'ts – don't do this, don't do that – don't bother is the one most people seem to pay most attention to. I remain convinced that for every donor who ever responded to a remote solicitation, several others nearly did but inertia (or call it what you will) got in the way.

Creative fundraisers can do a lot to overcome inertia by presenting their stories irresistibly, by making response easy, by demanding it in person (or suggesting that if you don't reply now by post someone from the fundraising department will telephone or, worse still, come round in person).

Insult, offend, plead, threaten, cajole, blackmail, expose – all these might help to overcome inertia. But perhaps not all are suitable for fundraisers.

Indifference

All of the above will put your potential donor off from making that all-important next gift (the one after the knee-jerk response and before becoming a committed donor – the second gift, the one that if you don't get means you've lost them forever). But it takes a rather dumb organisation to put its donors off through its own behaviour.

Yet research has shown (*see* chapter 3, pages 77–79) that the majority of former donors to a cause will leave because they feel the organisation doesn't care for them, or isn't interested in them – indifference. Tackling indifference is a really powerful case for the 90-degree shift. In practice, it doesn't matter what you really feel about them or whether you care for them. You can be as donor-led or relationship-oriented as you like. What matters is only what *they think* you feel about them.

So one of the greatest competitors for your charity is perhaps your own indifference to your donors, actual or perceived.

If you want to beat your competition, I recommend you cultivate your donors' trust, reassure them, do all you can to make them comfortable, remove any potential for criticism, stir them out of their lethargic inertia and into action, and make every effort to show them how much they are appreciated. That's not difficult, is it?

But perhaps there is one competitor even more dangerous, even more threatening than any of the above. This competitor is described fully by Regis McKenna in his book *Relationship Marketing* (Addison-Wesley Inc, Reading, Massachusetts, 1991). I can do no better than quote him here. The competitor he warns us against is the one closest to home… yourself.

> This competitor is the toughest of all. Machines and products don't compete, people do. People have to spot the market opportunities and take advantage of them. People have to develop the products and competitive strategies, and allocate resources and develop customer relationships.
>
> There are many ways people end up competing with themselves. When people underestimate their own ideas, just because the ideas have never been tried out before, they are competing with themselves. When, on the other hand, people develop an air of omnipotence and believe they can't fail they also are competing with themselves. When people are unwilling to listen, when they are unwilling to change, when they are unwilling to experiment, they are competing with themselves.
>
> People must leave themselves open to think creatively. With markets changing so rapidly, managers must be able to analyse new situations and apply creative approaches to them. Old approaches to new problems simply won't work.
>
> Above all, managers must pay attention to their customers. They must listen and respond to them. They must not underestimate their competition – or overestimate it. And they must continue to experiment. Successful companies are led by people who are never satisfied at being second best. Leaders make things happen. They have an attitude, a way of thinking that

permeates the company. If managers adopt this pattern of
thinking, this frame of mind, they can avoid the biggest problem of
all: turning themselves into a competitor.

In some places this might appear to be stating the obvious,
but it's worth thinking about. How many of us see ourselves
as potential competitors?

As a postscript to that last point, fundraisers might
consider the following salutary tale concerning Britain's
national airline, British Airways, and then ponder on how
they themselves think of, and talk about, their donors.

British Airways likes to think of itself as the world's
favourite airline. A few years ago, however, BA's image took
something of a knock when details emerged of its dirty
tricks campaign against rival Virgin Airlines, owned by
everyone's darling entrepreneur, Richard Branson (well he
was when this story came out).

British Airways soon found that an image expensively
created over time could be quickly and easily destroyed. A
damage limitation exercise was mounted during which one
national magazine reported a hapless PR man who, while
attempting to justify the dirty tricks to colleagues, was
quoted as saying 'we don't make profits out of escorting old
biddies to the gate'.

It was, of course, just the kind of soundbite that the press
loves and just the kind of quote that upsets millions of
elderly female passengers and their sympathisers – the very
people who, as British Airways has learned, do make all the
difference to its profit, or loss.

BA's underhand tactics with Richard Branson put me off
our national airline for quite a while. Whenever I flew I
would use another carrier, if I could, just to show that I was
on the side of the righteous.

Eventually, BA won me back, not only because there was
so often no practical alternative, but also by consistent good
service and offering me bonus points. (Moral: if being nice
fails, try bribery.)

But I'm still watching them. When a customer's belief in an organisation is shattered, recovery, if possible at all, is slow, difficult and rarely total.

That is more true for a not-for-profit organisation than for almost any other.

Five foundations of relationship fundraising

Deep thinking about what it means to be donor-led has caused many fundraisers to concern themselves with some areas that would be outside the normal province of books on fundraising. I include in this what Horowitz and Panak refer to in their book *Total Customer Satisfaction* (Pitman Publishing, London, 1992) as the soft tools of management – culture, leadership, motivation and inspiration, influence and communication. Soft tools they may be, but they are absolutely crucial to relationship fundraising and indispensable assets in transforming your fundraising organisation into one that puts its customers – its donors – first.

Organisational culture

I confess that I am an organisational culture vulture. I like organisations with strong beliefs, with visible principles and purposes beyond the mere making of money. My company, Burnett Associates, was founded on 13 principles that are issued to all employees when they join. We use them to guide our business practices.

Corporate culture is much more than just casual deference to an obscure mission statement that is tucked away on the inside page of successive annual reports and overlooked, or ignored, by most employees and customers alike. It is much more important and more powerful than concepts of corporate identity and the 'charity brand'.

Corporate culture is the character and personality of your organisation, the explanation of its philosophy and belief in what it is and who it is there for.

The corporate culture inspires and directs employees' efforts. In some companies it almost amounts to corporate religion.

The organisations fundraisers work for clearly have an advantage over commercial counterparts in terms of their ability to rationalise and justify their case for a strong corporate culture. Yet how many charities do? It is striking to see how often the employees of companies like The Body Shop, Toyota, Coca-Cola and even McDonald's have a stronger sense of corporate culture than some of the greatest causes in the land, and how their staffs are often vastly more committed to customer service than those of many charities.

Just like people, organisations can be strong or weak out of all proportion to their financial size and often this is a factor of the strength of their corporate culture. Organisations also can be friendly to customers, or hostile. As with people, the worst offence is indifference and it is also one of the most common.

Research among lapsed donors in America revealed that for every 100 donors who had discontinued their support of a once-favoured cause just one had been stopped by death (a fairly reasonable excuse), three had moved away, 14 had transferred their support to another organisation, 14 claimed to be dissatisfied and a staggering 68 left because they had had no contact with the organisation, or because of the organisation's indifference.

Fundraisers have no excuse for allowing a weak culture to lead to indifference or hostility in *any* part of their organisation and so sour their relations with supporters. But it happens every day. Of course it pays to understand your customers' expectations. With some notable exceptions, these are generally very low. Wherever these low donor expectations might come from, differing cultures do lead to differing expectations. For example, donors seem to expect Third World causes to be particularly economical, perhaps because small amounts of money buy a lot in developing countries, whereas by contrast environmental and wildlife charities have to do all their printing in glorious full colour, because the public expects it.

Our customers' low expectations could also be attributed to tolerance. In my experience many donors show remarkable goodwill towards their chosen charities and demonstrate this by being undemanding and very forgiving.

The situation is further complicated by the fact that donors often don't like to ask, or complain because they fear their demands will create additional trouble or expense. This means that often the fundraiser will be unaware if a problem exists, whereas in a commercial environment a similar problem would quickly be brought to his or her attention by an irate customer. This is really dangerous for those who are trying to be relationship fundraisers. It can lead to complacency that we are doing better than we actually are.

Being sensitive to real customer desires and concerns is particularly challenging for fundraisers. Do we know how many of our donors continue to support our causes not *because* of our fundraising activities but *despite* them?

Whatever the reason for our customers', or our donors',

low expectations, it seems to me that this is an opportunity which service-oriented, donor-led fundraisers can readily exploit.

In other areas, donors' expectations (again perhaps led by fundraisers) can be absurdly and unrealistically high. For example, in the belief that organisations can be run with little or no administrative costs and that fundraisers don't need to be paid properly. Of course, we don't want to delude donors or to collude with them in fostering a belief that we can perform miracles (of the '£2.50 will cure 100 babies' type). We do need to show that pound for pound or dollar for dollar we can provide extraordinarily good value for money. If we can get that message across cheerfully, efficiently and cost-effectively, it will be enthusiastically welcomed by donors. We should campaign to change our donors' expectations and make them more realistic. Both donors and fundraisers will benefit if we do.

Culturally fundraising organisations should be every bit as committed to customer service as any other business – if not more so.

Consider Club Méditerranée, the French international tourist resort company. From the outset, Club Med's representatives have been called *gentils organisateurs* – nice organisers. Imagine how some regional fundraisers would feel given such a title! But all Club Med GOs are on first-name terms with their clients and no GO is ever off duty. Their commitment to customer service is total. The GOs' objective is to forget that people are customers and make them feel as friends.

The UK retailer Marks & Spencer is another example that repays some study. The key to M&S's success is rapid reaction to changes in customer tastes and preferences. M&S doesn't innovate. It doesn't push products. What is important to M&S is that the customer should buy the product without being pushed. M&S's great strength is in monitoring any slight variations in customer purchasing patterns and then reacting to them rapidly. When it does promote it does so in a particularly customer-friendly way, such as suggesting a wine to complement a particular cheese, or providing a recipe for one central ingredient that will, of course, inevitably lead you to buying quite a few more.

Rather a fine example of being customer-led. And a very successful one too. From this it is easy to see the direct commercial advantages of being so much in tune with one's customers.

It's perhaps harder with some charities, but not always.

Corporate culture is more than just an understanding of procedures or everyone going in the same direction. To make an organisation into a distinct and singular entity involves agreement on common work habits and forms of behaviour. It also involves respect for staff and respect for colleagues. How people deal with their colleagues mirrors how they will deal with donors.

An effective corporate culture also includes politeness, ways of speaking, telephone manner and so forth. It involves standards of dress (an area much underestimated by some fundraisers) and issues such as consideration of others, turning up on time in the morning, being punctual for meetings, reliability, and a range of behavioural aspects that come with true professionalism. Precise communication is also part of company culture. For example, how many charities do you know that have detailed published corporate identity guidelines but no behaviour guidelines? An organisation's culture also encompasses its quality and orientation, systems of quality assurance, systems for hello and goodbye, attitude to value for money and more besides.

We fundraisers should get serious about our corporate culture. Your organisation's culture is a key component of your ability to put relationship fundraising into practice. As most charities have so far overlooked this area, here's another chance for you to gain a competitive edge – to be 15 minutes ahead. So take a lesson from the world of commercial enterprise – and make yours a strong one.

Leadership

I don't feel I need to say a great deal about the importance of leadership in implementing relationship fundraising in practice for I feel the case histories in this book amply demonstrate it.

The best ideas in the world will still fail without the right people to make them happen. Success demands knowledge, experience and technique, of course, but it also needs effective leaders, people who are capable of constructing the climate, environment and culture that will enable good ideas to flourish. Fundraising is a promising and exciting area to be in right now because it offers such interesting career challenges – for the right kind of leaders.

People with leadership qualities should be sought out and then nurtured, developed and, at all costs, retained.

I'm not talking about the old-fashioned 'over-the-top' type of leadership that in the past wasted so many lives during various wars. Nor, in this context, do I mean David Ogilvy's concept of 'the lengthened shadow', where one strong individual dominates an organisation to the exclusion of others. Leadership in today's business organisations strikes me as much more demanding than in these two examples. No one blindly follows orders now. And the fundraising leader usually has to work closely with, and as part of, a team. So leadership means example, inspiration and putting oneself second. Obviously this is somewhat removed from the self-serving leadership we seem to see so often nowadays, particularly in Britain's once publicly owned utility companies.

In his book *Understanding Organizations* (Penguin Books, Harmondsworth, Middlesex, 1976) Professor Charles Handy describes the main traits almost universally agreed to be essential to good leadership. These are above-average intelligence (but not genius), independent inventiveness or initiative, self-assurance and, what Handy refers to as the 'helicopter factor', the ability to rise above the particulars of a situation and perceive it in its relations to the overall environment.

You could easily add in a few others, including determination, clear thinking and the ability to stick to the original vision when all around have started to lose sight of it. Philosopher André Gide wrote that on any long sea journey it is necessary to be prepared to lose sight of land. It seems to me that several of the following case histories might easily be compared to a long and uncertain journey, and the careful reader may well be able to spot the point in these accounts when it was difficult, if not impossible, to see land. It is then that leadership unquestionably comes into its own. In some but not all of these cases that leadership has come through strongly and delivered the desired result, when without it the entire adventure might have foundered.

Leadership, of course, is not very fashionable these days. It smacks of élitism and privilege – all right for the army or political parties perhaps, but not really necessary in today's egalitarian society, particularly in charities. Or so people seem to think.

In the voluntary sector concepts of leadership have often been diffuse. Entrepreneurial verve is rare and seldom rewarded. Strong managers are frowned upon. So is taking risks. Collective management, a spirit of passive compliance and the meeting culture are the norm. Committees abound.

These have some advantages over more individually based structures and often work very well, but they frequently slow down the decision-making process and sometimes inhibit it altogether. Committees, particularly voluntary committees, are often more cautious so can dilute the entrepreneurial spirit that is invariably necessary if organisations are to take advantage of opportunities. However well qualified its members, I have yet to be convinced that committees make better decisions *per se* than any group of key managers. Most effective of all is the single manager or business leader who has the authority, the responsibility and the ability to work effectively with his or her team to get things done. To quote David Ogilvy again, 'Search your parks in all your cities, you'll find no statues of committees.'

Too often a committee is 'an incompetent group of highly competent people'. Many voluntary committees meet too infrequently to be of much use. The commitment of their members can be superb but more often is inconsistent and sometimes non-existent. Most chairs of voluntary committees don't issue job descriptions, or even terms of reference to their members, which means that the ability to control committees is strictly limited. So good, effective committees are rare.

However there are some, and they are worth working for. I have worked with several effective committees and with many truly first-class leaders who have served on committees. In my experience, committees work best when they don't seek to take decisions but rather act as approvers, or disapprovers, to the executive management team – supporting, challenging, encouraging and assisting them wherever and whenever necessary or desirable.

In this way committees can provide the inspiration and challenge of leadership. And can also give the organisation's real leader, or leaders, the strength and support that from time to time she, he, or they will certainly need.

Committee structures and procedures too are changing, generally for the better. Before long it will not be unusual for charity trustees in Britain to have written job descriptions, fixed-term contracts and targets. (The USA is already some way down this road. America's National Center for Nonprofit Boards publishes upwards of 40 detailed leaflets covering every aspect of not-for-profit management.) It is also expected increasingly that charity trustees will not only be inspirational donors themselves, they will also play a leading role in bringing in other major donors. As they say in America, charity trustees now are expected to give, get, or get off.

Sweet inspiration

No leader in the voluntary sector will be effective without
the ability to motivate and inspire. He or she must be able to
inspire all sorts of people from every station and walk of life
to believe in the cause and the imperative need to give to it,
as the old Jewish saying goes, 'until it hurts'. Nobody has to
be a donor. Yet tens of thousands of people give, and they
give to a vision, to an ideal, to a dream to which they have
been inspired.

Many fundraisers overlook inspiration, or neglect it.
Yet failing to recognise the essential role inspiration
plays in both staff and volunteer productivity is equivalent
to denying the fundraising machine its unique, extra
quality and edge. Of course, other businesses regularly
employ inspiration but fundraising has more claim to it
than most.

Cecil Jackson Cole (known as CJC), the estate agent and
furniture salesman who co-founded Oxfam and started Help
the Aged and ActionAid, was an irascible and difficult man,
notorious for his short temper and the tendency to over-
simplify problems and make outrageous demands on his
staff. Yet he had remarkable powers of inspiration, firmly
rooted in his own implacable belief in his causes. He
expected a great deal from his employees and he got it, often
far more than they themselves thought they could provide.
He got it, in part, because he pushed people. But most of all
he got it because, whatever they may have thought of him
personally, his staff were all imbued with an unswerving
devotion and loyalty to their cause, a loyalty required,
inspired, instilled and fed by CJC himself.

I know. He recruited me into fundraising. Working for
CJC was hell, but it was worth it.

Inspiration is the purest form of power, the ability to
change the attitudes and behaviour of others. Most
commercial organisations can persuade, motivate and
influence, and indeed constantly seek to do so through a

variety of marketing and sales activities, but few can regularly and consistently inspire.

Charities are different. To succeed they *have to* inspire, not just those who work for them but all those who support them. This is yet another fundamental distinction between the organisations fundraisers work for and the mainstream of commercial business life.

I stress the importance of inspiration when preparing any fundraising communication. Don't leave out the passion. And don't be shy. Don't hold back. If I were briefing a copywriter I would say, 'Unless your passionate conviction for the cause comes shining through on every page, your leaflet, or whatever, will automatically be assessed as just more junk mail. Just another nondescript addition to the spate of litter that nowadays comes flooding through your donor's letter-box.'

Fundraising publications must above all be inspirational.

It has long been acknowledged that changing people's attitudes is much more difficult than changing their behaviour. Fundraising would certainly be easier if in our relationships with donors we were more inspirational than we are now. Perhaps this is an area that would repay further investment of time and work from fundraisers.

Making friends and influencing people

In his famous book *Influence: the Psychology of Persuasion* (Quill Books, William Morrow & Co, New York, 1993), Professor Robert Cialdini cites six principles of influence.

■ Reciprocation. If you do someone a favour they will owe you.

■ Scarcity. If people can't have something they'll want it even more.

■ Authority. If an expert says it, it must be true.

■ Commitment. If they have already agreed to a small

request they'll be more likely to agree to a larger one.

■ Liking. People are far more likely to do business with someone they know and like.

■ Consensus. If lots of other people are doing it your prospect will feel he or she should too.

The summarising of these key principles is mine and I don't propose to go into Professor Cialdini's principles in much more detail. But I do urge you to read his book, for all fundraisers should be conversant with the basic skills and techniques of influencing. It's the logical extension of making friends.

The art of negotiation

No less important for fundraisers is the art of negotiation. Here I will digress slightly to impart a tale that never fails to cheer me up.

There once was a wary tourist who was visiting London's famous Petticoat Lane market. He had heard that whatever price they quoted you for anything you should automatically half it. Thus warned he sallied forth down the market, until he spied a stall that sported a pair of trousers he fancied, and asked how much.

'£10', said the stallholder.

'I'll give you £5', said the wary tourist.

'Are you mad? Feel the quality. Make it £8', said the stallholder.

'£4', said the wary tourist.

A small crowd was gathering.

'My life, who is this nut? Have them for £5 and scarper', cried the stallholder.

'£2.50', said the wary tourist.

A large crowd was gathering.

'You trying to ruin me or something? OK, have them for £2.50, only beat it', said the stallholder.

'£1.25', said the wary tourist.

> 'Look mate, take the bleedin' trousers for nothing', said the
> stallholder.
> 'I'll take two pairs', said the wary tourist.

I like this story not because it teaches you anything about
negotiating, but because for once the tourist wins.

Qualities also important for relationship fundraisers are
sensitivity, as in 'I can be very sensitive when I want to be',
and tact, the ability to see others as they see themselves.

Communication

Most successful organisations invest large amounts of time
and energy in ensuring that they communicate effectively –
the right messages to the right audiences in the right way at
the right time. Fundraisers have many more audiences than
most so need to be particularly concerned about
communication, not just to the obvious candidates but to
those hidden audiences that become apparent during that
process of deep thinking that I mentioned a few pages back.

These audiences are both internal and external. For
example, your switchboard has every individual and each
department in the organisation as its audience, as well as
all outside callers. Your finance department has all staff
(whom it pays) as its customers, and all suppliers. Head
office needs to communicate particularly carefully with staff
in the regions because they so easily feel left out. And
regional staff too have a need to communicate effectively
with head office. Trustees and boards of management
often complain that they are neglected when it comes to
internal communication, but, just as often, they neglect their
own communication responsibilities.

The relationship fundraiser is obsessive about her or his
communications – not only about their inspirational content
but also about what they say, when and how often. A
strategy is devised not only for each audience but for each
category or segment of that audience. Theoretically, a

communications strategy could be worked out for each individual, taking into account his or her experience, interests, past behaviour, preferences, and so on (*see* chapter 4 on communications strategies, where this subject is covered in more detail). This may be technically impractical and prohibitively expensive for some organisations at present, but may not be forever. The fundraiser's ability to individualise is increasing and, generally, is becoming cheaper all the time.

These communications – and the database necessary to deliver them in the right way to the right people at the right time – are at the core of any contemporary concept of relationship fundraising. So too is the notion that rapidly changing technology will increasingly improve the possibilities and reduce the cost.

To some it will seem idle to speculate on what the future might or might not bring, and cruelly tantalising to dangle imaginary scenarios that are unconstrained by costs, time, volume and other practicalities.

I don't agree. Second-guessing the future is a perfectly honourable pastime probably rewarded, it's true, by more 'wrongs' than 'rights'. If you never try you may never be wrong, but you'll certainly never be right and you stand no chance at all of being ahead of the game.

And, as I've said, fundraisers increasingly have to be one step ahead if they are to succeed – even if only 15 minutes ahead.

Writing for readers

I was a publisher before I was ever in fundraising and communications are my first and major love. So I'm going to digress a teensy bit and make some general observations about fundraising communications.

■ We lose half our readers by setting the type too small.

■ Most people are most comfortable reading body copy set

in 11 point on a 13-point leading.

■ Sans serif typefaces should never be used for body copy, or you'll lose up to 60 per cent of possible readers.

■ Older donors like large-appearing serif typefaces of 12 point or above.

■ Never, ever, set body copy in reversed-out type (some fundraisers, not content with making things merely difficult, persist in setting their body copy in reversed-out, sans serif type and then run it over a photograph).

■ Tell a story. Never forget that your publication – or letter, or leaflet, or whatever – is not about you, or your organisation. It is about the reader, and the people and projects they are helping by supporting your work. So remember your Kipling and his six honest men:

> I had six honest working men
> They taught me all I knew
> Their names were How, and Why, and When
> And What, and Where, and Who.

■ Use everyday language. Talk to your readers where they are, not where you want them to be. Be forward looking, not backward looking.

■ Find great photographs. And use them big, with clear descriptive captions. Break up slabs of text with dramatic headlines and intriguing subheads. Don't forget reading gravity. People naturally read from top left to bottom right. The easiest layout starts with a photograph, to draw the eye, has the headline underneath and the text leading downwards.

■ Heed the advice of that fundraising sage Si Seymour,

> Academicians relish lengthy paragraphs, it seems, but for purposes of coaxing readers any paragraph of as many as 10 lines may be a wee bit too long.

■ And be involving. Make your publications a dialogue

by adding points of contact, reply mechanisms, calls to action and other involvement devices.

■ Then train everyone in your organisation on how to use your publications. And monitor their ultimate effectiveness.

The reply form of the future

Anyone who receives a lot of paperwork will prize clarity above all else. Donors are no exception. And clear communications pay off in increased response, every time.

When American Express recently redesigned its statements for cardholders it was reassured to find customers started paying their accounts much more promptly. Barry Hill, senior vice-president for product development at AmEx, paid an interesting compliment to the design house that had wrought the transformation, 8vo (funny name, I think it's pronounced Octavo). 'They claimed that design should be transparent. It should allow communication to pass straight through to the viewer. Other agencies feel the design is the star.'

Well put Octavo. Next time you have problems with a prima donna designer, quote that at him.

American Express's instruction in redesigning its stationery was to reinforce customers' memory of why they had become American Express cardholders. Charities too should seek to do this in their reply forms. Also, as did AmEx, they should remove any unnecessary reference codes, which in practice will be almost all of them. Make your forms user-friendly, not technocratic. And, above all, set the type large enough for older eyes to read easily and allow enough space for anyone to write in what they need to tell you.

With the technology that now exists fundraisers of the future may be personalising individual and appropriate messages on to their reply forms. To quote Barry Hill again, 'If it's a good offer that's relevant to you, you don't need a glossy brochure when you can print 25 words or less on the statement.'

Bingo! Another nail in the coffin of junk mail. But organisations like American Express have one great advantage over us. A bill or statement is one piece of mail that is not going to be consigned straight to the waste-paper basket. That just means we have to work that much harder at these short and appropriate messages.

It's fundraising, Jim, but not as we know it

If we are really to aspire to giving our readers choices (*see* page 86) then perhaps the real issue for communications in the future can be discerned from the Peppers and Rogers' quote at the start of this chapter.

We speak differently to people we know well, reflecting what we know of them and how they like to be talked to, how best to approach them, and what makes them react positively. And the more we know them, the better we should get at understanding and communicating with them.

Fundraisers too should try to improve their communications as they get to know their donors better. It's unlikely that the relationship will develop properly if they don't.

Peppers and Rogers illustrated just how far this concept can go when people really know each other very well with the following imaginary conversation between a husband and wife. If computers are ever to hold conversations with humans, they reasoned, this is what they will have to aspire to.

> Husband to wife, 'OK, where did you hide it?'
> Wife to husband, 'Hide what?'
> Husband, 'You know.'
> Wife, 'Where do you think?'
> Husband, 'Oh.'

Now you may think it absolute science fiction for a

computer to learn to speak to people who are so comfortable after years of living and sharing together that they can converse almost without words.

But apparently it can be done. Computers can learn from experience, by listening to repeated conversations. According to Peppers and Rogers it's called a heuristic system and they claim it's currently under development in a number of research firms and universities.

What a world! It may after all be quite possible for our communications with donors to get much better as we get to know them better.

The logical extension of this, of course, is a computer that will automatically communicate with each donor individually, with thousands of donors all at the same time, telling them all exactly what they want to hear. Fundraising then will be easy – but perhaps not so much fun.

This future, I hope, is still some years away.

What do donors want?

The only way to find out for sure is to ask your donors, one by one. Their answers will vary and they will almost certainly change over time. So you have to keep asking them, one by one, over and over again. As I've said, it's neither easy nor cheap.

So, although I am a frequent advocate of research, I am also somewhat sceptical of it. Like a photograph of a dancer, research presents a frozen picture of something that is always moving, so the picture, while accurate, portrays only a part of the truth and then sometimes in a quite misleading light.

Nevertheless, we don't do enough research in Britain and so any picture, even if slightly distorted, usually reveals some insights. That's why I frequently find myself quoting research from America. It may be only partly accurate and possibly misleading, but it's often all there is.

But beware of ridiculous research, for it will simply

mislead. For example, don't ask silly questions such as, 'Do you want your charity to send thank you letters?' Few donors would answer positively to that – but few will be saying what they mean. Donors, by their very nature, are self-sacrificing.

With these reservations, it is worth considering some information gleaned from 'The Heart of a Donor', a survey of active American donors carried out by the Barna Research Group for the Russ Reid Company and reported by Holly Hall in the *Chronicle of Philanthropy* in February 1995. The primary interest in this survey seems to have been that it indicated that a significant portion of conservative donors give to liberal causes and a significant portion of liberal donors give to conservative causes. I found this unsurprising, as most donors are not extremists. This finding prompted the originator of the research to go on to comment that we must stop treating our donors as a mass. Well surprise, surprise! To my mind, the research became much more interesting when it went on to ask these donors what they wanted.

Again many of the results were not surprising, if you make the 90-degree shift.

■ 53 per cent of donors said their relationship with an organisation would improve if they were invited to participate in work projects closely related to the organisation's mission.

■ More than half said a 24-hour toll-free telephone number would have the same effect.

■ 47 per cent said their relationship would be improved if they were able to specify how frequently they received mail from an organisation.

■ Two-thirds of donors thought relationships would be improved if they were given the chance to express their views and ideas on the organisation and how it should be run.

■ More than half of donors indicated that they would respond favourably to the chance for their personal preferences to dictate communications from the organisation.

■ When asked to rate nine ways that non-profits might communicate with donors, the firm favourite was the newsletter.

■ Most other donor development initiatives were met with similar enthusiasm from responders.

Russ Reid himself observed that, 'The pattern may be indicative of a new generation of donors who expect more and are more critical and selective in their approach to non-profit giving.'

Professional conscience prickers

All this, I believe, points to significant changes in how fundraisers communicate with their donors, which is almost certainly a good thing. If relationship fundraising does nothing else, I hope it will encourage fundraisers to think more deeply and carefully about what they send and to save themselves the expense and trouble of producing anything that is not what the donor wants to read or receive.

But before closing this section on communications it makes sense to add a warning, again prompted by the 90-degree shift, about a valid concern that for me strikes rather close to home. As we become more and more competent at communicating with our donors we have to take great care not to appear to be too professional because the public, generally, dislikes professionalism in charities. They distrust it and are easily deterred by any sign of it. By professional in this context I think they mean slick rather than competent. But the term is confusing nevertheless. We fundraisers are always trying to be as professional as we can be. Donors don't see that as an advantage. In our context, true professionalism, therefore, is not to appear slick or polished but to let our passion show through.

This point was ably, if possibly misguidedly, made by one of Britain's most respected political commentators, Matthew Parris, in an article in *The Times* in October 1995.

> One senses the growth of a high-powered cadre of men and women who are good at what they would call 'communication' in the field of humanitarian charity – professional conscience prickers, if you like – whose skills are pretty much transferable between causes. The art of presentation swells in importance.

Now while you may say this displays a lamentable lack of appreciation of the need for professional and effective fundraising, it is a fair reflection of how many of our public see us. Parris's main concern is that as charities grow more professional might not the public grow more cynical and defensive about charity as a whole?

The answer is yes, it might. The challenge for relationship fundraisers is to ensure that we are so competent in communicating with our donors that the reverse is true and the public comes to believe increasingly that we are good and faithful stewards of their generosity, not just worthwhile but satisfying to support.

Times change, the basics don't

It is a shameful admission but when I wrote *Relationship Fundraising* I hadn't myself read the one great classic work on fundraising in the English language – *Designs for Fundraising: Principles, Patterns, Techniques* by Harold J (Si) Seymour (The McGraw-Hill Book Company, Chicago, 1966).

Seymour's book was first published in the year I left secondary school. Despite this great lapse of time, its relevance is bang up to date. What he says still applies universally to fundraisers.

Obviously since then there have been some rather important technical changes in the tools available to fundraisers. In Seymour's day carding systems were the state of the art method of storing and retrieving information on donors. Seymour well appreciated the importance of these things though. The purpose is the same. The advent of computers and word processors has just made more of it possible. (They may not yet have made life easier – *see* Michael Crichton's view on page 553.)

So what are the key components of relationship fundraising and what conditions must prevail before the concepts of relationship fundraising can flourish?

This list is not exhaustive but it contains what I believe are some of the most important.

■ Genuine liking for donors and their motivations.

■ Respect for the donor and the donor's rights.

■ A visible commitment to and passion for the cause.

■ A strong service-oriented, donor-led organisational culture.

■ Skills of influencing and negotiation.

■ Clear leadership.

■ The capacity to motivate and inspire.

■ A sufficiently large constituency of active donors.

■ Honesty and openness.

■ Good internal and external communications.

■ That these factors should involve the *whole* organisation.

And a little luck helps too.

Straight to the heart

How to create a donor communications strategy

> " Until well into the seventeenth century surgery was performed not by doctors but by barbers who, untaught and unlettered, applied whatever tortures they had picked up during their apprenticeship. Doctors, observing a literal interpretation of their oath not to inflict bodily harm, were too 'ethical' to cut and were not even supposed to watch. But the operation, if performed according to the rules, was presided over by a learned doctor who sat on a dais well above the struggle and read what the barber was supposed to be doing aloud from a Latin classic (which the barber, of course, did not understand).
>
> Needless to say it was all the barber's fault if the patient died and always the doctor's achievement if he survived. And the doctor got the bigger fee in any event. "
>
> **Peter Drucker**
> *The Practice of Management*

Wouldn't it be nice if we could find out exactly how, when, and on what subjects each of our donors would like to hear from us so we could only send to each of them what would be appropriate, welcome and likely to be read? Wouldn't that lead to happier donors? And wouldn't it lead also to the end of junk mail, less waste and much more cost-effective fundraising?

Of course it would. The scatter-gun approach of mass mailing is crude in the extreme. Sending the same message to everyone regardless of interest or acceptability is always going to be irritating and wasteful. The conveyor-belt system of direct mail fundraising, where every donor is inevitably subjected to a never-ending cycle of regular and untargeted blandishments, was always bound to lead to nothing as much as mountains of waste paper and was only ever likely to make direct marketing companies rich, rather than their clients.

But, despite this obvious wisdom and despite the rhetoric about targeting and segmentation that has been around for decades, most fundraisers are only just beginning to segment their mailings, and even those who do probably only offer a handful of different messages rather than any real attempt at matching their donors' needs and wishes.

The foregoing may all be quite true but it is a useless truth if you are one of the vast number of fundraisers saddled with an inappropriate database and denied the opportunity to do anything about it. Sadly, many, if not most, fundraisers seem to fall into this category and it is these people most of all that I hope will find something of value in the specimen donor communications diagrams that appear at the end of this section of this chapter.

But before considering how it might be possible to structure different communications for different groups of donors, from the most simple to the most complex of programmes, let us just spend a few minutes considering two other vital areas: research and database.

What do you want to know?

At first the connection between research and database might not be obvious. But they both hinge on the same vital question: what do you want to know about your donors?

Knowledge is power. For relationship fundraising, the more usable knowledge and understanding we have of our donors' interests and preferences the more effective our fundraising and relationship building will be. To properly answer the question 'what do I want to know about my donors?' you have to think of it in two ways: what do you really need to know about your donors, and what would be useful to know provided it doesn't cost too much?

Normally fundraisers have two sources for the information they need. Donors' previous behaviour, which can usually be found by analysing their own and other people's (ie profiling) databases or records and direct research (ie by asking the donors). The information from this research has then to be stored economically and accessibly alongside the behavioural data on the fundraiser's database.

The methods of achieving, storing and retrieving this information and the technical problems that have to be overcome along the way are not really our concern. We simply need to identify what in ideal circumstances the donors will want and then to strive to satisfy them.

'What does the donor want?' is, of course, just another way of asking the old question 'how should we segment our database?'

The information we put on our databases should, I believe, be considered in three ways:

■ Demographically.

■ By past behaviour.

■ By choice.

The first two are widely practised already, but usually imperfectly. Sometimes this is because the system used is inadequate, as often as not it's because the fundraiser doesn't know which questions to ask.

The third type of information, that which reflects the donors' choices or wishes, is very rarely available on fundraising databases, other than simple stuff such as opt-outs. Botton Village (*see* pages 160–162) is one of the few organisations I know that is systematically asking its donors and recording their choices (although the practice is spreading). Even at Botton, the choice is generally limited to frequency and type of mailing. This is 'third-level' segmentation, and we should make it our special concern for within it is the key to relationship fundraising – giving the donor what he or she wants and thereby raising lots and lots more money.

Demographics

These are mostly obvious: name, address, sex, status, date of birth (age), phone number, occupation, location, salary level and so on. We need to re-examine these to find the opportunities that this information will provide. For example, a short while ago no one bothered to record phone numbers. Now anyone can see how useful that information is, or would be. Hitherto we've done little or nothing with the information we have on the sex or age of our donors. Yet we know men and women react differently to different propositions and even respond differently to different linguistic styles. So why do fundraisers persist in sending exactly the same letter to the men and the women on their file? Some interesting work on gender splits is currently happening in the UK. The results are encouraging.

We also know older people have different values from younger people, that donors with families give to different causes than those without. Whereas many people give as individuals, some make their decisions to give in conjunction with their partner – as a couple. Even couples are not as straightforward as they used to be. The new households (gay, single parent, never married, etc) also have to be considered by fundraisers. Yet few fundraisers allow for writing to couples (not just in the salutation, but in letter copy and reply form too) and most persist in sending the same letter to everyone, or just segment by past behavioural patterns.

Behaviour

Donors' giving patterns in the past are clear indications of when and what they are likely to give to in the future. Many fundraisers now segment by recency, frequency and value. But most have no sophisticated scoring or monitoring system. Yet such systems could quite easily be introduced. It also seems logical to me to expect that in the near future, if not already, we could program our computers with the ability to analyse a donor's pattern of giving and automatically assign a communications strategy based on that pattern, with in-built upgrade components if desired. These might be either gentle or vigorous depending on the character of the donor and the sensitivity or ambitions of the fundraiser. (*See* Abel's day, pages 546–551.)

Choice

The process of offering donors choices is as important as whatever choice is made. We already have evidence that donors prefer to choose the number and time of appeals, and careful response to these choices can result in more cost-effective fundraising. Donors might also choose the type of appeals they wish to hear about (subject matter), how their money is used, how they might pay, who writes to them, even the number of enclosures and style of writing. What else might donors choose?

At present, most donors are offered the choice to receive reciprocal mailings or not. Many say no when they might be prepared to receive some, but don't want to receive all. They could be given the choice and may respond positively if they were.

Or they may not. Relationship fundraisers also have to assess which choices will make a real difference and which will not be worth offering.

Cost

Clearly there is a line between what is valuable information and what is not worth storing and manipulating. Collecting information is only useful if sometime – either now or in the future – it will be used. Otherwise the knowledge is useless and collecting and storing it an unjustifiable expense – and an unforgivable intrusion.

Where that line between usefulness and cost falls is largely a matter of choice, which may be further influenced by budget and the practical limitations of your system. An ideal system would at least store all the key demographic data plus behavioural information, which should include all recent gifts (by date, amount and subject area), affiliations, key relationships and recency frequency value score, which would automatically change with each transaction.

Research information should be from both direct (supplied by the donors themselves) and indirect (ie compiled from elsewhere) sources, and might include wealth indicators, reasons for joining, other charities supported, key motivations and opinions and so on. Preferences – also compiled by direct research – that should be included would be any opt-outs, best time to contact and choice of communication style and frequency.

Some possible questions/areas of choice for donors and databases

- All the demographics?
- Age and sex?
- How would you like to hear from us (the organisation)?
- Who do you know?
- Directorships? Clubs?
- Political/religious views?

■ Education?

■ Willingness to volunteer?

■ Questions relating to the issues dealt with by your specific charity.

■ Involvement in specific support schemes in your charity.

■ Other charities supported?

■ Financial status?

■ Family?

■ Relevant interests?

■ Giving preferences? (When, to what, and preferred method of payment?)

■ Choose from this list of possible reciprocal partners.

■ When should we contact you? (Choice of options.)

■ What should we contact you about? (Multiple choice options.)

■ How do you like to be contacted? (Multiple choice options.)

■ Attitude to legacies?

Planning a communications strategy

Anything that is horrendously complicated and hideously difficult to understand will inevitably look better and be easier to follow if reduced to diagrammatic form (the diagrams in trains and stations of London's underground system are much easier to follow than an actual map would be – unless you want to go from Bank station to Mansion House. The tube map suggests two changes and a half hour journey, whereas in reality the two are just a couple of hundred yards apart, by foot).

So with donor communications strategies, which are often frighteningly complicated, a not too complex donor communications' diagram can be very useful. My favourites are those with a relatively simple core that can then be added to, or overlaid as different options and directions are introduced. Although some strategies (*see* Greenpeace USA, page 394) are satisfactorily expressed in a linear fashion, most organisations have some sort of regular communications' cycle and so their communications will be better represented in the form of a circle. As different choices are introduced the basic circle may become progressively harder to discern. Someone once described a moderately complicated communications diagram as 'like the M25 and spaghetti junction put together, but on a very, very bad day'.

(Complex though they may be, these models are actually a simplification of what really happens. For example, the fairly crucial component of timing is omitted, for simplicity's sake.)

The circle (*see* figure 1, page 90), of course, was almost all there was in the bad old days, when donors were not specially thanked or welcomed, were given no choices and were immediately plonked on the conveyor belt of regular quarterly, monthly, or whatever, appeals. In those days, donors went straight in unprepared and there was no escape unless, in time, some bright and ambitious direct marketer decided to lapse them, reactivate them, or render them dormant. Even giving a much larger gift, whether cumulative or one-off, still wouldn't get you off that circle.

Nowadays, even with this circle churning away as of old, it is less likely that the new donor will find himself or herself dropped in it immediately without going through some kind of thank you and welcome procedure, with a variety of additional options being offered. This makes sense for the donor and also for the fundraiser, who finds that immediately after being thanked for their first gift is the time when many donors are most likely to give another gift, upgrade, commit to regular giving, or to volunteer for

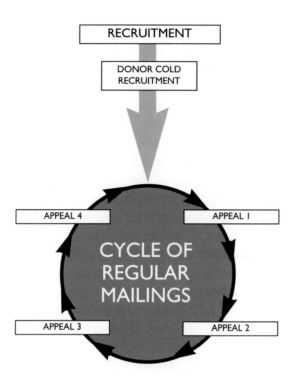

Figure 1 Donor activity plan – the basic cycle

various other ways of helping.

Immediately after the newly recruited responder has been thanked (*see* figure 2, facing page), a welcome pack should arrive including the various options. Larger donors, however, will be singled out for special treatment and enjoy a well-timed and well-managed telephone call, perhaps from one of the charity's big guns, who will personally offer a more élite version of the options on offer in the welcome pack.

How the new responder reacts to these options will determine when, how, and even if, he or she is returned to the main cycle of communication. If an appeals opt-out has been offered, he or she may be smoothly diverted into an entirely different kind of non-appeal-driven communications programme (*see* figure 4, page 93).

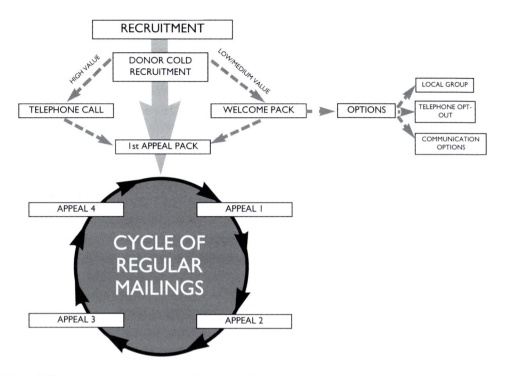

Figure 2 Donor activity plan – starting the relationship

Similarly, if he or she has said yes to monthly giving the main cycle will be bypassed and replaced with something more appropriate. (*See* figure 6, page 95.)

But with most donors the charity's main objective now will usually be to solicit a second gift. This may be by special approach to new donors or by including them in the next regular special appeal. Whether or not the donor responds to one or other of these appeals, further additional options will – or might – be offered along the way. These might include a regional appeal, a special communications option (*see* figure 4), a legacy (bequest) offer (figure 5), or any one of a range of other possibilities, each of which may – or may not – remove that donor temporarily, or even permanently, from the central cycle of communications. Committed giving offers and reminders (figure 6) will inevitably take our

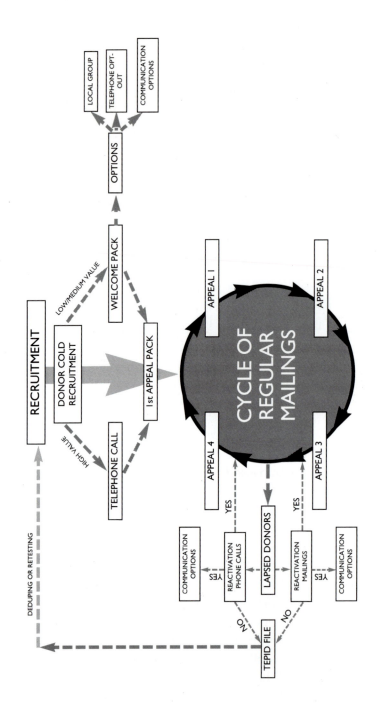

Figure 3 Donor activity plan – rekindling the relationship

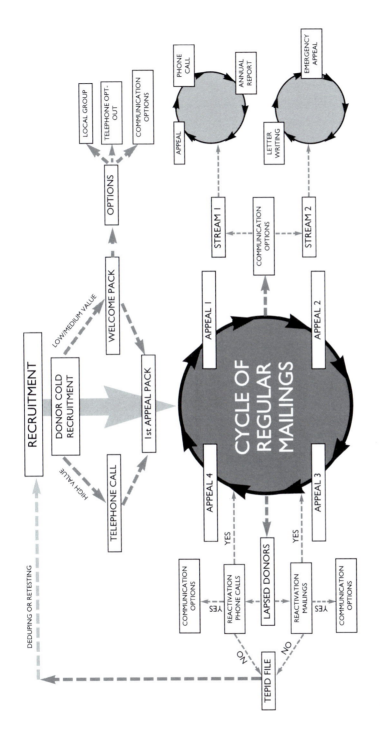

Figure 4 Donor activity plan – offering choices

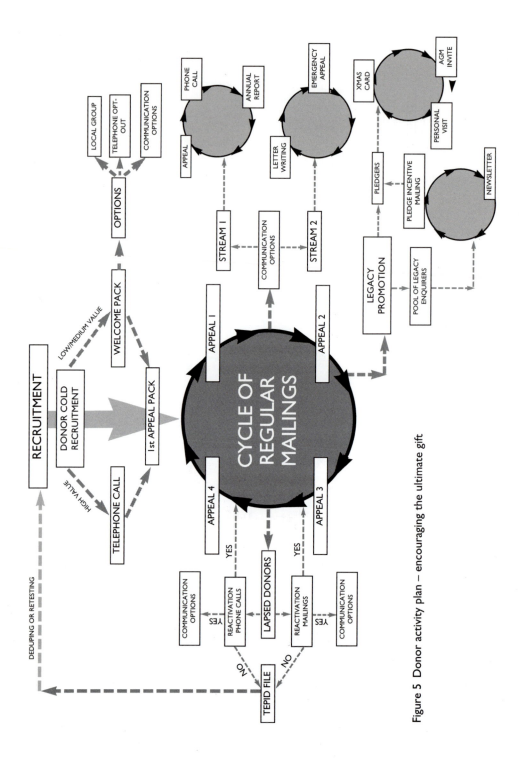

Figure 5 Donor activity plan – encouraging the ultimate gift

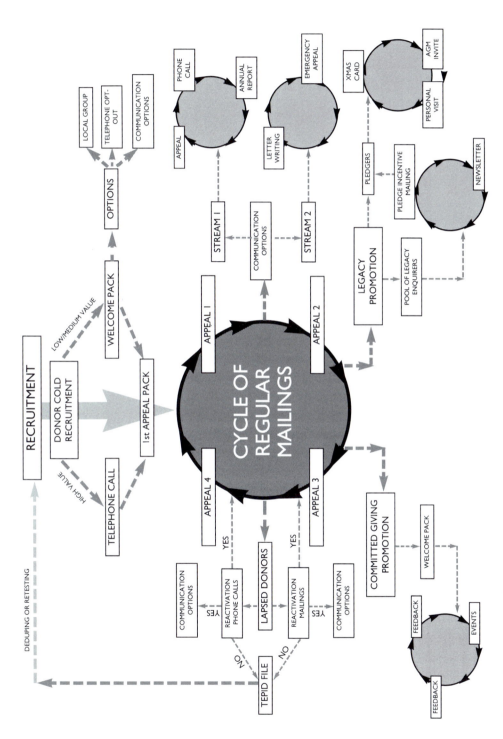

Figure 6 Donor activity plan – encouraging commitment

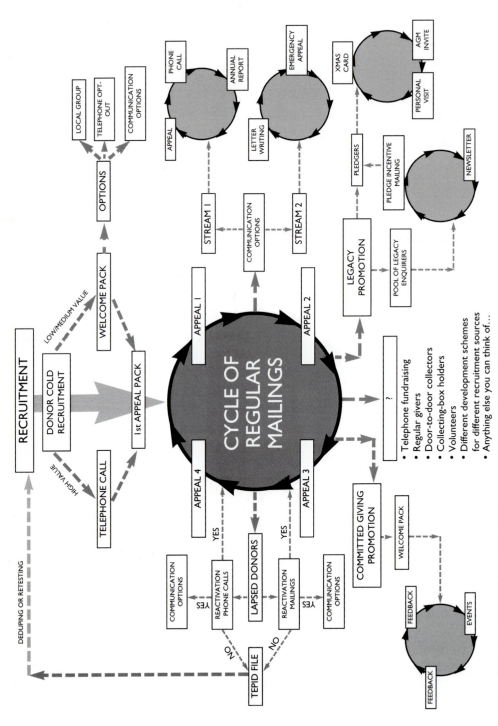

Figure 7 Donor activity plan – what else?

donor out of the cycle for a while.

But if none of these offers successfully tempts our responder she may be lapsed as a once-only giver. If she hasn't given for some time a variety of reactivation initiatives of increasing vigour may then be tried until this expensively acquired name is returned to a tepid file, which might be permanently rested or trawled from time to time with cold recruitment offers. (*See* figure 4, page 93.)

I predict these donor communications strategies will become increasingly sophisticated and the subject of much discussion, particularly in the sequence, timing and structure of specific plans. The ideal welcome strategy and upgrade strategy are already hotly debated topics when fundraisers get together.

In practice many donor communications strategies are very much more complicated than those I have illustrated. But adapting the diagrams to your organisation may help you to get a feel for however many different types and styles of communication you may be able to offer, now and in the future. And they will be useful too for explaining to your staff, your switchboard, or even your trustees, why and how you are making an effort to communicate effectively with your supporters.

And this kind of communications programme will help your donors to get more meaningful and relevant information about your work and how they can support it.

And that will lead to more successful fundraising for you.

What donors want

> One of the commonplace yet probably essential characteristics in the development of any new body of knowledge is the competing values of those who generate and use that knowledge. Those who are attracted to new areas of study are generally dissatisfied with the conventional wisdoms of more established disciplines. For the most part this is all to the good; new problems can be defined, new people encouraged to tackle them and new concepts and methodologies refined to meet the challenges of new situations.
>
> Difficulties start to occur, however, when the products of some of these new endeavours are communicated to the world at large...

Andrew Pettigrew from the foreword to
Understanding Organizations **by**
Professor Charles B Handy

I was once asked to prepare a seminar on what it is that motivates donors. I found it difficult at the time to locate any reliable research on the subject, with the inevitable exception of some interesting morsels from America. So I drew on my own experience and on that of several of my fundraising friends and colleagues. The next few pages are based on the information I produced for that seminar.

Why do donors give and what do donors want?

If we knew the answers to these two questions, then fundraising would be easy. But partial answers at least are within easy reach, although it constantly surprises me how often fundraisers overlook them.

Just for the sake of nostalgia let me just run through some of the basic tablets of stone about donors and donating.

■ People are the same, wherever you are. It is self-delusion to claim, 'but our donors are different', or 'that won't work here'. Such statements only serve to obscure poor performance and fool no one. Yet wherever I go in the world, some fundraiser or other will come out with one or other of those old shibboleths. Sure there are regional variations and cultural quirks but what inspires and motivates donors is universal. The basic interests and needs are the same, it's just the circumstances that might be different.

■ Not all of the people you talk to are really donors. Only a small number have the potential to become *real* donors. Therefore you have to identify and cultivate *your* targets: the people who are most likely to support you. You can comfortably forget about the rest.

■ People relate to people. People give to people, not to organisations Fundraising above all is a people business. Look at your promotional materials. Are you making best use of your people?

■ Fundraising is not about money. It is about needs. It's about bringing about change. People respond to needs, not achievements.They applaud achievements. (I see some evidence that this old and faithful truism is changing. People now seem quite keen to give on the promise of quantifiable results.)

■ The two most important words in fundraising are thank you. A short while ago this would have been a controversial statement. Now there is no argument. Basic politeness is fashionable once more. In fundraising it pays.

■ People respond more to projects that are closer to them. It follows, therefore, that the secret of fundraising success is to bring the problems – and the solutions – home to your donor. So it will pay you to make your fundraising local, relevant, exciting, touching, urgent and personal.

■ Timing is crucial in fundraising. Choosing the right time to ask, and the right time to wait, can make all the difference.

■ And, finally, donors need to believe in the causes they are asked to give to and in the people who do the asking. *This is vital.* The day of the detached, professional fundraising specialist didn't quite arrive and I believe now will never come. Donors need to believe that you, the fundraiser, care as much as they do about the issue you are both working to resolve. Before they will give, they need to see your enthusiasm and your commitment shining clearly through in everything you write, or say, or do.

Research I have quoted to back these points includes the by now legendary (but of unknown source) statistics about why donors stop supporting a once-favoured cause (*see* chapter 3, pages 62 and 63). Apparently a whopping 68 out of a 100 leave because of the charity's indifferent attitude to them. So mostly we lose them. They don't actively leave us. They just stop giving – and it's our fault. Here are some more reasons why donors don't give. There are probably multitudes of others but these strike me as among the most important.

Why donors don't give

■ There is too much choice. With the spiralling growth of competition in the 1980s, donors are now frequently heard to say that they can't give to everything. This feeling may lead to a donor giving to nothing. Who says all fundraising enlarges the market?

■ 'My gift won't make any difference.' Donors express this sentiment with equal frequency. It is often hard for donors to realise what their small gifts can do to ease the problems many charities face. Bridging this gap is a job for the fundraiser.

■ No recognition/no 'thank you'. Donors will rarely voice not being properly thanked as an objection. That doesn't mean they don't feel it. They may even expressly ask not to be thanked. I think you should thank them anyway – and explain why it's so important to you.

■ The charity hasn't lived up to its promises. Donors are unforgiving when a charity appears to get it wrong, or falls short of its own ideals.

■ The charity hasn't reported back effectively. Fundraising too often is a one-way street. Fundraisers frequently fail to go back to donors to update them on what their last donations achieved. Such reliance on blind faith alone asks too much of many donors.

■ The charity is obsessed with itself, doesn't listen to its donors so misses their signals and puts them off. To spot this tendency study charity annual reports. You'll soon see which reports are all about the organisation itself and its self-important officials. These publications have little to do with the donors and seem to say 'our annual report is about us, not our readers'.

■ Getting the asking wrong. Asking for the wrong thing (remember John's $1.7 million, page 55).
  – Asking at the wrong time.
  – Asking in the wrong way.
  – Asking for too much, or too little.

■ Inertia. Donors often don't give simply because they don't get round to it. This, I've explained elsewhere, is the biggest barrier of all and it's the hardest of all to climb. Couch potato syndrome. It's part of the human condition and explains why we have to make our promotions and propositions very compelling indeed. (Or switch people to automatic payments, where inertia works for us.)

(Please note. Lack of money is not really a valid reason for not giving. Obviously, if a potential donor lacks money he or she lacks one of the essential components of being a donor. But if the donor lacks money *at a particular time*, that is a problem of timing.)

What every donor wants

■ To be sought. Donors want to be wanted. With some people it's stronger than that: they really need to be needed. And they will respond better if you make them feel needed.

■ To be a worthwhile member of a worthwhile group. Most donors want to *belong*. They usually don't want to feel they're supporting you on their own. They want to belong to a small, exclusive group of similar individuals, or a group they might aspire to belong to. Si Seymour identified the above as the two most important requirements of every donor. I wouldn't like to contradict him. Although in the latter case I suspect some donors would run a mile rather than join in with other donors, so I imagine Si was referring to a spiritual rather than necessarily a physical sense of belonging.

■ Vision. The act of giving should be idealistic. Donors want an ideal. They are seeking a sense of magic, of wonder.

■ Every donor wants to believe his or her gift will be effective.

■ Donors want to see evidence of sensible use of resources.

■ Whether they admit it or not, most donors want recognition. Many North American fundraisers would unhesitatingly put this at the top of their list. They may be right.

■ Donors want to feel good. Why not?

■ Feedback. Donors like to know how their gift was used and what it achieved.

■ Prompt response. They may not always realise it, or may even say the opposite, but most donors don't want to be kept waiting or wondering what's happened to their gift. Did it arrive safely, or was it lost? Did some villain steal it? They want to hear quickly what you have done with their gift, and how much good it did.

■ And they like to be treated as an individual. Nobody wants to be just a number on a database, an entry on a computer file.

■ Donors want to have pride in their chosen cause.

■ Donors want cheerful, helpful service. As we have seen, most charities are customer-unfriendly. Donors may have tolerated this in the past, but the discerning donor of the future won't.

■ Good stewardship. Donors expect good financial management; careful and sound accounting of their gift. They won't stay donors for long if they don't get it.

■ Donors want to deal with people they like and trust.

■ And they want to believe the fundraiser is as committed to the cause as they are.

■ Donors need to be comfortable. Not to be pressurised.

■ Family and friends must approve (or not know). This can be vital. Any hint of potential disapproval and what appears to be a promising donation will evaporate.

This list is very general and it's not exhaustive. What donors want is probably not one of these things, but a combination of several. It may even be all of them.

One final suggestion: if a donor doesn't get what he or she wants, don't despair. But do encourage them to let you know. Give your donors every possible opportunity to tell you exactly what they think of your organisation. In particular, give them the opportunity, whenever you can, *to complain.* Remember Bob Worcester's observation at the start of chapter 1.

Perhaps something else that every donor wants is just someone to listen, someone who cares.

Upgrading

Every fundraiser wants to upgrade his or her supporters, all the time. We all need more money; that never changes. It is becoming harder and more costly to find new supporters so it follows that we should constantly be looking for ways to persuade our existing supporters to give more... and then to give even more again.

Upgrading simply means employing one or more of a variety of techniques to move a donor from his or her current level of giving up to a higher level, so that one way or another the donor will give more to your cause on a regular basis. Donors can be downgraded too although usually they do that themselves. Voluntary downgrading as donors lapse or as responders refuse to convert to donors may in fact be the most consistent and pervasive action in all fundraising.

I confess I am uneasy about the concept of upgrading. Most donors wouldn't like to be upgraded. For one thing it sounds like something you might do to an egg, or to a hotel room. Would you want to be upgraded, particularly if you knew it was going to cost you lots more money? Yet fundraisers mostly seem to assume that donors will enter their jurisdiction at the lowest level like lambs to the slaughter to be sequentially upgraded from enquirers to responders, then to donors, to committed donors and ultimately to leave a legacy. This of course is the concept we have been sold by our old friend the donor pyramid.

George Smith in *Asking Properly: the Art of Creative Fundraising* (The White Lion Press, London, 1996) describes this as 'the assiduous tradecraft of upgrading' and points out that adherence to this simple model deludes us into a self-fulfilling prophecy, that upgrading always has to follow this logical sequence.

People are rarely so predictable, or so logical. As Smith says 'It is a simple fact that most legacies are still left to charities by people totally unknown to the organisation concerned. How dare they be so generous when they have not served their time on the donor pyramid?'

Are you sitting comfortably?

So a little cynicism and scepticism about the process is probably healthy. Donors mostly can be upgraded only because they have not previously been asked properly or because they have not been offered sufficiently compelling reasons to give (and sufficiently automatic methods of payment) in the first place. Or because their circumstances have changed. But if a donor is giving at what they believe is their desired and comfortable limit (their comfort level) then they will indeed be difficult if not impossible to upgrade. And if you persist in deploying your various techniques and devices to change this you will perhaps persuade a few to upgrade, but at the price of making them feel distinctly uncomfortable. And you'll irritate the hell out of all the others.

Upgrading shouldn't ever be mechanical. It should always be approached carefully and with the donor's interest and recent history in mind. People don't give more because you want them to upgrade. They don't give to support your schemes, clubs, or giving societies. They give for a compelling reason; to support your work to resolve an urgent need that they care passionately about. Like all good fundraising, upgrading is finally about this thing called passion.

Monthly giving schemes can be the ideal means of stimulating a donor's passion – and that's why I'm so passionate about them.

Two fundraising propositions that can't fail

There are only three kinds of giving – spontaneous giving, prompted giving and planned giving. Spontaneous giving is when donors give without being asked in any way. This is very rare. Even at times of high emotion during a disaster or human tragedy, giving is usually prompted.

Prompted giving is what we fundraisers promote most of the time. We ask and people give. Often we imagine the gifts thus received indicate at least the potential of an ongoing relationship, but equally often the donor simply sees it as a one-off gift, with no implication or suggestion that there will ever be any more later on. As a result, when the inevitable follow-up appeal comes it is often resented. Because fundraisers have sold prompted giving rather badly – gift amounts are usually very low and response levels are falling almost everywhere – it has become steadily less and less viable for fundraisers in developed markets.

Planned giving is a more recent concept for UK fundraisers, although a minority of donors have always planned their giving on a regular, ongoing basis, without any special effort from fundraisers. The term is self-explanatory. Planned giving is reasoned, deliberate giving that takes place over a period of time. In America planned giving is traditionally thought of as involving insurance-linked schemes – annuities, or special legal structures and instruments, such as the charitable remainder trust. However, even in the United States 80 per cent of planned giving funds come in the form of bequests or legacies. (The two are virtually synonymous. In the USA they tend to use the term bequest, whereas in Britain we refer to legacies.)

For reasons detailed laboriously in *Relationship Fundraising*, the biggest untapped source of potential income for voluntary organisations is legacies, or bequests. With some trepidation, I will attempt to sum up that potential in a few of the following pages. But first I want to focus on a form of planned giving that I believe comes second only to legacies as the most reliable source of substantial long-term giving from individual donors: monthly giving.

Without doubt, the biggest challenge facing fundraisers as we move into the new millennium is to switch donors from prompted giving and on to planned giving. The two best prospects for doing this are propositions that almost any fundraising organisation can, and should, introduce: monthly giving and legacies.

Monthly, or 'committed' giving schemes, called monthly donor programmes, or programs in the US, are the second major potential for charities wishing to raise worthwhile sums from individual donors. Greenpeace and others have introduced versions of these schemes successfully in various countries around the world.

Let me qualify the optimism of my last subheading. Some fundraiser somewhere will be able to fail with these two schemes, because of Sod's Law and doing it badly. But they both represent high-value propositions that donors want. Any fundraising office not planning for them will be left behind.

Monthly giving – why it works

Most people are paid monthly. There are probably some exceptions to this, for example in America (where apparently many people get paid fortnightly), parts of Siberia, and maybe Vanuatu. But it remains generally true that most people in most developed countries are paid monthly. Pensions are often paid monthly too. It follows then that most people prefer to pay for things monthly. It isn't as difficult to find £5 a month as it is £50 in a lump sum, so most people tend to think that it doesn't sound as much – and therefore isn't. Some simple arithmetic will soon show it to be a lot more, but most people won't bother to work that out. Utilities, services, rent or mortgages are all paid for by the month. So are most major purchases. This is what people prefer, and find most convenient. Credit card advances are repaid monthly. Some time ago retailers came to realise that customers would often pay more for a product on 'easy' (monthly) terms than they would if they had to put down a lump sum.

This phenomenon is also true for charitable giving. Many donors prefer to give monthly, younger donors particularly. So monthly schemes are likely to become even more relevant in future. And most donors will give more through a monthly scheme. Many people who would not otherwise be classed as 'real' donors will become so quite happily through a monthly scheme. These aspects alone explain why monthly giving schemes are so successful and why they come second only to legacy marketing programmes in the fundraiser's list of 'must haves'.

Consider the really successful fundraising organisations of today: ActionAid, Oxfam, Amnesty, Greenpeace. All have successful monthly giving schemes and it's with these schemes that most find they recruit their largest number of 'big' donors and upgrade their best prospects. But there are many other reasons why monthly giving suits fundraisers.

A monthly giving scheme is usually a tangible, easily understandable and easily justifiable special cause. It is relatively easy to make a strong case to donors for a monthly giving scheme. It saves the charity money, is convenient for the donor, only costs pennies per day, and enables the charity to plan confidently for the long term. Donors keep control, they have an active voice and the charity is protected against financial crises. Most monthly giving schemes are sensibly priced. So promotion is relatively straightforward. And the unit value of each new recruit is high. This explains why monthly giving propositions can often be promoted successfully 'off-the-page'.

Monthly givers not only give more, it's regular, guaranteed income. Accountants love it because it helps cashflow. Donors get more involved because their support is ongoing and strong relationships are formed. The sheer convenience, particularly if the donors are on direct debit

(often referred to as pre-authorised checking, electronic funds transfer [EFT], or autogiro), means renewal is automatic. Monthly donors will give more than any other segment to your emergencies and special appeals, precisely because they are already giving more. And if you ever introduce an even higher level of support, your monthly givers are the first group to approach, because with them upgrading is easy. Such is the loyalty that monthly schemes build, many donors will happily volunteer for a wide range of other supportive activities, from lobbying to signing up their friends. But the best long-term justification of monthly schemes is that it provides you with a terrific base for legacies.

There is another reason monthly schemes work and it's not yet available everywhere – direct debit, which I mentioned briefly above. Automated collection of funds from your donor's bank into yours ensures no renewal programme is necessary and donors seldom lapse or miss payments. Thanks to inertia it extends their 'life' as donors from merely months to many, many years. Real donors willingly sign the simple paperwork, knowing it's in their interests and yours.

Because the banking systems of some countries have yet to catch up with this marvel I've often said that the most important campaign Greenpeace could mount is not 'stop toxic dumping', or 'save the whale', but 'change the banking system'.

It's not just monthly schemes that benefit from automated collection systems. Method of payment probably has more impact on the fundraiser's bottom line than anything else.

Ingredients of a successful monthly giving scheme

Monthly giving is committed giving. It must be very clear exactly what commitment is expected of the donor, and what is involved. So a structured scheme with a fixed price or range of prices is essential. It must be possible also for the donor to become actively involved in the scheme through some form of participation. The best schemes offer two-way involvement.

Payroll giving schemes – 'United Way', give as you earn, 'March of Dimes', and so on – are *not* monthly giving schemes. Nor can you draft donors into the scheme automatically when they give above a certain amount in a lump sum. They have to choose to be there. So you should also separate from your scheme those who just give every month but who don't want to join on a formal basis.

Certain components are essential if your monthly giving scheme is to succeed.

Passion
Your scheme will fail unless you and your staff believe passionately in its role, importance and potential achievements. It must help your organisation achieve its mission, in a substantial way. If it is simply a money-making device donors will quickly see through it. You must promote your scheme with passion.

A proposition people want to buy
However carefully you construct your scheme it will fail if the proposition is not right. Donors must be presented with a clear reason to give and to give in this way. People don't decide to give to a method of payment. They give to a specific proposition.

A good name
Successful schemes all have interesting and inviting names – Faith Partners, Village Neighbours, *Frontline*, Partners in Action, Friends of the Rainbow Warrior. Even something simple, like sponsor a dog, works well as a name. Schemes with badly chosen names, or with no name at all, can fail.

A list of tangible, worthwhile benefits.
Not just videos and teeshirts but also opportunities to visit, to see the organisation in action, to be on the inside, to see results, a private phone line, access to the top, and a host of others. Try to come up with practical benefits that will be unique to your organisation. Some very good and valuable benefits for your donors won't actually cost you anything. But give your donors the chance to opt out of benefits, as some won't want any of these.

Fixed price or range of prices
These are not negotiable. Your scheme will not work without one or the other. At the very least there has to be a minimum monthly gift, below which no one can join.

Recruitment strategy and materials
Your materials should reflect the kind of club or organisation you wish to start (ie they must be good). This includes welcome and thank you materials, and ongoing communications too.

Resources and ability to service the scheme properly
It doesn't take a lot, but it pays to do it right, with no compromise to donor service.

Renewal and upgrade procedures
The soundest advice I can offer any fundraising organisation is to set up the facility to accept and administer direct debits (autogiro, EFT, pre-authorised credits, or whatever) and then to promote this method of payment vigorously. The lifetime value of each donor will increase by 10 times or more over most other methods of payment. Bankers orders are good, but not as good as direct debits.

Communications and contact strategies
Individual or carefully segmented communications strategies are advisable, if not absolutely essential, as is a

Monthly giving in summary

- Regular and reliable money.

- Lots of it.

- Just goes on and on.

- Donors like it.

- Brilliant for getting people on to direct debit.

- Easy and cost-effective administration.

- Builds loyalty.

- Good source of volunteers.

- Automatic renewal.

- Reason to keep in touch.

- Additional appeals.

- Great for upgrading.

- Leads to legacies.

plan for personal (ie face-to-face) contact.

Anyone seriously thinking of starting a monthly giving scheme should read Harvey McKinnon's soon to be published book on the subject (*Monthly Giving Programs*, Strathmoor Press, Berkeley, California, USA).

See also the Greenpeace *Frontline* case history on pages 372–392.

Legacies – freeing the elephant

Legacy marketing is the last great fundraising opportunity. I suppose somewhere in Alaska or Upper Volta you might discover a fundraiser hidden away who hasn't been exposed to this insight over the last few years but he or she will be a very great rarity.

In 1992 in *Relationship Fundraising* I was able to write that despite being the largest and most important area for fundraisers, the area with the most potential and the least exploited, legacy marketing up until then had been so neglected that the whole area was virtually unexplored territory.

Well, that may have been true a few years ago but since then everything has changed. Legacies have rapidly moved to pretty near the top of most people's 'must do' lists and the field has opened out. Many new initiatives have been, or are being, tried. Now, if not fully explored and exploited, the foothills of legacy fundraising have at least been pretty widely trampled.

A lot of these excursions may seem like random meanderings to some people – and indeed they may be – but these are still very early days in legacy marketing. This is a time for pioneering, for innovation, for taking risks. Mistakes will be made. As yet it may be an area where we're more enthusiastic than effective, but that is changing fast. Progress will belong to the brave. Quite a few organisations have laid solid foundations that will stand them in good stead in a few years' time.

And it will take a few years, inevitably. Much has been made of the fact that the time between last will change and death has been estimated to be somewhere around four years and several legacy marketers (RNIB included, *see* pages 434–435) can prove direct results from their initiatives in even less than two years. Nevertheless, most organisations will find that it will be quite a long time before legacy marketing really takes effect and begins to repay its investment.

And rightly so, if you think about it from the donor's point of view. People just don't die to order, however impressed they might be with your relationship fundraising. You can't change a culture overnight. While there will always be exceptions, the kind of relationship that will lead to a substantial legacy is unlikely to be forged over a free booklet, a nice thank you letter, or a polite voice at the end of a phone. It is more likely to take a generation, or at least a decade or two. (For those who don't already know, a generation is about 30 years, according to the *Concise Oxford Dictionary*.)

This stands to reason. You can't sell legacies and you can't ever guarantee a quick or a certain return. It's like courtship. However much you like the girl and however nicely you ask, you shouldn't expect a lifetime's commitment on the first, or even the second, date.

Leaving a legacy to a charity, particularly to one you don't know very well, is for most people a very, very big decision. So perhaps the real key to legacy marketing is not to try to get people to make this big decision quickly, but to get them to see that really it isn't such a big decision after all.

Before I elaborate on this rather fundamental heresy, let me ask you to approach legacy marketing in true relationship fundraiser style by making the 90-degree shift and putting yourself in the shoes of your donors.

Why would you, the donor, ever want to leave a legacy to charity? It's quite illogical. There are loads of reasons, not just your immediate family, lined up against it.

On one of my now not infrequent trips to the USA I picked up a startling fact. (It always happens. America is that kind of country. Startling facts just leap out at you.) This startling fact is that someone has calculated that the cost of dying in the United States now is, on average, around $300,000. And it's going up, as medical costs escalate and medical science finds ever more ingenious ways of extending modern life. (By the cost of dying I don't just mean the necessary expenses of death and burial, but also the cost of providing medical and nursing care during the declining years.)

Ask yourself (donors' shoes remember): would you be generous to your favourite charity knowing you might have to come up with over a quarter of a million dollars not long after you next begin to feel a bit poorly?

Another startling fact is that apparently the average American female is now more likely to spend a longer time looking after an elderly dependent relative than she will have spent bringing up her own kids.

I think this is a terrible thought. In between, I suppose, is what could be called life.

Whoosh! What was that?

That was your life, mate. In between raising the kids and caring for your old mum and dad there wasn't really much time for you. Tough, I guess, but perhaps you can be reassured that your own son and daughter, now bringing up their own babies, will soon be looking after you. And mum's legacy when she passes on will make those long twilight years a lot easier.

So not a lot of comfort for legacy marketers in either of these developments. Still, as we slide into a new century several social changes do definitely seem to be going the legacy fundraiser's way. But equally, some others are not. The portents for legacy marketing are mixed.

■ There will be more old people. Thanks to the phenomenon of the baby boom generation (the huge number of babies born between 1946 and 1962) there will soon be more 'oldies' than ever before. Rather like a large meal passing through the digestive system of a long, slithery snake, this mass of babies that grew to become hordes of hippies and went on to cause runaway inflation in the housing market will soon be reaching prime donor age. Ultimately, just as the meal is digested and passes out of the snake, a rather larger than normal pile of older people will pass on to new pastures. But will they pass on a high proportion of their wealth to charities in legacies and bequests?

■ Donors are getting richer. Inherited wealth, again thanks largely to the baby boom, is growing each year (inflation has helped too). There are more and more millionaires, 60,000 plus in 1989 in the USA compared to just 4,281 in 1980. Yet in that same period the number of £1 million-plus gifts to charity only grew from 418 to 888. So maybe millionaires are getting meaner. Or is it just that being a millionaire isn't such a big deal any more? Nowadays, perhaps even millionaires can't afford to be too generous. Other social and demographic changes are about to happen and, as yet, the jury is still out on whether or not they will be benign for fundraisers.

■ People are definitely living longer. This is at best a mixed blessing for charities. Although it means there will be more donors many of these will be faced with not just having to pay for more medical and nursing care, but will have extra years to spend what an earlier generation might have left behind. My friend Betty was a victim of this. She had always enjoyed the good life and faced with a fixed income she calculated what she believed would be a reasonable lifetime, divided up her resources and proceeded to spend to her limit. But Betty miscalculated and lived until she was 86, the last six years being spent in thoroughly straitened circumstances. And she resented her longevity deeply, although all her friends were delighted. I don't suppose, however, that when she died she left more than happy memories.

■ The new-old, this vast impending generation of older people, will also be much better informed than their predecessors and will have considerably different social and moral values. They won't be so impressed by the so-called 'old-fashioned values' of pride, honour, duty and courage. They won't have an ingrained sense of social obligation. They won't automatically respect authority, or do what they're told. And they will really need to be convinced before they will believe anything. So the older, established, traditional charities had better watch out.

It is not likely that religion will play such a big part in

their lives. As many major religions include a moral imperative to give, this could be very bad news for fundraisers.

■ Tomorrow's older donors will have less techno-fear. They will have a different attitude to work, and to leisure. They will expect to be communicated with through the media they use themselves. And they won't make allowances. To get them you'll have to be on the ball. And very convincing. And very good.

So, donors' shoes again, why on earth should I plan to leave any of my money to your cause?

The answer, of course, can only lie with the fundraiser. He or she has to build the trust that is an essential foundation to that decision. He or she has to provide a clear understanding of the charity's need for legacies, how it will use them, how it can be so easy and painless to give a meaningful gift through a charitable legacy. He or she has to foster a climate of philanthropy that will sweep away the objections and encourage the maximum interest in this kind of gift. And he or she has to promote the proposition, the concept of a charitable legacy, so that it is seen as an automatic and natural thing to do. This calls for a spirit of social acceptability that is not quite there yet, something that is essential if my legacy to you is going to gain the approval of my family and friends. If it can't gain that approval almost as a right, a matter of course, then I believe that legacy marketing in the future will stand little chance of success.

So remember this: your donor doesn't want to leave you a legacy. She doesn't feel religiously compelled to, and she doesn't automatically trust you. Her bank manager has advised her against it. She doesn't know for sure if she can afford it. Her family are dead against it. She really isn't sure what good it will do. And anyway, doing it is expensive and a real hassle.

Now, for her, go and create some really compelling legacy marketing.

Working together...

So legacy marketing is far from easy, far from straightforward. It is also unlikely to be a rapid road to riches, whatever you do.

There are exceptions. Some legacy marketing is surprisingly easy. Greenpeace Austria recently received a substantial legacy from a woman specifically because 15 years earlier its director had written her a particularly good letter of thanks. Herbert Witschnig of SAZ Marketing in Vienna told me this story. He was that Greenpeace fundraiser all those years ago.

But real change won't come so easily. While I strongly advocate that every well-managed charity should have a strong and well-resourced legacy marketing strategy that it pursues consistently with commitment, I am also aware that individual charities ploughing their own, inevitably, self-centred furrow can only achieve so much.

For real and lasting success charities and fundraisers have to work together. We have to work together to stand any chance at all of elevating the status of the charitable legacy in the public mind – our public's mind.

What we need is little short of a culture change, so that the charitable legacy will in time become socially acceptable and even desirable – the measure of a person's humanity and concern for others. It has to become the 'right thing to do'. Such a change will only be achieved if we can work at it together.

We could do this – if only we believed we could. But, perhaps as a result of past bad experience, or perhaps because no one has yet taken the lead, most fundraisers I meet – and I meet a lot – hold little hope for such co-operation, however fruitful it might be, whatever the potential prize.

So I believe the charitable sector, in the UK at least, simply lacks the will to try. In this way, it reminds me of an elephant...

...to free the elephant

There once was a baby elephant who lived in a circus. He was a valuable little elephant and his owners were anxious that he shouldn't just wander about anywhere doing things they didn't want him to do. So they hammered a stake into the ground and tied the baby elephant to it by a long chain.

In time, as baby elephants do, this elephant grew. He grew and grew into a rather large elephant. But he was still tied by this now puny chain to a tiny stake in the ground. He could easily have broken free if he had wanted to, but *he didn't think* he could. The big elephant dutifully stayed put because he didn't realise how strong he had become. He didn't realise that things had changed.

I think that elephant is a bit like the collective weight of the fundraising profession. We don't realise how strong we have become. We don't realise what we could do if we set our minds to it.

Now is the time to convince the donating public that the best and easiest gift they can ever make is a gift that will live on after they have gone – a charitable legacy.

Now is the time to free the elephant.

Fundraising's big idea

I am convinced that this – freeing the elephant, co-operating jointly to make the charitable legacy part of our donors' culture in the next century – is the biggest single idea facing fundraisers everywhere. It may in fact be one of the best ideas since 1886 when John Styth Pemberton, an Atlanta pharmacist and patent-medicine man (whose earlier, less-inspired inventions had included Globe of Flower Cough Syrup), brewed up a concoction of cola nuts, coca leaves, caffeine and other equally dubious ingredients in an iron tub in his backyard, stirred it with a wooden oar from an old boat and called it Coca-Cola.

But having a big idea isn't enough. It's what you do with

it that counts. John Pemberton didn't make the best use he could have of his big idea – he sold a two-thirds interest in his new company for the curious and decidedly short-sighted sum of $283.29. The whole company was sold a few years later for just $2,000 and the Coca-Cola Company has gone on to make rather a large number of marketing mistakes since, including Coke-flavoured cigars and, as recently as 1985, the launch of the disastrously short-lived 'new Coke'. And this despite its undeniable cultural impact on some 195 countries around the globe, which has made Coke the world's best-known and biggest brand and, in marketing terms, one of the best 'big ideas' of all time.

I hope we'll do better with our big idea. Perhaps we might not raise as much money as Coca-Cola has (despite its mistakes the company has done rather well financially over the years). But we will do hugely well, and at least we can do better than Coke's inventor and make sure we see the fruits of our big idea.

Talking of a similar opportunity, Professor Charles Handy put it another way. Comparing the unexplored opportunity to a vast and bumpy plain or prairie, he suggested we could either all get into our buggies and try to make individual tracks across it – or we could get together to build a road.

Part II: The case histories

6

Botton Village

Donor-friendly from the start

The following seven paragraphs taken from *The Botton Story*, a short history of Botton Village prepared in 1990 and sent to all donors, provide a good introduction to what has become one of the most impressive and inspirational fundraising success stories this century.

In the austere 1950s the idea of a special village where mentally handicapped young people could lead happy, constructive lives was just a brave dream.

There was nothing like it in the world. But a group of parents and friends of handicapped youngsters at Camphill schools were determined to give their children the chance of a better future.

The unlikely site for their unique experiment nestled high in a dale on the North York Moors. Friends pooled their resources for the deposit to buy the estate, not knowing where the money would come from to build Botton Village.

But they had a vision – and tremendous faith that the public would support them.

Since then, financing the village has always been an uphill struggle, despite efforts to grow its own food and produce craft goods for sale. But in more than 40 years its friends have never failed Botton. Houses have been renovated, adjoining farms purchased and workshops built to expand the thriving village community.

Today Botton Village is home for 326 people, who all live and work together, each of them benefiting the whole community in a way best suited to their ability.

And Botton has gone on to provide a model which has inspired
many other village communities throughout Britain and around the
world.

By anyone's definition, Botton Village is a very special place.
Although it might appear to be as ordinary and as
typical as any small rural village could be, there's really
very little that is either ordinary or typical about it.
Botton is a one-off, an anachronism, a true individual.

It isn't old-fashioned yet it has a slightly lost or
misplaced feel about it as if it's not quite of this world. It
is a remarkable blend of traditional ways and customs
with the best of modern science and technology.
Nowadays it even has a successful and prosperous air,
but Botton and its people are as ordinary and
unassuming as they come.

All these apparent contradictions are part of Botton's
charm. It is a very unusual, as well as a very special,
place.

Botton certainly has something, a unique quality, which
gives it very wide appeal. Once reclusive and insular, Botton
Village has opened its doors. Such is its appeal that
hundreds and hundreds of people visit the village each year.
Genuinely ordinary people, they come by the coachload.
Some come for their holidays, others save up for months to
come, some come out of curiosity and others with deep
commitment. They all come to see Botton Village for
themselves – because they have been invited.

These people are donors. However long or short their
stay, Botton Village will have a special place in each donor's
heart by the time he or she leaves.

For Botton Village is not just a charity, not just another
appeal, another worthy cause. Botton Village is a way of life.

Botton Village is also one of the most attractive and
successful fundraising appeals of modern times. It is
attractive – and indeed successful – because it is simple and
because the people involved actually live it rather than just
take part in it. Its uniqueness as a fundraising case history

> My husband and I visited
> Botton Village some years
> ago when we were
> holidaying in North
> Yorkshire. We were so
> impressed by the concept
> and uniqueness of Botton
> that we decided to help.
> Naturally we receive
> satisfaction in giving but the
> purpose of giving is that
> others might receive.
>
> Mrs D Legge, Worksop

comes from when Botton started to raise money directly from the public – completely from scratch – just 13 years ago. At the very beginning it set the highest standards of ethics, responsibility and accountability to its donors. Since then Botton has consistently upheld this commitment to its donors while, at the same time, its paramount concern has been to protect the interests of those who live in the village.

Thirteen years is not a long time. Botton's achievements have been little short of spectacular. In this short time Botton Village has readily embraced the opportunities offered by changing technology and, almost without realising it, has pioneered many significant innovations in how to develop donor relationships successfully.

Its results alone eloquently make the case for a donor-oriented approach to fundraising.

The Botton community

Physically the valley that shelters Botton Village looks pretty much like any other part of the North Yorkshire Moors. But, as enthusiasts for this rugged and spectacular part of the world will tell you, these moors are always compelling and beautiful. If the weather is right, in both summer and winter, the landscape can be truly stunning.

Botton's valley enjoys surroundings no less beautiful than anywhere else in the region. To get to Botton the visitor has to cross the bleak and sheep-infested moors, up hill and down dale, until the road turns suddenly and sharply away to drop down a frighteningly steep incline into the valley. In winter warm air tends to settle in the valley, so often a snow-swept landscape above will give way to sunny, crisp, but clear countryside below. In summer there can be a thick mist above and sunshine in the village. At other times the mist will sit in the village and it will be quite clear up on the top.

But these are the impressions of an occasional and idealistic visitor. Residents of Botton Village will tell you till the cows come home of freezing winters, blocked roads,

Beautiful Botton Village, in Danby Dale.

power cuts, isolation and the many other social deprivations that go with living all year round in this exposed and isolated rural community.

Botton Village is the largest of the Camphill Village Trust communities in Britain. The Camphill movement was started by Dr Karl König, an Austrian doctor with an international reputation for his work with children with a mental handicap. Dr König had become increasingly concerned that the children he was working with would leave school only to end up in institutions, or return home to their parents, and possibly waste the talents that had been revealed during their education.

In 1955, with the help of the parents and like-minded benefactors, he was able to buy the Botton Hall Estate to create a village community where adults with special needs could live a normal life in a caring, open and fully supportive atmosphere. Over half the people living in Botton today have special needs and they are fully integrated into village life, working to the best of their abilities for the benefit of the whole community.

Like any village, Botton is essentially a varied collection of families, each with a character of its own. There are 30 houses ranging in size from six to 16 people. A typical household is run by a couple – house-parents – who, with the help of co-workers, look after up to nine adults with special needs, as well as their own children. There is no hierarchy. Everyone shares in making their house a real home where the needs of individuals are recognised.

> I am not associated with mentally handicapped people but I feel good and even privileged to support your work. The big difference between Botton Village and most other charities (dozens in the post around Christmas!) is that I feel good when I give whereas most other charities make you feel bad if you do not give.
>
> Bruno W Stalmans, Guildford

Botton is a community founded on firm principles. Everyone works and so everyone contributes to village life. The people of Botton believe that the dignity of work is a major contributor to the quality of life for both villagers and co-workers and it doesn't take long before the visitor is convinced of that too. Every job is viewed as an important contribution to the upkeep of the community, whether it is helping to run a home, tending the garden, milking the cows, doing the accounts – or fundraising. Yet no one, villagers or co-workers, is paid any sort of wage.

The people of Botton live their lives according to the philosophical, educational teachings of the Austrian philosopher Rudolf Steiner.

There is no television in Botton and many of the supposed benefits of modern living are conspicuously absent – no disco, no cinema, no pubs or restaurants. But there is a theatre, several shops, a school, a church and a small café, which contribute to the great and obvious sense of community.

Botton really is a working, functioning village. There are five farms, several gardens and 10 workshops, which allow it to make everything from bio-dynamic dairy products to fine, hand-crafted toys. Yet, although it has very modern facilities and equipment, it still retains a sense of Gippetto's* workshop.

All this combines to make Botton Village a very special place.

Botton Village is not only special for the people who live there. The following news item comes from the very first issue of *Botton Village Life*, published in the autumn of 1984.

> One of our auditors, a keen bird-watcher, surprised everyone by arriving at breakfast time to check the accounts. It transpired that he had already been in Botton since dawn. He said that nowhere else in the area has such a variety of bird and wildlife.
>
> The reason is that for the last 29 years Botton has farmed completely organically, using no herbicides or pesticides. This has resulted in Botton becoming healthy for wildlife, with the more unusual bird species such as tawny owls, herons, sparrowhawks and kestrels rubbing shoulders with the pheasants, pigeons, tits, cuckoos and multitude of other birds in Botton.
>
> Animals too abound – deer in the Honey Bee Nest woods, rabbits, hedgehogs, hares, ferrets and even the occasional fox, not to mention the vast number of cats, both domestic and farm types.
>
> Not everyone is happy about this abundance of wildlife, the farmers and gardeners are often dismayed when a field of young plants is ravaged by rabbits or pheasants. But, in general, the wildlife of Botton lives a peaceful and chemical-free life.

Despite its outwardly tranquil and idyllic appearance, in the early 1980s Botton Village had more than its share of problems. Much of the infrastructure of the village was out of date and needed replacing. Equipment and facilities in the

---

*Pinocchio's dad, Gippetto, was a toymaker who made his wooden toys with such love and care that one day one of them came alive. I saw Walt Disney's film of Pinocchio when I was about four years old. It made a deep impression, even though its point must have been rather lost on me as at that age I don't suppose I knew where real children came from. But I loved Gippetto's workshop.

workshops were obsolete, conditions in the houses were often below standard. There was pressure on places. Income was sporadic, to say the least. The village managed to get by, but only just. There was no capital, no emergency reserve, nothing to act as a safety net or to provide any little extras or luxuries. Government cutbacks loomed like a great cloud on the horizon then for all social work organisations. Under this cloud Botton struggled to meet its daily needs without giving too much thought to what seemed a bleak future.

Getting started

Timing is incredibly important in fundraising. To be in the right place at the right time, to choose the right moment to start, the right time to ask, the right time to hold back takes exemplary skill and consummate judgement. It also takes a great deal of luck.

An important component of Botton Village's success has been the character, personality and sheer existence of its fundraiser, Lawrence Stroud. Lawrence was 23 years old when he arrived at Botton Village in 1973. He stayed for 22 years, first as a co-worker and then as a house-parent and village maintenance man. Although he moved away from the village in 1994 he still works on its fundraising programme. As he explains, the village he entered then was very different from Botton today.

'Botton was founded in the early 1950s and for its first 30 years or so it was very isolated. When I arrived it was beginning to emerge into the twentieth century but it still had a very alien, monastic and inward-looking feel. It was very esoteric, very pure, but really the place was falling to pieces.

'There were only a couple of us involved in maintenance. Botton then had a total repair budget of just £8,000 a year and that used to get chopped because we never had the money. I can remember that the Lodge, one of Botton's many houses, hadn't been painted for 19 years.

'For some unknown reason, as I had no experience, I had been drafted into maintenance. I was thrown in at the deep end with an introductory spell in the gardens, the candle workshop, the wood workshop, and the creamery. I suppose I got involved in maintenance because I was technically inclined. I did electricals and plumbing and a chap called Piet Blok did roads and drains.

'After three or four years of that, out of the blue, the Government introduced its job creation scheme and for political reasons we found our application to be the area's manager for both youth training and adults suddenly coming into place. We started with 10 adults and 10 trainees. Within a year we were up to 120 adults and 100 trainees. And I suddenly found that instead of running everywhere with a spanner I was telling other people to run around with spanners. There was a great element of bluff because I really didn't know anything about joinery, building, or anything.'

In 1995 my daughter Mary gave me a parachute jump for my 50th birthday. I was anxious to put it to good use and thrilled at the generous response of large numbers of people I approached for sponsorship. A total of £2,700 was raised for Botton.

The single most striking impression I have of Botton is the 'belonging' of the residents. Everyone contributes and is important and valued.

Mrs Catriona Tremlett, Godalming

Cosmic fundraising

'Because there is no hierarchy in Botton no one was ultimately responsible for the financial side. I suppose we all were, and somehow we got by.

'Fundraising, as such, was non-existent, yet we managed to get a donated income of about £60,000 a year. It was a kind of cosmic fundraising – we needed the money and it would just come, as if from outer space. It worked remarkably well. I remember that once we needed £20,000 to pay for building materials for Trefoil House. Payment was due on the Monday and we hadn't got £20,000. But that very day in the post came an anonymous cheque for £20,000.

'And that was the way it had run for 20 years – relying on some kind of divine providence. It was uncanny that we survived as well as we did. But it couldn't go on.'

Lawrence is a realist. To a surprising degree, many of the residents of Botton Village are.

'One day I was sorting out some papers after someone had left the village and I came across an old file of trusts. I went through it and thought it looked interesting and that it might be a good idea to write to them, give them some news and ask them how they were. I was quite astounded to get, literally by return of post, about £10,000 in donations.' So Lawrence Stroud came to realise that cosmic fundraising could be even more effective if given a temporal hand. As with so many other charities, Botton's fundraising started with an electronic typewriter, a standard letter and an indispensable annual publication entitled the *Directory of Grant Making Trusts*. There was no selection, no individual proposals, no visits, but it worked reasonably well, and it gave Lawrence Stroud a taste for fundraising.

Providence clearly has a soft spot for Lawrence and for Botton because at this point fate kindly intervened again. Anxious to learn a little more about the techniques of fundraising, Lawrence responded to a leaflet promoting a seminar organised by the Directory of Social Change on the then-uncharted territory of fundraising by direct mail. It was held in London and entitled 'Direct mail – the last unexplored fundraising medium'. The year was 1982 and the key speakers were two enthusiastic chaps in suits called George Smith and Ken Burnett.

Lawrence recalls, 'At the seminar I remember thinking that this was it. A bit radical for us, maybe. In fact very radical, but that we had to bite the bullet. I thought that they might kill me when I got home, but went up to have a few words anyway.'

By that Lawrence meant he intended to talk to the speakers. He joined a line of hopefuls queueing up to find out more.

The brief meeting that followed stuck firmly in the minds of both participants, largely because it was so unlikely. Me wondering who this guy was and what he was going on about, while trying politely to come up with valid reasons against risking a day in North Yorkshire on what sounded like a wild goose chase for a very strange organisation.

And Lawrence thinking he was faced with some representative of Mammon, a London advertising person who couldn't possibly be interested in Botton Village and its problems – even if he could be persuaded to come up to the wild and frozen North.

Lawrence was persistent and as chance would have it I wasn't doing anything particular on the following Tuesday (times were hard then), so, on the strict understanding that Botton Village would pay my second-class rail fare, I bought a day return ticket and spent the train journey gainfully writing copy and unprofitably regretting the numerous gaps in my appointments book and my inability to say no on the spur of the moment.

> Thank you for a wonderful afternoon at Botton on Sunday. It was so refreshing to spend time in a beautiful location with lovely people and to admire the marvellous work of everyone involved… we will visit Botton again soon. A year is too long to wait.
>
> Joan and Cliff Lightfoot, Middlesborough

Of course, like many before me and many thousands after, when I arrived at Botton I was captivated. Being essentially an optimist, I could see that the day wouldn't be entirely lost as, if nothing else, it promised to be an enjoyable outing. But I was not enough of an optimist to believe that Lawrence and I could persuade his largely hostile community colleagues that this crazy idea called direct mail fundraising was possible, would work, and that Botton Village wouldn't lose its soul in the process.

Historically and emotionally the Camphill movement is rather against anything to do with public relations, publicity and putting oneself up front. From the outset there was tremendous opposition, but after full discussion and vigorous persuasion enough of the co-workers were prepared to give it a go. Lawrence and I prepared a very basic five-year plan. We knew we had to get it right from the start in every way. We wouldn't get a second chance.

An agreement of a sort having been reached, I decided that I would catch the late train back to London, leaving

Lawrence to cope with the details and the rearguard actions. From then on I simply stirred in technical, strategic and creative ingredients by remote control over the telephone, safely out of reach.

Only later did I find out that we had been flying in the face of an unwritten but important policy decision made some months earlier for the whole of Camphill Village Trust. This was that no professional outsider would be employed to help with fundraising. Looking back 13 years later, John Durham and others on the fundraising group feel destiny took over then, and set Botton on the road to discovering relationship fundraising.

Lawrence remembers those early days a little more ruefully. 'Our first mailing of 40,000 letters cost somewhere around £15,000. It seemed such a lot of money. Organisationally it was stop/start. Every time we did something I had to convene a meeting where dozens of people would chew every line to pieces, agonising over the wording. I tried to keep my head down. It was only sheer brutality and dogged determination that got it through it in the end.

'We had convinced everyone that the way things were going Botton Village in the future would need friends, supporters and money. By a painful, slow, but effective process we produced our first printed fundraising material and everybody was pleased with it [*see* illustration on the facing page]. We had printed tens of thousands of letters, leaflets, envelopes and reply forms. We had paid the postage and the mailing house and were all set to send it out. But would it work? Would anyone give us any money? Would any of the faceless, nameless, unknown people out there see anything in our work that merited their support, that would convince them to part with their hard-earned cash? At that time this was a very real and pressing question. It had to work.'

Luckily it did, and rather spectacularly well. In those days, of course, there wasn't nearly as much competition

Botton's very first mailing was simple, positive and very effective.

from other charities. Having gone through agonies of self-doubt about whether or not people would give (including advice from the direct marketing agency [me] whose professional opinion it was that mentally handicapped adults were a difficult cause, unlikely to appeal), Botton Village found that in fundraising terms its proposition had legs and would run and run.

And all the money that had been spent, after a little while and a little worry, had come back – only more so. This despite further erroneous advice from me. I said that the first few mailings would most probably make a loss.

From the start Botton's direct mail fundraising adventure comfortably exceeded targets, so Lawrence just rewrote the targets. A natural entrepreneur, he saw it was going well and decided to reinvest all he could, while he could. To make sure he wasn't taking undue risks he set about monitoring performance as thoroughly and rapidly as he could.

This was where Lawrence's technical bent, and his enthusiasm for and skill with computers were to prove invaluable. That skill, plus his capacity for hard work and the total absence of the nine to five convention in Botton, gave the fledgling fundraising organisation a substantial edge. Sunday phone calls and late night meetings became routine. Once started, Botton's programme of donor recruitment and development developed a life of its own. Its natural momentum took over and dictated a pace that was often hard for the rest of the village, if not Lawrence, to keep up.

'At that time we were trying to print most of the material we required – leaflets, mailing packs, newsletters – in the village itself, using the existing facility of the Botton Village Press. Obviously it soon became swamped as the volumes grew. Gradually we expanded production capacity at the press and a few years ago we built a completely new facility with up-to-date machinery and a capacity many times greater than the original press. Of course we were providing work in Botton and saving money by not using outside printers, but I've always felt that the real value was that it was "made in Botton". Our donors appreciate that we try to be as self-sufficient as possible.

'But it wasn't easy and there were often horrendous problems.'

Around this time, amid all this flurry of new and frantic activity, a committee was formed. The fundraising group or FRG, as it became known, took on all the responsibility for what we were doing and pretty soon caused me to revise my previously rather negative views about committees. They had a tiger by the tail and soon realised it. Although some members have come and gone over the years, the enthusiasm, cheerfulness and commitment of the core of hardened members of the FRG have never wavered.

Lest I inadvertently give the impression that all of Botton's fundraising was done by Lawrence with a little long distance help from me and my colleagues, here is the place to acknowledge the heroic contributions of John Durham, Nick Poole, Jeff Balls and Jos Smeele. Botton's fundraising success wouldn't have happened without them. Together they possessed the sanity to curb our excesses and the wisdom to back our risky but ultimately successful adventures.

After two annual rounds of direct mail recruitment Botton's sights had been set much higher. Lawrence believed that while the village could recruit new donors at a profit, or even at break even, then it should continue to do so as quickly as possible, because all the signs were that competition was increasing and this happy state of affairs – donor recruitment at break even – would not last.

From the outset Lawrence's vision set no limits. The initial objective had been to recruit 7,500 donors but, if cashflow would allow it, why not recruit 50,000 or even 100,000 donors? Lawrence knew how valuable these donors would be in the future, not just through their donations but through

> Having made a donation I received your warm and friendly letter. I must have forgotten to mention that I didn't require an acknowledgement!
>
> Nevertheless your letter was welcome, as indeed news of Botton Village always is. I do like the way you make us feel involved, even if we only send enough to buy a few doorknobs.
>
> Ms Evelyn Rowe, Huddersfield

introducing others, helping at events, even campaigning and, of course, ultimately by leaving a legacy. And he knew all about critical mass, that fundraising organisations have to have a certain number of donors to be viable. As the benefits of the direct mail programme began to make a visible, tangible difference to life in the village, Lawrence became increasingly convinced that the fundraising campaign would ultimately safeguard the long-term future of Botton and all its inhabitants.

Not everyone shared this belief...

Right at the start, for the very first mailing, the suggestion had been made that Botton should invite donors and potential donors to visit the village, to see for themselves. I reasoned that once people could see, feel, smell and taste Botton they'd be donors for life – and of course I knew (or rather hoped) that only a tiny proportion of those invited would actually come. But all those who didn't come would nevertheless be reassured to see such openness from this new and unknown organisation. It clearly had nothing to hide.

Others in the village were not so confident. Indeed the very idea that in its first mailing the village should invite 40,000 complete strangers to descend on Botton was regarded by many as the last gamble of desperate men. What if even half, or even a quarter, of them accepted? And if people did come might they not contaminate the village and all who lived there?

But this disagreement too, like all the others, was debated and resolved. Or so we thought at the time. However, as with many other issues in Botton, the decision was only temporary, the outcome was never finally decided and the problem resurfaced from time to time, to be raked over again. It still does.

There are some very good reasons why Botton's inhabitants are nervous about or hostile to donors' visits.

On the face of it the idea is brilliant. Botton is accessible, but not too much so. It is attractive, well worth a visit.

There's plenty of space and lots for visitors to see. And there are several events to which it is quite practical to invite donors. The best example of these is the open day, a summer celebration and sports day when everyone from the village plays host to the outside world in a fairground atmosphere around a multitude of fun events and things to do.

Lawrence has always invited donors to open day. Many come and are hooked. Others write to offer their apologies and usually send a cheque. A great deal of goodwill is spread.

But this kind of openness hasn't always worked. Tales abound of ungracious visitors who have been found poking around where they ought not, opening cupboards, rummaging through shelves, wandering into people's bedrooms, and so on.

> I am writing to tell you how much I appreciate *Botton Village Life*. It makes supporting Botton a much more personal thing. I enjoy reading about the work you do and the stories about the villagers themselves.
>
> Ms B J Smith, Cheshire

Says Lawrence, 'Yes donors should get the chance to appreciate Botton, why not? They've given the money to make a lot of it possible. But on the other hand if they barge into your house on Sunday afternoon while you are eating lunch to give you a £5 cheque then opinions can change. Sadly, some people are totally insensitive to others' need for – and right to – privacy. And whatever else Botton does, it will not allow fundraising to seriously impinge on the quality of life for anyone there. It hasn't done so far, but possibly it could.'

So there are tensions.

Subsequent research has shown that the chance to visit is highly valued by donors, not just by those who come – who thereafter are Botton's friends for life and would need a major disaster to see Botton cut from their list of causes that must be supported – but also from those who don't come, really won't ever come, but like to think they might one day and certainly really appreciate being asked. It's rather like the value of a 'room full' sign when a popular speaker addresses a conference or seminar. The people who are really impressed are those who could not get in.

Building on Botton's success

1983 – boost for Botton Bakery
Botton Bakery, started in a converted cow byre in 1975, was expanded from 600 to 3,000 square feet in 1984, thanks to donations by friends and building labour supplied by the Community Programme workforce.

The new bakery offers varied work for up to 14 villagers producing a range of chemical-free bread and biscuits.

As well as providing bread for the 300 people in the village, the 'baked in Botton' label can be seen in 17 shops across North Yorkshire.

1984 – Honey Bee Nest Farmhouse rebuilt
Botton Village Life, the newsletter for supporters of Botton Village, was launched during the winter of 1984 with an appeal to renovate one of the largest houses in the village. Our friends responded magnificently. Housemother Sally Martin recalls the project.

'Honey Bee Nest Farmhouse was always a house with a lot of character – one could feel the warmth left by many generations of Quakers who had lived here before. But it was also damp, dark and draughty, and very cramped for our extended family.

'Living with people with special needs is a full-time job and one needs the right living conditions for all members of the family to make this feasible. It is important to have space and proper facilities.

'Through your generosity, the house was extended and parts of it largely rebuilt. It is now dry, warm, light-filled and spacious – a very comfortable home for a family of 16.'

The Botton bakers.

1986 – creamery and food centre started
Like the bakery, Botton's first creamery was housed in a converted cow byre where it was sometimes difficult to keep up sufficient health standards.

As the reputation of Botton cheese grew, the old byre became cramped and totally inadequate.

The food processing centre was started in a farm outbuilding in 1975 with the idea of freezing excess vegetables and making a few pounds of jam. But when the operation grew to consume four tons of fruit a year, a proper food centre became a priority.

Botton's friends gave generously and a splendid purpose-built creamery and food centre were opened in 1986. Between them, the two new workshops provide work for 28 villagers.

1986 – Nook House joins our community
The constant pressure for places at Botton Village was relieved slightly when the community was able to purchase Nook House Farm in 1985.

A new Botton family was able to move in after extensive conversion of the 18th-century farmhouse. Both the purchase and the building work were paid for entirely by donations from friends of Botton.

Further development of the Nook House area into a full Botton neighbourhood is planned for 1991.

1987 – Stormy Hall brings room for growth
Botton's biggest step in recent years was the purchase of Stormy Hall Farm in 1987. The farm – next door to Nook House – was a natural extension to Botton Village.

It came up for sale on the retirement of Mr John Rudsdale and a loan of £200,000 was needed to buy and stock the farm.

In addition a huge conversion project was needed to make the farmhouse suitable for a large Botton family. Both the purchase and the conversion were possible thanks to the generosity of Botton's friends.

Buying Nook House Farm and Stormy Hall Farm has given Botton Village enormous potential for future growth to ease the constant demand for places.

Taken from *The Botton Story*, pages 4–5

Every letter deserves an answer

From the start Botton's fundraising activities have attracted a great deal of correspondence, most but not all of which has been positive.

'I made it a policy to answer every letter promptly and personally', explains Lawrence. 'It was demanding, but also fascinating and very rewarding. It could also be depressing. Correspondence generally falls into four types. Those who say Botton has changed their lives – the very enthusiastic; those who want details or to raise a practical query; compliments; and complaints.

'Of course Botton gets its share of "odd" communications, sometimes from people who seem quite disturbed. We also hear a lot from people who have relatives or friends with a mental handicap requesting information on how they can get a place in Botton for someone close to them. That's one more reason why whatever Botton writes, whatever is sent out, has to be honest, accurate and appropriate. If we paint too rosy a picture we can easily raise false hopes. We do anyway. Inevitably, the Botton story rouses hopes whatever we say. There simply isn't enough space in Botton to handle even a fraction of these requests, even if they fulfil our criteria.

'In one mailing we inadvertently implied that Botton catered for brain-injured people because the example we used, Terry, had been severely injured in a car accident and somehow had found his way to Botton. He is an exception, of course, but it opened a floodgate of enquiries.'

Botton's appeal

There are many aspects to Botton's appeal and different facets will reach different individuals, different audiences. But most are attracted by village life, by the personality of Botton itself. Its simplicity is appealing, aided by old-fashioned values of community, family, work and Botton's unique blend of cultural and social activities where everyone joins in. Glimpses of Botton Village hint at a quality of life as it once was in 'the good old days' (whenever they were). Stories from Botton are also about self-help and self-sufficiency, about real characters and personalities achieving independence and fulfilment, whatever their ability, by working and living together.

Even those who don't visit Botton can get a sense of what it is like and an understanding of the daily lives of the people through Botton's carefully planned communications. Village personalities come alive through *Botton Village Life* and other publications. The appeal also centres on value for money, on sound management and money well spent. For those familiar with mental handicap, Botton often represents a sensible middle way between rigid institutionalised care on the one hand and frequently unsupportive, sometimes non-existent, community care on the other, which can leave over-burdened and ill-equipped relatives to cope with little professional or State support.

For others, Botton is an idyllic place where an uncomfortable problem such as mental handicap can be dealt with in clear conscience in an atmosphere that is happy, productive and, most of all, out of sight.

Unlike most fundraisers, Lawrence Stroud actually lived his life as part of the cause. House-parents and co-workers live within the village seven days a week, almost every week of the year. Lawrence believes this is important. Until he left Botton, being such a close part of it underpinned every aspect of his approach to his job as fundraiser.

The database

In the beginning all data handling was supervised by Lawrence. It never occurred to him that specialist programs might exist for handling donations (and no one ever told him) so from the start he wrote all the programs himself. Initially his main requirement was that Botton's supporter records (it became a database much later on) should be suitable and acceptable for the people in the office. Any potential improvement would be considered and made, providing it might minimise their work and optimise their throughput. That was the priority then and it remains pretty vital now.

'In the morning', explains Lawrence, 'someone would ask if it would be better if something went up the screen instead of down. And by the afternoon going up the screen it would be.'

(By now several fundraisers must be thinking that Lawrence Stroud is a handy fellow to have around.)

Lawrence's computer program literally grew and developed with the staff who operated it. But they made some mistakes.

Lawrence explains, 'Had I known then what I know now things would be very different. I didn't even keep a donation history in the very early days, largely because I was so involved in all aspects of donations myself – opening envelopes, banking the cheques, sorting out everything – so I didn't think I would need it.

'We used to get overwhelmed licking envelopes – our lips would stick together. I remember going out and getting little brushes so we could paint water on them rather than lick them. It was a different world. And of course the quantities were much smaller then, although we all thought they were huge.'

A mixed blessing then came along in the shape of a generous computer manufacturer who wanted to help. The offer came in response to one of Lawrence's periodic trawls for support among the business community. No cash was forthcoming but '...our man in your vicinity will pop along to see if we can help you with some surplus-to-requirement computers'.

That sort of thing.

The man from the computer company did eventually come along and, of course, when he saw Botton he too fell for it, hook, line and sinker. So he thought he could do more for Botton than just unload one of his company's last year's models or slightly soiled demonstration equipment.

'What you need', he said, 'is a whole system...'

Of course he forgot to mention that the system, which in fairness was probably neither shop soiled nor last year's, would need very extensive support and backup if it was to work at all. And, as anyone knows, once you install any kind of multi-user system you have to be totally committed to it, or not at all.

So a multi-thousand pound, new, super-duper computer system was duly deposited on Botton – and left there. It came complete with five years' free maintenance and some essential support, but really it would have been much more suitable for a large corporation and had no fundraising software at all.

The fundraiser's dream

But here again Botton's unique asset in Lawrence Stroud came to the rescue. He simply rolled up his sleeves and got on with it himself. Botton purchased some off-the-shelf software, again adapted by Lawrence, and for some years it served Botton Village quite well, until it simply outgrew it. As with any machinery, there were limitations and problems. The entrepreneurial fundraiser quickly learns the need to compromise. Lawrence yearned for a new type of product that didn't try to fit fundraising needs to an already pre-ordained framework of what is and isn't possible, one that genuinely started and ended with the fundraiser's needs and the donor's desires. One whose writers saw it as their task to provide the flexibility to match those needs and desires in volume, in any given circumstance, across any range of circumstances.

Although he didn't realise it, Lawrence was dreaming of a new generation of interactive supporter databases. Meanwhile, in offices and laboratories in various other parts of the planet, computer software companies were slowly waking up to the needs of their customers and the benefits for them if they could satisfy even just a part of those needs.

One particular company – Westwood Forster – had already developed a software program specifically designed to maximise fundraising relationships. They had called their software ALMS. When they discovered what Lawrence and his colleagues were up to, they realised that Botton Village was some way ahead of them in anticipating donor needs. So they set about persuading Botton that ALMS could be adapted to do all that Botton might want. In convincing Lawrence Stroud of their product's potential they unwittingly took on the best possible chief test pilot. In true relationship marketing style, company and client joined forces to develop a new type of system that would potentially revolutionise the role of the fundraising database and bring true relationship fundraising within the reach of any fundraiser.

But that early enterprising software manufacturer was not alone. Relationship fundraising had been taken up as a concept by other software manufacturers who could see the writing on the wall.

It has been said before but can't be overstressed. The key to relationship fundraising is a flexible, accessible and affordable database.

The best investment you can make

Botton Village's wisdom in investing in growing its supporter base isn't simply a matter of financial providence. Quite apart from the obvious economies of scale, more donors mean more than just more money.

Lawrence Stroud again, 'I have always believed that in building Botton's list as quickly and economically as possible we were also building up a tremendous resource. Botton now has more than 55,000 current supporters and should the village ever need to call on them I have no doubt they will respond. It's unlikely, perhaps, but if ever there was a serious problem with the statutory authorities – with the registration office at the Department of Health,* for example – I can say that 55,000 people across the country, including a great many Members of Parliament and people of influence, are going to get a letter about this issue. We can ask supporters to write to their local newspapers or their MPs. Botton may never use it, but that list represents a powerful and influential weapon.

'We can, and do, call on our donors for many other things. We ask their opinions, we encourage them to introduce their friends, we use them in press campaigns and for PR, we invite them to events, we sell them things, many of them raise funds for us, we use them to explain and to justify our very existence.

'And ultimately, because our needs here are limited by our size and lack of space, we can be confident that this same group of people will provide for Botton's villagers into the foreseeable future through the gifts they will leave us as legacies in their wills.'

In terms of legacy promotion Botton is still a fairly new appeal, but the signs for long-term income are very encouraging indeed. Income from legacies has grown steadily from almost nothing a few years ago, and hardly a week goes by without at least one legacy enquiry from a donor or solicitor.

'At some point', explains Lawrence, 'legacy income may become Botton's primary source of income. And then fundraising perhaps need not be so active. Botton will always need to keep its fundraising programme going, however, to maintain and protect its list and to develop its relationships with its donors to the maximum mutual benefit, for both them and for Botton.

'They represent Botton's future.'

Think small

Botton is not insignificant as fundraising organisations go. Of course it is certainly not big, but it raised about

---

*The office responsible for the statutory provision of care to people with a mental handicap in the UK.

£1.9 million in 1995, net of costs, and that amount is growing, so it is certainly not small. Botton Village has benefited from its small-scale approach to its personal dealings and problem-solving.

Lawrence clearly recalls the early days, 'I remember I visited a very large charity to look at their new computer system. I was taken by the fact that they were still using Cheshire labels when their new system laser-printed addresses so well and I asked them why. The response I got was "well, we in the computer department have been telling them up there in marketing for years that we can do it". I found rival, competitive departments in the same organisation. They were more concerned with their own power struggle than getting the best for their charity.

'What's needed is to break down the walls. There is no such thing as a specialist need. People shouldn't see themselves as marketers, or computer specialists, or whatever. In fundraising you have got to be multifunctional.

'I remember in another large charity I visited the fundraiser was lamenting the fact that he didn't get time to change addresses because people in his accounts department were so anxious to bank the money that they grabbed everything as soon as it came in. His department was membership. Of course, he didn't have time to say thank you to people because, again, accounts just grabbed everything. This is crazy.

'The flexibility at Botton is very important. If I wanted to restructure the database I just got on with it. I have actually done it – just like that. It took me just one morning.'

Long-term service too is a great asset. 'Yes, it is very important to have new blood from time to time and change can be very beneficial. But when people change jobs every two years or so and the newcomer wants to change everything, so he or she can make their mark, the overall effect can be disruptive and expensive.'

In establishing a long-term relationship with tens of thousands of donors, continuity is a great advantage for

Botton Village. While most fundraising organisations won't be able to offer the incentives that keep people in Botton, it is perhaps worth their while to look more closely than they have at ways of retaining staff as long as possible and to set up procedures and systems that can't be easily changed at the whim of some 'here today, gone tomorrow' newcomer.

Opportunities for promotion and career development simply aren't on the village's agenda and from Lawrence's personal point of view this might be a mixed blessing. 'My problem was I couldn't pass it to anyone. Nobody else wanted it. There were no power politics, no fighting or jostling for my position. In many ways that is a bad thing.' Eventually, after over 20 years, Lawrence simply felt like going in a different direction. So he left the village. But not the direct mail programme.

In Botton Village's case the lack of career progression inhibited neither drive, ambition, nor creative urge. Even though the need for funds is lessening, there is no sign in Botton's current programme of stagnation or complacency.

But Lawrence is not convinced that a fundraising career at Botton has more to offer a young tyro than some of the more mundane of jobs outside.

'We were recruiting a while ago', he explains, 'for an office junior.* A young man from one of the local banks applied. I had to explain to him that he might grow to become an office unjunior, but there's nowhere else to go. And what, I asked him, are you going to learn? At least in the bank there are huge training resources. So I persuaded him out of it.

'After that came the recession and even the banks started laying people off. For all I know he may have been made redundant, so perhaps he would have been better off at Botton.'

I think Lawrence may also have been neglecting the fact that a couple of years' experience with Botton would have given the young enthusiast a training and background that any fundraising organisation would willingly snap up. But

---

*It has become necessary for Botton to employ a small number of paid staff.

whether or not an ambitious career fundraiser would be right for Botton or its donors is a moot point.

Communicating with donors

Success in direct mail fundraising came steadily and as something of a surprise to Botton Village. As the number of donors on the list grew, as funds began to flow in, and as project after project was successfully funded and completed, Botton began to be less and less concerned about whether or not the money would keep on coming and more and more concerned about the people who were sending it and what they were getting out of it. Everyone on the FRG was keen that donors should not be taken for granted, that they should not be written to or dealt with inappropriately, and that Botton should at all costs avoid any sense of an exploitative or one-way relationship.

This was not a sudden realisation. It had always been there, but it came increasingly to the forefront as Botton steadily improved the systems and extended the capabilities of its database.

Segmentation had been a priority from the start and over the years Botton had introduced as much segmentation as most of the country's large-scale users of fundraising direct mail. Then, as a direct result of the coincidence of improved database potential with an increasing awareness of the possibilities of relationship fundraising, Botton's fundraisers began to rapidly push forward the frontiers of segmentation.

Flexibility is the key

Lawrence says, 'The theory of the new database is that any one of our people – he or she doesn't have to be a computer specialist – should be able to sit down in front of a screen and say, for example, "I want a report on donors in the town of Crewe, who are female, who are over 45, who are of the star sign Aries, who have a giving pattern of x, who received the white book but didn't receive the postcard, who have not completed the renewal form they were sent but did receive a telephone call, and who should be written to next week because that's their best time..." and get the report exactly as she wants. I can't think why we should want to write particularly to that type of donor, but I can't imagine how we can do real relationship fundraising without that possibility.

'Flexibility is the key, infinite flexibility. There is no reason why such flexibility should not be possible and available to fundraisers now.'

In the early days at Botton mistakes were made. Methods of identifying donors and segments that seem so obvious now were simply not used because no one thought of them. Whole groups of donors were lost.

Now Botton codes responders and donors according to where they are in the programme. Zero means they have just entered the programme and had a thank you letter. One means they've had their first letter and first issue of *Botton Village Life*, and so on. If at any time during the first eight stages they give a second donation they are then moved into the next category. They will then cease to be responders and will become donors, fitting into one or other of Botton's donor categories. There, of course, they will be treated appropriately and developed on, hopefully, to further categories. Or if donations cease they will be dropped back to a lapsed category. Nobody stays still.

It seems obvious, but for Botton the system is quite recent. Many other fundraisers have no system at all.

'We still move people generally because of their financial performance', says Lawrence, 'rather than for any psychographic, or even demographic, reason. I think that is wrong. We will do even better when we treat people not according to how much they have given, but according to their expressed desire for involvement and their interest in our information.'

Segments within segments

Jackie Fowler, client services director at Botton's agency, Burnett Associates, took over responsibility for working with Botton in 1990. She has equally ambitious intentions for Botton's segmentation.

'In the next series of letters to our donors we intend to take some samples out of several of the larger segments and try another approach, so we can test within segments. This makes sense because we know that, by whatever criteria we segment, obviously not everybody within a given segment will be the same, or will behave in the same way. We want to develop the ability to include each donor in several different segments simultaneously.

'We know from work with other clients, for example, that the Pareto principle* not only applies across a whole database, but also applies within each segment of that database. This is only one criterion and a financial one at that, but it does show how important it is becoming to segment within segments.

'We've even got a word for it – cross-segmenting.

'Logically, of course, we will then need to find a way of segmenting within the subsegments, which sounds daft but is actually not far from writing individual letters to each of your donors.'

NSPCC's Attila project (*see* chapter 7, pages 196–197) was a good example of this. A subset of every group was identified from each of certain higher level donor categories and earmarked for different treatment.

In the NSPCC's case, the Attila donors were sent personal, hand-prepared letters and information – no junk mail. The purpose was to monitor over time the reactions of identical groups of donors to two completely different styles of communication.

Fundraisers could just as easily try more radical donor contact programmes and test, for example, sending a video, making a telephone call, visiting at home, invitations to

---

*The curious phenomenon in most businesses that says 80 per cent of your sales will come from 20 per cent of your customers and vice versa.

events, tape cassettes (or even sending a Botton Village cheese). Packages could be constructed in a variety of mixes and the tests run simultaneously over a period of time, at the end of which it may be possible to see which is the best communications mixture for a given group of donors, both from the donor's perspective and the fundraising perspective.

Lawrence Stroud believes increased segmentation and increased personalisation will at last enable him to get away from the 'dreaded' tick boxes, those ubiquitous squares with leading gift amounts, one of which is always blank for £_____ other.

'The sheer range of choice indicates that you don't know very much about your donor. I appreciate that donors like gift amounts to be suggested, but I feel sure that with consistent givers, whose giving level we can clearly establish, it should be quite easy to write about needs within or just above that level and send an already completed reply form that just relates to them and doesn't suggest a lot of higher amounts that are out of reach, look greedy and leave the donor feeling bad.

'This is no exaggeration. I have often had letters criticising us for the leading nature of our reply forms. Most of our donors are thinking people. They feel tick boxes insult their intelligence.'

So the boxes were dropped.

Jackie Fowler was not entirely happy with this decision, mainly because its effect had not been tested. 'It would be fairly easy to show examples of how specific tick boxes have increased average donation values and improved return on investment but, of course, that's not what it's all about at Botton.

'But there are concerns if response appears to be down so I have lobbied for testing of prompt levels, but this has always been turned down by the FRG. Fortunately, or unfortunately, response always picks up, so the discussion becomes rather academic.'

The error factor

The fundraising team at Botton Village is well aware that dangers lurk within the increased personalisation they seek to impose.

'The more we personalise', says Lawrence, 'the more possibility there is for error. Errors are irritating at best and lose us donors at worst, so we have to weigh up the error factor when we decide just how sophisticated we want to be.'

Lawrence's nightmare is that after spending hundreds of man-hours making sure that the body of the letter is exactly right, with the right donor history, that the correct 'push-up' levels have been built into the appeal, and all the right cross-references have been included, his wonder letter goes out misspelling the donor's name.

> I was delighted to hear from you. The letters and pamphlets we get from Botton are excellent because they are not merely appeals but explain so much about the people and the new developments at Botton. I have been to Botton some years ago, and have been trying to get there again to see all the wonderful progress Lawrence Stroud writes about.
>
> Peter Jellinek,
> Buckinghamshire

Once there was an error. It was just before Christmas and every donor in one of the top segments inadvertently received three identical mailing packs – and very rapidly thereafter a hastily scripted letter of apology from Lawrence, who had almost instantly spotted his error. This letter was a triumph of disarmingly sincere contrition. Lawrence humbly accounted for his shortcomings and included, without any sense of trying to excuse himself, that he had been distracted from his duties as he was playing God in Botton's Christmas play and this had clearly over-occupied his mind. A few donors complained, but many more than usual responded with generous gifts. Results from this segment were the best ever. (I don't recommend this as deliberate fundraising practice, but it does show the power of apology.)

Some outside help

Jackie Fowler and Philip Dilks, copywriter, have both played important parts in developing Botton Village's communications with donors. Philip has been visiting Botton almost since the fundraising programme started, and he loves it. He regularly takes his family to Botton for holidays. Everybody in the village knows and likes Philip, which is so valuable and useful when he comes to prepare material for *Botton Village Life*. Philip identifies totally with the people of Botton, he knows them all and quite a lot about them too. People talk to Philip and confide in him, which of course he respects but inevitably this background adds colour and authenticity to his writing. Not only has Philip written nearly all issues of *Botton Village Life*, he has also written most of Botton's leaflets and the majority of its letters to donors.

The benefits of immersing the writer in his or her subject and ensuring their ongoing commitment are immense. It takes time and requires a considerable initial investment, but it pays off. Botton and its agency have also invested by sending account managers and production editors to spend days in Botton getting to know the people and the place. It pays dividends later through their commitment and the quality of their work.

Jackie Fowler has been a regular visitor to Botton for the past six years. Whenever possible she stays in the village, joining one of the households and taking part in the daily routine just like anyone else.

Jackie's role is strategic and supervisory. The year-round Botton communications programme ensures that there is always a range of projects currently in production. Many will be established publications with clearly defined schedules but there is always something new, something challenging. With a programme of this scale nothing can be taken for granted and everything is run on a tight budget and time deadline.

'It's fun', says Jackie, 'and it's very interesting. Botton gives me the chance to practise a wide number of fundraising marketing disciplines for a cause in which I believe, in an enjoyable, productive atmosphere. We have

Lively, newsy and a great fundraiser. *Botton Village Life* gives donors a regular window on what their help achieves.

had a chance here to be very innovative, to try lots of new approaches, particularly in donor development and relationship building.

'It is the perfect environment to see relationship fundraising in practice because the people of Botton are such natural relationship fundraisers. They have a great commitment to their donors and wouldn't mislead or abuse them for the world.

'We are convinced that we should give donors what they want and so far all the evidence we have gathered since we started putting this into practice shows that when we give donors what they want they give us more – and get more out of it themselves.'

If you want to know, ask

Jackie, Lawrence and the FRG between them have supervised a programme of file segmentation that started over four years ago and is still going on.

Jackie explains, 'If technology will allow us, we want to keep pushing segmentation forward, so we are always reviewing and, if possible, improving the relevance of what we send. We may never reach the ultimate, which is a tailor-made communication programme for each individual, structured precisely to meet that individual donor's perceived interests and desires, but we have already gone a long way towards it.

'It's encouraging because once we started writing appropriate letters people noticed it and responded warmly. It also saves money for Botton and stops us from irritating donors with unwanted mail. It shows Botton in a good light to donors, who appreciate hearing from a charity that is obviously anxious to avoid waste as well as inconvenience.'

Botton decides its segmentation by the most obvious and reliable method. It asks its donors. Curiously this is the one approach most fundraisers overlook.

Clearly there are risks in asking your donors. They may

not say what you want them to. They may tell you something else entirely.

To many fundraisers it seems the height of folly, for instance, to allow donors to decide that they want to hear from you just once a year. Imagine that, whatever next? Well, how about giving them the opportunity to tell you that they only want information – *no appeals*? Or even how about giving them the opportunity to say they never, ever, want to hear from you again?

Botton does all these things. The logic is that if someone, even a valued donor, decides he or she doesn't want to hear from Botton then Botton should respect that. Anyway, the village doesn't want to spend its postage budget writing to people who don't want to hear from it and who probably therefore won't respond.

Much better to let donors self-select. Some will want to hear more regularly, others less. In theory it should cancel itself out.

In theory.

In practice, of course, life rarely works out like that.

In practice Botton's approach has turned out to be even more warmly welcomed by donors than was expected. Donors have written to say things like, 'I wish other charities I support would treat me like you do.'

Of course, these are early days and this, the biggest test of all, may yet have some surprises in store, but after four years indications seem to point strongly towards substantial financial benefits from asking, and listening to, your donors.

Further adventures in segmentation

Jackie Fowler takes up the story of Botton's experiences in segmentation. 'The first segmented mailing went out in April 1992. Lawrence and I came up with a list of the main groups we felt we'd like to monitor and who we felt could do with different treatment. The list totalled 12 segments, most being very obvious ones like companies, trusts, groups, large covenanters, multiples, and abroad.

'Even that first time we were amazed by the different response rates from those initial broad segments, from 27.7 per cent (average donation £119) from large donors and 45.12 per cent (average donation £17.08) from multiple donors, to 10.7 per cent (average donation £31.49) from "normal" donors. Suddenly we could see how the single average figure we'd always had from warm mailings broke down – who was doing what.

'I began to see that past average figures in fact didn't represent any of our main groups of donors. It's rather like the chap with his feet in the fridge and his head in the oven, his average temperature tells you very little about how comfortable or otherwise he is.

'From there we began to segment further and in particular to break down those who weren't giving. On analysis, we had discovered that at any time around 40 per cent of Botton's file was inactive. We broke these down into once-only givers, those who had given more than once but subsequently stopped, and recent, first-time donors. We also included both lapsed segments – those above plus covenants due for renewal and those that had expired – and a programme to take a first-time donor through a series of "welcome" stages to discover the pattern of when people "convert" and how many.'

The results from appeals in April, June and September of 1992 were helpful but didn't show any real increase on past results. But Christmas 1992 came as an amazing surprise.

The Christmas appeal, which goes out around the beginning of December, has always been the best appeal time for Botton and income from the Christmas 'warm' mailing to donors has always exceeded the others. Over the years various 'barriers' have been a good barometer to the success of each appeal. Early on it was the £100,000 barrier – when the appeal total exceeded £100,000 that barrier was broken. As the years passed by so too was the £200,000 barrier and eventually the £300,000. In Christmas 1992

I'm sending you some of my photos of me with my friends at Botton village! I like living here. I want to stay forever. Lesley

Dear Friend,

Lesley Simmonds is part of a caring family. She has many friends and a job she loves. She also happens to have Down's syndrome.

Here at Botton Village in the North York Moors, Lesley and other people with special needs make the most of every minute of their lives, contributing fully to the rich and varied activities of a unique community in a way that would often simply not be possible elsewhere.

Lesley came to Botton Village 20 years ago when she was 21. Her mother, now in her eighties, was increasingly worried about no longer being able to care for her daughter.

Now Lesley is a member of the Rowan House family where my wife Anke and I are houseparents. We are one of 28 extended families who live in Botton Village.

For Lesley and everyone at Botton, the day usually starts with breakfast together at 7.30 am. Then we all have our different jobs to go to around the Village.

Lesley's job is cleaning our house. She calls herself Anke's right-hand helper and is literally the heart and soul of the household. She loves her job and enjoys making herself useful. She is always offering to help others and will stop for a chat over a cup of coffee at the drop of a hat.

Other members of the family work in different parts of the Village. There is a Food Centre, a Weavery, and a Gardening Team. We have five farms, a Bakery, a Wood Workshop, and a Candleshop. We also have our own Printing Press and Workshop. We create beautiful wooden toys, engraved glass and woven scarves, and we make bread, jams and cordials. We eat much of the food we produce and sell the rest along with our crafts in our two Village shops and to buyers in Britain and abroad.

Everyone at Botton does the job which suits their ability and personality, but nobody receives a wage. We are all happy to work for the benefit of each other and the community as a whole.

Botton was founded in the 1950s by the pioneering doctor, Karl König. He believed that people with a mental handicap should have the chance to discover and use their talents to achieve their full potential in a safe and caring community. Since then, the Village has gone from strength to strength. Today it is home to more than 320 people, over half of whom are adults with various forms of mental handicap. Everyone lives in extended families like ours at Rowan.

Botton Village

Danby, Whitby,
North Yorkshire YO21 2NJ

Switchboard (0287) 660871
Helpline (0287) 661294
Fax (0287) 660888

Always colourful,
never dull. Botton
sends its donors
letters they want to
receive.

to: Jos Smeele,
Botton Village Appeal Fund,
FREEPOST
Botton Village,
Danby, Whitby,
North Yorkshire
YO21 2BR

I want to help Lesley and her friends stay at Botton

Here's my donation of
£19   other £

I enclose a cheque made payable to the
Botton Village Appeal Fund

or please debit my   Access   Visa   CAF Charity

Card no.   /   /   /

Exp. date   /

Signature

Please send your gift with this reply form in the freepost envelope provided. Thank you.

If there are any errors in your name or address,
please amend them here and accept our apologies.

Thanks for being our friend
Do visit us soon if you can!

Lawrence Stroud was hoping that the surplus income from that one appeal to donors would exceed the £400,000 barrier – a very significant milestone.

Determined to write as appropriately as possible to Botton's donors, Lawrence and Jackie had come up with 19 different segments all of which required an individual letter.

Five different types of preprinted computer stationery were involved. Personalisation was not just by name and address number, but by type of giving, by recency of giving and by size of last donation. Bar code identifiers were used for the first time. And instead of one letter with a few minor variations, 19 different communications were sent to Botton's 60,000-plus donor file, each letter reflecting the status or expressed interest of the donor who received it.

As responses began to come in the excitement at Botton was more intense than usual. A lot was at stake. Everyone

Key segments – Christmas 1992

1. Donor – banker packs.	11. Companies.
2. Large/multiple donors.	12. Groups.
3. Covs/BOs/GAYES.	13. Responders – 1st *BVL*.
4. Renewal covs.	14. Responders – 2nd *BVL*.
5. Expired covs.	15. Responders – 3rd *BVL*.
6. Christmas-only covs.	16. Anxious reminder.
7. Christmas-only.	17. Once-only inactive/newly inactive.
8. Information-only.	
9. Abroad.	18. Past donor inactive.
10. Trusts.	19. Christmas-only inactive.

expected to break the magical £400,000 barrier, but by how much?

In the event the £400,000 barrier was a bit of an anticlimax. Income shot past it so quickly it was barely noticed and within days the unimaginable £500,000 barrier had already been left far behind. Profit from that one mailing eventually reached more than £580,000, a real increase of 46 per cent on the previous year.

> Talking about Botton Village to friends and acquaintances is important, and might produce further help.
>
> Mrs D Legge, Worksop

The Christmas-only segment produced a 54 per cent response and a very much higher than average gift value. Lawrence quickly calculated that this one mailing had achieved a higher income than it would have done had he sent the usual four appeals throughout the year to those donors who had ticked the 'Christmas-only' box. One rather than four mailings to that segment had meant a great saving in postage. And all those donors hadn't been irritated by unwanted and unwelcome mail.

Instead Botton had strengthened its long-term relationships with these donors by asking what they wanted and then delivering it.

(It occurred to us, of course, that 46 per cent of people who said they wanted to hear from us only at Christmas had not responded – why not? This certainly would be well worth finding out. And could we not go back to these people quite urgently, and perhaps quite forcefully, to suggest that having asked for that once-only contact each year they had now just missed their only chance to give?)

The 'information-only' segment of the Christmas 1992 mailing produced perhaps the most positive and most surprising result.

These people, remember, had at their request received only a copy of *Botton Village Life* and a friendly, newsy letter, no appeal. They weren't even given a reply form.

Yet 12.5 per cent of this group responded spontaneously with a donation and at a higher than average level of gift. Evidence again that when you give people a choice and then do what they want, they will respond positively. Donors are like that.

So what of Christmas 1993? Were these early encouraging results supported by further progress the following year, or were there signs that initial enthusiasm had waned? Despite the apprehension with which these results were awaited, when they came they were equally spectacular. And so were Christmas 1994's.

Although percentage responses in the second and third years of the experiment were not quite up to the first year's phenomenal total, they were only slightly down. And they were still streets ahead of what most other charities would expect.

These results alone seem to indicate that the donor-based approach works rather well.

Donor choice

'As time goes on', Jackie explains, 'the donor base has become more "pure" in only being current, active givers. Lapsed donors are weeded out and treated differently. More and more people opt for information only, currently 2,200 out of 43,000 donors, and Christmas only – three segments totalling 19,100 out of 66,580. The response rates from these last continue to astound. In June 1995, as a one-off opportunity that we justified by a full explanation, we sent covenant forms to information-only people. The segment has so far responded at 16.84 per cent, average donation is £119, and 32 new covenants have been taken out. Net surplus earnings from that segment alone are £38,000.'

Botton has always been generous in sharing the results of its experiences with other fundraisers. Lawrence justifies this simply, 'When we started we were helped enormously by the openness of other charities. Now we try to help others as much as we can.'

On testing generally

Botton Village must have tested every possible variable in direct mail communications and not just once, but many times. Sometimes the results were helpful, but just as often they were contradictory or confusing.

Jeff Balls is a long-standing (even long-suffering) member of the FRG and manager of the Camphill Press, which handles most of the print production for Botton's complex programme of donor communications. In one mailing there were 71 different tests.

'One thing we learned for certain', he says, 'is that testing is a pain. Our mathematical abilities have frequently been stretched to the limit, and sometimes beyond. Most challenging will be when we have a result of sorts, but then Lawrence and I would have different views on whether it had worked or it hadn't, or whether the thing we were testing made a substantial difference or not. Usually it's clear, but not always. Direct mail is very flexible and split tests can be introduced across a variety of segments, but don't expect mathematical precision from donors, or even consistency from one group to another, or from one time of the year to another.

'The longer I do this the more convinced I am that people are individuals and their behaviour, collectively, is hard to predict. The only certainty is that as long as they still believe in us they will keep on giving. More than that is not a matter of mathematical certainty but a question of gut feeling. And you have to be prepared to be wrong.'

Lawrence agrees. 'I wouldn't say testing is a waste of time but I don't think fundraisers should become obsessed with it. We have tested all sorts of things: messages on envelopes, stamps, personalisation, long letters, short letters, fewer enclosures, more enclosures, any number of creative approaches including some really quite wacky ideas. The results have not been hugely encouraging in that most increments were marginal and when retested frequently

> Thank you for the card from the Castle House family. I came in from my window-cleaning round cold, wet and windswept feeling fed up and then I opened your envelope. I can't tell you how much it warmed and cheered me up.
>
> Ted Francis,
> Gainsborough

went the other way. Once when we tested individually hand-typed and stamped outer envelopes we found this actually depressed response, which is bizarre.

'For nearly five years we tried a seemingly endless variety of creative approaches, trying to beat our "banker" cold donor recruitment pack. Whatever we tried seemed to make little or no difference. Then, without much optimism, we tried a different concept, a roll-folded leaflet that broke the convention of long copy by going for big photographs with little more than extended captions. This package featured one of our most appealing residents, Frances, and it performed about 20 per cent better than our banker – a huge jump. I think we have probably sent out about 5 million Frances packs since then. Frances has since left the village to live in another Camphill centre, but a similarly designed mailing featuring Lizzie, one of Botton's most popular residents, is working just as well.

'Later we achieved similar success in a much simpler way – we sent a small, more basic, easier to complete reply form. However, even though response increased substantially, we have found it more difficult to convert these "responders" into real donors.' (Botton doesn't regard anyone as a donor until they have given at least a second gift.)

So testing may be hard work and sometimes confusing, but it does pay.

Testing in segmentation

Together Jackie and Lawrence regularly reviewed the segments, changing them as they felt appropriate, testing new ideas, looking at results and donor behaviour. They have also introduced other segments such as 'information-only' (introduced in September 1992), which offered people the chance not to receive appeals, and 'recent' donors (March 1993), to acknowledge a recent gift and make a softer ask.

They also tried a hard-hitting final letter to persuade

Seven ways Botton can help you

Your support means a great deal to us and we want to help you in any way we can. Please complete the questions below if you wish to change a previous decision or would like additional information. Just tick the relevant boxes and we will keep in touch the way you want us to.

1 By letting you decide when you'd like to hear from us
We usually produce four issues a year of our newsletter, *Botton Village Life*, but you can choose one of the following options.

I would prefer to hear from you just once a year at Christmas.
I would like you to keep me up to date with Botton's news through Botton Village Life, *but I do not wish to receive appeals.*
At the moment I hear from you just once a year:
I would like to receive all four regular issues of Botton Village Life.
I want to catch up on news at Botton with the past three issues of Botton Village Life.

2 By sending you free advice
We produce *The Simple Guide to Making a Will*, which is full of useful, impartial information. Of course, if you do decide to remember Botton in your Will we would be very grateful.

Please send me my free copy of The Simple Guide to Making a Will, *currently only applicable to England and Wales.*
I would like the   standard print   large print version.

3 By showing you and your friends life in Botton
Our video, *Botton Village: A Very Special Place*, tells the story of our community through the lives of three villagers. It'll help you to get to know us better, especially if you haven't had the chance to visit us yet.

Please send me your video on a month's free loan.
Please send me my own copy. I enclose £5 (see payment details overleaf).

Botton Village is part of The Camphill Village Trust, a non-profit-making company limited by guarantee 539694 England and registered as a charity, number 232402.

4 By inviting you to visit us
Visitors are always welcome at Botton. If you can, please give us a ring in advance on (01287) 661294. We can supply details of the opening times of our workshops and a guide to the best village walks.

Please send me your information for visitors.

5 By giving you information on Botton's history
We have been producing our newsletter, *Botton Village Life*, for eleven years. Past issues feature lots of interesting stories from the Village's history.

Please send me a set of back issues (1–20), or issue(s) no(s) _____ (between 21 and 33).

6 By respecting your wishes
From time to time we agree with other carefully selected charities to write to some of each other's supporters. This can be a very valuable way for us to find new friends.

I would prefer not to hear from any other organisations.

7 By sending you information only if you want it
I would prefer you not to write to me again.

Do let us know if you have moved to a new address, if we are sending you more than one copy of our newsletter by mistake, or if there is anything else you would like to tell us.

The basis of segmentation: this unique reply form asks what Botton can do for the donor, rather than the other way round.

responders to overcome their inertia. It didn't work well.

'Recently we've been experimenting with the telephone as a final stage in the "conversion" process', says Jackie. 'The phone is an obvious way to start a dialogue with people who don't respond to letters, and we are trying it on larger-value, first-time givers. The conversation tends to lead people either to give again, or to request to receive information-only, or once-a-year mailings.

'Those who Botton doesn't speak to on the phone are sent a series of *BVL*-based mailings, which contain more direct and specific asks during the later stages. If they haven't responded after about 18 months they are transferred to receiving just one contact a year at Christmas. If they then don't respond for several Christmases they join a pool that is mailed from time to time with a cold pack. This segment then responds rather well.

'There has been very little testing within segments, for example testing of prompt levels or shopping list items. Although the agency has suggested this, there is resistance from Botton's fundraising group, which believes strongly that donors should be allowed to choose how they respond and not to have the level of their giving too much led by the charity. The fundraising group is extremely ethical about how donors should be treated, which might frustrate some perfectly acceptable direct marketing practices but which surely would be widely appreciated by Botton's donors.'

I hope and advocate that Botton Village may resist the temptation to hire professional 'money-raisers' with *Reader's Digest* style letters, telephone canvassing and market research.

Bruno W Stalmans, Guildford

Making best use of the phone

'This too is typically "Botton" says Jackie. 'Instead of using a telephone marketing agency, which Botton felt would not be quite "them", Julie Upton, the daughter of a member of staff, was given specialist training from a professional telephone fundraising consultant. Julie now makes calls from her home in the evening, liaising with Botton over which donors to call and afterwards what their responses were.

'The script, which Julie can depart from at her discretion as the conversation develops, has always been deliberately "soft". A typical debate for the FRG would be whether the ask should be more direct and where the balance lies between donor comfort, cost and income.'

Creative on the segments

Over the years Botton has tried different kinds of stationery, allowing for different reply form backs and for one- or two-page letters. Jackie explains, 'We've learned to use the letter front copy, to angle it and tailor the ask in different ways for different types of people.

'We have selectively lasered a message on the reply form about covenanting depending on the segment. A covenant form is then included, or not.

'However, the range of tick box options has remained constant between all segments.

'Sometimes the number of creative/copy variations has to be dictated by volume in order to be cost-effective. For instance, it's very expensive to create a separate letter variation for 70 people. Also, producing different base stationery had to be questioned on the grounds of cost. In the end it wasn't really worth it.'

Recent developments in personalisation and segmentation

Botton's welcome and conversion cycle continues to evolve. The segmentation plan is still being reviewed regularly and tailored each time to specific segment quantities, time of year and other needs. The programme is working well but keeping it operational requires an ever-increasing amount of work. Relationship fundraising may indeed be successful, but it is not easy.

Botton Village will soon be testing a new, larger reply form to explain various costed needs associated with the current appeal project. Although this isn't a conventional 'prompt' tick box, it will at least give the donor a clearer idea of what a certain sum could achieve. However, as yet there is no suggestion at all of how much a donor should give or what that might achieve. The interesting thing is that, mailing by mailing, the average donation continues to vary a great deal across the segments, but to remain roughly consistent within a segment.

This discomfort about leading people's giving, or creating élite categories has also led Botton Village to reject any kind of committed giving scheme. For Botton every active donor counts, however often and however much they choose to give. A great deal of thought goes into ways of deepening the relationship, giving donors greater understanding of the village and its way of life, giving them control of the relationship and respecting their wishes.

So on balance the FRG doesn't feel that a special committed giving scheme would be right for Botton. If there were to be a great and ongoing need for funds then perhaps the subject might be revisited. But at present that need just isn't there and the existing fundraising programmes currently meet all of the village's requirements. So, inevitably and quite correctly, new initiatives are now not viewed with the pioneering enthusiasm that characterised Botton's early days.

Where next for Botton's fundraising?

For some time a lively debate has occupied the village about how much it should be fundraising. While people acknowledge what it has achieved, there are some who yearn for the good old days when life was less secure and you just made do. Also people feel that the pace of change and rebuilding might become disruptive to life and could threaten to take control of how the village develops. Obviously, when money comes in you find ways to spend it. There is a worry that in the foreseeable future the pace of development will be determined by the fundraising income, rather than the other way round.

As registration (the process of formally meeting Department of Health standards) demands a huge amount of upgrade work, this argument, at the moment, is academic. Botton Village still needs money. But the debate probably will continue for some time at Botton, until needs change one way or another. Legacy income is now increasing rapidly and, while it cannot be relied upon, there is a strong feeling among the fundraising literate at Botton that there will soon be a lot more legacies coming their way.

> When we received your invitation to the open day we decided to make the effort and see Botton Village for ourselves. We had a most enjoyable, delightful day... It is very gratifying to see people's donations put to such good use.
>
> Joyce Sandell, Hertford

So for several years now there has been a policy of maintaining rather than growing the database – recruiting to replace attrition rather than increasing the number of active donors. This continues to be the case. (In practice the number of donors has grown a little. Response to the current cold pack is the best ever and an active reciprocal programme recruits relatively large numbers at a profit.)

Equally with the 'warm' appeal programme it is very much 'carry on what we're doing', but with few new initiatives. Response to the regular appeals accompanied by *Botton Village Life* does vary by the mailing (June 1995 looked very poor for a long time but has since picked up to £315,000 net surplus), but taken year by year the trend is still upward. And at present Lawrence, Jackie and the FRG are working on a methods-of-payment mailing and special thank you letter to send to newly converted donors (who've just given for the second time), showing them how their support helps and explaining different ways to give.

> Since being retired and with only small savings I've had to cut down on donations to causes. Your attitude has made sure that Botton Village is not one of those cut out.
>
> Ms Evelyn Rowe, Huddersfield

The fundraising group is now engaged in active, prolonged and uncomfortable discussion about the level to which Botton should be prepared to support other Camphill communities with its fundraising resource – its donors. Some feel this is a responsibility and the only ethical thing to do. Others clearly feel worried about the possible effect this could have on Botton's own fundraising. This discussion typifies the perhaps healthy but opposing tensions that now confront Botton. There is a desire to be able to rely on donated income and not to do anything that may threaten it that conflicts with a feeling of moral pressure to look outside Botton's own needs as they are now well catered for.

It is a dilemma borne from a not inconsiderable success. For the first time, Botton recently sent a mailing to 10,000 of its donors asking them to support a new Camphill community in Estonia. *Botton Village Life* had already run a short feature on a co-worker, Christian, who had worked in the Botton Creamery and who has now gone to Estonia to help start the new community. Lawrence and Jackie are now tracking the effect of this mailing on regular donors to Botton, to see if helping Camphill in Estonia might negatively – or positively – influence giving to Botton.

At the moment, guidelines for a 'third-party' appeal are being drafted. So far they suggest a third-party appeal only once every three years to part of the list, maybe 20 per cent of the total database. As with the Estonia mailing, Botton will create and manage each third-party mailing. Although the address of the recipient community will probably appear on the pack, donors' names will never be passed on by Botton.

Research

The fundraising group at Botton Village has always placed great value on research, but only recently have resources been allocated to find out on a formal basis what donors really think, what turns them on, what turns them off, what they want.

Of course, Botton had been listening to its donors for years on the basis that the best research is free and conducted on a personal one-to-one level. Members of the FRG have regular opportunities to meet donors when they visit Botton, to talk to donors on the phone and, of course, to read what they say in the flood of letters that come in daily to the Botton Village office.

Not surprisingly small organisations have an advantage over larger ones in that everything is closer to hand, so it is easier for the fundraiser to keep in touch with what is going on. Daily visits to the postroom, listening in to how the phone is answered, meeting donors face to face – these are all indispensable ways of finding out what concerns and interests your donors. Fundraisers from bigger charities need to find ways to get this feedback or they risk becoming dangerously out of touch.

Botton's experience with more formal research began with a detailed postal questionnaire sent to 4,000 donors selected at random. A very high percentage returned it, which showed a high level of donor interest. And what the donors said was very positive too.

Quite a few enclosed a cheque with their completed questionnaires. Donors are sometimes just wonderful.

Since then there have been occasional focus group sessions and several questionnaires. But Botton's most consistent and reliable source of feedback from donors is in its regular ongoing correspondence and its openness and willingness to listen to donors and to welcome their interest and concern.

A happy ending

The early days of Botton's adventures in fundraising now seem a very long time ago. So much has changed, mostly for the better.

A stroll around Botton Village now is a somewhat different experience. For a start, it's larger as, over the years, Botton has acquired some neighbouring farmland. The natural beauty that so long ago warmed an auditor's heart is still there, in abundance. And so are the villagers, the real life and soul of Botton, who seemed so happy and well placed then and seem no less so now.

Fundraising success may have some disadvantages that are not easy to see, it's true. But there are also plenty of tangible advantages. If you were to continue on that imaginary stroll around Botton these would soon become apparent: the recently built creamery and bakery, the superbly refurbished houses, the Thomas Weihs Centre – a purpose-built facility for older people with mental handicaps, the modern printing press, the new and spectacularly beautiful, award-winning church, and lots more besides.

One other major benefit from fundraising would not be seen from this stroll around the village but it might well be felt anywhere – the care and commitment of the tens of thousands of new friends, real friends, that Botton has found over the last few years, who, come what may, will care for Botton's welfare and well-being now and into the future. Many of these people have themselves benefited enormously as they have come to love this special place that has raised funds for this very worthwhile cause with so much integrity and with such commitment to them, the donors.

Botton Village Life

Central to Botton's communications with donors is the, usually, quarterly newsletter, *Botton Village Life*. It first appeared with Botton's first 'warm' mailing to the donors recruited from the initial cold mailshot. It has consistently advertised its provenance as being printed at the Camphill Press in Botton and is a cheerful, reassuring, positive news-sheet that donors genuinely seem to welcome and appreciate. Indeed, if it is ever late many will write in worriedly to enquire what's happened and make sure they've not somehow inadvertently missed an issue.

The newsletter has a fairly simple but consistent editorial policy. It should offer donors a slice of village life and an introduction to its characters. In each issue the lead story usually reports on what has been achieved in the village as a direct result of the most recent appeal. The back page sometimes features an illustrated trailer for the next appeal, which is almost invariably described more directly and in more detail in the accompanying letter and reply form. The centre pages focus on life in Botton Village, to show readers as much as possible of the personality of the village and the daily interests and concerns of the people who live there.

Interviews with various individuals are a regular feature and each issue carries a profile of one of Botton's workshops, farms, or other activities. Important issues, such as health and hygiene for older people with mental handicap, are also given brief coverage. From time to time *Botton Village Life*'s editorial reflects on Botton's foundation and its philosophical basis in the teachings of Rudolf Steiner. But nothing in Botton Village is ever covered in very great detail. The intention is that photographs (only cheerful and of high quality) should occupy at least 40 per cent of each page and that each four-page issue should have as many as 12 to 14 separate pieces, some up to half a page in length, but most little more than 'snippets'.

It works. The readers have loved it from the start.

An early and popular feature in *Botton Village Life* involved an interview with a 'character' from Botton's wide selection. I remember the very first was with a wonderful man called Peter Street. Philip Dilks, who wrote the interview, sent the draft material, as he always did, in to the editorial department at Burnett Associates. Now the qualified and experienced editors there did as they were trained to do. They edited it, corrected his grammar, rearranged his words into proper Queen's English and, of course where necessary, corrected Philip's spelling and punctuation. The result was grammatical, sanitised – but it wasn't Peter Street.

The article was duly returned to its original, unedited, reality. We learned a valuable lesson then and tore up the rule book when it came to *Botton Village Life*. As a result the true personality of the village comes shining through its pages and donors love it. We've applied that lesson to interviews done for many other clients since. Sometimes it gets us into trouble...

Language, of course, is a living, breathing, changing thing. Its purpose in the kind of writing we do is to express ideas, actions and emotions with ease and impact. So all rules should be viewed with suspicion and a willingness to bend or break them is healthy, even necessary. Shakespeare couldn't spell his own name, but he knew how to write. I believe all producers of publications (which includes most fundraisers) should beware of linguistic pedants who would confine our language in the cold, glacial halls of computerdom. If people relate to people then we need to be able to write the way people speak otherwise, whatever it is we are writing about, it isn't reality.

Television learned this long ago. But when it comes to the printed word, it is amazing how many people seek to impose rigid and inflexible rules that remove the heart from the language. My advice to fundraisers is don't let these people prevent your donors from meeting the likes of Peter Street.

A day in the life of Peter Street

'I come up to Botton Farm at 8.30 a.m. John and I take the milk up to the creamery at Roger House. We bring the churns back for milking at night and put them into the dairy for Chris. We go and move the electric fence for the cows, then we get the cows. Buffy the cow took the wrong turning, then she didn't. She always does sometimes.

'Yes we bring them. Then we go for the dustbins, one had a hole. We take one dustbin to Rock House, one to Roger House (I remember that), two scruffy old ones to Amber and two clean ones to Tour. Then I do my muck piles.

'We put the muck in a tidy heap. We throw the muck on the top and mix up the straw and muck. We are making some more compost areas. You can put lime on top of compost. I know you can, we did it in the Grange too. You can put brambles and bracken in a compost heap, it is very good stuff.

'A load of straw comes at 12 o'clock. I throw the straw off, then I belt off when the bell goes because I must not be late for lunch.

'I come back to work at 2.00 p.m. We all go down the field to dig out a trench. Then we can lay the pipes – it's a big operation, what a struggle! The ditch goes all right. We clear black earth out and the water goes down into a drain, one of those little red pipes.

'Stephen feeds the calves and gives milk to them. Sometimes on a rainy day he tidies up.

Peter Street.

'Then I come up to help Chris with the milking. I empty the churns – it's quite true! At 6 o'clock I leave Botton Farm. I should leave earlier because I am always late.'

Peter Street

Botton Village
Danby
Whitby
North Yorkshire YO21 2NJ
United Kingdom

Tel: + 44 (0) 1287 660871
Fax: + 44 (0) 1287 660888

The National Society for the Prevention of Cruelty to Children

Making the 90-degree shift

The National Society for the Prevention of Cruelty to Children is one of Britain's oldest, most popular, and most respected charities. Born 112 years ago during the golden days of Victorian philanthropy and with a dramatic and colourful history since, the NSPCC nevertheless has a reputation as a thoroughly modern organisation, constantly in the forefront of developments in child care and protection. It has a record of achievement and innovation that far exceeds its size or resources.

So too in fundraising. The NSPCC has frequently led the way in fundraising development in Britain: in direct marketing, in trading, in legacy promotion, in schools fundraising, in affinity marketing, in regional fundraising and, perhaps most famously, in the classic big gift campaign, the NSPCC centenary appeal, which was the first major appeal in Britain to be structured along the now-familiar lines followed by capital fundraisers throughout the land.

Now the NSPCC is innovating again, this time in donor development.

The NSPCC is a major British national charity engaged in a very broad range of fundraising activities. For this book I'm going to focus mainly on its experience in developing high-value donors. But first I want to say a little about the history and philosophy of the NSPCC's approach to fundraising, principally because it has had a profound influence on me. In so doing I hope also to explain the basis of its approach to major donors.

I have been a regular visitor to the NSPCC's headquarters in London since the beginning of the 1980s. In that time – nearly as long as I've been a fundraiser – I've seen many changes in the charity, but I can't recall anything quite as dramatic or fundamental as the change that's transforming the NSPCC right now. The '90-degree shift' is the term coined by the NSPCC's deputy director and head of appeals, Giles Pegram. He uses it to describe a process of change that he is encouraging, rather than imposing, on the entire organisation. The shift he is seeking is for all NSPCC people to see their work and their objectives for it from the donor's, rather than the organisation's, point of view.

By voluntary organisation standards the NSPCC is quite a big organisation – 1,000 social workers or child-care staff, 290 fundraisers and 130 support staff. It ranks number eight in the UK's top 200 table of voluntary organisations by size of voluntary income. Encouraging such fundamental change in such a large and complex organisation is no easy task.

The NSPCC has a strong and emotive fundraising proposition. Its work focuses directly on the child – vulnerable, frightened and alone, the child in danger from the most sinister and repellent threat of all: deliberate abuse by an adult that the child should be able to trust, perhaps even its own parent. Such is the public abhorrence of child abuse that many people prefer to deny its existence, to shut it from their minds in the hope that if they don't acknowledge it, it will go away.

It doesn't, of course. Instead, in the last years of the

Being a supporter of the NSPCC means a lot to me. I have seen the effects of abuse first hand and my mother's interest in the NSPCC taught me to support them. Having been to a local centre where parenting skills are taught I was very impressed with the level of care.

I have always found the NSPCC has time to answer any questions I've had and also to be very interested in my views.

Mrs Pat Cann,
Brentwood, Essex

twentieth century, horrific crimes are perpetrated against small children behind closed doors. Physical abuse, emotional abuse, neglect and sexual abuse are the daily fare of the NSPCC, an agenda it seeks to bring before its donors and potential donors confident that when they know about the issues, the problems and the solutions, these donors will willingly respond. It is to the NSPCC's credit that it has done so much over the years to bring these dark, taboo subjects to the British public's attention. By confronting the conscience of the nation, the NSPCC has pressed the people and, ultimately, the government into action. Many achievements stud the NSPCC's history of ceaseless campaigning for the rights of children.

I have never forgotten a story that illustrates this point, which I came across while researching the history of the NSPCC, now more than 10 years ago, for a special publication produced to mark the Society's centenary. The story concerns the first-ever prosecution for ill-treating a child at a time when there were no laws to cover the crime of child abuse. A little girl, Mary, was brought before the court wrapped in a horse blanket because, while there were no laws to say what you could or couldn't do to your children, there were laws regulating the treatment of your animals.

It was against this background that the NSPCC was founded in London in 1884.

The making of a career fundraiser

Not many can claim a childhood ambition to be a fundraiser although Giles Pegram's introduction to the business comes close. Like many others his entry point was via another professional interest, journalism, or more accurately, the ambition to be a press magnate. The fact that he was just 10 years old at the time is coincidental but does distinguish Giles as one of the earliest career fundraisers.

The journalistic endeavour resulted in a school

Oxford Committee for Famine Relief

274 BANBURY ROAD · OXFORD · TELEPHONE OXFORD 54333   TELEGRAMS · OXFAM. OXFORD

CHAIRMAN EMERITUS: Rev. H. R. Moxley, M.A.   CHAIRMAN: Canon T. R. Milford, M.A.   VICE-CHAIRMAN: Michael H. Rowntree, M.A.
HON. TREASURER: R. H. Langdon-Davies, D.F.C., F.C.A.   HON. SECRETARY: C. Jackson Cole.   DIRECTOR: H. Leslie Kirkley.

18th July 1963.

Giles ████████, Esq.,
2 Heath Close,
London N.W.11.

Dear Giles,

I am writing to you on behalf of the Oxford Committee for Famine Relief to thank you most warmly for your kindness in sending us your cheque for the magnificent sum of £80, being the proceeds of a Jumble Sale held at St. Barnabas Church Hall on Saturday, July 13th. I am so pleased that the Jumble Sale was such a great success. Would you please thank all those who worked so hard to collect together articles for sale.

Your kind gift will be a great help to us in our fight against hunger in the world. I think you will be interested to hear that last month we made a grant of over £20,000, a substantial Freedom from Hunger grant, to buy seeds, fruit tree saplings and fertilizers for training and demonstration purposes, which will be sent to 28 different countries in Africa, Asia and Latin America. The seeds will be distributed through existing training centres and colleges and trainees will return to their villages to demonstrate new methods of farming. It is only through the continued support of people like yourselves that we can commit ourselves to these important long-term projects.

I am enclosing a copy of our Annual Report which gives a general picture of our work. I am also sending you some posters and leaflets for your holiday effort. If you would like further copies of anything, we will be pleased to send them to you. I am afraid that you must be 16 years of age before you can be a house-t -house collector.

I know that Jenny Olson and our Schools Department would be delighted to see you whenever you and your friends find yourselves in Oxford. Perhaps you could write and suggest a day.

With best wishes.   Yours sincerely,

Director

Few organisations nowadays write such personal donor-friendly letters.

newspaper written by the young Giles, typed by his mother, copied on the school duplicator and sold to classmates in his primary school playground for just one penny a copy. That's pre-decimalisation money when there were 240 pennies to the pound and pounds were worth having. So even at this early stage he demonstrated that almost universal shortcoming of the professional fundraiser – underpricing his product.

Several issues and at least 1,200 copies later Giles had made a profit of £5 – a small fortune in those days. He remembers it well. 'The school was collecting for Oxfam so I sent the money I'd raised off to them. Oxfam responded well, so I got some friends together and organised a jumble sale, which raised £80. I sent it off. Almost by return of post I got a letter back. In those days getting a letter was a rare event for me and this letter was actually signed by the director of Oxfam, H Leslie Kirkley.'

(By one of those strange coincidences that pervade any small world such as fundraising, both Giles Pegram and I were destined, several years later, to work closely with, by then, Sir Leslie Kirkley CBE, one of the most distinguished figures in British voluntary action. He died in 1989.)

This letter from the director of Oxfam impressed Giles Pegram greatly. 'It must have been written on one of those early tape-driven automatic typewriters that preceded word processors. Organisations could write multiple standard letters just by individually typing in each name and address then pressing a button. In this case, it was the first paragraph that was personal to me and talked about the proceeds of the sale and thanked me for my gift. It went on to tell me about current Oxfam projects and what my gift would achieve, about the work they were doing with the money I had raised.'

The speed of the response, the fact that it came from the very top and the firsthand evidence of what his gift had enabled Oxfam to achieve all made an indelible impression on the young Pegram.

'I was so taken by this that when I went to my secondary school I continued fundraising for Oxfam – right up until I went to university. We did lots of things – jumble sales, sponsored events, the lot. But I never did relaunch my newspaper.'

This is not just a touching little anecdote. It has a significant lesson for all fundraisers. It shows the importance of a prompt and personal word of thanks, even for the smallest of gifts. Who could tell that this small boy with his small gift would go on to make such a contribution to Oxfam, eventually to work for Oxfam, and to become one of the leading fundraisers of his day? Sir Leslie Kirkley certainly couldn't, but he was a relationship fundraiser at heart and he would have realised that given the right encouragement anything might be possible. He must have written thousands of similar letters to thousands of similar youngsters many of whom would have quickly moved on to some new enthusiasms, as children do, and many more of whom would have continued their giving, eventually to become regular donors and perhaps lifelong supporters of Oxfam, or of other equally worthwhile causes.

That letter of thanks may not have been justified by an immediate cash return, but who can say it's not justified in the long run? It is ironic that now, more than 30 years later, fundraisers rarely get their relationships with new donors off to such a good start as Leslie Kirkley did all those years ago.

Giles Pegram got off to such a good start that he not only continued as a volunteer fundraiser for Oxfam, he later became a paid member of its staff (where he had the privilege of working alongside Guy Stringer and other great fundraisers). On leaving university Giles went to work as a fundraiser with Help the Aged, the international charity for elderly people founded by Cecil Jackson Cole (CJC), co-founder of Oxfam.

Help the Aged in those days was something of a university for the fundraising profession as some very good fundraisers came out of it. CJC's zeal for the cause made a further deep impression on Giles Pegram's attitude to fundraising.

'If I had to decide on specific influences that lead me to my belief that fundraisers should be "donor-led" then the top two would be Leslie Kirkley's letter and CJC's fervent commitment to the cause. They made me realise that voluntary organisations are really a bridge between donors and the cause. It's not just that fundraisers exist to get the money for their organisations to meet urgent needs. That seems to me to portray a begging-bowl attitude to fund-raising. Fundraisers exist also because there are people out there *who want to give.*

'Donors are not just passers-by who drop coins casually in a tin. Real donors use their giving to bring about change. They continue giving because they believe that change will be effective – and will last.

'One of the key things fundraisers have to understand is what motivates their donors – why they give and why they don't. Our job is to facilitate their giving. We want them to give as much as they can afford in the most cost-effective way. We want them to give to us rather than to someone else but people will only give if they themselves have needs that can be met by their giving. That seems to me to be the most professional thing that has to be understood about fundraising.'

When Giles Pegram joined the NSPCC as appeals director at the beginning of the 1980s it was one of the most important child-care charities in the UK. Yet the Society approached its hundredth birthday in a parlous state. Its annual income was low and many of its traditional sources of funds seemed under threat. Its image was worthy, but old-fashioned. Many of its fundraising structures were archaic and inflexible. Voluntary committees of the great and the good were sometimes not as commercial or as effective as they might be. And each year the Society was spending more than it was raising. Something had to be done.

Giles Pegram came in at a senior level, with authority to change things. But early on he met resistance.

'There was a misplaced but perhaps not surprising resistance to investing in fundraising. I'll never forget one child-care director, shortly after I'd joined when I had rapidly increased our fundraising income, complaining to me that the increased money spent on fundraising was taking away money he could have spent on child care. It was true, the *percentage* spent on fundraising had increased. But he failed to see that the result of this expenditure was a far, far bigger cake that would enable him to spend much more on services to children.

'People tend to see these things very simplistically – if you let them. So for many years now I have spent time explaining in presentations and workshops to our trustees and to colleagues from other divisions what the financial realities of fundraising are and why we do what we do. The tendency among the public – including trustees and other staff – is just to assume the money comes flowing in. Of course it doesn't and wouldn't without substantial direction and encouragement from fundraisers.

'At a donor reception recently a woman asked me why we spent 11 per cent administering her gift. I explained that we didn't, but I asked her: "If you give me £100 will you allow me to spend £11 of that to raise a further £100?" She then saw the point and everyone in the audience agreed. One donor said that it not only makes sense, it's brilliant value for money. But it needs to be put that way because that's not the way people will look at it if left to their own devices.'*

> I support the NSPCC not to derive any personal satisfaction or good feeling but simply because the NSPCC does good work and alleviates suffering. I am not sure I consider myself to be a 'relationship funder' of the NSPCC. I am a long-term supporter but this implies a financial rather than a psychological relationship, in general.
>
> Simon Duffy, London

A remarkable campaign

What the NSPCC needed then was an entirely new approach, one that would enable it to break out of its

---

*The NSPCC's expenditure on administration is four per cent. Its cost of raising money is 13 per cent of total income.

traditional treadmill of annual deficits, to create instead a
special long-term fund that would underwrite the future of
the organisation. What was needed was a massive, one-off
capital appeal that would not only provide this endowment
fund but also transform every part of the fundraising
organisation so that, even when the appeal had reached its
target and been forgotten, fundraising activity would be
kicked up several notches to operate permanently at a
higher level.

That opportunity presented itself through the NSPCC's
centenary year in 1984. Redmond Mullin, a senior and
respected fundraising consultant, worked closely alongside
Giles Pegram to plan and implement the strategy that
resulted in the NSPCC's centenary appeal. He explains the
significance of this remarkable campaign, the likes of which
had never been seen before in Britain.

'In itself, the anniversary provided no reason why
anybody should pay special attention or give extraordinarily
generously. But it was an opportunity that could be made
the occasion for a reappraisal and reaffirmation of roles. It
was also a chance to increase public understanding of issues
relating to cruelty to children. And, most of all, it was a
chance to raise a significant amount of money during the
centenary year and to increase the NSPCC's long-term skills
and resources for fundraising.'

The two laid their plans well in advance, starting more
than three years ahead of the actual 'year'. Their plans were
bold and ambitious. They set a target that would challenge
staff, volunteers and donors to unprecedented levels of
performance and generosity. They set out to uplift
significantly the Society's self-perception and performance
and they called for an investment and single-minded
commitment to success from the upper echelons of the
NSPCC, commitment that had to remain steady for months,
even years, before the initial investment would be seen to
pay off.

At this point one of the Society's committees, perhaps

influenced by inherent conservatism, recommended that the target for the year should be set at £5 million, as that might be achievable and for prestige purposes they wanted the campaign to be a visible success.

Giles Pegram stuck to his guns, demanding a £12-million target. His simple logic won the day. 'I reasoned that we might indeed fail to make a £12-million target. Perhaps we might only raise £10 million, or £8 million. But an £8-million failure is better for children than a £5-million success.'

The strategy for success

Both Redmond and Giles realised that the success of the centenary and all they were building around it would entail some very major changes within the NSPCC. (This acceptance of the need for fundamental change was to be just as essential nearly 10 years later when the NSPCC prepared to undergo a similar but less obvious metamorphosis on the introduction of relationship fundraising – the donor-led approach.)

Redmond Mullin takes up the tale again. 'During 1981 experiments were carried out in four locations to test the concept of local big gift campaigns and to establish organisers' (local fundraising staff) requirements for training and support. The strategy was refined. By the end of that year we had completed basic planning for a corporate committee subdivided in 12 commercial sectors, a network of new area committees, a national centenary committee, an appeal chairperson and a vice-chairperson. The Duke of Westminster – one of the most influential men in Britain – agreed to become chairperson. This set a trend that helped the centenary appeal to succeed in another of its objectives – to encourage the most powerful financial and social leadership nationally and locally.'

Prospect lists were prepared, a strategic timetable was set, targets totalling £12 million were agreed for the six major sectors (national industry and commerce, regional committees, wealthy individuals, trusts and foundations, public appeals/national and youth organisations, and sponsorship and promotions) and were accepted by their appropriate committees.

Other new initiatives were put in place. The Friends of the NSPCC, a new quasi-membership scheme, was launched. Direct mail activity was stepped up, a special reception was put on for major 'askers' (not donors) at 10 Downing Street, hosted by the then Prime Minister, Margaret Thatcher.

Getting the major committees to perform was a potential headache. An early incident with the industrial committee showed the duo's (Pegram and Mullin) capacity to turn adversity to advantage. At a crucial meeting of the industrial committee only one person, Sir Maurice Laing, a leading industrialist, turned up. The minutes of that meeting, however, are a model of an effective committee's productivity. A number of key decisions were made – Sir Maurice simply made them himself – and much progress was reported. The minutes conveniently neglected to mention who had attended, but strengthened the resolve of absentees to be there next time.

Keeping their collective nerve during these crucial stages was not easy for the appeal's key players. Many had to be deflected or dissuaded from making an appeal for funds. That would come later. Everything had to be securely in place first. One industry leader, Sir Terence Conran, was invited to accept leadership of the retail sector. By this time word of the campaign and its thoroughness had got out. Conran commented that it was like being asked to join the Cabinet. He accepted the honour.

Months of patient relationship building were paying dividends.

Throughout 1983, events, receptions, promotions and printed communications by the million helped to keep the assembled network of motivators and key players in a constant state of excited animation. Area chairpersons met on their own initiative. As Redmond Mullin succinctly put it, 'They formed a competitive, mutually supportive determination to succeed.'

At times like this the idle outside observer might be forgiven for imagining that with so much activity going on from so many prominent and hard-working volunteers the relationship fundraiser isn't really needed very much. Here the fundraiser can smile wisely from the background secure in his or her knowledge that he or she had set up the whole thing from the start.

By now the campaign had developed considerable momentum across almost all its many fronts. Thanks to a carefully constructed press advertising campaign and extensive PR work, massive press coverage was sustained during the key months of the centenary year itself. Having so carefully structured the campaign and so painstakingly assembled each and every individual component, Mullin and Pegram could now stand back and watch their strategy steamroll through its original target of £12 million, to become by far the most ambitious and successful capital campaign for a UK charity. At the same time a blueprint was created that many others have successfully followed. The NSPCC centenary appeal eventually raised around £15 million, and normal income that year was also increased.

But more than that, it boosted the Society's fundraising performance into a new league. The NSPCC itself was an organisation renewed, determined never to slip back into underachievement. (To set the achievement of the centenary appeal in context, the NSPCC's income has grown from £5 million in 1981 to more than £44 million in 1996.)

Innovation is the norm

There are two opposing schools of thought about innovation – 'the early bird gets the worm' and 'pioneers don't live long'. Pioneering certainly is expensive and high risk. It can also be lonely and divisive. Pioneers set themselves up for criticism and ridicule should they fail and frequently don't get fair credit when they succeed. Isn't it better and more prudent to let others break the new ground, watch what they do, and when they've proved their new idea will work, promptly plagiarise their methods from the sidelines, without all the risk and expense?

Or does success, recognition and reward belong only to the brave, who by being first can pick the best and leave the rest?

Much can be said on both sides. The NSPCC, however, has a tradition, even a culture, of innovation – but always as a means to an end. This innovation is not confined to fundraising. It is applied to personnel policy and across a diverse range of child-care issues, including the Society's regional structure and its whole approach to working with children, which is perhaps best described as 'needs-led'. The NSPCC's deliberate search for new developments has led to many firsts and these have brought many benefits for the Society, its staff, its supporters and the children it helps.

Radical, but amazingly simple

Giles Pegram is careful to emphasise that for the NSPCC innovation must never be an end in itself. 'The biggest innovation for us, the move to being donor-led, coincided remarkably with the Society's simultaneous decision to listen to children more deliberately and to ask them what *they* thought about our services and how we help them. We had learned – and this is real innovation in child-care terms – that in some cases what children wanted from our services was very different from what we thought they wanted. We were sometimes making judgements about children and their priorities that were wrong. And we only learned this through the remarkable, radical, but amazingly simple innovation of listening to children.

'Of course, with hindsight it seems obvious. So too with

donors. Quite by chance, through various influences, I was already thinking seriously about what it means for fundraisers to be "agents of the donor" and how we should structure ourselves according to the donors' needs rather than according to our activities.

'It sounds easy, and obvious, but in fact it is a policy fraught with difficulties. For a start we have to make judgements in terms of how far we will go in listening to each individual donor and in responding to his or her needs. Similarly, this is an even more pressing concern with child-led social work. Children may not know what is in their best interest, or may choose an easy way out when some other course may clearly be better for them. But these difficulties serve to illustrate the importance of being donor-led, or child-led. They make it even more valid as a policy and more important that we listen well – and get it right.

'One example of listening to children springs to mind because it is so shocking. The NSPCC did a survey of children who had been abused and who had then gone through the court process as part of society's effort to punish the abuser. Seventy-five per cent of those children said the court process was so awful that had they known what they would have to endure they would never have revealed the abuse in the first place. In terms of indicating a child's needs that points very clearly to the direction the NSPCC has to take. That's why we are now actively campaigning to reform the system so that society *truly* protects the victims of abuse.

'Of course, as with donors, we still constantly need to make judgements about what children need from us. But now we can make better judgements – because we listen to children.

'Our other key word at the NSPCC is partnership. We constantly work in close partnership with local authorities and with the statutory services, but in recent years we have extended the concept of working in partnership to a host of other agencies, including many charities that not so long ago were thought of as competitors. But if the best way to serve children is for the NSPCC to work in partnership with Barnardo's, or NCH Action for Children, or whoever, so be it. That's what we exist to do – to serve children. And that, as with any other innovation, is the only real reason I can give to justify our move to be donor-led. I believe it is the best way for us to serve children.'

Donors are owners

Donors really appreciate being treated as owners. This means the ultimate responsibility for success or failure stops with them. They cease to be mere supporters and assume for themselves a tangible role as part of the organisation. Some monthly giving schemes bestow this sense of ownership very effectively and cultivate it in their reporting back and their explanation of needs. The effect on donors' giving can be phenomenal. Many donors don't need persuasion to accept the mantle of ownership. Rather they will jump at the chance. Of course there can be a downside to this, as too strong a sense of ownership can place the fundraiser in an awkward position.

The NSPCC's appreciation of the power and the value of donors as owners goes back many years. During the centenary appeal the total campaign target was cunningly divided up among carefully selected groups and sub-committees, each with its own centenary appeal chairperson whose prime function was to take ownership of their part of the appeal total. Many of them took this responsibility so seriously that they were prepared to go to almost any lengths to avoid failure.

Giles recalls, 'I remember one area chairperson particularly. Towards the end of the year it became clear that his area wasn't going to make its target. He was almost in tears when he came to see me to explain the situation. He was so committed to his target and so appalled that he'd failed that he promised he would make up the shortfall out of his own cash over the next 12 months.'

A less inspirational example of donor ownership came during the same campaign when publisher Robert Maxwell called Giles to his office at around seven o'clock one evening and *told* him how to run his direct marketing campaign. Such was his degree of ownership of the appeal's success that he thought he could come in and do anything. And he did indeed raise a considerable sum towards the target.

Of course, Robert Maxwell was infamous for his dictatorial style of management and would probably have behaved in a similar way with any enterprise that took his interest. Many other senior business people are similarly confident of their contribution even if their knowledge of fundraising or direct marketing might be limited or non-existent. To control and direct their conviction and their contribution demands great skills from the fundraiser.

Many organisations, however, are very cautious about giving away ownership and, while they want their donors to give, they are not prepared to give donors the participative role that goes with ownership. The relationship fundraiser should not be afraid to at least share ownership, subject to necessary controls. That much is implicit in the fundraiser's role as agent of the donor and the cause.

While on the subject of ownership it is worth considering the role and attitude of trustees to this issue. Not many trustees, perhaps, would share the NSPCC centenary appeal committees' sense of ownership and chip in from their own pockets if their organisation failed to reach its targets. Yet sometimes it is these same trustees who are most reluctant to share the ownership of their cause with donors. Perhaps there is some scope here for a re-evaluation of priorities?

So it is undesirable for trustees to exclude donors from ownership, and equally it is a shame if donors feel more of a sense of ownership of the cause than do the trustees.

The concept of trustees as major donors is quite new in Britain and many charities feel it is foreign and not at all welcome. But the concept is well established in other countries, particularly in the USA, and can be very appropriate. While size of donation alone is not sufficient criterion for board membership, trustees who are not donors – particularly the well-heeled variety – could hardly be said to be demonstrating the best kind of commitment to the cause, nor are they inspiring by example, as they should.

Fundraisers as fundraisers

Another shift in NSPCC thinking involves recruitment policy. Rather than rely on outside experience and qualifications, the charity now puts most emphasis on identifying the important qualities and attributes that will fit an NSPCC employee for direct donor contact.

'We have moved away from the belief that we should employ specialists – direct marketers, strategists, sales professionals, and so on. Now our most important criterion is fundraising aptitude and ability. We look for relevant experience and proven track record, of course, but we are also increasingly "growing" our own fundraisers because most important to us is motivation towards our particular style of donor-led fundraising – an understanding of what motivates donors and an ability to see things from a donor's perspective.

'This is not to suggest that fundraisers don't need to possess a wide range of technical skills – far from it. Fundraisers nowadays need to be accomplished planners and financial managers. They need to be fully conversant with information technology and with all aspects of communication and marketing. Their financial skills must include targeting, forecasting, risk analysis and all the rest of it.

'But first and foremost they must be fundraisers. That means they must possess what you might call "the people skills". We are looking for individuals with the best in people skills but who can also graft on the necessary technical skills as well.

'When many fundraising organisations write their recruitment advertisements they place their emphasis on technique, but that overlooks the essential core of fundraising, which is building relationships.'

Some time ago the NSPCC changed from referring to its local appeals staff as 'organisers' to calling them 'area appeals managers' (AAMs). The move was partly to give local fundraisers more status but unfortunately there has been something of a backlash, particularly from volunteers. Some volunteers, it seems, feel the title gives too much importance to the professional fundraisers and that some AAMs behave as if they're a cut above the volunteers. Also volunteers may worry that such a title will give the professional fundraiser the idea that the volunteer is there to help the professional, rather than the other way round.

So titles can be important, particularly in how they are viewed from outside. This explains why many organisations are now changing some of their titles and positions to make them at least sound more donor-friendly.

> The NSPCC seems to have a policy of soliciting the opinions of its supporters on a variety of issues and keep them frequently updated on the work of the Society. This helps make me feel a part of a large group of people all working to help children's needs. While it alerts me to the darker side of life, the caring way in which the NSPCC relates to the children and their supporters renews my faith in the good side of human nature.
>
> Miss Lucy Vincent-Daviss, Evesham, Worcestershire

The 90-degree shift

The mid-1980s were a time of comparative prosperity for charities in Britain. It was also in this period that fundraisers across the land were enthusiastically importing a variety of marketing activities from more traditionally sales-oriented sectors of commercial life. Thanks to the buoyant economic climate of the time and the novelty of the techniques for fundraising, most of these new promotional methods worked well, for most of the time.

Marketing activities at the NSPCC burgeoned then and extended to include perhaps the largest (and arguably most successful) direct marketing department in any UK charity, with responsibility for press and radio advertising, posters, direct mail, television and radio advertising, telephone fundraising, and departments for publicity and public relations, marketing, corporate fundraising, trusts, major donors, mail order, shops, special events, regional fundraising, local group support and much more.

The NSPCC sought to employ the very best people it could for these important tasks. Salaries were generally considered to be competitive within the voluntary sector and the NSPCC was proud of this. It reflected the Society's commitment to do all it could to attract and retain the best – again in the interests of serving children.

The NSPCC's growth of income during the mid-1980s testifies clearly to the effectiveness of these techniques. But nagging doubts were forming not only in the mind of the director of appeals, but also among some of his colleagues and associates. These had to do with the domination of technology, the mass-marketing techniques the charity was deploying so successfully, and the feeling that the whole machinery was geared and structured solely towards the needs of the NSPCC and had very little to do with donors and what they wanted.

Giles Pegram summarises his feelings at the time. 'I had sat in on all the seminars and read the articles of the industry's gurus of the time. I had listened to the words of wisdom from the likes of Harold Sumption and Guy Stringer. I'd seen others nodding vigorously in agreement and heard them saying how absolutely right it was. I'd even written it all down myself. But then we all went back to manage organisations that were structured by activity and technique for reasons somewhat removed from donors and their wishes or interests. I remember thinking that there was something fundamentally wrong. I decided that we, the NSPCC, had to change. We had to become donor-led, to structure our fundraising not by our needs nor by the myriad of techniques available but by groups of donors and how we could respond to *their* needs.'

This is Giles Pegram's unique contribution to relationship fundraising. Others like him had seen what needed to be done. Some others articulated and presented it. For the first time here was the head of a leading national fundraising organisation who was prepared to say, 'Hang on, how should we – the big organisations – structure ourselves to really make that change?'

Giles Pegram was not only the first head of fundraising in Britain to think in this way, he has committed his entire organisation to restructuring, to show that it can be done and that it will work.

Considerations beyond fundraising

'One of the things that is different about a charity', says Giles, 'is that whereas a commercial organisation can afford to alienate a large part of the public so long as enough people buy its products, the NSPCC can't afford to alienate anyone because anyone could be a user of our services.

'One of the reasons we recently cancelled our off-the-page advertising in national newspapers is that we realised we were stigmatising clients and turning off possible users of our service. However successful these ads may have been in fundraising terms, we couldn't justify that.

'So there are other considerations beyond fundraising. But, having said that, I would argue vehemently against there being any purpose to the process of building relationships other than long-term financial gain.

'There are a number of worthwhile by-products of the 90-degree shift. Perhaps coincidentally these can lead to more effective fundraising. Staff are generally happier when their job is relationship-oriented. Donors too are very often noticeably happier, even if the relationship fundraising approach hasn't been explained overtly they are very quickly aware of it and much happier about it. Happy staff means more productive staff and happy donors give more. But these rather agreeable by-products of happier people are none the less just that – means to the end rather than the end itself, which has to be more money for your cause.'

The Attila project

Attila the Hun is well known to schoolboys and students of management techniques as the authoritarian, despotic leader of unruly barbarian hordes whom he mercilessly bullied, cajoled and coerced into a hopelessly over-optimistic and intrinsically suicidal attack on the grandeur that was Rome. And they won. (Or was it the Visigoths?)

Anyway, the Attila project was so named by some of the senior staff at the NSPCC because they seemed to draw some similarities between the ancient demagogue and the way this particular project was imposed upon an unwilling NSPCC by its director of appeals. It is not a parallel that Giles Pegram understands but nevertheless he calls it the Attila project too. And, although it was discontinued after about two years, he considers it to have been something of a success, if a little difficult to measure.

The Attila project is not as glamorous as it sounds. Its purpose was to demonstrate the difference that would result when one group of donors was sent individually prepared, personalised letters as opposed to mass-produced, mass-mailed appeals. Two identical groups were isolated for the purpose of the test. The first group was sent appeals in typed envelopes, with stamps, and hand-signed letters that looked like letters. The control group was sent the normal direct mail appeals. The subject and content of each appeal were supposedly identical but strict comparison was difficult of course as inevitably the test group received less designed, less illustrated and less appealing promotions. Rather they received more personal, more human, communications. The test was proving difficult and costly to administer and in time it came to an end. But not before detailed research among both groups showed that those who had received the more personal communications knew more and were happier about the NSPCC, and had a more positive view of the communications they had received. Although it would be difficult to prove, it seems likely that this group would be more inclined to support the NSPCC in the longer term.

'What Attila showed us was that this personalised non-junk mail approach didn't increase our income in the short term and did significantly increase our costs, but it improved the donors' attitudes towards our organisation. There were signs that, in the long term, this would have led to improved relationships and improved returns. We couldn't afford to implement it wholesale, but it hasn't been abandoned. The Attila project altered both the way we communicate with our direct donors and the way we measure success. Much of what we learned from it has been adopted and implemented.'

> I think there is a tendency for there to be too many letters. Assurances have been given that this will be reduced, but I don't honestly believe the delivery is in line with that promise.
>
> Anonymous donor (BWF member)

The value of goodwill

'While companies place enormous value on the goodwill attached to their business and some even pay large sums to acquire it, the intangible, but very real asset of many service industries, goodwill, is not something that you will find on any charity's balance sheet.

'Clearly goodwill is something charities benefit from enormously, probably more than any other commercial sector, but until that fund of goodwill is translated into a donation or legacy it is never taken into account, or planned for, or anticipated. Yet building a fund of goodwill may be very valuable indeed for a charity and placing some value on goodwill may become important for fundraisers. We all know the damage that can be done by *bad* will, as evidenced by a lack of confidence or adverse publicity. But what about the goodwill that can be built up by a programme of relationship fundraising? This is the x-factor, the measure of how much better donors feel about you now than they did at the start of the year.'

The donor as an asset

'Of course we are always trying to quantify the effect of our move towards building donor relationships, our 90-degree shift. But it is extremely difficult, partly because these things are intrinsically hard to measure and partly because, as we are growing so fast, analysing historical data is difficult because things change so rapidly.

'But we are working on it. We are still a long way away from measuring the value of our "work in progress" as a commercial enterprise would do. It is very hard to measure the asset value of a donor base, but there are some indicators, such as the percentage of committed donors and levels of quantifiable donor satisfaction.

'We know what it costs us to find a new donor. And we know how profitable each donor is while he or she is with us. But calculating, for example, how much relationship fundraising increases the lifetime value of a donor, or if your 400,000 donors feel significantly better about you at the end of the year than they did at the beginning, what is that worth in financial terms? We don't know. But perhaps one of the most important things we have to do now is to try to quantify that so we can measure both the short- and the long-term effects of relationship building.

'It might be said of course – and it is in *Relationship Fundraising* – that the ultimate value of these relationships will only show after the passage of several years – in legacy income. I hope that is true, but we need to measure it and can't wait for years before we know the answer for sure.

'We have 400,000 direct donors and many tens of thousands of volunteer supporters in the field, yet last year we received just 700 legacies. We have got to bridge that gulf somehow.

'I believe that the building of better relationships is the answer. But I'm looking forward to proving that with figures – and soon.'

Acquiring and developing donors

Like any charity with a large donor base, the NSPCC's various recruitment methods are permanently under review. New approaches and avenues are regularly tested to replace any of the established means that, for whatever reason, have ceased to be viable, or to support established and ongoing recruitment practices that after a time have become 'tired'.

Off-the-page press advertising, from which the NSPCC withdrew, is a perennially difficult area for fundraisers to justify, even with its indirect benefits of encouraging staff and supporters, and increasing visibility and brand recognition. Apart from disaster advertising or sponsorship-type propositions, few organisations are able to use the press as cost-effectively as the NSPCC. Thanks largely to its direct proposition, off-the-page advertisements have recruited tens of thousands of new supporters for the NSPCC in the past. Recently even the NSPCC has found the high cost of donor recruitment through the press hard to justify. Now that this avenue has been cut off, where does this leave the NSPCC in terms of donor recruitment?

During the fundraising heydays of the 1980s the NSPCC rapidly expanded its donor file through the vigorous deployment of direct mail. In this area the charity has been something of a pioneer in the sheer scale of its direct mail programme and also in the sophistication of its testing, its list selection and its constant donor profiling. If any prospective donor drew breath anywhere in the United Kingdom, the NSPCC and its agency WWAV Rapp Collins would find him, or her. The targeting was superlative and the delivery consistent – and persistent. Creatively, the NSPCC's direct mail has verged on the conservative – good, solid, workmanlike packs that follow all the guidelines, make no mistakes and predictably deliver the message, every time.

> As children are our future it means a great deal to me to be involved in an organisation that helps them to grow up in a safe and happy environment. I truly believe that prevention is better than cure.
>
> Mrs Trina Brenton,
> Cheltenham,
> Gloucestershire

199

Giles Pegram has no difficulty justifying this use of mass mailing. 'I think we acquire new donors quite effectively through direct mail. Some of the problems we are facing need to be presented in a dramatic way, to get people's attention. With a mailed letter we have room to tell our story fully and powerfully. We present the need, the solution and the offer – £15 can help save a child's life – that is our proposition. And it works.

'But, of course, like almost all charities we are now seeing a steep rise in the cost of finding new donors. And there is obviously increasing public resistance to direct mail. So we must look at other ways.' (Recently several major recruiters, including the NSPCC, have been achieving much lower costs per donor through door-drops – unaddressed packages delivered to every home in selected postcodes by the Post Office. Inevitably, as this becomes more popular, costs will rise. And so the wheel turns...)

Maintenance of a large supporter file is a continual process. With 400,000 current donors at varying stages of development, just standing still requires constant new recruitment at quite a high level. And the NSPCC has never been content to stand still.

At this point the charity's commitment to innovation began to pay off spectacularly. The NSPCC started to recruit donors cost-effectively in large numbers, using one of the most controversial of all fundraising media – television.

Turning on TV

British charities have only recently been allowed to advertise on television. Although most pundits at the time predicted that the exorbitant cost of air time and the lack of a direct-response culture on British television would mean it would be unlikely to work for UK charities, and might lead many to produce expensive commercials that would never run, there was nevertheless a long line of optimistic charities who couldn't wait to try out fundraising through the television.

Predictably, very much towards the head of that line was the NSPCC.

NSPCC's press advertising agency, Saatchi and Saatchi, prepared a series of highly creative 30-second appeal commercials that over a period of time were tested in various regions at various times of day upon the good viewers of Britain.

> I do get the feeling sometimes that if I see one more piece of paper I'm going to cancel everything and save a tree.
>
> Anonymous donor (BWF member)

Results of such tests are often hard to ascertain and sometimes not very helpful. (Since those early days more sophisticated systems of response analysis have been developed, particularly a call analysis system pioneered by the NSPCC's direct marketing agency, WWAV Rapp Collins. Most response to television of course is by phone, not by letter.)

Much of the production costs for early appeal ads were underwritten by agencies and production companies keen to develop a new client sector. If direct response was low, research might reveal other benefits, including significantly increased awareness and also which techniques were merely bad and which were downright awful. But the key sign of whether or not something works is repeat showings. If charity ads really work well (ie come close to covering their cost) you might expect to see them come out of the obscure regional stations where they've been hiding amid the equally obscure daytime programming and start appearing on the big stations, networked, perhaps, in peak spots such as the break during *News at Ten*.

For charity advertising this hasn't happened, or has happened with such rarity that for once it seemed the pundits were proved right. (This may not simply be a factor of responses not covering cost. The other dilemma for direct-response television fundraising is the difficulty of volume response handling. Responders' interest rapidly flags if they aren't answered within a few minutes. Each call takes around three minutes on average to answer properly, and one line/operator will only be able to answer two calls before response falls away. So successful direct-response fundraising from the telly demands an awful lot of lines and operators. That's why the few charity TV ads that work are still to be found on somewhere like Channel 4 in the afternoons.)

But contrary to the trend, the NSPCC has made television work. How they did this is a classic tale of fundraising folk showing those advertising types in suits how to do it right. It deserves to become a part of fundraising legend.

Brilliant at shifting products and concealing the defects in political parties, Saatchi and Saatchi's fourth and final attempt at a 30-second sell from the NSPCC had actor Michael Caine (a lovely man and staunch NSPCC supporter) in a funny shade of green and tilted at an alarming angle of about 35 degrees, walking across a severely cropped screen saying things like 'child abuse makes me really angry' and 'not a lotta people know that'. It rather obviously wouldn't work, and it didn't.

Not a lotta people know this

Now the fundraising specialists at NSPCC (Giles Pegram and former marketing manager Dennis Kingshott) had a chance to have their say. They wanted a longer commercial, at least one and a half to two minutes, and they wanted to use all the time-worn, tried and tested techniques that had been proved to work so well in every other type of fundraising – emotion, direct proposition, a clear link between the donor's gift and the need. And what television is best of all at: living sound and vision, the recorded sounds and actions of a real child presented as needing *your*, the viewer's, help, right there in your own living-room. It was the television equivalent of the long copy versus short copy argument, and they knew it would work.

To make this new commercial Dennis and Giles went to Britain's largest direct marketing agency, WWAV. Up until then WWAV (now WWAV Rapp Collins) hadn't made many television commercials, but it had handled the charity's

Ellie. It's impossible to watch and not be moved.

direct mail programme very effectively for 10 years and its experience of fundraising is second to few.

So the Ellie ad was created. Ellie is a little girl who is left alone and neglected at Christmas. It's very difficult to watch this short film and listen to the brilliantly interwoven music without getting a lump in the throat and a tear in the eye. Thanks to the clear voice-over at the beginning and end it is even more difficult to keep your credit card in your pocket and to duck out of dialling the freephone donation line.

Television donors appear to behave significantly differently to those recruited by other means, such as direct mail. With WWAV's help, the NSPCC is now developing new ways to build relationships with these donors, as clearly they have different needs and interests and will respond to different things.

Speed of follow-up is critical when dealing with an emotional and perhaps transient response. Acknowledging a credit card gift weeks after the event is of little use, as is any attempt then to secure further involvement. One Canadian child sponsorship charity has estimated that every day that passes between the gift and thank you reduces response by three per cent.

Donors recruited by television appear, generally, to give lower-value gifts and to suffer a higher rate of attrition. But there is evidence that they can be very responsive to committed giving propositions and some claim that as a result they may have a greater overall lifetime value than donors recruited by more conventional means.

This debate will run and run, but one thing is sure: through its pioneering use of television the NSPCC developed a new and cost-effective way to bring in large numbers of new donors.

But despite this kind of success, recruiting new donors seems likely to be a perpetual problem for large charities such as the NSPCC. An integrated and flexible approach is clearly needed, rather than one driven by technique. As donors become more and more expensive to find, making sure they are developed to the optimum becomes more and more important. This, rather than recruitment, is the crucial area that most charities neglect. Research has shown that it costs five times as much to recruit a new donor as it does to develop – and keep – a donor you have already got. Yet many fundraisers still devote most of their energies and resources to trying to find new donors. Inevitably with costs being so critical charities can justify using whatever hooks will work to get people in the door in the first place, provided they can be confident of recruiting mostly *real* donors and not just knee-jerk, one-off responders (however important these may be).

Once the potential donor is 'in the store', as it were,

communication and development take on entirely different aspects. Impressions are more important. Donors have time to digest, and reflect. Service and value become important concepts. The task for the fundraiser is much broader, and more challenging.

Making life difficult

'It is in our regular communications with donors', says Giles Pegram, 'that I'm really concerned about the junk mail image of what we send, rather than in our cold, or acquisition appeals. Our intention is to progressively move our donor communications towards the relationship building, information, cultivation style of communication – letters our donors actually want to receive. We are certainly more sophisticated now. It is a question of striking the right balance in tone and content, in how we say what we need to say to different groups of people.'

But surely there is a dilemma here for all charities?

Donors won't give unless they can see the need presented to them dramatically and convincingly. Many charities, including the NSPCC, will inevitably shock and even cause distress when they confront their donors with the full detail of what their work involves. How can this dramatic presentation of reality be reconciled with the desire to send donors what donors want to receive?

This is not an easy question and there is no simple, universally applicable answer. It is a sign of how difficult life is becoming for the fundraising copywriter, who has to achieve the nearly impossible balance of keeping the funds flooding in while crafting communications that donors will welcome.

One avenue is to vary the style of communication and consciously to avoid constantly hitting donors with the same relentless message.

'We have identified that the vast bulk of our income comes from appeal mailings concentrated on just four months of the year. The rest of the time (on average, the NSPCC writes to its donors once each month) we are struggling to keep our income levels up.

'So increasingly we are going to make the successful mailings harder hitting, more appealing, but at other times of the year we will do more in the way of donor cultivation.'

Donor care by post

'Another route is to give donors the chance to receive less. Or at least to allow donors to choose when they will hear from the charity, if not how.

'We have tested this and it looks very promising. Twenty per cent of the people in our test opted to receive fewer mailings. Some of our people were terrified by this. They thought that we were going to lose all those people from our list. I think it's brilliant. As we monitor and develop these people I think we'll see *more* income from this group over the years, not less.'

The proof of the pudding

There can also be an implicit understanding with those who opt for once-a-year-only communication that when they get their annual appeal they will give. So if the charity doesn't get a 100 per cent response it can write quite sternly to those who haven't given to remind them of their commitment (or perhaps more tactfully to point out their oversight).

Mailings don't always have to be appeals, they can offer donors lots of other opportunities for practical and often lucrative involvement. Donor-care mailings are now being planned into the NSPCC's annual cycle of communication that encourage donors to choose from a list of other ways to help, in addition to their general giving.

Giles Pegram is quite firm about the way ahead for the foreseeable future. 'Clearly much of our reaction to these developments is subjective. We want these donor-care initiatives to work, and logic – and listening to our donors – tells us they should. But we can't risk our £11 million a year direct-response programme on suppositions, however logical they may be. Now what we have got to do is track how the relative segments are performing over a period of time and see if they have given more, or less, or the same as a comparable segment would have done had we continued with the traditional "conveyor belt" of donor mailings.

Children's charities play an important part in encouraging society to improve. NSPCC enables me to do something about an issue I feel strongly about even if I haven't the time personally to give.

Anonymous NSPCC supporter, Croydon

'I am confident that the new initiatives will work – our donor-care mailings have paid for themselves even when there was *no* reply form – no opportunity to give. But it will take a long time to quantify this, and to prove it conclusively.'

But what will happen if some donors do give less? Will the NSPCC still stick to its plan? For example, there may be a short-term penalty to pay when listening to some donors, but legacy income may increase. Can fundraisers afford to take the chance? And, even if they do, can they afford to wait?

Individual organisations will need to evolve their own response to these questions, but the NSPCC is not losing its nerve at this stage.

Giles is convinced that a further benefit will derive from this kind of 'donor-care' mailing. 'I believe that the first appeal letter we do after the donor-care mailing will see an increased response from the group who received the donor-care package. The donor-care mailing talked to people intelligently and gave them sensible and useful opportunities. It will have enhanced our donors' view of us, so the next time we appeal I expect they will give us more.'

Because of this Giles has reservations about allowing donors, or lapsed donors, to opt out completely from all future contact.

'We know the very act of contacting people produces a positive response so I'm very reluctant not to contact people who certainly once cared about our work. One of the most interesting lessons from our telephone work* is that those people who have said no over the telephone to all our suggestions perform noticably better to our next mailing than a comparable group of people who *haven't* been telephoned.

'There seems to be no logic to this at all, but I am sure people feel better about the organisation if it has contacted them directly – provided that contact is well handled. Perhaps they may feel some guilt at having said no.'

This experience is borne out by other organisations, including Oxfam, ActionAid and Greenpeace. Direct personal contact at least shows that the organisation cares, that it is interested enough to get in touch, and perhaps gives some kind of reassurance that the organisation will accept no if it is told.

'Because what people do and what they say they are going to do are often quite different things we have to be a little careful at times as to *how* we listen to them. This is in many ways the same kind of caution and judgement** that we have to exercise when we listen to children. We have to establish not just what they really want, but also what will simultaneously be best for both them and us. I think it could well be counter-productive if we actually wrote to people and asked them how many times a year they want to hear from us.'

So much, Giles believes, of the listening has to be indirect, or at least not in response to direct questions. Listening, for example, to comments received in correspondence, to complaints and criticisms and to research. The NSPCC is committed to dealing with its donors in person, the human touch, treating them always as important, real people. That means training staff to the highest standards in face-to-face relationship building, use of the telephone and letter writing.

'We know that by and large our donors welcome direct contact. They enjoy it and gain from it. We know it strengthens their commitment and increases their giving. So

---

*The NSPCC uses the telephone very successfully to welcome new donors, to contact lapsed donors, donors whose covenants have expired and to renew members of the Friends scheme.
**Mentioned earlier, *see* page 189.

we must make absolutely sure that when a donor has telephone contact with, or meets someone from, the NSPCC – and those contacts may take place hundreds of times in a day, every day – then we must make sure that our contact is of the highest possible standard and quality.

'That means training.'

The future

Relatively speaking the NSPCC can be well satisfied with many of its successes. Its recognition among the British public is extraordinarily high. (Peter Davis, then managing director of Sainsbury's and now chairman of the Prudential, sponsored the NSPCC's study of brand and image awareness. Ninety-seven per cent of people knew of the NSPCC. 'That's higher awareness than Sainsbury's', said Peter.) The NSPCC enjoys frequent media coverage, which ensures that whenever an issue arises relating to child abuse, or child care generally, the first point of contact for journalists will often be the NSPCC press office. Recognition and concern among the public for child-care issues have never been higher thanks largely to the high profile and campaigning efforts of the NSPCC. Some million people support the charity regularly as donors and volunteers. In commercial terms the NSPCC has exceptionally high brand identity and more than its fair share of the fundraising market.

Many fundraisers would be quite satisfied with that. While Giles Pegram certainly takes pleasure from what has been achieved, he firmly believes that the NSPCC is under-achieving in its development of many donors and that a large proportion of the charity's hundreds of thousands of donors could be giving more – substantially more. Like many of the lessons he has learned about fundraising, this view is based on something he's seen in the USA.

'I have visited many fundraising organisations in America. They tend to be smaller than us, more local and more specific, so it's always a bit dangerous to draw conclusions as we're not comparing like with like. But so many of these American organisations have identified their core donors and, in many cases, are getting half their income from them.'

By core donors Giles is referring to the élite that seem to be found in most donor groups. These are the '$1,000 a year club' donors, people who give substantial amounts regularly – committed donors. They are usually enrolled in some kind of special scheme or club, often referred to in the United States as 'giving schemes'.

'One of my obsessions', admits Giles, 'is the Pareto principle. It applies to so many areas within NSPCC. We discovered that in our Friends of the NSPCC scheme the top 20 per cent of Friends give the vast bulk of the money, so we converted them to Gold Friends. But even within Gold Friends Pareto still works – the bulk of Gold Friends' donations comes from the top 20 per cent.'

Pareto points to potential

The Pareto principle also applies generally to the NSPCC's main file of direct donors, but within this group, who were all recruited on the '£15 can help save a child's life' proposition, is a huge group of donors who still give but only at that level. The NSPCC had historically concentrated on the 80 per cent, not the 20 per cent. This has tended to give the NSPCC a rather flat pyramid of giving. Giles Pegram sees this as positive, 'I think it shows us where our real potential lies.'

He may be right. If anything can disturb the ratio identified by Pareto it will most likely be in the opposite direction.

Many American organisations would claim Pareto was a little conservative in his estimate and that as society has changed so have the ratios in Pareto's principle. It is not unusual in the USA to find that 95 per cent of an organisation's income is coming from just five per cent of its supporters. This may not be so much a social phenomenon as simply offering the more wealthy, more committed donors propositions that relate to them, excite them and are comfortable for them. (When I say wealthy I am not referring to absolute wealth, but to substantial disposable wealth. People whose wealth is committed, eg to their children, or tied up, are not likely to make exceptionally good donors.)

To help raise the pyramid and redress the imbalance in the NSPCC's version of Pareto, the charity has established a department specifically to deal individually with major donors and with supporters who have the potential to be major donors.

The major donor development department should be the epitome of relationship fundraising in practice because its origins are firmly rooted in the 90-degree shift. It was created specifically to be donor-led.

Developing major donors

The NSPCC's major donor development department is unique. Innovative and experimental, it is nevertheless based on long experience of what makes donors tick and is firmly rooted in the NSPCC's tradition of individual donor development. Substantial investments of both faith and finance have gone into this experiment in the certain knowledge that many months and even years would pass before any signs of return would be seen. If the donor-led approach forms the foundations of the department, then its structure is held together by the belief that when individual and personal attention can be justified the investment will be repaid through stronger mutually beneficial relationships that will substantially increase fundraising income.

Giles explains, 'The department is still in its infancy and it's evolving, but we've already had some noteworthy successes. A little while ago we received a donation from a man who had seen one of our television appeals and had sent in £1,000. At one time he would have received a very nice letter to say thank you, but that would have been about it. Now he gets handled personally.

'As I had written the personal letter of thanks to him, he rang me to tell me how impressed he was with our service. During the course of the call he asked if he could come to see me. I, of course, was delighted and arranged to meet him with one of my colleagues from major donor development. A little later I arranged for him to meet some of our trustees.

'A lot of trouble perhaps. But, in fact, following that meeting he made a five-figure gift and has told me he intends to give a similar sum on a regular basis. I did a little research into him and he can certainly afford to do it.

'But perhaps if we'd just sent what used to be our standard response that would have been that. Or he may have given £1,000 again, which we would have been jolly pleased with.

'Another donor had been sending us £5,000 each year for several years. Now, thanks to our 90-degree shift, he gets the major donor treatment. Having been briefed by the department, I telephoned and specifically thanked him for his long, consistent and substantial support. The following week he sent in £10,000.

'I phoned him again and discovered that he had never been to an NSPCC event before, so like a shot, I invited him to our annual council meeting. Our relationship with this donor is now much closer – and much more fruitful, both for him and for the charity.'

What is a major donor?

Initially some principles had to be established for the major donor development department, and some fairly arbitrary lines had to be drawn.

What constitutes a major donor? Clearly someone who has shown the capacity to give at a substantial level, not just once but repeatedly. After much discussion, the NSPCC decided that an annual single or cumulative gift of £500 would qualify the giver to be identified as a major donor. Any figure would inevitably have to be arbitrary but there was no practical alternative. So a donor giving £500 would qualify as a major donor, whereas one giving £499 would not. But the second donor could nevertheless be treated as a prime prospect for upgrading.

> If there's any way they can maximise my contributions then they should tell me. That's common sense.
>
> Anonymous donor (BWF member)

In practice the randomness of this division led to problems. Experience has taught the NSPCC that being a major donor is not about a specific level of giving, it's about a principle. It's about providing appropriate service to someone who wants and deserves individually tailored treatment.

Some individuals, of course, were already giving at levels well above £500 a year. Giles was already convinced that the Pareto principle would also apply to major donors and that 80 per cent of the income from major donors would come from the most generous 20 per cent of them. It was agreed to identify these prize individuals as 'core' major donors (as a guide, people giving £2,000 plus) and to give them even more special attention and treatment.

Trusts and foundations were identified as a special group of major donors with distinct and individual needs for personal service and development. So the major donor development department was set up with three sections: trusts, core donors and individual major donors. Its purpose was quite simple: to enlarge all of these groups and to increase funds from the individuals within them by developing mutually beneficial long-term relationships. (In time the NSPCC's major donor staff came to realise that trusts behaved very much like – and were often directed by – individual donors, or groups of donors so this distinction became less important. But there are still core trusts and major donor trusts.)

First principles

Central to the original vision of the major donor development department was the concept of individual and personal attention. If the direct donor marketing department was likened to a large and efficient supermarket then the major donor department would be the corner shop – small, personal, caring, recognising each customer individually and providing not only an old-fashioned blend of quality and service but comfort and reassurance too. The staff would be selected for their commitment to donor service and their 'people' skills as much as for their professional fundraising experience. Perhaps the original concept for Harrods would be a better analogy.

I'm a member of this Benjamin Waugh thing.
Anonymous donor (BWF member)

The ethos for the new department can be summarised in six key principles.

■ Each donor would be assigned an individual member of the major donor development department staff – his or her 'key worker'.

■ Communications would be much more individual and personalised wherever possible. There would be no mass mailings.

■ Each donor would be offered opportunities for involvement and the chance to share 'ownership' of NSPCC projects. Positive feedback would be given. Donors would feel involved and recognised.

■ Key workers would seek to discover and develop the interests and potential of each of their donors.

■ Relevant, structured products and propositions would be offered.

■ Major donors would be encouraged to join the Benjamin Waugh Foundation.

The Benjamin Waugh Foundation, named after the NSPCC's

founder, was an internal device for major donors, loosely based on the traditional American concept of a giving society. The Foundation had been around for some time and its function was neither widely understood nor appreciated, either inside the Society or without.

Although the development took some time, the arrival of the new department was to give the Benjamin Waugh Foundation a new direction and lease of life.

> I think of myself as a supporter or donor rather than a member, because to claim membership you've got to be more active than I am.
>
> Anonymous donor (BWF member)

Recognise and advance

Donors in Britain are unfamiliar with formal structures that recognise their philanthropy and many are uncomfortable with any process that appears to reward their generosity. Perhaps this is why philanthropy, which was so strongly prevalent in Britain in Victorian times, is regarded by most British people as a passé and old-fashioned concept.

North Americans, on the other hand, celebrate and encourage philanthropy, placing it among the highest ideals and noblest aspirations, the pinnacle of objective for the fully civilised and rounded individual. Perhaps this goes some way to explain the difference between individual giving levels in North America and Britain. The concept of philanthropy may be even less warmly embraced or understood by some other nations, for example the French, or the Italians.

If so it is a shame. But, for whatever reason, the notion of the North American giving society as embodied in the NSPCC's Benjamin Waugh Foundation had not transplanted well. When the major donor development department was revitalised it found the BWF among its armoury, languishing somewhat dolefully, under-used and misunderstood. Some donors, it transpired, assumed the Foundation was another organisation, entirely separate from the NSPCC.

Working with its agency, the new major donor development department set about injecting a renewed sense of vision and purpose into the Benjamin Waugh

Foundation. A mission statement was drafted, to be promulgated to all donors. A new identity was introduced incorporating the NSPCC logo and an explanatory strapline. Specific projects were selected that the Foundation's supporters could identify as 'theirs' and around which future communications, support opportunities and feedback could be built.

For some years now an annual information day has been held to encourage members of the Benjamin Waugh Foundation. Later an evening reception was also added. These tend to be sparsely but very enthusiastically attended (about 50 come to the information day, which is the department's main annual event) and the presentations of key aspects of the NSPCC's work, which form the main part of the programme, are widely acclaimed and appreciated. Only the very dedicated – or very mobile – come to these receptions, but these people are clearly affected by the experience and inevitably go away renewed.

> I must admit on a practical level I'm always being invited to things and always having to fill in cards to say that I can't and it takes ages!
>
> Anonymous donor (BWF member)

Such occasions attract a strange mix, from builders to stockbrokers, from young couples in their twenties to a pair of elderly sisters. They come from near and far – the North of England is not unusual and once someone came from Switzerland. These sessions provide donors with a unique chance to see the inner workings of the NSPCC and to debate with actual practitioners some sensitive issues at the leading edge of child care, for example children who abuse other children and how children should give testimony in court. Many of the NSPCC's staff are astonished to find how well informed some of their donors are.

Running these major donor receptions produces quite a few lessons for the NSPCC. Obviously the most enthusiastic and outgoing donors will come to such events, but others no less committed are clearly inhibited. How do you reassure the nervous donor, perhaps someone who might be shy of being alone among strangers, or put off by the prospect of being on the fundraiser's own turf, surrounded and

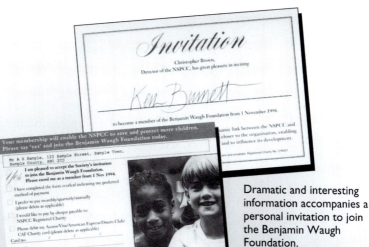

Dramatic and interesting information accompanies a personal invitation to join the Benjamin Waugh Foundation.

Our Ref: CB/SA

7 October 1994

Mr A B Sample
123 Sample Street
Sample Town
Sample County
AB1 2CD

Dear Mr Sample

LAST YEAR JUST A FEW HUNDRED PEOPLE ENABLED THE NSPCC TO TRANSFORM THE SHATTERED LIVES OF ABUSED AND NEGLECTED CHILDREN.

THIS YEAR, TO HELP SAVE AND PROTECT EVEN MORE CHILDREN, I AM INVITING YOU TO JOIN THE BENJAMIN WAUGH FOUNDATION.

Seldom have I written to the NSPCC's valued and trusted supporters with a more important purpose.

That's why I trust you will give this letter your careful and immediate attention. I am writing to ask you if you would consider taking an important step. It is my great pleasure to invite you to join our most committed group of donors - the Benjamin Waugh Foundation.

During the past year the members of the Benjamin Waugh Foundation have together enabled the NSPCC to give real hope to many abused and neglected children. On the attached sheet I have listed just a few examples of the vital work they have made possible. If you agree to join - as I sincerely hope you will - we will be able to achieve even more in the future for some of our society's most vulnerable children.

Your joining the Benjamin Waugh Foundation now will mean a great deal to us. Quite simply, it will make possible a range of vital and pioneering work for children at risk.

Here are a few of the challenges the NSPCC faces in the near future:

* Our free Child Protection Helpline provides immediate access to help for anyone worried about a child in need of protection. At the moment we can only answer seven out of every ten calls. We desperately need to ensure that we can respond to every child who needs our help.

* To stop abusive children from growing into abusive adults we need to put more funds into projects around the country working with children who abuse other children. For example, the Phoenix Project is just one initiative making real progress in this challenging area.

* We need more resources to change public attitudes through nationwide education campaigns. Our recent 'Home Alone' leaflet is one example. Many more issues need our voice.

NSPCC National Centre, 42 Curtain Road, London EC2A 3NH
Telephone: 071-825 2500 Facsimile: 071-825 2525

The NSPCC was founded in 1884 and is incorporated by Royal Charter. Registered Charity No. 216401. Printed on recycled paper.

1993/94

Benjamin Waugh Foundation: challenges and achievements

Just to keep our current services going costs more than £2 million every month, which is an enormous challenge in itself. However, thanks to the reliable support of members of the Benjamin Waugh Foundation, each year we are able to fund a range of key projects. These projects are specially selected, either because their vital daily work needs support to survive and grow, or because their pioneering work will help children at risk in new ways.

During the past 12 months members of the Benjamin Waugh Foundation made possible many new and existing projects to help children at risk. Here are brief snapshots of just a few of them.

Helping children who abuse other children: the Phoenix Project

The Phoenix Project in Sunderland is a ground-breaking new scheme that provides intensive long-term counselling for children who have abused other children. This distressing, stressful project demands remarkable commitment and resources of the three staff who have dedicated themselves to making it work, but it is already proving to be very rewarding. It's rewarding because it seems to be working. Results so far show real hope that the project will actually stop children from growing up into adult abusers. And that will save an untold number of children from abuse in the future.

The average day-running costs of a project such as Phoenix are approximately £250 per day.

'Now we can clearly see success I would dearly love to expand our work to help more children. But I know that without the support of our donors even our existing level of work cannot be guaranteed.'

Carl Docking, the Phoenix Project

Training Centre support

A gift to the NSPCC's National Training Centre in Leicester reaches far beyond the NSPCC to a wide network of people specially trained to protect children and prevent child abuse. This is because NSPCC training is recognised as a national resource. It provides not only specialist teaching for qualified social workers but also training for the trainers themselves, developing and passing on child-care training skills that will ultimately help child-care specialists to be more effective in their jobs.

Last year the NSPCC's National Training Centre cost £291,126 to run but this was offset by fees earned to the value of £207,080. So the net cost to the NSPCC was £84,046 – a truly superb investment both in child care and in the prevention of abuse.

defenceless in the face of, presumably, inevitable requests for even bigger gifts? To combat this natural resistance the NSPCC has tried many initiatives, including offering crèche facilities, explaining in detail what will be involved and reassuring shy donors that they wouldn't be expected to contribute. These have some success, so the process will continue.

> The BWF is important to me in that it gives me more information. I imagine it also gives more revenue to the charity.
>
> Anonymous donor (BWF member)

There is clearly a substantial information and explanation job to do with major donors simply to get them to understand what being a major donor means and to relate to the supposed benefits and entitlements that this status might bring. As there is little relevant experience anywhere to guide them the NSPCC's staff has had to learn by doing. The process clearly underlines the old truism that fundraising first and foremost is about people.

Now they can tell their own story.

Angela

Angela Cluff joined the NSPCC as head of major donor development in 1995 from the British Heart Foundation. She was immediately made aware of the issues and challenges that then confronted the department.

'I chose to see them as opportunities, which is very much the way the NSPCC sees them. After all the department has set itself very ambitious objectives. As far as I am aware no other charity in Britain has invested as much in time and resources in this area – and all the signs are that it is paying off.

'The main issues and opportunities we can see for major donor development are, first, how to increase the numbers. Several hundred possible major donors are automatically upgraded each year from the NSPCC's direct donor activity. But the active file is still in the low thousands. We have tested many approaches to recruit major donors directly, with some success. But it is limited. At this level the numbers coming in tend to be small, but very valuable. In terms of volume our best approach is still to grow our own – but we are working on it.

'Second, to keep the department integrated. We want to offer donors the right thing at the right time, picking up all the clues and information we have without appearing obvious or intrusive to the donor. Our aim is to deliver a seamless service to donors, regardless of which segment they are in and how often they might move between segments. This demands excellent integration between and within departments. For example, the major donor welcome programme must elicit information as to how a major donor should be managed, but it mustn't replicate information provided in the welcome programme for lower-level donors because most major donors are recruited from existing lower-level donors.

I must admit that if you do make regular contributions it's sometimes galling to have another letter to say there's even more agony out there, can you send more money?

Anonymous donor (BWF member)

'Third, to find out how best to develop each donor's potential. Are they best served by being encouraged to join the Benjamin Waugh Foundation? How do we recognise a potential core donor? What is the best way to welcome people? We have a lot of experience and information on these, but we are still evolving answers.

'Fourth, renewals and upgrading. Renewing major donors is often difficult as many donors don't see their major gift as an annual or renewable thing. So at what point do we downgrade a donor? The questions are the same as in any direct marketing programme, but because we are dealing with people more individually the answers are usually far from straightforward.

'Fifth, the communications programme. Its variety and structure is a constant challenge. Income alone isn't an accurate guide. Sometimes we have raised as much money by sending out an invitation to an event as we have from a really strong appeal based around a dramatic child-care issue. What choices should we give donors? We want to keep them close and regularly in touch, but don't want them to feel bombarded. What is the right balance?

'Finally, to maintaining real personal service as we grow. Increased service leads to raised expectations so we have to retain that personal approach while handling greater numbers. The process of segmentation has had to be structured too – we can't leave it to what individuals remember any more.'

> It wasn't something I looked for. I feel it is almost a burden because I get *more* literature now. It has increased since I fell into this category.
>
> Anonymous donor (BWF member)

Angela Cluff is convinced that it's the personal, donor-led approach that has contributed to the NSPCC's success to date, so it must be continued. 'It works. We are looking at gifts increasing by several times in just a few years since we started treating people in a different way. We are fundamentally taking donors to different levels of giving.

'A recent example comes readily to mind. A couple in the North of England had given major gifts before but no one knew their potential, no one was sure what else we could do with them. They were taken to see an NSPCC child protection team, which impressed them hugely. They then committed to fund a project worker for the next three years, a gift worth a six-figure sum.

'That certainly wouldn't have happened without a personal, donor-based service. And I imagine they – the donors – are very thankful for it.

'So you could say this department now has completed its first phase. We've tested the proposition and know it works. We'll refine what we do as we go along, of course. That's the beauty of one-to-one relationships.

'But now we're ready to roll out.'

The major donor development department now undertakes a complex range of functions and activities, many of which would not be found in any other British charity. Seventeen people are employed in areas as specialised and diverse as research and face-to-face fundraising.

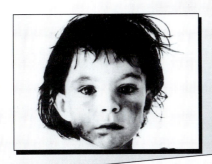

NSPCC CHILD PROTECTION HELPLINE INTERNAL MEMORANDUM

TO: Christopher Brown
FROM: Head of Child Protection Helpline
DATE: 1st September 1994
SUBJECT: Helpline Statistics · 1.7.93 - 30.6.94

A steady increase in calls to the Helpline has started to make important inroads into the prevention of child abuse in 1994. Callers ranged from distressed parents, feeling unable to control their anger and needing advice on how to cope, through to neighbours and relatives who suspected, heard or saw child abuse.

We recorded 77,661 calls in the 12 months ending June 1994.

8,313 of these calls were requests relating to serious child protection concerns. Of these 76% were passed to the police, social services, or NSPCC child protection staff for a final decision on the action to be taken. The remaining 24%, after further consultation, needed no further action.

The remaining 69,348 calls related to requests for advice, counselling or information on matters related to the care of children, and were dealt with by Helpline staff.

REQUESTS FOR SERVICE RECEIVED BY THE NSPCC FOR THE PERIOD 1.7.93 - 30.6.94 CLASSIFIED BY TYPE OF ABUSE

Neglect	27%	Emotional Abuse	7%
Physical Abuse	34%	Other	11%
Sexual Abuse	21%		

With the lines we have at present, seven out of every ten people who try to call can get through. But those remaining three may well be in severe crisis - we cannot afford to take the chance. We desperately need to ensure that we can respond to every child who needs our help.

COST

In 1993/94 the Helpline cost £2,764 per day to run.

CONCLUSION

The growth in the number of recorded calls to the Helpline, although a positive sign of its success, reveals a need which we can at present only partially answer.

ACTION

a) We need resources to maintain the service at current levels.
b) We must consider investing in order to increase our service to answer more calls.

The Helpline is a vitally needed service, and we must ensure its maintenance and growth.

Registered Charity No. 216401

FROM THE RIGHT HONOURABLE THE LORD MACKAY OF CLASHFERN

HOUSE OF LORDS
LONDON SW1A 0PW

Child cruelty is an evil which few of us objectively or dispassionately. In my position Chancellor I am only too aware of the growing numbe abuse cases passing through Britain's courts. The ap disturbing nature of these crimes never fails to mov is why I am keenly interested in the work of the N.S am delighted to serve as an Honorary Member of its

It is tragically clear that child abuse widespread in this country than most people would The N.S.P.C.C Child Protection Helpline provides a with a direct link to the N.S.P.C.C, so that action to protect threatened children.

I hope that the information enclosed by Christopher Brown will give you a clear insight into the work of those whose daily task is to prevent cruelty to the nation's children - and why that work is so vitally important.

A letter from the Lord Chief Justice, local child abuse statistics and a tape recording of calls to the NSPCC Helpline are combined to recruit new major donors from cold.

Alison

Alison Montgomery heads the research unit of two people. Their task is to ferret out relevant information about current supporters and specific individuals and, through research, to locate new contacts who may turn out to be of value to the NSPCC.

'Our job', says Alison, 'involves assessing how wealthy an individual might be in terms of what they could possibly give us financially. For example, if someone owns a stately home they may look very wealthy on paper, but if they have to spend a lot on the upkeep of that property, or their wealth is tied up in assets such as land they may have little to give away.

'The starting point is to research background biographical details, such as company directorships, trustee positions, names of wife (or husband) and children, and so forth. Then we add information from various sources, particularly what is learned from a meeting with one of our core donor team.

'The NSPCC has over 400,000 donors nationally, held on a central database. Part of my job is to evaluate our donors beyond their donation histories to find people *capable* of giving £500 or more. Getting the criteria for selecting information from the database is critical in this process. In the past we have tried a variety of approaches, from location – although living in a rich area is not always a good guide – to spotting names of celebrities and titled people. Now we have refined the process, part of which is the monthly review of names, networking and increasingly sophisticated research methods. But we still feel there is a lot more we can do to improve the process.

'We are also helped by MAID, an electronic system that scans the daily national and international press. And, of course, the key to it all is building our own flexible and accessible database.'

Angela Cluff underscores this view. 'People so often don't appreciate the value of database and see it as an administrative burden. For us, database is, quite simply, the future of our fundraising.'

Peter, Kerry and Sue

Peter Knowles is responsible for all major donors not currently identified as core donors. Working with him are Sue Adams and Kerry Cutting, who have been with the major donor development department since it was formed. Kerry now works with those donors who are members of the Benjamin Waugh Foundation – most of the non-core file. Sue concentrates on those who have given at the required level but have not joined the BWF.

'In the early days,' says Sue, 'if people gave you £500 that was it. They were made a life councillor and all we sent them from then on was an invitation to the annual council meeting. We just didn't ask them for any more. We were then part of what was known as central projects. I remember putting all the life councillors' names together and so we created a list of who were our best donors. That was the start of the development of major donors.'

The changes since have been dramatic.

Kerry Cutting explains, 'At first it was difficult to explain our approach. There weren't any leaflets or promotional material, it all seemed vague and a bit hollow. But as we developed and began to get results it became increasingly obvious that donors did want to become a part of it.'

Peter Knowles joined more recently and with a particular purpose. 'I was attracted by the degree of specialisation this job offers. It is direct marketing, of course, but in a very small and highly specific area. And, unusually for the voluntary sector, it is very well resourced. So we all feel we are developing something here that will be very important.'

Kerry and Sue are both aware that aspects of the specialist experience that has come into the department have helped them get over some of their initial problems. 'I was initially worried about face-to-face fundraising', says Sue, 'about whether our donors would want it. But now it seems to be really taking off.'

The need for close co-operation internally is reinforced frequently. Kerry says, 'Every so often one of our colleagues from core donors, guided by research from Alison's unit, will come to us and take a dozen or so names from our file for individual contact. Recently they approached a man who had been on our file for some time, giving £500 every second year or so. They took him to see one of our projects and he followed this with a gift of £20,000. And he is now much more motivated.'

Peter appreciates the opportunity this kind of work presents, but is anxious not to elevate the types of donor he deals with. 'They are giving at a higher level because they can afford to and because we have motivated them and made them feel involved. But that doesn't make them a different kind of person. Generally they are more discerning and they are making a conscious decision to give at a significant level. For some, £500 is a lot of money.

'The big challenge over the next few years will be to develop the ability to assess at a very early stage the kind of relationship donors want with the Society, and then to find a way of automating communication that will meet their needs and so maximise their giving, while retaining a genuine personal touch. No one thinks it will be easy.

'Some people don't want to be valued or feel special, but others do. The Benjamin Waugh Foundation, while it's not ideal for all situations, provides a useful means to secure the initial commitment and remains true to its original purpose of being a structured scheme that allows people to feel their contribution matters to us.

'The main thing is that we constantly review and analyse, not just by talking to donors but by asking the right questions and then acting on what they tell us. This is vitally important to ensure that they are comfortable in the Benjamin Waugh Foundation and, if not, to identify what approach will meet their needs. It also provides a key opportunity to identify donors' potential to upgrade their giving to core donor level, or to explore other opportunities to develop their support.'

Hazel

Hazel Weiss works as part of the team developing core donors. She joined the NSPCC in 1985 and has been involved with major donors since before the department was formed, when the most generous supporters were dealt with by central projects. She remembers the excitement of those early days, when fear of the unknown mixed with the challenge of breaking new ground.

'I was quite apprehensive. We didn't know how donors would react to telephone calls, far less visits at home. We were worried that we might lose some support as well as gain some – but also the process was so new and somewhat daunting.'

Early successes soon convinced Hazel and her colleagues that their new initiatives were taking them in the right direction.

'We had one donor who was working abroad, enjoying a tax-free lifestyle. He had regularly supported the NSPCC at quite a high level for a while, then wrote to inform us he was coming back to England. We wrote back suggesting a meeting and went to see him at his office. He was so interested in our approach that he offered to give us introductions to some of his professional contacts. Then he volunteered that he would like to see some of the NSPCC's work at first hand. So we took him to his local child protection team – a very impressive team. He was so interested he kept his chauffeur waiting an extra hour. Now he knows us so much better, its effect on his future support can only be good.

'Sometimes we have to be a little persistent. One day a letter from a firm of solicitors brought an entirely

> I realise I am a member of this society that is abusing children and should do something about it. But what? My personal practical contribution is pretty ineffective so I pay NSPCC to work on my behalf.
>
> They always show great appreciation for my donations but don't lean on me which would be counter-productive. We have excellent relations which I very much appreciate.
>
> Mr L A Potter, Shipston-on-Stour, Warwickshire

225

unexpected cheque for £30,000 from a client but, almost as if to save the charity trouble, we were asked not to write. One of the Society's specialists from major donor development, therefore, decided to phone the solicitors' office and to offer to send their client further information on the NSPCC's work. They responded that it would be very welcome. Just how welcome could be measured by the cheque for £100,000 that arrived within the week.'

Helen, Amanda and Daniel

Helen Owen leads the core donor team, which concentrates on developing relationships with the cream of NSPCC's major donors through face-to-face meetings. She was trained in one-to-one major donor work in the United States, where the practice is far from unusual.

Helen also has responsibility for face-to-face legacy marketing, following up on donors' requests. 'This', she explains, 'is another area where the NSPCC sees huge potential for one-to-one relationship building. But the donors here are very different to major donors – not necessarily well-to-do, more typical of the general donor file – and have come in not because of a substantial gift but through an expressed interest in making a will or leaving a legacy to the NSPCC. So although both activities involve face-to-face fundraising they are quite separate and may well evolve separately in the future.

'Initially there was some feeling in other departments that face-to-face fundraising was unlikely to work. I was aware that visiting people at home is just one aspect of it. You then have to do something with that person once you have established a relationship.'

The process with core donors begins with a phone call to qualify their interest and the appropriateness of a visit. Unlike legacy prospects who have specifically requested a follow-up, core donors may have been supporting the NSPCC for years with sporadic donations and aren't expecting anything else. But they usually react positively to the idea of a meeting.

Helen continues, 'Following the qualification stage the process of deepening the donor's involvement continues with, perhaps, a meeting (probably at the donor's home), or a visit to an appropriate project, or the donor may be encouraged to get involved further by attending an event or meeting a senior member of staff. Involvement is key to the relationship from here on and the level of involvement needs to be defined by the donor – who is, of course, prompted by the core donor manager about ways to become involved.

'In the early stages of the relationship, particularly, it is a learning process in terms of getting to know the donor and getting to understand his or her needs. As these needs become more understood, it is the role of the core donor manager to ensure that the donor is involved and kept informed on a regular basis, in most cases at least monthly.'

Amanda Saunders and Daniel Batt develop core donor relationships through face-to-face visits. Daniel came to the department in 1995 from both a fundraising and commercial sales background, while Amanda came from fundraising. Both see their jobs as breaking new ground.

Daniel believes that in a few years the area will be much more competitive but that at the moment the NSPCC benefits by being ahead of the field. 'Most of the donors I see support four or five charities, but the NSPCC will invariably be the only one to have visited them at home.'

Amanda agrees, 'I was surprised at the number of people who have wanted to see us. And equally surprised at how much they are prepared to tell us about themselves.'

Daniel continues, 'Occasionally they confide in us rather a lot. It is a two-way process and clearly they benefit. Sometimes we find that a visit to a project will encourage donors to use the opportunity to talk about their own childhood experiences.'

'People do make disclosures to us', explains Amanda,

'and often we have to be more than just a fundraiser. The organisation has backed us in this with training and counselling.

'We are fortunate that we have 140 projects nationwide so we can always put donors in touch with work near to them. And we ourselves have spent time visiting NSPCC's work so we can talk from experience to inspire our donors. Without doubt it's the work that inspires, more than any follow-up material.'

Success in this work is always difficult to predict accurately, but the department now is consistently beating its targets, often by quite large margins. In core donors the target set was for 60 per cent growth, but the year ended with the team nearly doubling its own ambitious estimate.

'The main challenge', says Helen Owen, 'is to find the really big donors, particularly new donors. I did find one cold prospect recently who has now committed to a £50,000 gift – but most of our growth is from within our existing donors. So far at least.

'One route to new donors is to encourage existing major donors to act as influencers for us, to help us develop more peer-to-peer contact.'

Sara

Traditionally, fundraising from trusts has been highly cost-effective for the NSPCC. Originally part of corporate fundraising, the trusts section became part of the major donor development department as it was realised that trusts were not corporate bodies but groups of individuals. Sara Hertz manages the trusts section within major donor development.

'Our trusts strategy is built on relationships too. Inevitably there is some cross-over with core donors as we too seek to develop face-to-face relationships and many trustees could also be individual donors.

'We don't do blanket mailings to trusts. Instead, we

review the smaller trusts regularly to ensure our communications programme is always effective. Core trusts, those giving £10,000 and above, get a multi-tiered approach and each trust has an individual donor plan.

'To me, relationship fundraising is about common sense. How would I like to be treated? So it's about listening, remembering, being creative and flexible. I see myself as a facilitator and will use the right people to set up the best relationship – even if that doesn't involve me. We have a range of ways of involving donors and I often use the NSPCC's own trustees to help cement a relationship with the trustees of a particular trust.

'Relationship building with donors is like building a friendship in your personal life. It should flow naturally. You have to put yourself into it. When I worked in the United States some donors sent me gifts after the birth of my son and some came to my leaving party. Of course donors must be committed to the cause, but it helps if they are also committed to you.'

The last word

Angela Cluff, NSPCC's head of major donor development, deserves the last word.

'Our development of major donors has spin-off benefits in some unexpected areas, for example with our child protection teams. They may not have been wholly enthusiastic when the idea of visits from major donors was first suggested, and some probably still need persuading, but most are now surprisingly positive about it. They value the opportunity to talk about their work and the chance to show what they do to interested and appreciative visitors. And they can see the effect this has on the donors and on their willingness to support their work. So after a visit I'll often get a call from a child protection team leader saying how good the visit was. I like that.

'When a donor makes a major financial commitment to

support a charity like ours, they don't want that to be the
end of it. They often look for further involvement, even
though it may mean more effort for them and, inevitably,
will lead to their being asked sooner or later for more
money. They welcome that. These major donors want to
have some further relationship with the Society and that
alone justifies our work here, helping them to find the most
fruitful, most rewarding way to do it.'

NSPCC
42 Curtain Road
London EC2A 3NH
United Kingdom

Tel: +44 (0) 171 825 2500
Fax: +44 (0) 171 825 2525

The Royal National Institute for Deaf People

Part 1 – putting the customer first

Just as this book was passing for press I followed a recommendation from George Smith and attended a rather surprising session at Britain's National Fundraisers' Convention. It was presented by Karl Holweger, who was then director of public affairs and national services at the Royal National Institute for Deaf People, one of Britain's old established and I would have thought probably more conservative charities. Karl's presentation proved otherwise.

Over the last three years RNID has been quietly implementing a thorough and ambitious programme of customer care and development that would warm the heart of donors like my friends Myles, Rebecca, Agnes, Dora and Camilla. More than that, it has been taking some trouble to monitor and evaluate the effects and the value of its customer care initiatives. Inspired by a hope that now I might be able to include something more positive about donor service than the generally damning conclusions of my opening chapter, I pressed Karl into telling his story here. I think it well worth the slight inconvenience of a delayed production schedule to outline RNID's pioneering steps in donor and customer care.

A little background

The RNID is the largest deaf-related organisation in the UK. Established in 1911, the RNID has gone through many transformations in its history, perhaps the most exciting being in the late 1980s when a new chief executive officer was appointed and the RNID started the slow transformation from a typical charity to a leading not-for-profit service provider.

Today, the RNID employs over 1,000 people and has a turnover approaching £30 million. It is primarily a provider of services that cover residential care, deaf awareness training, communication support or sign language interpretation, information, Typetalk – the national telephone relay service and assistive devices for deaf people. Eighty per cent of its income comes from the sale of these services to private individuals and to organisations within the private, public and voluntary sectors. The rest comes from voluntary giving, chiefly raised by direct marketing and from legacies. The dynamics of the RNID's income demonstrate how far the charity has come in its aim to be a service-providing organisation. This reliance on service income means that, as with all service organisations, front line workers and, most importantly, customers need to be right at the centre of management concern.

Therefore in 1993 the RNID embarked on a journey to create a customer-led voluntary organisation. At the time, the organisation was unsure as to where this journey would end, but the RNID was convinced that the journey was both worthwhile and necessary. During the journey the RNID was not alone. It was guided both by organisations who were already practising the mantra of customer care and by two individuals, Mahatma Gandhi and Machiavelli – but more of these later.

The journey

The journey was to travel the road of customer care – to reach the goal of creating a truly customer-led, or customer-focused organisation. It is a goal that many organisations, be they voluntary, public, or commercial, have striven for but few have really achieved.

The first issue that the RNID had to resolve was to define what it means to be customer-led or focused. Without a clear idea or definition it becomes very hard to tell if you are travelling in the right direction and to know when you have arrived.

The RNID's simple definition of being customer-led is an organisation that is totally driven, managed and organised to ensure that it understands and meets the expectations and needs of its customers. An organisation that is committed to and does put its customers first.

The second issue that the RNID faced was to identify who exactly were its customers. In a commercial organisation customers are relatively easy to spot – they buy your products or services. But what about in a charity? As a large part of RNID's turnover comes from the sale of services and products, primarily under contract, to the social services, health authorities and commercial organisations, spotting some customers in a commercial sense is easy to achieve. But what about the thousands of deaf people who may use RNID's services free of charge and even people who give money, either individually or through companies and trusts? At the RNID all these people are defined and called customers. To the RNID a customer is someone who purchases a service, uses a service, or who donates. All are customers and all are equally important.

> I would like to congratulate the RNID on their helpful leaflets. I am a primary school teacher and I have used the excellent information they have given me to highlight an awareness in the children I teach about communication, deaf issues and cultures.
>
> RNID information customer

Why customer care in the voluntary sector?

The case for customer care in the commercial sector is easily understood. Enter our first guide, Mahatma Gandhi, perhaps one of the earliest proponents of customer care and someone who has neatly summarised the importance of customers. The following quote from Gandhi is regularly used whenever the subject of customer care is presented within, or by RNID.

> A customer is the most important visitor on our premises. He is not dependent on us, we are dependent on him. He is not an interruption of our work, he is the purpose of it. We are not doing him a favour by serving him, he is doing us a favour by giving us the opportunity to do so.

Commercial organisations know and understand the reality and importance of caring for their customers. Their survival depends on it and competitive advantage is won, or lost, on the basis of providing the service that customers want better than their competitors.

But why should the voluntary sector take customer care seriously and, more to the point, why did the RNID put this initiative at the heart of its long-term business strategy?

There were four key reasons for this that are valid, not just for the RNID but for any voluntary organisation involved in service delivery.

■ Customer care is in line with the charity ethos.

■ It offers a strategic response to the overall rise in customer expectation.

■ The approach can be used to shape staff attitudes and behaviour.

■ It underpins the service profit cycle that drives all service organisations, including charities.

Customer care and the charity ethos

Private sector organisations are primarily driven by the bottom line, the need to ensure that the company maximises its profitability and share dividend. In these circumstances satisfying customer needs can often take second place to financial and profit considerations. Obviously, this isn't always the case as some of the best examples of good customer care are found in this sector. Focusing on retaining customers and building their loyalty is increasingly fashionable in companies. Time and again companies have demonstrated that it is significantly more cost-effective to keep existing customers than to recruit new ones. In addition, relatively small changes in customer retention can have a large impact on overall profitability. However, it is still the exception to find a company that is brave enough to put customer service and satisfaction above profitability.

The public sector is primarily driven by regulatory and statutory responsibilities. In the past, very few statutory bodies have been required to deliver satisfied customers. The emphasis in these organisations has been on processing people and services. Again there are some in this sector who are producing extraordinary results around customer service, including some of the Government 'next step' agencies and health trusts, but they are the exception, not the rule.

> The RNID directs people to Sound Advantage even when they don't carry the most appropriate equipment... The RNID should not claim to be meeting the needs of the hearing impaired and also have a retail outlet.
>
> RNID customer

Voluntary organisations are not primarily driven by bottom line or statutory responsibilities. Voluntary organisations are value-driven – they are established and run to meet the aims and objectives set down in their constitutions. As value-driven organisations their *raison d'être* is in essence to service the needs of their respective customer groups.

A customer-care approach or customer-focused strategy is directly aligned to this purpose. Caring for customers is a value-led approach – care implies a relationship much deeper than that around financial or statutory obligations.

Caring and serving their respective customer groups is the very essence of what it is to be a voluntary or charitable organisation.

Customer expectations

Customer expectations are on the rise. Never before have customers expected so much from the organisations they deal with. The reasons for the general increase in customer expectation are primarily threefold.

Firstly, government legislation and policy in the UK has increasingly moved to define and provide people with rights as consumers. In Britain the political debate about the nature of being a subject or citizen has now shifted – increasingly we are seen, defined and behave as consumers, not citizens or subjects. Consumerism has set the context for how we interact with organisations and the State. Classic examples of this have been the spate of legislation to protect customer rights and the introduction of public sector service initiatives such as the citizens and patients charters, which for the first time have laid down basic service standards the public (customers) can expect from public bodies.

Secondly, when organisations get customer service wrong the power of today's media ensures that everybody gets to know about it – fast. Examples in the UK include the Hoover free flight promotion fiasco and the poor level of service and commitment to customers exhibited by newly privatised utilities. Customers affected by these organisations have been quick to exert their rights and use the media to highlight the offenders. With a highly effective media in the UK and more vocal, demanding customers, you can run but not hide from a breakdown in customer service and a failure to deliver on your promises to customers.

Finally, with dramatic and continual advances in technology and product development, most companies are now making products that are often indistinguishable from their competitors'. So to offer a competitive edge companies are turning to the level of service they provide in association with a product. This has driven up the level of service offered to customers by all sorts of companies. Some traditional product companies now sell and position themselves on their service, not their product. The Korean company Daewoo, a recent entry into the car market, is a good example of a company that manufactures cars but sells them on the basis of its customer service.

All of these factors drive up the expectations of voluntary sector customers who use services or donate to expect an equal if not a better level of service from charities when compared to others. It must be remembered that very few people are customers of our organisation only. The excuse of being a charity to explain away poor service will no longer suffice.

> …last year I posted eight letters to organisations for deaf people. Only two replied within eight weeks, one of those without the information I had asked for… it is difficult to keep enthusiastic when most deaf organisations are unwilling to communicate beyond sales and promotion.
>
> RNID information customer

Shaping behaviour

The RNID chose to use the language and ethos behind customer care as a tool to shape and change staff attitudes and behaviour.

The voluntary sector is littered with the language of dependency, which is inappropriate to the ethos of customer care. Charities call people 'users', 'clients', 'beneficiaries' – the language of patronage, disempowerment and disrespect. This language can often lead to unhelpful attitudes, values and behaviour from staff who work in voluntary organisations. Comments such as ' I am a professional, I've been doing this for 10 years, I know what people want' display a level of arrogance and prejudice towards customers that if not dealt with will cause damage to the organisation and its relationship with customers. The relationship between an organisation and a customer is powerful and special and involves empowerment, respect and responsiveness. When you ask staff to recognise people as customers they readily understand what this means, primarily because they will have been treated as customers themselves when receiving products and services in their own daily lives. So they will shape their behaviour to deliver the exceptional levels of customer service that they as customers would expect and want to receive.

The service profit cycle

The RNID has used the service profit cycle (*see* figure 1) as the defining case for customer care and has placed it at the heart of its business strategy.

> Overall the operators
> are marvellous.
>
> RNID Typetalk customer

The service profit cycle* describes and defines the relationships between profitability and income generation, service quality, staff morale, customer satisfaction and loyalty within a service organisation.

The key drives within the cycle act upon each other to produce a positive effort. Profit is driven by customer loyalty, which in turn is dependent on customer satisfaction. The prime driver of customer satisfaction is staff satisfaction. Happy, motivated staff lead to happy, pleased customers. Staff satisfaction is attained and sustained by appropriate and fair rewards and by creating quality services for staff to deliver. Profit and income are required to do this. Thus the cycle continues.

> I have recommended the
> information service to friends
> who have also been helped.
>
> RNID customer

Customer loyalty drives profit

In the commercial sector it is recognised that real increases in profitability are highly dependent on customer loyalty. By loyalty we mean the three Rs.

Retention (of customers), repeat (business from customers from the same service and other services), referral (by customers of the service or organisation to other people).

*J.L. Heskett, T.O. Jones, G.W. Loveman, W.E. Sasser and L.A. Schlesinger, 'Putting the Service Profit Chain to Work' in *Harvard Business Review*, March–April 1994.

Figure 1 The service profit cycle

The three Rs are just as important to voluntary organisations. If you were to ask any fundraising direct marketer about his or her priorities you would almost invariably receive the reply that the key challenge is to keep customers donating, to get them to give larger gifts, covenants and, finally, legacies. Charities like the RNID will succeed in this if they can retain their customers, persuade them to use the charity's services and to donate, and get customers to recommend the charity to other potential customers. Like all charities it is important for the RNID to retain its donors, particularly as it costs the charity £10 net to recruit a new donor from cold. So the RNID needs to maximise its donors' lifetime value through repeat donations, covenants and, ultimately, legacies. Where appropriate, the RNID also encourages donors to use its services and encourages service-users to donate, thus building a real relationship with individuals, which over time encourages repeated use of services and donations. Finally, we want our customers to be so happy with the process of doing business with us that they refer us to other people, either to use services or to

> The knowledge, interest and professionalism shown by RNID trainers throughout the day was excellent. A course I'd recommend to anyone.
>
> RNID training customer

donate. In other words, these highly satisfied and loyal customers become our most powerful sales force and advocates. The term for these super loyal customers is apostle and that is the charity's aim: to create customer apostles for the RNID.

Customer satisfaction drives loyalty

How do you actually achieve customer loyalty? The answer is through customer satisfaction – very satisfied customers become loyal customers. Today many organisations set corporate targets for customer satisfaction – in fact two highly successful companies, Rank Xerox and hi-fi company Richer Sounds, put them above everything else, including financial and profit targets. Satisfying all the needs of your customers should become the number one goal of any organisation determined to put its customers first.

> How does one convey the feeling of euphoria when, having been deafened over 20 years ago, I can at last make phone calls by myself? I remember after my first Typetalk call charging round the house, yelling, jumping and punching the air and throwing myself into the arms of the plumber who came in through the front door, shrieking that I had made a phone call all by myself.
>
> RNID Typetalk customer

Staff and the value they add drive customer satisfaction

Voluntary organisations are value-orientated and all the services and activities we deliver are value-laden. Customers too expect high value in services from the organisations they deal with – just providing standard products and services is no longer good enough. In any service environment happy, well-motivated staff will, time after time, deliver added value to the services and products they produce. This is the key to delivering customer satisfaction.

Service, quality and rewards drive staff satisfaction

The vast majority of employees want to do a good job. What they ask for are the tools to do this, in the form of resources to provide high-quality services and products and, for themselves, appropriate levels of reward and recognition.

Staff like to provide high-value, high-quality services to other people. Services that they can take pride in. The same is true, if not more so, within a charity, where staff will often go the extra mile to advocate and promote the cause and issue the organisation stands for. However, as in any organisation, staff will expect appropriate reward and recognition for their efforts, which will be difficult to resource without increased income and profit.

> We felt that the RNID representative was not only most charming but created a sense that her mission was to help to the maximum, that you were a very important person to her and that you have her undivided attention. If all the RNID staff are of this calibre we are confident that you give a wonderful service.
>
> RNID customer

These are the dynamics and links in the service profit chain. The RNID has recognised over the past three years that understanding, communicating and driving these elements are crucial to its success. The service profit chain is the reference point for all it is currently doing and is the lever for future growth.

Creating a customer-focused organisation

Creating a customer-led organisation was obviously not going to be a simple task and when the RNID embarked on this in 1993 there was little idea or experience in how to go about it. Rather than starting completely from scratch, the RNID decided the best course of action was to learn from others and set up an internal team with the following tasks.

■ To identify key customer-led organisations.

■ To arrange to visit the organisations to identify how they had introduced a customer-led strategy and what they had learned.

■ To create an appropriate strategy for the RNID using what had been learned from others.

Over a dozen organisations with experience of customer

care were identified, including British Airways, British Telecom and Rank Xerox. In all cases the organisations approached were more than willing to share with the charity their ideas, experiences and thoughts on how to create a customer-led organisation.

From the exercise RNID drew up four key lessons, important points and principles which had to be addressed if the RNID's approach was to be successful.

- Practice total commitment and communication.

- Become process focused.

- Develop a comprehensive measurement strategy.

- Allow front line staff to drive the process.

Total commitment

All the successful organisations the RNID spoke to were totally committed to their own customer care programmes and initiatives. It was never seen or viewed as simply the latest idea or business fad. Customer care had become an integral part of the organisation, its purposes and its mission. In companies like Rank Xerox, customer satisfaction was the key target for all business units and profit centres.

Profitability is relegated to second place. People live, eat, breathe and believe in customer satisfaction – performance, both individual and team, is judged on it, rewards and recognition are set by it.

> The information unit at RNID is very difficult to get hold of and has restricted opening hours.
>
> RNID information customer

Process focused

Customer-led organisations had recognised that in the past they did not have the processes and procedures in place that made it easier for customers to interact with them.

In fact, this is not particularly surprising. As they grow,

most organisations will naturally tend to evolve
bureaucracies that make it easy for senior managers to
control staff and resources, or make it easier for employees
to carry out their daily functions. Unfortunately, nine
times out of 10 the processes that evolve and flow
from this, by their very nature, do not make it easy for
customers to interact with staff and the organisation.
Many of the customer-focused organisations that the
RNID spoke to had examined all of their procedures
and processes from their customers' point of view and
asked a simple question, 'does this process make it
easy for customers to do business with us?' Processes
that failed this test, or which were overly complex were
either cut or changed. To help examine all of their different
functions and areas, some organisations also broke down
their services into seven key process areas.

> Delivery is hopeless, exacerbated by not being able to use a credit card. I phoned and explained I live alone and would appreciate speedy delivery. Delivery was a month in one case and more in the second.
>
> RNID customer

- Attracting customers.

- Handling customer enquiries.

- Dealing with customer orders.

- Providing and delivering the ordered service or product.

- Invoicing the customer.

- Handling complaints.

- Maintaining an ongoing relationship with the customer.

Each of the process areas can then be looked at in any
service function to determine how each rates in terms of
ease for customers to interact with staff and the company.
With each process, surveys should be carried out to
determine both the level of satisfaction and its importance to
customers. Significantly, these process areas apply to
virtually all types of commercial and voluntary
organisations.

Measurement strategy

Successful customer care initiatives ensure a regular measuring and reporting of satisfaction data, which is crucial for any customer-friendly organisation, thereby maintaining the focus and momentum of the initiative. Without momentum there is a danger of results being shelved and other organisational priorities taking precedent.

> Instructions for the Uniphone are a mess. I have a degree in electrical engineering and yet it took me weeks to successfully make and receive calls via Typetalk.
>
> RNID Typetalk customer

Driven by the front line staff

The experience of other customer-led organisations is that the key staff who will drive any customer care initiatives will be those who deal directly with the public, staff who daily deal with customers, or who are intimately involved with service delivery. Only these front line staff are in a position to understand the needs and issues around customers and service. Middle and senior managers, far removed from customers and service delivery, are the worst people to recommend and drive the changes that will be necessary to improve customer satisfaction. Too often they address and push changes or activities based on their own biased assumptions and experiences. Engaging and expanding the role of front line staff is often the biggest challenge and most likely contributor to success in creating a customer-focused organisation.

Putting principles into action

After 12 months of research and analysis of the theory behind customer care as well as studying the practice of leading organisations, the RNID was ready to embark on its own customer care journey, to implement the learning and principles it had acquired.

Gaining commitment and communication

The first step was to ensure that the RNID's trustees, its chief executive officer and its senior managers were all aware of what the organisation was about to embark on and were fully committed to it. To reinforce this targeting, reporting and monitoring processes for customer care were put into place for senior managers and the trustees.

The customer care initiative was explained to all middle managers at a special one-day conference. This was then followed up with a series of roadshows around the country to drive home the message to staff at all levels. Events like this were crucial to allow staff the opportunity to ask questions about the initiative and start to develop employee ownership of the programme. One of the additional benefits was the identification of staff who were particularly enthusiastic about the initiative. These staff formed a pool of 'customer care champions' for later work involving the management of change within particular services.

Identifying and measuring customer satisfaction

After the staff roadshows, the priority was to develop the questionnaires and surveys to be used for measuring customer satisfaction.

First qualitative research was carried out with small focus groups of staff working with each of the RNID customer groups and a variety of customers themselves, ranging from contract purchase managers in social services, personnel managers in commercial organisations and deaf sign-language users. The purpose of the research was to identify from customers what the key issues were for each service. What were the areas that really pleased them and what caused the most dissatisfaction? The same approach was undertaken with staff working in the services to determine their understanding of customers' concerns. This helped to continually build a sense of ownership of the initiative

Table 1 Customer type and measuring frequency

Customer type	Frequency
Service	
Residential organisations	Annual
Deaf awareness training, organisations	Quarterly
Deaf awareness training, individuals	Quarterly
Information, individuals	Quarterly
Communication support unit, organisations	Quarterly
Communication support unit, individuals	Quarterly
Typetalk, deaf individuals	Quarterly
Sound Advantage, individuals	Quarterly
Sound Advantage, organisations	Quarterly
Fundraising	
New donors	On joining
Regular donors	Bi-monthly
Covenantors	Quarterly
Pledgers	Annual
Corporate donors	Quarterly
Trust donors	Quarterly

among staff. It was surprising how often each group highlighted similar issues, re-enforcing the view that front line staff have a better view of customer needs and concerns than senior managers.

The information from customers and staff groups was used to develop draft customer surveys for all the RNID services, including fundraising. Next, each survey was piloted with customers to ensure that the questionnaires and language used were appropriate. In particular, it was important to test out questionnaires with profoundly deaf people, as English may not be their first language. Adjustments were then made from the pilot exercise to produce finalised questionnaires ready for the actual surveys.

Who is measured?

Table 1 lists all the key customer groups who are sampled (a random selection from each group is researched by questionnaire). Typically each customer group is sampled every quarter. Regular reporting ensures that the momentum is maintained on reporting and follow-up action. The gap between reporting and measuring allows time for the impact of service change to show up in results. Any more frequently and there is a danger that staff would become disillusioned before the effects of their work and the changes would be seen in the next set of results.

Results

The RNID has found that the regular data and feedback coming in from customers are invaluable. For the first time, overall customer satisfaction can be measured along with customers' future re-use intentions and willingness to recommend us to others. Figures 2, 3 and 4 provide

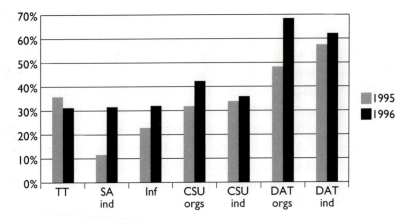

Figure 2 Overall satisfaction – 'very satisfied' (%)

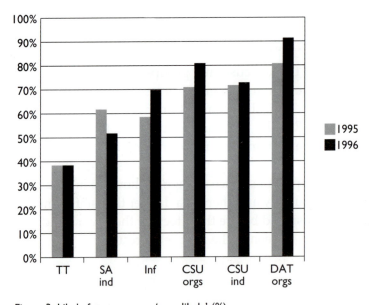

Figure 3 Likely future usage – 'very likely' (%)

Key for figures 2–4
TT: Typetalk customers; SA ind: Sound Advantage customers; Inf: customers seeking information; CSU orgs: communication support units, organisations; CSU ind: communication support units, individual customers; DAT orgs: deaf awareness training, organisations; DAT ind: deaf awareness training, individual customers.

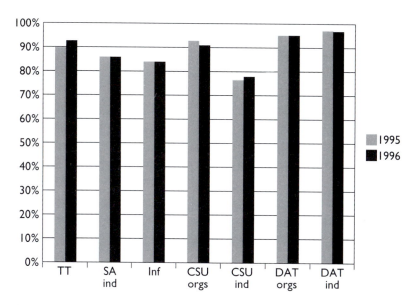

Figure 4 Recommend to others – yes (%)

Key – see opposite page

illustrative examples of these results for customers of our services and how they can be tracked over time with comparisons for scores between 1995 and 1996.

Managing change

Of all the companies visited in the benchmark process, Rank Xerox appeared to have the most effective and versatile customer care management process. So the RNID borrowed its management process for changing customer satisfaction from them. Customer care teams, which drive the whole initiative within the organisation, are the most important component of Rank Xerox's programme. The RNID followed suit. For each service and process area the RNID set up a customer care team. Membership of each team was drawn from front line services and key process areas, such as information technology, finance and marketing. A prerequisite for staff on the team is to have firsthand

knowledge of customers and services. Managers are
excluded. The purpose of the teams is to analyse in detail
the results from the customer satisfaction reports and to
identify the key areas that drive dissatisfaction, so they can
develop appropriate action plans to change this. The
management strategy has also been facilitated at the RNID
through the creation of a new position: the dedicated
customer satisfaction officer. Within the whole process, the
most useful data tool is the customer satisfaction
scattergram, which visually plots the satisfaction and
importance of the different issues within a service. (*See*
figure 5 for a typical example of a scattergram, in this case
for the Typetalk telephone relay service.)

The scattergram highlights at a glance which areas
should be prioritised. In general, one would want areas of
low importance to score low in satisfaction. Obviously, it
would not make sense for an organisation to spend
resources on areas of low customer importance. However,
areas of high importance require high satisfaction. Low
scores of satisfaction with high values of importance
highlight problem areas that require urgent attention. With
the scattergram the customer care teams are expected to
generate action plans to improve customer satisfaction,
using the detailed results behind the data overlaid with
staff's own knowledge and experience.

These action plans are then passed to senior managers
within the RNID. It is the job of management to accept the
plans and ensure the recommended points are put into
place. This is the opportunity for the chief executive officer
and directors to put their commitment into action. The
temptation to change or reject plans has to be overcome.
Management is required to accept that these front line staff
have the knowledge to know how best to solve customer
problems.

The customer care teams track the impact of their plans
and highlight problems to senior managers if obstacles are

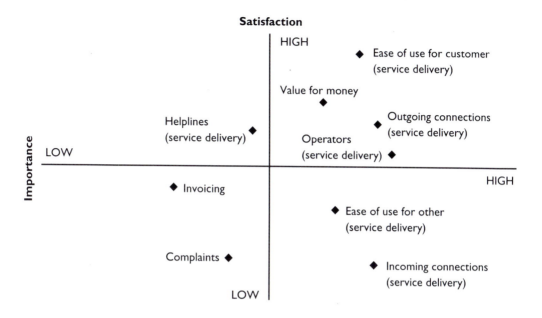

Figure 5 Typetalk – satisfaction vs importance

hit. At the RNID, these teams are the engine behind the customer care initiative. Their inspiration and hard work have kept the initiative alive and running for two years. If you were to talk to any of these staff they would tell you of the stimulation and responsibility they feel – staff empowerment in action.

The satisfaction of customers who donate

As explained at the beginning of this chapter, 80 per cent of the RNID's income arises from the sale of services and products. Customers of these have therefore formed the main focus of the initiative to date. However, the RNID has recently extended its customer care initiative to include customers who donate. For the first time it has been able to establish just how satisfied its donating customers are and what makes them happy or unhappy when they support the RNID.

Comparisons to other charities

One of the key areas was how donors would compare the RNID to other charities they support (*see* table 2). Only seven per cent thought it better than other charities they donated to, the majority believed RNID to be the same (79 per cent) or worse (13 per cent). The aim had to be to improve this so that at least 50 per cent of customers would rate the RNID as better than any other charity. To achieve this RNID identified through questionnaires which charities were consistently rated above them. The practices and policies of these higher-rated charities were investigated and changes made to procedures to match or exceed the level of service these charities were providing.

Table 2 Customers who donate – satisfaction with the RNID compared to other charities	
Better	7%
Same	79%
Worse	13%

Satisfaction and the link to levels of giving

Initial results show that satisfaction with supporting the RNID is high (*see* table 3). Not surprisingly the financial commitment of donating customers to the RNID is highly dependent on their level of satisfaction. Thus legacy pledgers who have been regularly donating show the highest very satisfied score (43 per cent compared to regular donors at 24 per cent).

Table 3 Satisfaction with the experience of supporting the RNID

| | Type of donating customer | | | |
	New	Regular	Covenantor	Pledger
Very satisfied	31%	24%	25%	43%
Satisfied	44%	56%	61%	39%
Neither nor/ dissatisfied	9%	13%	9%	6%

This confirms that the RNID can only hope to maximise the lifetime value of supporters if it satisfies and delights them. But what is it that makes customers who donate either very satisfied or dissatisfied?

What drives satisfaction?

The scattergrams that the RNID produced showed that the charity currently is good at satisfying donors in areas that are relatively less important to them (*see* figure 6). The top three priorities for customers who donate were identified as communication, appeal presentation and staff competence. If the RNID were really to start delighting these customers, the fundraising customer care team had to analyse the information they were now gathering, to develop an understanding of which issues needed to be addressed.

> I'd rather have a pack once a year with all the updates on everything, rather than having stuff coming through the door all the time.
>
> RNID donating customer

Communication with donors

For regular donors communication is the biggest single influence (44 per cent) on overall satisfaction. The charity discovered that most donors felt that they were receiving too many appeals (*see* table 4),

> Thank you replies are a waste of money and extra expense for them as well. You know it's got there, that's good enough.
>
> RNID donating customer

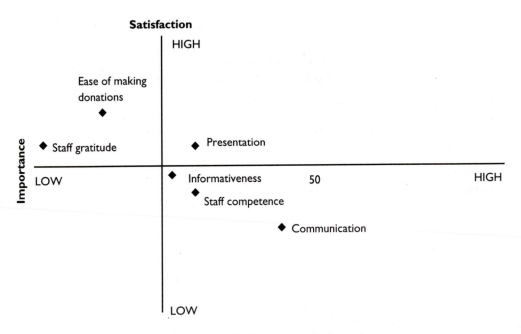

Figure 6 Customers who donate – satisfaction vs importance

Table 4 Frequency and desired frequency of receiving appeals from the RNID		
	Actual	*Desired*
Once a month	4%	*
Once every two months	20%	3%
Once a quarter	30%	29%
Easter and Christmas	8%	32%
Once a year or less often	4%	26%
Don't know	35%	10%

with 55 per cent perceiving that they were getting four to five appeals each year which they would prefer to be cut to one or two. In reality these donors were being sent up to eight appeals each year, which illustrates a common feature of donor care – the marked difference between reality and perception.

The RNID is currently testing a series of initiatives to try to bring mailing frequency in line with customers' needs, without of course damaging the amount of income raised. The initiatives include more positive opt-outs, reduced mailing frequency to donors who rarely respond and methods to reduce donor perceptions of mailing frequency.

The RNID's thank you policy was also an area of concern. The charity currently thanks all donors giving £10 or more by letter, with larger gifts being handled separately and more personally. But the research showed that only a small proportion of donors think it is important to receive a thank you and 42 per cent think it is unimportant. Twenty-six per cent think the £10 cut off is too low and 11 per cent think thanking donors is a waste of money.

So the RNID is looking at a number of measures including opt-out thank yous, increasing the cut-off level and thanking donors just once a year in a special update mailing. Each option will be carefully evaluated to track the impact on customer satisfaction and support.

> Some charities are greedy. You give and they come back in three months asking for more. They give you reams of literature and you don't have time to read it. As far as I am concerned the less literature you send, but with the facts written down in a matter of fact way, the more likely I am to give.
>
> RNID donating customer

> We had a follow up two weeks after having given.
>
> RNID donating customer

Presentation

The big issue around presentation was that significant numbers of donors believe their mailings to be too long. Most flicked through the appeal rather than read it (46 per cent vs 36 per cent), and while 79 per cent felt there were clear instructions on how to donate, only 29 per cent rated the length of the letter as very good (*see* table 5). This appears to challenge the generally held view among direct

Table 5 Customers who donate – happiness with the appeal	Very good	Good
Clear instructions on how to donate	79%	17%
Easy to understand	58%	34%
Easy to read	54%	37%
Identified how your donation would help deaf people	51%	37%
Presentation	43%	40%
Length of letter	29%	38%

Table 6 What customers who donate did with the last appeal letter	
Did not read	5%
Flicked through	46%
Read thoroughly	36%
Can't remember/don't know	13%

marketers that long letters are best. The RNID believes that it would ignore its customers' views at its peril so will be testing shorter letters as well as investigating other issues such as typeface, type size and layout.

The last appeal brought some good news about a prototype of a new hearing aid they wanted to test. That's a real encouragement to give.

RNID donating customers

Another challenge for the charity and its advisers is to improve donors' views of the organisation. Currently only 60 per cent of customers who donate think their money is spent wisely (*see* table 7). The

Table 7 Customers who donate – impressions of the RNID

	Agree	Disagree	No answer
Is a professional organisation	72%	1%	22%
Provides good advice and information on issues about hearing loss	64%	1%	27%
Uses money wisely to help deaf people	60%	1%	31%
Is an efficient organisation	56%	1%	33%
Is less aggressive than other charities in its fundraising	49%	5%	28%
Is an approachable organisation	48%	1%	43%

Table 8 Customers who donate – their impressions of RNID staff

	Very happy/happy	Neither/unhappy	Don't know
Helpfulness of staff	68%	9%	23%
Staff doing what they say they will	51%	8%	41%
Ability to answer questions	57%	7%	36%
How much staff care about the service	45%	9%	45%
How grateful staff were about your donation	55%	6%	41%
Overall satisfaction	80%	10%	10%

objective is to rapidly increase that to 90 per cent or more.

Staff attitudes

The third priority area highlighted in the scattergram was staff competence (*see* table 8), specifically the ability of staff to both do what they say they will do and to demonstrate that they care about the service they provide. The RNID provides appropriate customer care training for all staff who come into contact with customers and equally importantly it provides leadership and motivation to ensure that all staff have the training and attitude to deliver exceptional levels of customer service.

> Nothing was too much bother... helpful, friendly advice... very pleasant indeed.
>
> RNID information service

The importance of delighted customers and complaint handling

> The phone calls to you gave us all the information necessary for which I was extremely grateful. Thank you *very* much for this service. It ensured that money was well spent.
>
> RNID Sound Advantage customer

The RNID has gained two general pieces of key learning from all the results from both customers who use the services and those who donate. The first shows how important it is to go that extra step to delight customers and the second shows the need to identify and resolve customer complaints successfully.

Satisfied isn't good enough

Generating satisfied customers isn't good enough, only very satisfied customers will do. For RNID customers who donate this is clearly demonstrated when comparing their likelihood to donate again against their level of satisfaction (*see* table 9). The intention to re-donate of very satisfied customers is approximately 200 per cent greater than that for dissatisfied and satisfied customers. The message is very clear, delighting customers is of prime importance and the only factor that keeps customers loyal.

Table 9 Satisfied isn't good enough – the importance of delighting customers

Intention to give again	Very satisfied	Satisfied	Neither satisfied/ nor dissatisfied
Definitely	65%	27%	21%
Very likely	22%	39%	31%

The importance of successful complaint handling

Complaints by customers need to be successfully and effectively handled. Failure to do this will cost the RNID lost customers and money.

From an examination of both RNID's services and its fundraising, it is clear that customers who do not complain have higher levels of satisfaction and re-use intentions than those who do complain. This obviously makes sense – people who complain will do so because something has gone wrong and would, therefore, expect to score lower on satisfaction. However, the situation is not that simple. Further analysis of complaints, particularly looking at the difference between those customers whose complaint was successfully resolved versus those whose weren't shows some startling points. If a customer complaint was successfully resolved then the customer's overall service satisfaction and intention to re-use are higher than customers who didn't complain.

> I would be lost without Typetalk. Overall it is wonderful. I hope my criticisms are taken as they are meant (ie constructively). I know you are striving to improve an already excellent service. Thank you.
>
> RNID donating customer

However, customers whose complaints were not properly resolved are likely to be significantly less satisfied and half as likely to re-use the service compared to those who didn't complain (*see* table 10). The learning message from this is clear. Making sure you resolve complaints to the customer's

Table 10 The benefits of identifying and resolving customer complaints

	Satisfied	Intention to re-use
Complained	69%	32%
Not complained	87%	41%
Complaints successfully handled	89%	43%
Complaints unsuccessfully handled	43%	21%

satisfaction is a sure way to increase overall satisfaction and retain more loyal customers. (This rather proves Bob Worcester's point, *see* page 16.)

And finally

The RNID's experience of customer care has been an immensely exciting learning event. The RNID truly has embarked on the road towards customer satisfaction and now is starting to reap the benefits. However, we are painfully aware that we have only just scratched the surface and plenty more work needs to be done.

First and foremost has to be winning the hearts and minds of all the staff at the RNID to turn customer care ideas and work into reality. It is at this point that we frequently refer to our second guide who summarises the problems we face but provides the inspiration to carry on.

There is nothing more difficult to plan, more doubtful of success, nor more dangerous to manage than the creation of a new system.

For the initiator has the enmity of all who would profit by keeping the old institutions, and merely lukewarm defenders in those who should gain by the new ones.

Machiavelli

Royal National Institute for Deaf People
19-23 Featherstone Street
London EC1Y 8SL
United Kingdom

Tel: +44 (0)171 296 8000
Fax: +44 (0)171 296 8199

World Wildlife Fund Canada

Thank you and welcome

I first came across World Wildlife Fund Canada in the autumn of 1995. I was running a six-hour, so-called masterclass on donor development at the International Fund Raising Workshop in Holland. I was a little disconcerted as one of my students that day not only seemed familiar with most of my concepts of donor relationship building, she had been putting them into practice for some time.

Along with others, I sat spellbound as she described the innovative welcome programme she and her colleagues had been developing over the previous two or three years. She was – and still is – Gwen Chapman and her organisation then was World Wildlife Fund Canada.

The rest, as they say, is geography. I found myself in Toronto, Canada later that year, where I met Gwen again with David Love, senior vice-president at WWF Canada, and their colleague Ana White, who is now WWF Canada's director of membership. A brief history of these three appears on page 282.

Over a glass of Canada Dry they told me what they were doing. As I had expected, it struck me as the best example of relationship fundraising in practice that I had then found outside the UK. So I invited David and his colleagues to tell their story in this book. Here it is, as they tell it themselves.

The good old days...

'Damn! There goes the phone. How can I do my job if I am always interrupted? After all, I am doing important work and people should be happy with that.'

Maybe there were times years ago when employees of charitable organisations could say this. Indeed maybe in the 'good old days' the phone never rang at all. Perhaps the donors just wanted to give money to good people to do good work. There was no need to bother these folks as they worked their magic. A donor might even distract them from their crucial job.

...are gone!

Today charities are accountable to their supporters. In fact, the public expects them to be more accountable than any other organisation. Why this happened and how one charitable organisation responded is the subject of this chapter.

Like all charities, World Wildlife Fund represents a tangible hope for a better world. WWF's particular mission is to save life on earth, including people. Those wishing to share this dream become supporters of WWF.

Supporters is a loaded term though. These people do not simply support the organisation – WWF. They feel part of our mission and they share our passion to achieve it. That is why we think of our supporters, or donors, or customers as *partners*.

The words we use often reflect what we think. By using partners, we recognise the fundamental relationship between the mission of WWF and the individuals who want to invest in that mission. Our partners see themselves joining with WWF to save nature.

All this wouldn't matter much if we could still go about our business without paying much attention to our partners.

> This is a sign of the new philanthropy. Rich people are not going to hand over a cheque and say goodbye. Joan wants to be a full partner.
>
> The days of just throwing a cheque at people are gone.
>
> Taken from a news story about a wealthy family who had been supporting the Ontario Arts Council for 25 years and then notified them that they were not going to give them any more money

Why don't they just leave us alone? What happened? Four things changed the world of charities forever.

The new reality – your donors are watching

In 1968, the unrest surrounding the major political conventions in the United States signalled that the world was undergoing a fundamental change. Never again would authority be vested in anything – a person, an institution, even a government – without question. The demonstrators in the streets of Miami and Chicago were shouting 'show me'. And people have been demanding accountability ever since. Especially from charities.

I subscribe to several organizations but none are as appreciative as you for contributions.

Margaret Gillard,
Victoria, British
Columbia

Another major influence was the growth of charities with large memberships. Suddenly organisations became effective through the support of many thousands and, in some instances, even a million people. Whether they knew it at the time, these organisations were heading for a new challenge – forming partnerships with their supporters. If they didn't, they would lose them.

Third, there were suddenly thousands of charities. All around us, clever articulate people were developing their own vision for a better world and they were aggressively marketing that vision. WWF was not the only game in town and people who cared about wildlife and wilderness had a choice. If we didn't deliver the goods they'd find a group that did. (In 1995 5,000 new charities in Canada brought the national total to over 72,000. At the last count, over 2,500 of these are environmental organisations.) Whether we liked it or not, we had competition.

We are not in competition *against* other charities. We don't want to limit the number of dreams we can have for a better world. *The competition is for the partners.* For people who will share our mission and who will stay with us as we work feverishly to achieve it.

Finally, the explosive growth of charities brought with it increasing public scrutiny. Unfortunately, a number of high-profile scandals were uncovered that rocked the world of non-profit organisations. By the end of the 1980s, the climate for charities was dramatically different.

At WWF Canada we recognised these factors in 1989 and we made our first foray into the area of 'customer service'. We took the bold step of asking our partners what they wanted. Our first attempt was comprehensive – and ridiculous. From a database of about 5,000 people we received 2,000 replies for 2,000 different things! We had offered far too many opportunities for 'write-in' requests that we could do nothing about. But we learned one thing – our partners were keen to talk to us. We just needed to figure out a better way to do it.

Step one: the 'we're listening' guarantee

One of the issues that came through loud and clear in our first communication with our partners was their concern about junk mail. As a conservation organisation, we were obliged to satisfy this concern.

As a result, we created our exclusive 'we're listening' guarantee, which invites our partners to take a role in establishing their relationship with us. We sent the 'we're listening' guarantee with the first thank you letter or welcome letter to our partners.

The guarantee was our first specific acknowledgement that our relationship with our partners was changing and that, if we did not think carefully about this relationship, support for our conservation mission could slip. (WWF's first 'we're listening' guarantee appears on page 266.)

In the autumn of 1992 listening to supporters caught the attention of Canada's national newspaper, which ran a feature article about it and 'customer care' at a non-profit organisation became national news. (The *Globe and Mail* article is reproduced on page 266.)

And WWF continued to work on developing the relationship with our partners.

> Firstly, let me tell you that we are proud to be members of WWF. We view it as the 'foundation' of our wildlife activism and of the many animal, nature and similar organizations to which we belong. We congratulate you on your dedication, talent, enthusiasm, personal approach and responsiveness.
>
> Christine and Hayden Bush, Bedford, Nova Scotia

Right: Canada's press starts to take notice of
WWF's donor development initiatives.
Left: proof that WWF Canada means what it says.

Step two: welcome booklet no. 1

At about the same time, our director of membership returned from a fundraising workshop with other members of the WWF family. At the workshop she saw an example of a donor's welcome booklet that she immediately recognised as an excellent way to deepen the relationship with our partners. As a result, we launched our first welcome booklet.

Here is a quick summary of the contents of that first booklet.

Front cover 'Welcome' logo and photo.

Inside front cover
Names of membership contacts.

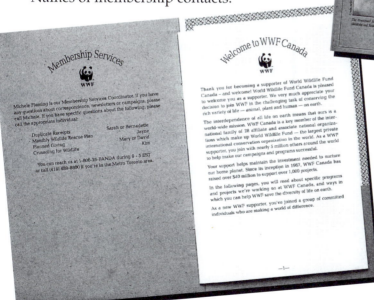

Welcome to WWF Canada
Who we are and what we do.

Full-page, cute photo
Something for the right brain!

Around the world, wild cats are in jeopardy. Through conservation projects in many countries, WWF is working to save tigers, leopards, jaguars, cougars and other wild cats.

-3-

Despite WWF's efforts, the Polar Bear remains a species in jeopardy. Like many large carnivores, the polar bear is taking its last stand in Canada

Your Membership Card

WWF

Your personal WWF Canada membership card should be kept in a convenient place; you can use it in a number of important ways.

The front of your WWF Canada membership card lists your name and below, your Membership Number. You will want to refer to your membership number when taking advantage of exciting "members-only" offers — for example, limited-edition WWF Canada posters, and T-shirts. Currently, we are negotiating special opportunities for WWF supporters with some of our corporate supporters. We will let you know the details as soon as they become available!

On the back of your card, you will find a toll-free 1-800 telephone number for WWF Canada, and a list of contact names. Please keep your card handy and refer to it when you want to talk to us.

Your membership card
What is the card for and what are the benefits of membership?

Working for Wildlife
An introduction to our quarterly newsletter.

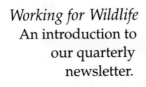

WWF was among the organizations which led the battle to make South Moresby in the Queen Charlotte Islands a national park. This conservation victory came about because of the nation-wide concern for our unique wilderness areas.

"Working for Wildlife"

WWF

You can follow WWF Canada's activities in "Working for Wildlife", our quarterly newsletter exclusively for active WWF supporters. Your first issue will arrive soon.

You will read about local campaigns, international programs, volunteer efforts, government response and the many ways that your contribution is making a difference to wildlife. Also, you will find details of special opportunities and merchandise available only to WWF supporters!

"Working for Wildlife" not only keeps you abreast of WWF Canada's activities, it lets you know exactly how your contribution is working to save wildlife.

Saving life on earth
A broader look at WWF's conservation programmes.

At WWF Canada, supporters like yourself make a real difference. There are a number of ways you can help save wildlife.

Join WWF's Monthly Wildlife Rescue Team. You can help ensure a reliable and predictable income for wildlife, by authorizing WWF to draw an amount from your chequing account each month. This is an economical and convenient way to make donations and it also helps reduce paperwork.

Tell your friends about WWF. One of the easiest and most valuable ways you can help is by simply telling your friends about WWF, and encouraging them to become supporters.

Be a part of our Earth Day events. If you're in the Toronto area, you can hike to the top of the CN Tower as a fun and fit way to raise money for WWF Canada. Other Earth Day activities include a climb up Signal Hill in St. John's and a Calgary tower climb.

Become a Wilderness Crusader. You can use any activity you enjoy, from walking to baking, as a fund-raising and/or public awareness event to help save wildlife.

Use the power of your Pen. Mail or fax letters to the appropriate politicians to express your concern about the urgent need to protect our wildlife and wild places.

Become a Guardian of the Rainforest. For only $25, you can help protect an acre of valuable tropical rainforest in Latin America or Canadian wilderness.

"Buy" Shares in WWF. You can purchase shares in WWF by investing in our Conservation Endowment Fund. This natural investment provides financial resources for wildlife far into the future.

–8–

From the Yukon to the Prairies to the Maritimes, over 250 species of plants and animals have become sufficiently threatened to be included on Canada's list of Species at Risk which is released each year by WWF Canada.

The list is determined every year by The Committee on the Status of Endangered Wildlife in Canada (COSEWIC), and currently includes the beluga whale, eastern cougar, peary caribou, harlequin duck, coastal plain wildflowers, blue ash and wild hyacinth. After careful consideration, COSEWIC assigns each species a particular status, ranging from "Vulnerable" to "Endangered" to "Extinct".

Each year we make this list of endangered species available to active donors like yourself in an exclusive poster format, with a beautiful illustration of WWF's featured species such as the sea otter.

WWF Canada's action projects speed the recovery of wildlife on the endangered species list. We're making real progress for many species, including peregrine falcons, harbour porpoises and swift foxes.

Much of the success of these efforts is due to supporters like you helping to lobby elected officials. You may want to take a moment and write a letter to the politician responsible for wildlife in your province or territory, urging greater protection for endangered species. For information about who to contact in your area, please refer to the information request insert at the back of this booklet.

–7–

Endangered species
WWF in action saving species.

Triumphs and achievements
Some conservation results.

Although the challenges are great, WWF Canada has an admirable record of success.

The white pelican is no longer threatened, and the wood bison is no longer endangered. And more than 500 projects worth almost $5 million have been supported since 1988 through the Endangered Species program.

WWF's book *Endangered Spaces* was a Canadian bestseller, and was sent to over 1,000 elected representatives across Canada. The Endangered Spaces campaign boasts more than 280 groups as participants, and almost 600,000 Canadians have signed their names to the Canadian Wilderness Charter.

Through the *Guardian of the Rainforest* program, WWF Canada has been able to protect 200,000 acres of Costa Rican rainforest. In Canada, more than 100 new parks have been established, including BC's magnificent Tatshenshini wilderness area.

In 1988, WWF was able to help the Kayapo Indians in the Brazilian Amazon successfully defeat hydro development proposals which would have flooded many acres of their tropical forest home.

As a result of WWF's efforts, the world's first Jaguar reserve was established and then dramatically expanded in Belize.

–16–

Saving Life on Earth

Protecting Canada's vast and varied wildlife poses a unique challenge. In keeping with our mission statement, WWF Canada's task is to protect this diversity, enabling Canadians to live in harmony with their environment. WWF Canada is working towards this goal through three programs:

• Endangered Species Program – increasing the chances of survival for Canada's endangered wildlife, through careful, thorough research, specific species recovery plans and practical field work to rebuild the numbers of depleted populations;

• Endangered Spaces Program – completing a network of protected areas representing all of Canada's biologically unique regions by the year 2000;

• Wildlife Toxicology Program – protecting Canadian wildlife and wildlands from harm caused by toxic chemicals.

• International Program – providing funding through the *Guardian of the Rainforest* Program to support conservation projects aimed at stopping the loss of the tropical habitats in Latin America.

You can help WWF get results
Opportunities to help WWF – with some non-monetary ideas.

–6–

You can make a difference
Some suggestions for personal action to help
the environment.

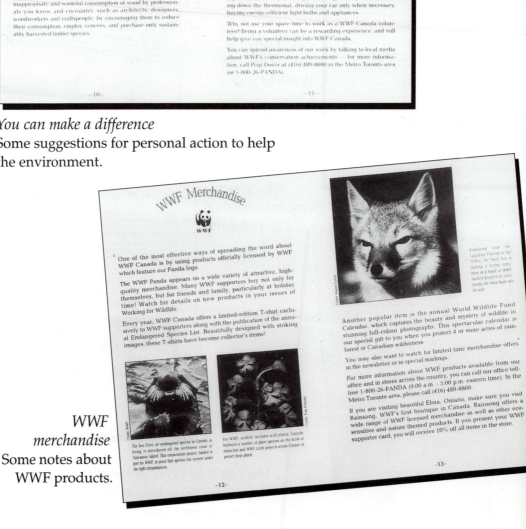

WWF
merchandise
Some notes about
WWF products.

Other Things You Should Know

WWF

As a supporter of WWF Canada, you will be kept up to date on our activities in a number of ways. You may notice that your address label on these items includes certain codes and numbers. The 7-digit number above your name is your membership number.

If you move, please let us know eight to ten weeks before to avoid missing any of WWF's important publications. Simply send us your old address (or your mailing label) and your new address (including your new postal code) and the date it becomes effective.

Should you receive two copies of the newsletter or another mailing, please let us know. Occasionally, a supporter's name will appear twice on our mailing list, perhaps in a slightly different form. To help us correct this situation, please return both mailing labels to us, indicating which one is accurate.

Our ability to exchange your name for another will help build our supporter base, adding to the many people who support the conservation of wildlife and wild places through WWF. Exchanging our list on a one-time basis with that of other reputable charitable organizations is the most cost effective way to find new donors. There is absolutely no obligation for you to support these other organizations. But by allowing us to exchange your name, you are helping build a stronger constituency for wildlife conservation in Canada. Of course, if you do not want to participate, please let us know, and we'll be sure to exclude your name from any exchanges.

What happens when we exchange a name?
1. WWF arranges a one-time exchange of names and addresses with a registered charity. (Only names and addresses are exchanged.)
2. The exchange names go to an independent mailing house, so the exchanging charities never see each others lists.
3. You receive a mailing from the other charity inviting your support, and you decide whether to respond. Only if you respond to that charity's mailing do you go on their mailing list.

Other things you should know
Some details about confidentiality, moving, etc.

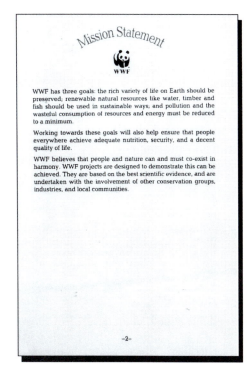

Mission Statement

WWF

WWF has three goals: the rich variety of life on Earth should be preserved; renewable natural resources like water, timber and fish should be used in sustainable ways; and pollution and the wasteful consumption of resources and energy must be reduced to a minimum.

Working towards these goals will also help ensure that people everywhere achieve adequate nutrition, security, and a decent quality of life.

WWF believes that people and nature can and must co-exist in harmony. WWF projects are designed to demonstrate this can be achieved. They are based on the best scientific evidence, and are undertaken with the involvement of other conservation groups, industries, and local communities.

–2–

Mission statement
The mission of WWF
around the world.

Inside back cover
The 'we're listening' guarantee,
information request and new
member survey.

Back cover
Logo, address and charitable
registration number.

Making donors feel they have made the right choice

Looking back at the first booklet after four years it seems institutional. While its purpose was to welcome new members, its emphasis was on information that we thought our new donors needed to know – there is even a section called 'other things you should know'.

Even so, the booklet produced results. Our increasing retention rates proved that the booklet was a success and we began work on improvements. Many of these were suggested by our partners. For instance, a common suggestion was that, since we had three inserts, it would be helpful if we included a reply envelope.

The acknowledgement of success came when WWF Canada won a Gold RSVP award from the Canadian Direct Marketing Association for our acquisition package, which included the welcome booklet. And then came the ultimate tribute. A number of organisations (and not just charities) began to send welcome booklets to their customers.

Fuelled by an invigorating response and some new information about our partners, in 1995 we completely rewrote the welcome booklet.

We know that half the people who give to WWF Canada once give a second time. However, when a partner gives a second time our retention rate is over 90 per cent. While these may seem like large numbers, research inside and outside the charitable sector shows this to be the case in many customer transactions. (Actually our retention rates are higher than those of many organisations.)

Our new welcome booklet needed to take a fresh approach. We must do all we can to make our partners feel that they have made the right choice and to work to see if we can get the second gift because, as they say, 'a donor isn't a donor until they give a second time'.

Step three: welcome booklet no. 2

Front cover
Bigger 'welcome' and 1-800 number featured.

There is new hope for the survival of the endangered burrowing owl as a result of World Wildlife Fund's work with landowners in Manitoba, Saskatchewan and Alberta.

1-800-26-PANDA

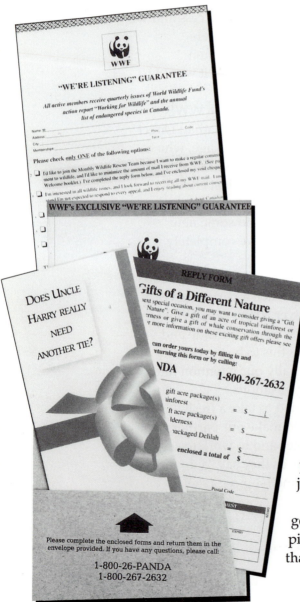

Inside front cover
Inserts were:

A new 'we're listening' guarantee. We rewrote the guarantee and added a number of important things, including a 'do not call me' option. We also repositioned the guarantee as the cornerstone of our relationship with our partners, not simply a justification for the mail we send.

A reply form – an attempt to get the second gift. This was a key piece of the new booklet. We knew that the best time to get the second

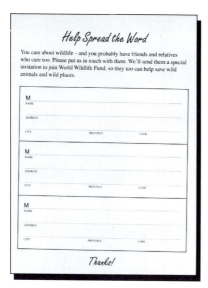

Help Spread the Word

You care about wildlife – and you probably have friends and relatives who care too. Please put us in touch with them. We'll send them a special invitation to join World Wildlife Fund, so they too can help save wild animals and wild places.

M
NAME

ADDRESS

CITY   PROVINCE   CODE

M
NAME

ADDRESS

CITY   PROVINCE   CODE

M
NAME

ADDRESS

CITY   PROVINCE   CODE

Thanks!

gift was right after the first one. But we felt that to ask for more so quickly might be a tad greedy. So we positioned a 'symbolic gift' as a more subtle and less threatening way to ask for a second contribution. Hence the leaflet 'Does Uncle Harry really need another tie?' It offers donors the chance to buy their friends and family some unusual but unquestionably useful presents: a rainforest, some Canadian wilderness, and so on.

We moved these inserts from the back to the front of the booklet to try and get an immediate second contact. Send back the guarantee, make a second gift – anything to strengthen the relationship at this crucial first stage.

The membership card with membership contacts on the back is put under tabs on the inside front cover.

Table of contents
One of the most common suggestions about the booklet was to include a table of contents to position the booklet as a handy reference – 'your personal guide to WWF'. Both versions of the booklet had page numbers.

TABLE OF CONTENTS

WWF

"We're Listening" Guarantee
"Gifts of a Different Nature" Reply Form   Front Pocket
Welcome to World Wildlife Fund Canada   Front Pocket
Getting Involved as a WWF Member   Pages 2 - 3
Conservation Triumphs and Achievements   Pages 4 - 5
How Your Donation Goes to Work   Pages 6 - 7
Endangered Species   Page 8
WWF in Canada and Around the World   Pages 9 - 10
You are an Important Part of the WWF Family   Page 11
Moving? Card   Page 12
Information Request Form   Back Pocket
New Member Survey   Back Pocket
                                                  Back Pocket

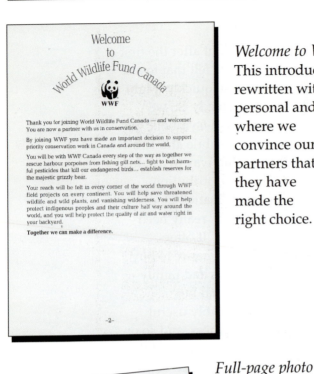

Welcome
to
World Wildlife Fund Canada

WWF

Thank you for joining World Wildlife Fund Canada — and welcome! You are now a partner with us in conservation.

By joining WWF you have made an important decision to support priority conservation work in Canada and around the world.

You will be with WWF Canada every step of the way as together we rescue harbour porpoises from fishing gill nets... fight to ban harmful pesticides that kill our endangered birds... establish reserves for the majestic grizzly bear.

Your reach will be felt in every corner of the world through WWF field projects on every continent. You will help save threatened wildlife and wild plants, and vanishing wilderness. You will help protect indigenous peoples and their culture half way around the world, and you will help protect the quality of air and water right in your backyard.

Together we can make a difference.

-2-

Welcome to WWF Canada
This introduction was completely rewritten with an eye to making it more personal and less institutional. This is where we convince our partners that they have made the right choice.

Around the world, wild cats are in jeopardy. Through conservation projects in many countries, WWF is working to save tigers, leopards, jaguars, cougars and other wild cats.

-3-

Full-page photo
We still believe in appealing to the right brain!

Getting Involved as a WWF Member

WWF

Your Membership Card
Your personal membership card is on the inside flap of this booklet. The card lists your membership number. You will want to refer to this number when taking advantage of exciting, exclusive offers — like our limited edition posters and t-shirts. On the back of your card you will find WWF's toll-free telephone number. Please keep your card in a handy place.

Newsletter
You ca...
quarte...
issue...
grams...

Mer
Many...
additi...
your b...
names...

Eart
You w...
ties ac...
Tower...
these e...
ness p...

Collecting names on petitions
You can collect signatures on WWF's petitions to show decision-makers that Canadians want our governments to protect our natural world. Almost 600,000 Canadians have signed WWF's Canadian Wilderness Charter expressing their desire to see Canada protect its vanishing wilderness.

Wildlife Rescue Team
You can help ensure a reliable income for wildlife by authorizing WWF to draw a donation each month from your chequing account or credit card. This is an easy way to spread your support of wildlife throughout the entire year, and help us respond to urgent wildlife issues the moment they arise.

Northern Stars Circle
The Northern Stars Circle recognizes the outstanding generosity of individuals who contribute a minimum of $1000 on an annual basis to WWF. Members of the Northern Stars Circle are offered unique benefits, including guided wilderness trips and briefings with WWF conservation staff.

Give WWF a gift that keeps on giving
How can you make a gift that keeps on giving? A bequest in your Will, a life insurance policy in WWF's name, or other assets can help save wildlife and wild places for future generations, and provide tax benefits to you as well.

To receive more information on any of the above, please see your Information Request form in the back pocket of this booklet.

-5-

Getting involved as a WWF member
These two pages about involvement with WWF are much more donor-centred. The second welcome book uses the word 'you' 70 times in the text of the booklet and another 64 times in the inserts. (The 'you count' was much lower in the first booklet.) This section tries hard to build a relationship between our partners and our mission.

Conservation Triumphs and Achievements

In the last year, World Wildlife Fund Canada funded over 130 priority conservation projects. Here are just some of the results we achieved during this period, thanks to the support of members like you.

In the Classroom...
Canadian Wilderness education materials reached over 400,000 students in over 11,000 schools and youth groups across Canada.

In Local Communities...
World Wildlife Fund Canada trained 3,052 people from over 26 communities in techniques of sustainable land use in the Arenal Conservation Area of Central America.

From Coast...
In the past year alone, close to 100 new parks were established in Canada including 317,291 hectares in British Columbia's Kitlope Valley.

To Coast...
Because of disturbances around the endangered piping plover's nests and the dune systems, WWF worked with local maritime communities to secure a summertime ban of destructive All Terrain Vehicles (ATVs) from the beaches of the Magdalene Islands.

In Canada...
Thanks to an intensive lobbying campaign, which included tens of thousands of signatures on a petition, WWF convinced the federal government to adopt stronger regulations to help stop the illegal trade in Canadian black bear gall bladders on international black markets.

And Around the World...
WWF Canada helped negotiate a debt-for-nature swap that converted $22.8 million of Costa Rican debt into $11.4 million of local currency for conservation projects.

-6-   -7-

Conservation triumphs and achievements

Our partners support us because we get conservation results and reporting those results to them is our greatest challenge. This centre spread looks at tangible results across Canada and around the world. 'Wow! This organisation is out there doing it.' In the earlier booklet our achievements were expressed as part of our programme structure. This is not interesting to partners – results are. The new section shows our partners that in the classroom, in the lab, on a mountain top, or in the boardroom they are with us every step of the way.

How your donation goes to work

Increasing competition for the charitable dollar – especially among organisations doing similar work –

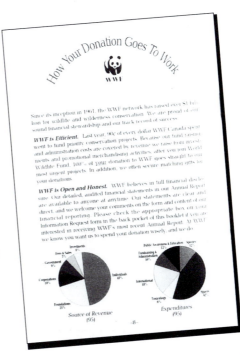

How Your Donation Goes To Work

WWF

Since its inception in 1961, the WWF network has raised over $1 billion for wildlife and wilderness conservation. We are proud of our sound financial stewardship and our track record of success.

WWF is Efficient. Last year, 90¢ of every dollar WWF Canada spent went to fund priority conservation projects. Because our fund raising and administration costs are covered by revenue we raise from investments and promotional merchandising activities, after you join World Wildlife Fund, 100% of your donation to WWF goes straight to our most urgent projects. In addition, we often secure matching gifts for your donations.

WWF is Open and Honest. WWF believes in full financial disclosure. Our detailed, audited financial statements in our Annual Report are available to anyone at anytime. Our statements are clear and direct, and we welcome your comments on the form and content of our financial reporting. Please check the appropriate box on your Information Request form in the back pocket of this booklet if you are interested in receiving WWF's most recent Annual Report. At WWF we know you want us to spend your donation wisely, and we do.

Source of Revenue (95)

Expenditures (95)

-8-

has prompted new awareness in efficiencies and value gained per dollar given. WWF Canada has an excellent story to tell and we take a whole page of our new booklet to tell it. This again confirms for our partners that they have made the right choice and addresses how WWF spends *their* money.

Endangered species
This section was rewritten to be more donor-friendly. Again, our first version was quite institutional in its approach – talking about committees, etc. The new text makes the point that our conservation programmes are closely linked and each one offers opportunities for our partners to take action. We also introduce our partners to the breadth of our conservation work using the subject they most associate us with – endangered species.

WWF in Canada and around the world

This section was also suggested by our partners who wanted to see that WWF was at work around the world on global issues.

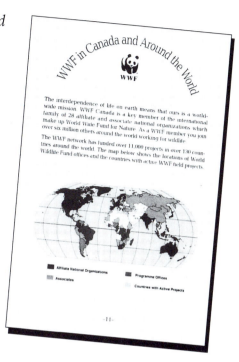

You are an important member of the WWF family.

This section used to be called 'things you should know'. It now looks at the elements of our customer service for partners. We shifted focus from us to them – moving from 'we' to 'you'.

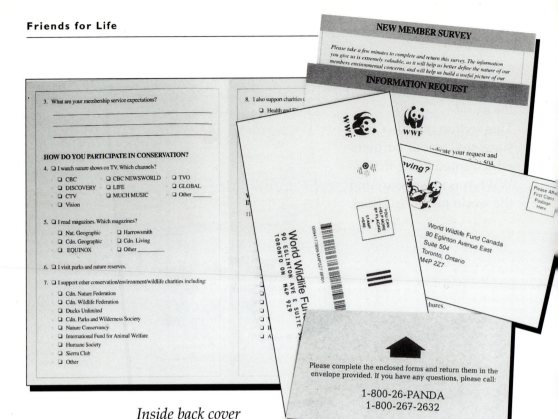

NEW MEMBER SURVEY

Please take a few minutes to complete and return this survey. The information you give us is extremely valuable, as it will help us better define the nature of our members environmental concerns, and will help us build a useful picture of our

INFORMATION REQUEST

3. What are your membership service expectations?

HOW DO YOU PARTICIPATE IN CONSERVATION?

4. ❑ I watch nature shows on TV. Which channels?
   - ❑ CBC
   - ❑ CBC NEWSWORLD
   - ❑ TVO
   - ❑ DISCOVERY
   - ❑ LIFE
   - ❑ GLOBAL
   - ❑ CTV
   - ❑ MUCH MUSIC
   - ❑ Other _____
   - ❑ Vision

5. ❑ I read magazines. Which magazines?
   - ❑ Nat. Geographic
   - ❑ Harrowsmith
   - ❑ Cdn. Geographic
   - ❑ Cdn. Living
   - ❑ EQUINOX
   - ❑ Other _____

6. ❑ I visit parks and nature reserves.

7. ❑ I support other conservation/environment/wildlife charities including:
   - ❑ Cdn. Nature Federation
   - ❑ Cdn. Wildlife Federation
   - ❑ Ducks Unlimited
   - ❑ Cdn. Parks and Wilderness Society
   - ❑ Nature Conservancy
   - ❑ International Fund for Animal Welfare
   - ❑ Humane Society
   - ❑ Sierra Club
   - ❑ Other

8. I also support charities
   - ❑ Health and E...

...ing?

World Wildlife Fund Canada
90 Eglinton Avenue East
Suite 504
Toronto, Ontario
M4P 2Z7

...dicate your request and ... 504

Please Affix First Class Postage Here

YOU CAN HELP MORE BY PLACING A STAMP HERE

World Wildlife Fund
90 EGLINTON AVE E SUITE
TORONTO ON M4P 9Z9

...hures.

Please complete the enclosed forms and return them in the envelope provided. If you have any questions, please call:

1-800-26-PANDA
1-800-267-2632

Inside back cover
Included a business reply envelope, moving card, information request and a new member survey – the survey was redesigned to ensure that we could do what we said!

Back cover
WWF mission and a note about production. The WWF merchandise section is omitted because we found that the stuff was simply not available and we risked creating expectations without being able to deliver any value.

World Wildlife Fund's Conservation Mission

WWF has three goals: the rich variety of life on Earth should be preserved; renewable natural resources like water, timber and fish should be used in sustainable ways; and pollution and the wasteful consumption of resources and energy must be reduced to a minimum.

Working towards these goals will also help ensure that people everywhere achieve adequate nutrition, security, and a decent quality of life.

WWF believes that people and nature can and must co-exist in harmony. WWF projects are designed to demonstrate this can be achieved. They are based on the best scientific evidence, and are undertaken with the involvement of other conservation groups, industries and local communities.

WWF

World Wildlife Fund Canada
90 Eglinton Ave. East, Suite 504, Toronto, Ontario M4P 2Z7
Charitable Registration # 0308270-54

This entire booklet, as well as the enclosed inserts, were printed on recycled paper using vegetable oil based inks.

Step four: questions for the next booklet

There are certainly other options we can provide for our partners. But are they important? Can we deliver them?

Should we address the competition more directly? Is it a fact that donations to other charities mean less for WWF? What should we do about this?

The relationship is between each partner and the mission. How can we strengthen this relationship?

Can we make the booklet easier to read?

Is there a role for endorsements from corporate partners?

At the time of writing this chapter, WWF is getting results from a comprehensive survey of our partners. Some significant challenges are coming from this work, which we will address in the next version.

> I was most impressed when I filled out the form inquiring about my desire for mail. I requested that little mail be sent to my home. You complied exactly. You listen, you implement, you care! That committed me to WWF for life more than anything you could have done. Thank you!
>
> Tracie Pasubio, Richmond Hill, Ontario

Seek and ye shall find

The good old days will never return. Nor should they. Charities will only accomplish their mission through a meaningful partnership with those who contribute to them. As charitable organisations become more accountable they will attract more fervent supporters, who in turn will contribute more.

In addition, by forming partnerships with individuals and institutions who share their mission, charities will discover better ways of expressing and even accomplishing their mission. These powerful new partnerships will not only be financially profitable, they will refine and focus the mission.

But this will only come with a new vigilance on looking after partners. It's all so simple really – it's all about listening. And we always learn more when we're listening.

Brief biographies

Most charities don't seem to listen to my requests to decrease the amount of mail they send. I'm amazed by the number of duplicate mailings I receive which tells me that most charities don't have their acts together. WWF is not like that. I feel like they really care about my donation and give me the personal attention I want.

Kathy Nosich, Toronto, Ontario, Canada

Gwen Chapman was the director of membership for WWF Canada from 1990 to 1996. During that time, Gwen directed an aggressive acquisition campaign and she developed an extensive house campaign. Gwen has moved on to the Canadian National Institute for the Blind where she continues to work her database marketing miracles.

David Love is the senior vice-president of WWF Canada, in charge of fundraising and communications. When he joined in 1979, WWF had a staff of three and a budget of $170,000. Today, WWF has a staff of 45 and a budget of $10 million.

Ana White is the new director of membership at WWF Canada. She joined in 1990 and was largely responsible for redrafting the welcome book from version one to two. Ana is constantly looking for ways to 'get the second gift' and to deepen the relationship between our partners and our mission.

A final note

We are keen to hear any comments from readers of this book. Please feel free to contact our director of membership at the address below.

WWF Canada
90 Eglinton Avenue East
Suite 504
Toronto
Ontario M4P 2Z7
Canada

Tel: +1 416 489 8800
Fax: +1 416 489 3611
E-mail: general@wwfcanada.org
Web address: http://www.wwfcanada.org

Children's Aid Direct

Taking the donors along too

In July 1996, a month before the public announcement, Feed the Children's executive director, David Grubb, wrote to donors with the following news.

> From the beginning of next month our lorries will leave our Reading warehouse carrying a new name on the outside. On the inside though they will still carry the same aid and they will still represent the same hope to children in desperate need all over the world.
>
> Over the last six years, supporters like you have helped us provide a lifeline for many thousands of children around the world. Six years on, the need for our collective help has never been greater. And never more diverse.
>
> We are still called upon to feed children but we support them in many other ways too. We now provide no fewer than 20 different kinds of essential aid – from delivering emergency food supplies in Bosnia, to reuniting families in Rwanda, or providing basic child welfare in Haiti.
>
> Of course children need food in emergencies, but they may also need shelter to protect them from the elements, shoes to cover their tired and blistered feet and care and affection to help them come to terms with their grief. And once the immediate crisis is over they need help to find their families, they need help to come to terms

with the trauma of war, and they need a pencil and paper to help them catch up with the education they've been missing. We recognised these needs some time ago. And for some time we've been attending to them.

That is why we are changing our name – to reflect the changing pattern of need and our changing response. From 1 August, Feed the Children will be called *Children's Aid Direct*.

We are still the same people, with the same passion running through our veins and the same unshakable sense of purpose. But we're now being called upon to do much more than feed children.

I believe our new name, *Children's Aid Direct*, embraces the wider range of our work. All of our activities are uniquely for the benefit of children and their immediate carers, proving aid to help children survive and recover from a crisis rather than encourage them to depend on our efforts in the longer term. And, importantly, the aid we provide is placed directly into the hands of those who need it most.

The fundraising described in the following pages took place before the name change, when the charity was already creating a considerable name for itself as Feed the Children Europe. Clearly they intend to make even more of a name for themselves in the future so from now on I'll refer to this remarkable organisation by its new and more appropriate title – Children's Aid Direct.

A small room in Reading

Gordon Bacon, a 53-year-old former policeman from Lanchester in county Durham, England and now Children's Aid Direct field director in Bosnia, former Yugoslavia, was midway through a lecture about general conditions in war-torn Bosnia and about the charity's work there. He stood before a great multicoloured map in an otherwise bare, cramped, but sunlit office above Children's Aid Direct's central warehouse in Reading, just west of London. It was late in 1994.

Packed with him in that unassuming office were 15 men, their ages ranging from early twenties to almost 70. Apart from being all male and all white, a more varied bunch of people could hardly be imagined – there were former teachers, professional truck drivers, an ex-civil servant, three people from an advertising agency, several from the ranks of the unemployed, a window cleaner, and others. With the exception of the agency people, who just happened to be visiting their client that day and had sat in at the meeting to see what they could pick up, the only thing the rest of the group had in common was that they had all applied to join Children's Aid Direct's aid delivery team as drivers to take the charity's regular truckloads of aid into Bosnia. Each of these men had voluntarily applied for one of the most dangerous jobs going. They had all come to see if they had what it takes to brave the risks that go with working directly in the front line of humanitarian assistance, doing what Children's Aid Direct was rapidly becoming famous for – taking the aid direct.

Or at least they all thought they wanted the job, until Gordon Bacon started talking.

Gordon Bacon must have been a wonderful policeman. Formerly a senior police officer with Durham County Constabulary and with experience fighting corruption in Hong Kong, he appears to be a candidate for the British 'bobby' sent straight down from central casting. Gordon is typical of the international image that the British policeman once enjoyed, a solid professional but still someone who everybody loves and trusts, someone you could tell your troubles or confess your misdemeanours to, sure of a fair hearing and a concerned and equally fair response. He exudes solidity, reliability and humanity. Good qualities for an aid worker too.

Every face in the audience was a study in concentration as they listened intently to the speaker's every word. It wasn't so much that they, interviewees and advertising agents alike, were each on their best behaviour, anxious to create a favourable impression. They were simply staggered by what Gordon Bacon was telling them.

A little historical background

Feed the Children was started in 1979 in the United States by a Southern Baptist preacher called Larry Jones. He had been shocked by the poverty and deprivation of children around him in America's Southern states and by the apparent contradiction at the same time of agricultural surpluses. He had the essentially simple but practically challenging vision of converting these surpluses and excesses directly into feeding programmes for poor children. His message was simple: 'Look, you've got poor people on your own doorstep and you can with your own unwanted produce do something about it.'

Over the past 17 years Larry Jones has built this concept into a multimillion-dollar organisation working in 19 countries across the world.

In July 1990, on the initiative of James Tysoe, at that time international vice-president, Feed the Children Europe was established with a start-up grant of $200,000 from the parent organisation and David Grubb, a former headmaster and national appeals director for the child-care agency Barnardo's, was appointed as its first director.

Feed the Children Europe was an independently established charity with its own distinctive personality, mission and terms of reference, working in partnership with its parent organisation rather than as a wholly owned subsidiary. To maintain its own personality and to preserve effective autonomy, the initial grant was promptly repaid and Feed the Children Europe (now Children's Aid Direct) began its own programme of expansion and development.

The charity started operations at a time of great international upheaval. This was the period when the maps of Eastern Europe and the Soviet Union were being hastily and frequently redrawn. It was a time when most of the

PAGE 24   Daily Mail, Monday, April 5, 1993

HOW ONE SMALL AGENCY STRUGGLES TO EASE BOSNIA'S SUFFERING

Children of war who cry out for a reason to smile

Haunted: Srebrenica's young victims

By ANNE BARROWCLOUGH

AT first glance they are a sorry sight — but it takes more than a glance to take in their plight.

Forget the straggly hair, the grubby faces and dirty fingernails.

It is the eyes that tell the true story. In them, there is a depth of suffering that many adults can only imagine.

These are the children of the former Yugoslavia. They have no home. Many have no families. Even the most basic rights have been denied them.

The desperate images have filled our TV screens. Who can forget the screams of little Amer Dsebo as a surgeon removed shrapnel from his back, without anaesthetic? Who can forget the crying child who fell from a truckful of refugees fleeing a besieged town, and who frantically ran beside the convoy to make sure he wasn't left behind? Who will ever forget the starving children of Srebrenica, scrabbling to eat straw?

Starving

They are children who have seen love, security and innocence replaced by deprivation, suffering and unspeakable horror.

They are exhausted. You see them in their hostels, sitting in tight circles, unmoving. They don't play, they don't laugh. They don't even cry any more. Their energy has been drained — not just by what they have witnessed, but because they are starving.

Fuel, food and blankets are in desperately short supply. Shoes are a distant memory. Despite the best efforts of aid agencies, despite relief convoys shuttling across tortuous mountain tracks, few civilians know when they will next eat.

Doctors are used to operating without anaesthetic, sometimes even without bandages. And it is getting no better. Only yesterday, Moslem leaders in Srebrenica refused to allow a UN convoy, which had delivered 78 tons of food to the mountain settlement, to evacuate civilians.

Feed The Children is a small agency. It has none of the power of the Red Cross or the UN. But it is one of dozens of smaller agencies quietly taking food and medical supplies to villages and towns that have nearly

Lost: A group of children band together in a world full of pain

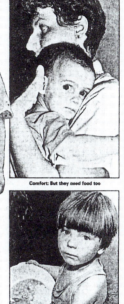

Comfort: But they need food too

A hot meal in a cold and cruel world

lost hope. Yesterday, aid workers from Feed The Children were loading up their small vans and trucks in Vitez to re-supply villages in Bosnia.

Since June last year, workers have been to Croatia, Slovenia and now to Bosnia. Supported by the Cheshire Regiment, who sometimes escort their convoys and always keep them up to date on troublespots and even regional weather, they have delivered aid into the most inaccessible areas of the country.

During the two years the agency has been in operation, in Eastern Europe and amongst the Kurds, they have learned the best types of aid for the starving. Food that needs no cooking and can be eaten straight from a container, 'family packs' that include toothpaste and soap because a full belly alone doesn't give self respect.

Feed The Children operators don't work in large convoys — they feel the safest method is one which may appear piecemeal but is actually highly organised.

They go silently, often under cover of darkness, and sometimes under mortar attack, in small vans, four-wheel-drives, even sometimes on bicycles, into villages where they leave their supplies with the promise they will return. And they do go back — returning to the same places time and again to ensure the people are not forgotten.

In these villages, where only the very young and the very old live, the effects of the war are made painfully clear. 'Over and over, you see

that the people have been totally reduced, spiritually and physically,' said David Grubb, executive director of the agency.

'Amongst the children, there is a tremendous passiveness and it is because they are shattered. They can't believe this is happening to them and they don't know where to go.

'Usually in refugee situations parents and teachers set up playgroups or try to create a schoolroom — but that doesn't happen there. The adults don't have the energy to do something like that, even though there are teachers amongst them.

'In a way, too, setting up a school in a refugee hostel would be admitting they were settling there, giving up hope of going back to their homes.'

So the children do nothing. 'It is

as if everything has slowed right down. The women and children sit in circles, very close together. They keep their voices low, and there is no sound of children running about or playing.

'Many of them have been kept in basements and shelters for months on end. If they do play, they play at war. They vandalise ruined buildings. When you see a 14-year-old sitting there empty, hollowed out, it is truly alarming.'

In parts of Bosnia and Croatia, experts believe that children have starved to death. In villages on the border of Serbia and Bosnia, Mr Grubb says the agencies know that children held there were dying of hunger.

Feed The Children is now making special efforts to get food into Srebrenica. It will remain in the Yugoslav republics until the hostilities end, and then it will stay on longer to help families' rehabilitation.

When he thinks of that future, Mr Grubb talks of playgrounds and toys — but it will be a long time before these children will play happily, in peace. Until then, at the very least, they can be helped to live.

The struggle to deliver life-saving aid into war-torn Bosnia has never been far from the front page.

conventional aid agencies were already widely stretched in areas more familiar to aid workers abroad and donors at home, such as the Sudan, Ethiopia, Cambodia, and other parts of the developing world.

Flexible, quick and effective

By an accident of history, the new charity was set up just when the Cold War was finally coming to an end, the Berlin Wall had at last come down, and a range of extreme social problems that had previously been so firmly suppressed was emerging on a confused and largely unprepared world.

From the very start Children's Aid Direct was plunged headlong into the centre of some of the most urgent and challenging needs the world had ever seen, in Romania, Bulgaria, and working to assist Kurdish refugees.

Children's Aid Direct was determined from the outset to be flexible, quick to respond and above all effective in its aid delivery. It was soon to have the chance to prove itself.

One of the early destinations for Children's Aid Direct's help became clear when Albania suddenly opened its doors after decades of silent and determined insularity. The death of the last great communist dictator, Stalin's friend Enver Hoxa, finally allowed the world to see behind that country's ideologically driven standoffishness. And what emerged was a country in dire poverty, its infrastructure non-existent, its flimsy framework of government shattered, with huge chunks of its population in desperate need. And as always, the greatest need was among children.

There was a great deal else disturbing the world at that time. David Grubb realised that he needed the help of the media if he was ever to enlist the help of the people of Britain. They had to know what was going on.

Behind closed doors

The major coup came when the charity secured the support of Britain's *Sunday Times*, who launched its own appeal for Albania through a major and very powerful feature article in which it promised to channel funds directly to those in need through the then-unknown charity Children's Aid Direct.

The appeal was an instant success – 10,000 people responded immediately and the appeal went on to raise more than £1 million. Thousands of British schoolchildren collected writing materials, school furniture and enough money for three lorryloads of new books. They were touched by news that in Albanian schools children lacked even pencils and paper to share. In the months that followed, Children's Aid Direct distributed £3.5 million worth of food, medicine and clothing. The story was featured three nights running on BBC television news. BBC's Bill Hamilton described the speed of delivery as a miracle.

Children's Aid Direct suddenly felt it was on the map. David Grubb and James Tysoe now had sufficient confidence to recruit a permanent member of staff to head up the marketing of what they were determined would be a significant and distinctive cause.

In time, Stewart Crocker, formerly development director at the Royal Agricultural College, was appointed to the position. By now some 13,000 people had given to a variety of urgent appeals. But no one kidded themselves that the charity possessed 13,000 donors. Most of the people who had responded had very little knowledge of, and even less loyalty to, what was then, Feed the Children. They had given their money to Albania, or to Romania, or to the *Sunday Times*, or whatever. They had given to feed children in need, not to Feed the Children the charity.

Developing meaningful, lasting and fruitful relationships with these donors and with the thousands upon thousands who would come after them was to become a priority, even an obsession, for Stewart Crocker.

Developing a unique proposition

One of the ideas Children's Aid Direct borrowed from its parent organisation was crucial in helping the charity to distinguish itself from similar organisations. This was the notion of direct delivery or, as it became known, 'taking the aid direct'.

In the USA the charity ran a substantial trucking operation and this direct and tangible activity clearly had strong donor appeal. Children's Aid Direct determined not to run a road haulage operation – that wasn't to be its core business – but to make direct delivery of services its unique selling proposition.

Stewart Crocker explains, 'We could see a great deal of mileage, if you'll forgive the pun, in focusing clearly on the direct delivery of aid, but we didn't feel that limiting ourselves to trucking would be helpful. Instead delivery has to be a means to an end. We need to think broadly about the best, most cost-effective means of getting from A to B.'

But one thing Children's Aid Direct did identify was the public's willingness to donate goods, particularly foodstuffs. Whereas most agencies decline this type of aid as troublesome, inappropriate, or not commercially viable, Children's Aid Direct has exploited this gap to tremendous effect.

Although its principal purpose is the procurement and delivery of urgently needed, even life-saving, primary aid, everyone at Children's Aid Direct believes that if the agency is only concerned about meeting immediate needs, if its only role is answering today's urgent request, then it really isn't fulfilling its proper function and potential.

Unless it is also trying, in a catalytic way by influencing other individuals and organisations, to close the currently enormous gap that exists between the demand for emergency aid and its supply, most Children's Aid Direct people will feel they are only partially achieving their mission.

In the long term, what Children's Aid Direct seeks to do is to shift public opinion towards much more sharing of resources and a much fairer distribution if not of wealth then at least of basic needs.

That's why, whatever the practical difficulties, Children's Aid Direct is anxious not to turn off or to deny the public the opportunity to give relevant goods – food, clothing, consumer durables – whatever has a use or value in the emergency area. Demand for aid is continuing to rise faster than supply, so Children's Aid Direct believes that if the public is prepared to give in this way then Children's Aid Direct should be flexible enough and resourceful enough to enable them to do it. If it tells the public it can't be done then it is going the wrong way.

'The important issue for us', says Stewart, 'is that the donated goods need to meet the priority needs of the intended recipients, and that they should be more cost-effective at the point of delivery than goods manufactured near to the need – or even in the country.

'Of course, we are dealing with public donations, even if those gifts are not always money. So the charity's central duty is to add value to what it receives, to be cost-effective, to get the best possible value.'

If Children's Aid Direct can make cost-effective use of donated aid, it might just help to narrow the gap a little and, ultimately, to do what every charity should be trying its utmost to do – put itself out of business, make the aid supply business redundant.

In enabling people to give what they have the charity accepts that it must undertake a constant process of informing and educating them. The items that are really most needed overseas on the whole have to be bought. They are just not available in people's wardrobes. Children's Aid Direct doesn't need to ask for clothes because clothing is readily available and, generally, supply exceeds demand. The urgent need is for hygiene materials and food, particularly dried food.

Within these reasonable limits, if you have what is needed to provide emergency aid to a hungry child, Children's Aid Direct will undertake to take it there for you with all possible speed. All you have to do is to give.

In practice, the charity quickly learned that it needed to operate a mixed-load policy of carefully planned proportions between donated and procured goods to ensure that the aid it delivered was always demand-led rather than supply-driven.

Stewart Crocker says, 'We have developed skills in buying particular goods at best prices, often heavily discounted prices, to complement donated aid and ensure that what we are delivering is what the people we are helping really need, rather than what we happen to have in our warehouses.'

Clearly this distinction encourages charities towards money collection, with all its advantages of flexibility and transferability, rather than donated goods that inevitably depend on what the public is prepared to part with at the time.

'Wherever possible and providing it is appropriate', says Stewart, 'we encourage people to donate what they can. People love to do it. It provides valuable resources that otherwise would not be donated, it is a channel for people's spontaneous compassion that too often is prematurely closed. And often donated gifts can be a life-saver if carefully monitored and closely controlled.

'Sometimes the very success of this kind of fundraising (aid-raising) can be almost overwhelming.'

In the autumn of 1992 one of Britain's commercial television companies, Granada Television, decided to try to interest its viewers in donating humanitarian aid for direct delivery to people suffering in former Yugoslavia.

Stewart takes up the story. 'Granada got in touch with us as one of the few agencies able to offer the facility of direct delivery. We were attracted both by the potential to procure substantially more aid than we were currently sending and by the opportunity for valuable publicity.

'We estimated that a few minutes of prime air time might lead to 30,000 parcels of donated aid plus additional cash donations of £30,000, which would be sufficient to pay for the delivery of the aid and more.'

In the event Granada gave three minutes of air time to the appeal. It also arranged for British Rail's subsidiary Red Star Parcels to accept the donated goods and deliver them to Children's Aid Direct's warehouses free of charge. This removed any financial disincentive that might have discouraged would-be donors from giving their aid.

'The great British public responded with 150,000 parcels, five times what we'd anticipated. It was truly over-whelming. Red Star simply couldn't cope and had to stop accepting them.

'It was a marvellous, marvellous response. But it left us with a huge problem. We hadn't raised anything like the cash we would need to transport this mountain of generosity to former Yugoslavia. Having done its bit, we couldn't interest Granada in paying the bill, so we had to find the money ourselves.

'It was a moment of crisis. Here we were faced with a need to send out three truckloads of aid a day when we had budgeted for just one truckload a week.'

After some worrying days, during which a variety of potential sources were explored, the charity eventually secured a contribution of £150,000 to the transport costs from Britain's Overseas Development Administration. The justification used to secure the grant was that the ODA would be funding the will of the public at large. (A fairly good justification, as it happens, for this kind of charitable support.)

But the experience highlighted some of the peculiar difficulties and risks associated with appealing for donated goods.

'Not only was the volume unpredictable, the quality was too', Stewart says ruefully, 'and this time the variation didn't

work in our favour. Our televised appeal clearly asked for
food items and some hygiene materials but what we
received from the public was a high proportion of clothing,
not all of it very usable.

'It demonstrates that often people will give what they
want to give, rather than what you might ask for.'

Carried too far this tendency can lead to high-bulk loads
with low practical value in terms of delivered aid. And of
course the cost of delivery doesn't reduce, so it is possible
for an agency such as Children's Aid Direct to find itself
paying more to deliver the aid than the aid itself is worth.
Clearly aid agencies have to protect themselves against such
a dilemma. This further illustrates the limitations of donated
goods as a form of aid.

Lorryloads of enthusiasm

Such experience taught Children's Aid Direct many valuable
lessons. It realised the potential power of the public's
response with donated goods, and the need to be realistic
about how specific the request for goods could be, and with
what likely result. The charity also accepted that before it
could guarantee delivery of donated aid it had to have
sufficient funds available to pay the delivery costs.

Stewart explains, 'This is not something donors always
appreciate. Shortly after the Granada appeal – in fact as a
direct spin-off from it – dairy roundsmen in Northern
Ireland took it upon themselves to collect food from the
doorsteps of their customers, asking them first of course.
Their intentions were the best in the world, but it landed us
with a headache. I remember they phoned joyfully one day
to say they had eight containerloads of food for us to collect.
It was brilliant and we couldn't help but be carried along by
their enthusiasm. But the cost of transporting eight
containers of food from Northern Ireland to Yugoslavia is
not inconsiderable.'

Once again Children's Aid Direct found an institutional

As winter approached in Britain, Feed the Children hit the public with a vivid description of what that might mean for Bosnia's children.

donor to pay the transport and the spirit of voluntary aid was saved from any embarrassment. Nobody wants to say to dedicated donors making sacrifices of their own worldly goods, 'Sorry we can't take that. It's no use to us.' So perhaps without realising it, Children's Aid Direct was beginning to make a habit of delivering. And word gets around. Thus are reputations formed.

'Not long after the Northern Ireland incident we had a call from the National Dairy Council, who had heard about the initiative of their colleagues across the water and wanted to replicate it across the country.

'We estimated that they could expect to collect £4 million worth of aid, but that to transport it to where it was needed would require a further £1 million to cover all logistical and transport costs. We simply didn't have that kind of money. So we put it to them that they would have to find those costs up front.

'We're working on it. It could still happen. But the important thing for Children's Aid Direct is that having learned from past experience we were able to see and decide what we could do, and what we couldn't.'

You can rely on donors

Turning adversity to advantage has always been a strength of Children's Aid Direct. The low point in the tale of the Granada/Red Star avalanche of goodwill parcels came at a time when instead of sending just one truckload per week three full containerloads were leaving Reading every day, heading for former Yugoslavia. The cost was crippling Children's Aid Direct and it appeared inevitable to the charity's senior management that, at a time when the need in former Yugoslavia had never been greater, they would be forced to close their doors, to suspend the entire aid programme because they didn't have the money to pay for the trucks to get it through.

In this moment of despair Children's Aid Direct reviewed

the situation at a meeting with its direct marketing agency, Burnett Associates. Much of the talk at these meetings in past months had centred on the need to build donor relationships based on trust and open communication. What more natural and more obvious place to turn to at such a time of need than to the donors, to Children's Aid Direct's friends?

Marc Nohr, creative director at Burnett Associates, takes up the story. 'Here, if ever there was one, was a good reason to contact donors directly. The need could hardly have been more urgent, or more clear. But there were two complications. Firstly, the normal November appeal mailing was already at an advanced stage of production and was scheduled to land on donors' doormats in just three or four weeks. The risk was that an emergency appeal so close would dilute response to what was expected – and budgeted – to be an important money-maker.

'The second complication was simply timing. We had to get this emergency message to donors quickly or it would be too late for them to help. Children's Aid Direct's relief programme would already be stopped and would be difficult and expensive to restart.

'We thought about using the telephone but Children's Aid Direct was cautious about the suitability of telephone fundraising and we wanted to test it first. It seemed too big a risk to take, particularly as we didn't have a trained and experienced network of callers in place.

'Then – at that meeting – we came up with the idea of the Telemessage. The Telemessage is a trademark of British Telecom and is, in effect, the successor of the inland telegram. Guaranteed next-day delivery, its appearance is inevitably important and its message often urgent, so opening and reading it is as much of a certainty as can ever be. It was simple, immediate and uncomplicated. The only trouble was it had never been used with a reply coupon before and neither we nor Children's Aid Direct could be sure that it would work.

'Success would depend on a number of factors – and everything had to happen very quickly.'

Exceptionally quick response and turn-round times were to become a consistent hallmark of Children's Aid Direct's direct marketing activities, with spectacular results.

On this occasion, just about everything went right. The Telemessage emergency appeal was written within a day. British Telecom was contacted and not only agreed to include a reply form but offered to produce the Telemessages at no cost, charging Children's Aid Direct just normal postage.

The short and carefully worded emergency message to donors was delivered through their doors just five days after that meeting at the agency. Faced with this threat to the programme and offered the chance to keep the lorries running, Children's Aid Direct's donors reacted with predictable, immediate and generous help. The appeal was an astounding success, far exceeding either Children's Aid Direct or its agency's expectations.

Two weeks later these same donors also received their November letter, and a further urgent request for funds. Response to this second appeal exceeded expectations too.

Proof indeed that if the reason and the explanation are good enough, donors will respond – and happily.

With hindsight, it's obvious

Now I know I said a few paragraphs back that we weren't sure it would work, and that later I contradicted myself by claiming that Children's Aid Direct's donors responded with predictable generosity, but both these statements are true. Donors – real donors – can be relied upon to respond generously in times of need. But so many other factors can affect response, and for a new charity like Children's Aid Direct absolutely nothing can be taken for granted. Also the Telemessage hadn't been used like this before. Perhaps donors would consider it offensive, one marketing ruse too far.

So maybe it would be more accurate to say that, with hindsight, Children's Aid Direct's donors behaved predictably.

Ladies and gentlemen of the press

In these early and formative days, Children's Aid Direct was also learning valuable lessons about the role and motivations of the press – how they could make or mar an appeal and how the secret of successful press involvement was to coincide their interests with those of Children's Aid Direct.

Of course it has to be remembered that the advertising departments of the British press are among Children's Aid Direct's best and most consistent donors through their gifts of heavily discounted advertising space. But such generosity is the province of different functions, different departments, different people. The journalists and editors who compile and present the news often can be equally generous and concerned but generally have their own quite different, selfish agenda – but one that can be of great value to such as Children's Aid Direct.

Being attuned and responsive to the needs and interests of the press is a vital part of Children's Aid Direct's fund-raising strategy. As in most other areas of its work, rapid response is essential. To have a clearly defined and effective rapid-response strategy in place demands a particular kind of commitment and, of course, round-the-clock availability.

That strategy is perhaps best illustrated by an anecdote that shows rapid response at its best, both in advertising and in press development. It is the story of the Grand National fiasco of 1993.

No racing certainty

The Grand National is Britain's favourite horse-race, its premier steeplechase. Bookmakers everywhere love it because this one event never fails to bring out the punter that lurks within all of us and the bookies inevitably make a killing when a nation of amateur gamblers risks a flutter on the gee-gees.

This collective gambling fever appears without fail each spring, when half the country gathers round its television sets to watch the race and count its winnings, or losses.

Without fail, that is, until the Grand National of 1993, which will go down in the history books as the Grand National that never was, the race that ended before it started in utter shambles, watched by an incredulous nation – a grand national disaster.

Innumerable action replays, post-mortems and even an official enquiry established what went wrong and duly apportioned blame and meted out retribution.

But to the millions who watched from home it just looked like a nasty case of over-excitement. A bunch of jittery horses mounted by jittery riders making a false start, thanks to a very jittery starter person, which then couldn't be fully stopped. As only half the field noticed the false start and the others couldn't be recalled, the event ended in chaos, leaving millions of pounds of punters' money where it was always expected to be, with the bookies. Only this time they had to return it.

Sitting in his London office watching the unfolding fiasco was a very bright journalist from the *Daily Mail*. He was the first to realise the improbability of all those returned bets.

Adversity to advantage

Here was a great story. All those disappointed punters had already psychologically said goodbye to their money. No one really believes they can beat the bookies, all they cling to is a forlorn hope – a rank outsider.

How brilliant it would be, thought the enterprising journalist, to unite this inevitable headline grabber of the next day with another media hogger of the moment, the crisis in Bosnia. So there and then, as the dazed race marshals were still picking up the pieces, he came up with the only winner of the day, the idea of returned bets for Bosnia.

The concept was simple but stunning – adversity to advantage. All those millions of returned, useless bets could be immediately applied to save starving children in Bosnia. And the orchestrator and originator of the event would be – the *Daily Mail*. The newspaper that cares – or whatever. Tomorrow's extensive coverage of the Grand National disaster would instead be a conduit for a spontaneous outpouring of concern and assistance. A message of hope, not failure.

Some time over the rest of that Saturday, the story was 'sold' to the *Daily Mail* and it became front-page, headline news scheduled for the very next edition on Monday morning.

At the same time someone realised the need for a strategic alliance with an organisation already operating in former Yugoslavia who could deliver the expected aid to the children who needed it. The result was an early morning phone call to David Grubb and to Stewart Crocker to secure their co-operation. They were only too happy to oblige.

Stewart Crocker takes up the story, 'We put the whole appeal together during the Sunday and one of the things the *Daily Mail* appreciated about us was that we reacted immediately and worked very closely with them to get all the details sorted out during the Sunday, ready to launch it on the Monday.

'On Sunday afternoon I rang our agency and briefed them to prepare an ad, hoping if we moved quickly we could get something in Tuesday's papers when the *Mail* would start to develop the story – and their readers' response – in earnest. By early Monday morning we had a choice of three ads ready to run in all the other nationals to support the massive coverage promised by the *Daily Mail*.'

At this stage, it hadn't occurred to the *Mail* that the story 'had legs' (in other words, it could run and run). David and Stewart found themselves selling the newspaper the idea of further follow-up, particularly to report on how the money was being spent in the field – and what it was achieving.

'We encouraged them to send a reporter and a photographer to Bosnia who would report back through stories and pictures that would keep the appeal going. So we were making the most of the photogenic nature of our work, keeping it very visible. As a result the *Daily Mail* was encouraged to keep the story running for several weeks, which wasn't the original idea.'

Soon Children's Aid Direct had raised more than £200,000 from several thousand new donors, or rather, at this stage, responders (once-only givers).

The *Daily Mail*'s massive and sustained support was much appreciated. But it was also frustrating at times and again several lessons were learned. There seemed to be a new journalist on the story every few days, which made maintaining interest and involvement quite difficult.

And at a crucial time, when Children's Aid Direct felt everything was in place for a concluding feature thanking readers for what they'd done and illustrating what had been achieved through human interest case histories, the *Daily Mail*'s interest waned.

'It clearly reached the stage of being old news for the journalists,' says Stewart, 'and there was nothing we could do to resurrect it. We weren't ungrateful of course, far from it. The appeal had done an enormous amount of good.'

But the *Daily Mail* had also benefited, generating lots of quality copy at low cost while promoting its own image. Stewart Crocker and his colleagues are aware of this but accept it without resentment.

'To work at its best the relationship between charities and media has to be mutually beneficial. They have their jobs to do and if it isn't news it won't work for them, or for us. So we recognise that all newspapers are essentially in it for themselves and if they can do some good while telling their

Yesterday's media urged readers and listeners to use their returned Grand National bets to feed starving children in former Yugoslavia. Here's how **you** can help today.

A grand national gesture

Let your returned bets feed starving children in Bosnia

Every £1.00 you give will be used by Feed the Children to deliver at least £2.00 worth of food aid directly to starving babies and children in war-torn Bosnia.

Donation line 0891 234 240

Feed the Children, 1 Priory Avenue, Caversham, Reading RG4 7SE. Registered charity number 803236.

Yes I'll make a grand gesture, and let my returned bet save a starving child. 040
Here's my donation £50 ☐ £20 ☐ £10 ☐ £5 ☐ £ ☐ (other)

(Please make your cheque payable to Feed the Children) OR debit my ☐ Visa ☐ Access card

CARD NUMBER | | | | | | | | | | | | | | | |

EXPIRY DATE | | | SIGNATURE

NAME (BLOCK CAPITALS)

ADDRESS

POSTCODE TELEPHONE

Please send to: Feed the Children, Freepost, Reading RG4 7BR.

FEED THE CHILDREN
TAKING THE AID DIRECT

A response to what was a comparatively small national disaster. The campaign raised at least £200,000.

stories then that has to be a better use than the press usually enjoys.'

Building loyalty

But some newspapers, or rather some editors, can be very short-sighted. They can appear to have little interest beyond the next day's paper and often, having started an appeal, will offer their readers no follow-up, immediately moving on to the next breaking news.

Stewart thinks they could learn a lesson or two from fundraisers.

'Sometimes the press doesn't seem to understand the importance of developing relationships at all. They haven't yet grasped the value of building loyalty with their readers, particularly when it comes to encouraging humanitarian aid. Just as we have a duty to report back to donors, and in doing so we encourage continued involvement and loyalty, I'm sure it is the same with a newspaper's readers.'

There is some truth in this. How often has your interest been piqued to read in your newspaper of Mrs So and So hanging on to life by a thread after some dreadful incident and then that's the last you ever hear of it. Mrs So and So and her life-and-death struggle drop silently and entirely from view. She is no longer news, which isn't quite the same as saying people are no longer interested. So far it has always been that way and few readers can see any point in complaining. Perhaps, as with some fundraisers a few years ago, some newspapers haven't yet realised the strength of people power.

But the Grand National appeal clearly showed that this kind of fundraising is (please forgive yet another pun) a matter of horses for courses. The great lumbering battleships of established international charities could not have taken advantage of that kind of opportunity. It takes a nippy little speedboat like Children's Aid Direct, unencumbered by lots of baggage and undeterred by the need to take risks, to reap these kinds of benefits.

Again, however, experience showed that you don't always get what you ask for.

Although there had been some donations, the original request for returned bets from the Grand National hardly worked at all, neither from the press advertisements nor from the editorial coverage. The distinction of returned money being redeployed to help children seemed to have almost no donor appeal.

But thousands of people did respond, simply because these articles had highlighted a need. They saw, and they gave. (It may be that the punters and the donors are quite different types of people, united only by the fact that they read the same daily paper.)

How many of them can be developed by Children's Aid Direct into subsequent donors and from there into regular and loyal supporters remains to be seen. But the signs are quite good.

Developing a personality

The ability to mount a rapid and effective response is clearly a part of Children's Aid Direct's personality, part of its so-called unique selling proposition (USP), that which helps distinguish it from other similar but different organisations that might also be calling for a donor's help.

Another part of that USP is Children's Aid Direct's deliberate decision to stay exclusively in primary aid and not to take the tempting but possibly diverting option of extending its interests into long-term development.

The charity believes it has developed specialist expertise in a distinct and very important niche area. This enables it to project a sharply focused image that has positive fundraising advantages. To further diversify would put this advantage at risk.

The single focus also has other fundraising advantages, not least of which is the availability of donated supplies from individuals and the corporate sector, as well as generous discounts on transport costs that enable Children's Aid Direct to claim that it can convert every £1 of cash donations it receives from supporters into at least £2 worth of delivered aid overseas. In addition, the charity can use its donors' money to unlock government funds of at least matching proportions. The attractiveness of this proposition is not lost on either Children's Aid Direct or its supporters.

Strategy first, structure second

The Children's Aid Direct proposition has very broad appeal. It lends itself to a wide range of audiences and every possible type of fundraising. At a very early stage in its development, the Children's Aid Direct board decided that planning strategic priorities would be crucial. The new charity simply couldn't hope to tackle all its possible opportunities at once.

So Stewart recommended that its first priority should be to build and develop a donor file principally through direct marketing. Only once that activity was firmly established and running smoothly would the charity move on to its second priority, which was identified as community fundraising. Then, when community fundraising was similarly successfully established, the charity would be able to move on to its third identified priority – corporate fundraising.

Stewart Crocker explains, 'We believed that it was really important to think about this strategy before any formal fundraising was started, to decide what we should *not* be doing as much as what we should be doing. New charities have to resist the temptation to try to do everything at once. If they don't the chances are they will end up doing everything badly.

'So when the strategy has been decided first, then the necessary structure naturally comes second.'

With its direct donor programme well established,

Children's Aid Direct began to implement its original strategic decision to develop community fundraising.

The emphasis for the new staff being recruited for this activity was again on developing effective one-to-one relationships, but this time increasingly on a face-to-face basis.

Now stronger and with sound experience behind it, the charity is confident enough to move forward on more than one front at the same time.

'We now have a growing team of people', says Stewart Crocker, 'working on one-to-one relations in community fundraising. We are also starting to develop a strategy to work with corporate supporters.'

This activity will help to tie in Children's Aid Direct's continuing work with a small number of specialist suppliers as well as large corporate and institutional donors.

'We have taken on a corporate liaison manager whose prime objective is to develop our relationship with 12 substantial companies, many of which are already supplying our aid. He is also looking at the most effective ways to involve employees in fundraising, how to make best use of our senior people, celebrity contact, and so on.'

Creating an identity

Children's Aid Direct's supporters are not very different from those found on most charities' books. They tend to be well educated, from the social categories B and C1, compassionate people with some disposable income, promiscuous in their giving to a wide range of charities, but probably with a discernible preference for overseas aid or basic needs causes.

The trouble and the challenge for Children's Aid Direct in its formative years (then called Feed the Children, of course) was that while these same people would know immediately if you asked them whether or not they supported Oxfam, or Save the Children, or ActionAid they most probably would not know that they were, or once had been, supporters of Feed the Children.

For any new organisation, creating a positive and lasting identity among this kind of target audience is a formidable and daunting challenge. For Feed the Children improving its recognition and reception among donors was a top priority.

'We know from telephoning, for example, some of our large donors', explains Stewart, 'who, perhaps, have failed to return their Gift Aid forms, that many of them don't remember our name at all, even some of those who have given us several hundreds of pounds.

'The name Feed the Children didn't particularly help. We sounded more like an action, an activity, rather than an organisation. It was only when we reminded them that it was for former Yugoslavia, or Albania that the memory came back.'

Stewart and his colleagues all hope that the change of name will make a difference. Clearly such distinctions, which are of great importance to emerging organisations like Children's Aid Direct, are of little import or interest to donors. This proves the well-worn fundraisers' maxim that donors give to the cause not the organisation, and organisations should be very careful not to come between the donor and the cause.

Stewart Crocker recognises that from the donor's point of view this set of priorities is no bad thing. So his aim is to position the organisation as a strong brand identity, with a clear personality and proved efficiency as a reliable conduit of aid, a good steward of its donors' resources.

'We're at something of a disadvantage', asserts Stewart, 'when establishing ourselves in a donor's mind. Some causes are almost synonymous with the organisation's name, for example CPRE, the Council for the Protection of Rural England. If you care about the preservation of the British countryside, then that's the organisation you'll support. But that will never be the case for Children's Aid Direct because the cause the people will be supporting will be constantly changing as we move from one emergency, or trouble spot, to another. It's part of our mission, in a way, to be deliberately changing. So I think our building of relationships will always be a tough and uphill task.'

To remedy, this Children's Aid Direct is concentrating on building its brand personality, consolidating and publicising its achievements in the field and communicating its successes and its unique approach to its donors and supporters through a carefully planned and structured programme of relationship fundraising.

Although press advertising is Children's Aid Direct's most cost-effective and largest method of donor recruitment, postal communication is by far the most widely used method of relationship building. To some extent this is a matter of necessity as much as of choice. The charity's growth in its first years had been spectacular, and was largely demand-driven rather than planned. The pressures this placed on the small staff were considerable and recruitment of additional staff barely kept up with the rate of growth.

So many of the longer-term and more personal forms of relationship building, such as one-to-one meetings, receptions and even detailed telephone work, were inevitably put on a back burner until the rate of expansion showed signs of slowing.

Hence the initial emphasis on postal communication. Within that area a great deal of attention has been placed on customer service, thank yous, upgrading, reactivation and on ensuring donors receive relevant, interesting and well-targeted communications.

At the start of 1993, Children's Aid Direct had some 15,500 donors on its list. By the end of the year that number had grown to 319,200. On average these donors were not recruited at a cost to the organisation, but at a net contribution of £2 – each and every one of them. A year later the total had risen to 50,200 and 13,000 responders had been lapsed (18 months since their last gift).

Lively appeal mailings retain the style and pace of news stories.

A justifiable investment?

Despite this happy situation, Children's Aid Direct still has
to think twice before spending its donors' gifts on apparent
luxuries such as donor development initiatives. If the charity
decides to divert funds into such activities as welcome and
thank you strategies, it has to be able to justify that decision
not only to its donors, but to children in need.

Children's Aid Direct's senior management is absolutely
convinced that this sort of investment in building
relationships with donors is not only justifiable, it is
essential.

'Fundamental to building those relationships', says
Stewart, 'is the commitment to treat everyone who relates to
Children's Aid Direct with respect and courtesy. That means
thanking them promptly when they offer any sort of support
whether it's time, donated goods, or money, or anything
else.

'So we have set up a policy where we acknowledge
different gifts in a structured and very consistent way. We
telephone those people whose size of gift makes them
eligible to give it under Gift Aid – always on the same day
we receive the gift. People are delighted. It gets the
relationship off to a superb start, so there's really no
question about whether it's justified or not. We *like* to do it.'

Children's Aid Direct is anxious to strike the right
balance between conserving its scarce resources and
investing adequately in the materials it needs to effectively
develop donor relationships.

The charity is concerned not to save money, or to cut
corners, or to economise for the sake of it, but to get genuine
value for money.

Stewart continues, 'Even if we were spending to recruit
new donors, I think that investment in donor development
would be essential. In fact, probably more so because it is
essential to protect and preserve your initial investment
when getting the donor.

'Not to do so would be rather like buying an expensive motor car then leaving it outside in all weathers, because you couldn't afford a garage roof – or at least a tarpaulin.'

Often these initiatives lend themselves to sponsorship. When Children's Aid Direct wanted to upgrade and expand its flagship publication, the annual report, it went in search of a sponsor before committing itself to the additional expenditure.

'But we had a very clear picture', says Stewart, 'of what we wanted to do and what we wanted to say, before we asked any potential sponsors. We wanted to tell our story in a passionate, emotive, highly readable way that would inspire our readers, literally, to share our dreams and to help turn those dreams into reality.

'So we showed our sponsors exactly what we had in mind and our proposition to them, therefore, became very straightforward and quite appealing. We asked them to make our achievements and dreams for the future become tangible, in print. They became the catalyst. For a comparatively small investment they could play a vital part in making those dreams come true.'

So Children's Aid Direct now has an excellent communication and recruitment document for very little cost (most sponsors won't cover *all* costs associated with a large publication such as an annual report).

Not only does their new-look report encourage Children's Aid Direct's staff and provide an easy-to-use, comprehensive briefing for journalists and new contacts from a variety of sources, it also has two additional vitally important and very valuable functions according to Stewart.

'Through our annual report we report back in detail to our donors in an accessible and attractive way, reassuring them that their gifts of the past year have been well used and that their continuing support is justified. That reassurance alone would directly repay any cost in producing the report, but its additional prime function in my view is its effectiveness as a tool to actually recruit more new donors, particularly in the corporate sector – companies and grant-making trusts.'

Trustees of foundations, company directors, journalists and editors – these are all just people in disguise and, like all people, they respond to an emotive, moving story and to powerful, appealing images. And they will give generously if they are moved by what they see and what they read.

The other major publication in Children's Aid Direct's communications strategy is its appropriately named newsletter, *Feedback*, which is produced four times each year to coincide with and support appeals. The timing of these is dependent on events but they are at roughly quarterly intervals.

Feedback has two purposes. As its name suggests, it reports back directly, in newsy style, on how donors' funds have been used and what, through the charity, they have achieved. Its equally important function is to vividly support the accompanying appeal letter and reinforce its key messages, describing in detail the subjects of the current appeal. Children's Aid Direct achieves huge responses to its now quite extensively segmented appeal mailings to donors and the feedback to *Feedback* is almost universally positive.

As the charity has become more sophisticated it has produced tape recordings of short, simulated radio documentaries, which are sent with *Feedback* to key segments (mainly those who have given to that appeal area before). The first featured Gordon Bacon in Bosnia. The second was an interview with David Grubb on the crisis in Rwanda. Tests show that they lift response.

In 1995 the Children's Aid Direct database was segmented by gender. Women were sent a proposition designed specifically to appeal to women. Men were sent a similar proposition, but here the proposition was designed to encourage donors to identify with the plight of fathers. Results were excellent, but not conclusive. Direct comparison with other appeals would be dangerous, but the possibility will continue to be tested.

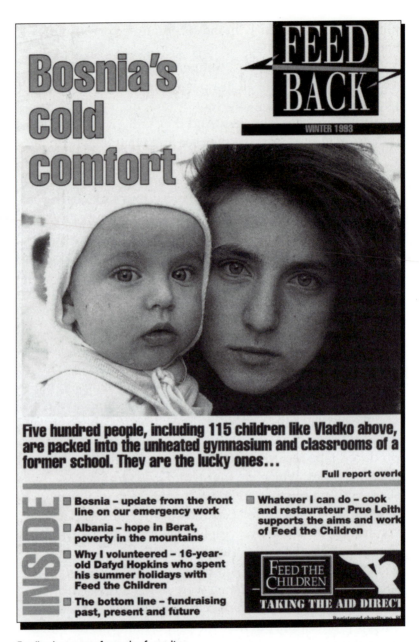

Feedback reports from the front line,
showing donors what their gifts achieve.

Hello, how are you?

Despite initial reservations about telephone fundraising, Children's Aid Direct has now developed several successful ways of using the phone to strengthen ties with donors and to increase their support. Existing and new supporters have been telephoned and invited to sign up to the DART committed giving scheme (*see* panel on the next page). Not surprisingly, this has proved particularly effective at times of high-profile emergencies. Lapsed donors, too, have been successfully reactivated following telephone calls. New higher-value donors (giving more than £250 a year) are now routinely called immediately after receipt of their gift by one of four staff members, who then maintain contact with that donor as the donor requires.

Stewart's own experience with calling donors at home was initially not very encouraging. 'I have telephoned a number of our donors and almost without exception the results have been disappointing, for one simple reason. As soon as I got through and the donor realised it was Children's Aid Direct calling, he or she assumed I was asking for money and immediately became defensive. It was rather distressing when I wasn't asking for money at all.'

But relationship building can be a huge mountain to climb, particularly in the early stages. The comfort and safety of more remote contact, namely by post, therefore may be preferred by many donors, at least until a certain level of trust and mutual understanding has been established.

One of the clearest signs of this for Children's Aid Direct has been in its early attempts to invite donors to events such as special receptions or briefings. There it seems the initial hurdles also apply.

Very often donors won't attend an event, not because they don't want to or would not be prepared to, but because they don't know what to expect, or because they have a suspicion that at some time or other in the evening, or

Regular giving ensures rapid response

Whenever a cry for help goes out in any part of the world, Children's Aid Direct has to respond immediately – not tomorrow, or the next day, but right there and then.

News reports have to be assessed, risks have to be calculated, casualties have to be verified, sources of help have to be located and 101 other complex and important tasks have to happen, tasks that cannot be held up if help is to get to where it's needed as quickly as humanly possible. There just isn't time to wait until sufficient funds have been raised.

The difference between need arising and funds being available could easily be a major problem for a rapid-response agency like Children's Aid Direct. Instead it turned it to advantage by creating DART – the direct action response team – and used the compelling logic behind its inception as a platform to launch its committed giving scheme.

DART offers donors the chance to get involved right at the cutting edge – before a problem becomes a crisis. DART is Children's Aid Direct's instant response capability, already funded and operational in anticipation of need. If emergency support for children fleeing a monsoon has to be dropped in the Far East, or if supplies have to be mobilised quickly for Africa, DART can respond first and sort out longer-term fundraising and other issues later.

Donors make this possible by paying a monthly subscription of £12 or more (they can pay less, but get fewer benefits). In return they receive briefing documents from the field, priority news of Children's Aid Direct's emergency actions, an enamel badge and a striking photograph of a child that features the special DART logo. They also get an opportunity to visit Children's Aid Direct's warehouse for a unique open day where they can meet the DART team and even pack a box of aid.

Perhaps not surprisingly, the charity has found that response to the DART proposition is highest at times of high-profile emergency. 'We also find the telephone works best for DART. It is quite a complex proposition', explains Roger Lawson, Children's Aid Direct's direct marketing manager, 'so the phone fits in well because donors can get immediate answers to their questions.'

One year after its launch, DART was consistently receiving high responses from the charity's donor database, particularly when the telephone was used. Some segments achieved response levels of 16 per cent, with a further 15 per cent making one-off donations.

afterwards, they are going to be subject to a hard sell. Most donors are well aware that there's no such thing as a free lunch.

Fundraisers need to be aware of this, however established and trusted their organisation. When an insurance company or a mortgage broker invites you to a cocktail party it's not so much that you wonder if there's a catch, you assume there *must* be.

Although it may be difficult to get all but a few of your donors to actually come to a donor reception or development event, there is nevertheless a great, if hidden, advantage to be gained just by inviting them.

If Children's Aid Direct invites donors to come and see round its warehouse, or to come and hear one of its specialists who has just come back from Bosnia, then, even for those who cannot attend, the invitation contains a reassuring message. Clearly there is nothing to hide in that warehouse. The charity is happy and relaxed about opening its doors. That chap just back from Bosnia has a good story to tell... And so on.

And very frequently (as Botton Village finds on its open day) many of those donors who don't come will send a donation with their letter of regret because they really appreciated being asked.

Charities are just beginning to appreciate the importance of their requests and invitations on those who *don't* respond. Some commercial organisations have understood this for a long time.

The privileged few

Take American Express. It is forever inviting cardholders to expensive wine tastings, or visits to stately homes, or high-ticket social nosebags, where you can hobnob with society types and have a jolly time, while going some way towards wearing out the numbers on your little piece of plastic. Most people would rather fly in the air than go to one of these events. Yet AmEx keeps on hosting them, even though only a very small number of people can ever go. And it continues to invite the rest of us, without fail. Why?

Because it builds the image it wants to project of the company as exclusive and very upper crust, even though most of its punters are just ordinary Joes like you and me. Also it creates and constantly reinforces the tangible nature of belonging to American Express. And it has quite correctly divined that there's commercial advantage to be gained by cultivating that feeling of belonging, particularly to an exclusive club.

So all the thousands of American Express members will continue to be invited to these events that are beyond their desires, as well as their means. And as those members sit out yet another invitation, from time to time, secretly in the backs of their minds, they'll hear themselves thinking, 'I wish I had the courage to go to an event like that.'

Whether or not the people come, invitations can be very

The launch of DART – the direct action response team.

good for relationship building. (I don't yet know of anyone who has hosted a donor development event to which *nobody* came.)

'Those helpful people at Children's Aid Direct...'

Their experience with incomplete Gift Aid forms and other similar situations has encouraged Stewart Crocker and his colleagues to believe that there are considerable benefits to be gained by being proactive in donor service. When a charity takes the initiative in solving problems, or anticipating queries, donors are usually rather grateful.

'It arises commonly', says Stewart, 'with bureaucratic procedures such as Gift Aid, covenants and the like. Donors, not surprisingly, aren't interested in such things and often find them confusing. Here the telephone is such a useful medium for overcoming objections and misunderstandings.'

Donor recruitment at Children's Aid Direct

Children's Aid Direct's biggest single fundraising investment each year will be in advertising, the bulk of it paying for spaces in prime positions in a limited list of national British daily or weekly newspapers. From time to time, the charity also continues to test the relative cost-effectiveness of other media, such as radio and direct-response television.

It's not only the fundraising department's biggest expenditure in financial terms, it also takes the most time, energy and commitment.

Maintaining a year-round direct marketing recruitment campaign that is effective, opportunistic and responsive is no easy matter. Yet Children's Aid Direct has been more successful at it than most.

The response figures demonstrate just how successful. When most charities are struggling to recruit new donors at costs they can both afford and justify, Children's Aid Direct is running radio campaigns that produce new donors at break even or better and press advertising campaigns that are bringing in hundreds of new donors each month with an average *surplus* gift (income less cost) of £22.

But Children's Aid Direct is acutely aware that the principal factor contributing to its fundraising success has been the extremely bad news coming almost daily, and for months on end, from former Yugoslavia, Rwanda and, to a lesser extent, from other trouble spots in Eastern Europe. These ongoing tragedies confront donors as they watch their televisions each night and read their daily newspapers, creating a natural swell of awareness and compassion that forms the ideal background to Children's Aid Direct's entrepreneurial fundraising.

As in any disaster or world-scale emergency that attracts international media attention, the secret of successful fundraising is to move in quickly alongside the news coverage with strategically placed advertisements to give potential donors an immediately available and grateful channel for their concern. Faced with a seemingly overwhelming catastrophe, many people feel they should do something. And the only practical thing they can do is to give their money to someone who promises to put it to good use on the spot.

Natural, or even man-made disasters tend to appear suddenly out of the blue and occupy our television screens for just a few brief minutes across a few brief days, if that. Opportunistic fundraisers have to have a plan set up in advance of such an emergency. When the story breaks, they have to first judge its likely scale. Will it stir the public? Will it last? Then, if appropriate, they must get quickly behind it with rapidly prepared but effective ads so that they can, in effect, cream off the fruits of the public's compassion before it is diverted by the next soundbite.

What happened with Bosnia, and later in Rwanda, was very different. Both of these situations, rather like the Ethiopian famine of 1984, were disasters that, it seemed, wouldn't go away. In both cases the tragedy was man-made and the victims often seemed to be the perpetrators, guilty of committing atrocities while suffering atrocities themselves.

The donating public was frequently confused, particularly by what appeared to be happening in Bosnia. But as always in every conflict, in every crisis, children are the most vulnerable and wherever else the blame and guilt may lie it certainly isn't with the children. They are the innocents and the wars in Bosnia and Rwanda were remorselessly and continuously dispossessing, orphaning, starving, maiming and killing children. On not just one but two fronts. Here was a ready-made role for Children's Aid Direct.

As war raged in former Yugoslavia, providing basic necessities – food and medical aid – became the immediate priority for all aid organisations. Through inaccessible mountainous terrain, often in appalling weather and with a devastating war going on around them, the major humanitarian agencies, UNHCR (United Nations High Commission for Refugees) and the Red Cross provided an often fragile but undoubtedly life-saving supply route for the thousands upon thousands of civilians caught up in the fighting, or simply cut off from the normal necessities of life.

Its commitment to be fast, flexible and responsive meant Children's Aid Direct was often among the first into formerly besieged towns and villages. The charity soon developed a reputation for its ability to deliver aid quickly to where it was needed most. Appropriate aid too: Children's Aid Direct chose to specialise in food for babies and young children in Bosnia because no other agency was supplying it and the need was almost overwhelming. Incredibly, in 1994 this new and small agency was responsible for providing regular supplies to 180,000 children and their carers in Bosnia alone.

Against the background of the British media's intermittent but continued coverage of the ongoing tragedy in former Yugoslavia, Children's Aid Direct set about investing some of its slender resources in donor recruitment. Given the unevenness of press coverage, the ambiguity of some of the stories coming out of Bosnia and the possible confusion in donors' minds, press advertising would inevitably be a risky investment. But Children's Aid Direct had ways to minimise the risk.

The charity was well aware that press advertisements would only work in a few high-quality, national newspapers. Conventional wisdom also dictated that for best results it would have to use small spaces – tests in emergency situations have repeatedly shown that 20 cm deep by two or three columns' width is almost invariably the most cost-effective size for this type of advertisement – and would need to secure good positions in the early part of the paper, hopefully on a right-hand page. Being next to relevant editorial matter – if it could be arranged – would often be worth the extra payment that usually would be asked.

Children's Aid Direct's experience did differ somewhat from the conventional wisdom so that, in one area at least, the rules were rewritten. At the height of Bosnia's crisis the charity was able to deploy larger, page-dominant ads that not only had greater impact, so recruited far more donors, but also competed cost-effectively with the traditional 20 x 2 ads.

Most fundraisers spend a great deal of time and energy in getting the message right (copy, photographs, text and coupon) without realising that often careful media selection, timing, choice of size and position and, above all, vigorous negotiating on price will be far more likely to influence the cost-effectiveness of a newspaper or magazine advertisement.

Handled in the right way, spaces in 'banker' media (tested, proved publications that can be relied upon to work) can often be negotiated down to a fraction of 'rate card' cost. In its 1995 campaign, which used 115 spaces in 20 different

Developing a fundraising product – the baby box

The inspiration for Children's Aid Direct's now famous baby box was found in a dark corner of Bosnia in October 1993 when Marc Nohr visited the country to see the charity at work in the front line. Surrounded by almost overwhelming shortages of just about everything, one of the aid workers remarked that he'd love to give each mother a box of basic essentials for her baby.

Shortly after, the first baby box mailing was produced. The proposition was simple – £20 from you, the donor, will ensure that a boxful of (listed) necessities will be promptly delivered to an anxious mother in Bosnia. (The amount was later increased to £30.) The idea was presented compellingly in a fax from Gordon Bacon in Bosnia to David Grubb in Reading, outlining the needs of very young children. David simply wrote his comments on the fax and sent it on to donors, with a response card in English and Serbo-Croat that allowed space for the donor to send a message, drawing, or photo to the mother in Bosnia.

Children's Aid Direct's donors did the rest. Fifteen thousand baby boxes were sent to Bosnia in the following year, along with some touching and simple, but widely appreciated, messages of hope. One young mother in Bosnia responded with her own message of thanks to a donor in Windsor. The exchange made headlines in the local press.

Press advertisements in 1995 (see opposite) neatly and graphically summarised the proposition and quickly repaid their costs, then shot into surplus – acquiring hundreds of new donors along the way. Proof indeed that donors will respond to a tangible, logical product and a very direct way to give.

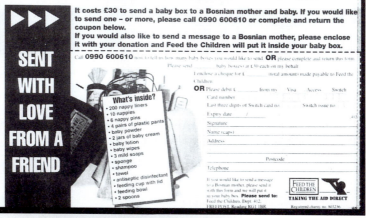

The award-winning baby box press advertisement.

publications, Children's Aid Direct, through its agency, was able to negotiate discounts off rate card averaging 63 per cent. In other words, it managed to pay just 37 per cent of what most other advertisers paid because of who it was and what it was doing.

Making the ads work

Such discounts do not come easy. They require determination, painstaking hard work and the creation and nurturing of numerous relationships within the media. They also demand the ability to make decisions and to implement them very, very quickly.

Children's Aid Direct and its agency are so attuned to quick responses that they undertake to have camera-ready copy for existing advertisements with any British national newspaper within one and a half hours of agreeing to take space.

Ernst Goetschi, media and planning director at Burnett Associates, explains, 'This means we are set up to take advantage of what is known in the advertising world as "Friday night specials", late space that becomes available and needs to be filled quickly – where the advertiser can often dictate the price.'

Without the effective negotiations that this speed of response makes possible, Children's Aid Direct's response figures would look very different indeed.

'We are constantly testing different approaches', says Ernst, 'and meticulously recording every detail of test results. We know that one creative approach can work as much as 19 times better than another in identical conditions, so getting the creative right is *very* important.'

So too is that other vital ingredient of successful off-the-page recruitment – the reply mechanism. Years of experience and refinement have gone into Children's Aid Direct's reply coupons. Nothing is extraneous and not a millimetre is wasted.

Unlike many other successful off-the-page fundraisers, Children's Aid Direct's message was inevitably influenced by rapidly changing events overseas, so throughout its fundraising history advertisements have had to change to reflect those changes rather than because they would necessarily generate better response.

Maximum emotional impact is a consistent feature of every Children's Aid Direct ad. With a small amount of space for their complex message and confronted by an audience with limited attention spans, the ads have to instantly recall the emotional impulse that we know lurks within every potential donor. But despite the convenient response mechanism and the ease with which responders can post or phone through their cash, cheque, or credit card, turning that emotional energy into a donation there and then is far from easy and will only work with a tiny minority of the readers of that carefully crafted and positioned ad.

Lessons have been learned about which subject works best. Does baby food out-pull the looming threat of a harsh winter? What type of photographic image is most effective – single figure or group, head and shoulders or full form, looking directly to the camera, or away? And, most importantly, who is the message coming from? One of Children's Aid Direct's most effective advertisements featured an 'advertorial' style of presentation (where the layout is deliberately designed to look like a piece of newspaper editorial) and was presented by a third party, a public personality speaking on Children's Aid Direct's behalf. The advertisement featured BBC news correspondent Martin Bell, a well-known presenter of television news and associated at the time in the public eye with Bosnia through his daily reports from the war zone, where he was frequently caught up in the action and once was seriously injured.

Respected as a concerned and caring reporter, Martin Bell was familiar with Children's Aid Direct's work at the front line and was able to give the charity the strongest possible

How you can save lives in Bosnia now

Martin Bell reports from Tuzla

Whoever is guilty of creating the hell that is Bosnia today, Adisa Ekrem and thousands of children like her are the innocent victims.

I discovered the six-year-old girl in an overcrowded makeshift refugee shelter near Tuzla. Orphaned after a devastating mortar blast, Adisa herself was now fighting for her life. The shelter was desperately short of food, particularly the food needed by young children.

At first hand, I witnessed the work of Feed the Children, the aid agency which delivers food and medical and hygiene supplies direct to children in immediate need.

They're bringing hope to hell. Their work is fast, efficient, extremely well-targeted, and often carried out in very dangerous conditions. They've saved Adisa's life – and the lives of countless more children.

But every week, yet more are made homeless. Feed the Children has pledged that if military action threatens aid deliveries to any area, they will continue to distribute supplies wherever they can in former Yugoslavia.

To do this, they need more support from people in Britain. *Telegraph* readers can make a real

BBC's Martin Bell: witness and advocate of Feed the Children's life-saving work

difference. With £25, Feed the Children can feed 45 hungry infants for one day. I strongly urge you to help.

I won't watch children die. Here is my life-saving donation. (087

£250* ☐ **£100** ☐ **£50** ☐ **£25** ☐ **£** _____ ☐ (other)

OR debit my ☐ Visa ☐ Access card

CARD NUMBER | | | | | | | | | | | | | | | | |

EXPIRY DATE | | | SIGNATURE

NAME (CAPS) MR/MRS/MS

ADDRESS

POSTCODE   TELEPHONE

OR please phone our donation line **0272 767700**

*A gift of £250 or more is worth an extra third to us under Gift Aid.

Please make your cheque payable to Feed the Children and send to: Martin Bell, c/o Feed the Children, FREEPOST, Reading RG4 7BR.

Reg. charity no. 803236.

FEED THE CHILDREN

TAKING THE AID DIRECT

The 'advertorial': the editorial style and authority of the writer produced exceptional direct response.

endorsement. By copying each paper's typeface and by-line style and specifically addressing each newspaper's readers in the headline, plus personalising his appeal with real case histories from his own experience, Martin Bell's powerful message was hard to resist (*see* facing page).

Martin Bell was a natural choice when it came to record Children's Aid Direct's first radio commercial, which he willingly agreed to do. These appeals were widely broadcast and, like the newspaper ads, were very noticeable. Just as press ads piggybacked on editorial, so radio was booked before and after the news.

Sadly for Children's Aid Direct – and for the people of Bosnia – Bell's assistance came to the notice of his employers, who decided this humanitarian activity might jeopardise his impartiality as a reporter and called upon him to stop. Other journalists, including some from independent broadcasting companies, who had volunteered to promote Children's Aid Direct were similarly muzzled.

So the advertisements and radio announcements that featured Martin Bell were summarily stopped. But Stewart Crocker wasn't bitter. 'Look at it this way,' he says, 'we had the public endorsement of Martin Bell for six weeks and during that time he told the world about us and helped us raise more than £200,000. That's six weeks and £200,000 more than we might have had.'

New approaches were applied to the advertisements, and when it came to finding a safe and reassuring voice to replace Mr Bell what better than the strong, comforting, reassuring tones of Gordon Bacon, the ex-policeman from Lanchester whom I introduced you to at the start of this story?

And very effective radio announcements and newspaper advertisements they were too.

Two years later, following the fall of Srebrenica in July 1995, Children's Aid Direct took the 'advertorial' ad concept a stage further. The story broke on Saturday. By Monday page-dominant advertorial ads were ready to be placed. One insertion alone brought in 1,350 responses and donations totalling more than £55,000.

Some British newspapers carried a photo-story showing a young woman who, unable to live with the horrors that had befallen her, had hanged herself. Marc Nohr was so horrified when he learned of this tragedy that he wrote an ad on a Sunday, using the story to dramatise the fall of Srebrenica. He phoned his idea through to Stewart Crocker, who accepted it on trust. By Monday the ad had appeared in the press. Two days later Stewart decided to withdraw it, not because of public reaction – that was mostly supportive – but because Children's Aid Direct's staff were uncomfortable with the image. The charity here showed courage, both in running the ad in the first place and in later accepting that because of staff sensitivity a winning ad should be dropped.

Through a combination of its adroit placement of its carefully prepared and skilfully purchased messages and the sheer weight and power of the news context within which it appeals, Children's Aid Direct is more successful than most at acquiring new donors through radio and press.

Direct-response television, which has proved to be such a graveyard for optimistic fundraisers, has also been made to work in a limited way for Children's Aid Direct. Such are the mechanics of television production that it is difficult to see how the charity will ever be able to use it for the kind of rapid response it employs in the press – but the medium is never far from mind and is likely to be tested in a variety of ways in the future.

Children's Aid Direct has benefited spectacularly from television coverage in other ways. When the charity was featured in 'the week's good cause' appeal it raised the second highest amount ever from this type of announcement, despite the fact that the broadcast went out at a traditionally poor day for fundraising, Christmas Eve.

The real value of giving

In today's competitive climate it is rare for a new charity to rise to national prominence with the speed and style shown by Children's Aid Direct. If league tables are anything to go by, Feed the Children, as it was then called, was the fastest-ever climber in the fundraising world's equivalent of the pop charts. Britain's Charities Aid Foundation annually compiles a table of the top 200 not-for-profit organisations by total voluntary income. Unsurprisingly, for the first few years of its life Feed the Children didn't even register. Then in 1994 it shot in at position 37. Children's Aid Direct is certainly not a new organisation. It will open its doors as one of Britain's biggest charities.

In his letter informing donors of the new name, which I cited at the start of this chapter, director David Grubb reassured supporters that the new name for the charity would not be accompanied by triumphalist advertising campaigns or glossy literature. All that matters, he said, is that the organisation – whatever it is called – should continue to help the most vulnerable victims of emergencies and war, the children.

This letter to donors, he went on to explain, would count as one of the few exceptions to that rule. Here's how he justified this exception to the charity's donors.

> Your support has been essential to our success. So I believe it is only right that you should be among the very first people to hear of this change. By helping us provide so many vital needs you have helped us evolve into an organisation that does so much more than just feed children.

Children's Aid Direct
82 Caversham Road
Reading
Berkshire RG1 8AE
United Kingdom

Tel: +44 (0) 1734 584000
Fax: +44 (0) 1734 588988

Habitat for Humanity International

Building relationships that last

Millard Fuller was a millionaire when his wife left him. His business and personal lives were the epitome of the American dream, but the Fullers weren't happy. So, in a desperate attempt to keep his family together, Millard Fuller decided to give all his money away and to point his life in a new direction. That new direction led to Christian missionary work and, in time, to the founding of Habitat for Humanity International. Sandra Byrd, vice-president, communications and development for Habitat, takes up the story.

Habitat – the early years

'Habitat for Humanity began in 1976 in a converted chicken barn at a small Christian community called Koinonia Farm in south-east Georgia. A few months later the first office of Habitat was opened in one room of Millard Fuller's modest law office in Americus, Georgia. There were no mailing lists full of anxious-to-give supporters, no strategic plan, no field

Habitat's founder Millard Fuller is helped with the building work by a high-profile supporter, former President Jimmy Carter.

staff. There was just a dream, a vision in Millard Fuller's mind that every person, regardless of station in life, deserves and has a right to a simple, decent place to live.

'A couple of years later when he hung a sign in front of a small house next door, which had become the headquarters of the budding work, proclaiming Habitat for Humanity International the folks in town thought it humorous and ridiculous. Little did they know then what Habitat for Humanity would become in just 20 years.'

Millard Fuller's direct marketing background

Millard Fuller was an entrepreneur from childhood. His college and law school days were supplemented by a myriad of successful money-making ideas, from raising pigs, rabbits and chickens to selling firecrackers. He sold

Christmas trees, student telephone directories and a
birthday cake service offering to deliver cakes to students –
a business he promoted through the mail to students'
parents.

Despite his ultimate rejection of the normal fruits of
commercial success, this entrepreneurial spirit was to come
in very useful for the Fullers when, after a three-year spell as
missionaries in Zaire, they started Habitat for Humanity
International.

Sandi Byrd describes those precarious early days. 'A
handful of volunteers, attracted by Millard's vision, spent
hours out back of the first office in a storage shed hand-
stuffing mailings to likely supporters. The response to these
mailings often meant the difference between whether or not
there were nails and boards to work with that day.'

It took Habitat for Humanity International 15 years to
build the first 10,000 houses. The next 10,000 came in just
two years, the next 10,000 in only 14 months. By 1995
Habitat was building 10,000 houses a year and 1996 was the
year when HFHI completed the grand total of 50,000 houses.

Giving people what they want

From the very beginning, with those painstaking storage-
shed mailings, Habitat has been dependent upon income
from the mail for its existence. Even today, mail receipts
represent about half of Habitat for Humanity International's
annual income. But direct mail 'Habitat-style' is not typical
direct mail.

Even before Millard Fuller imagined Habitat for
Humanity he was customer-sensitive. He found out what
his customers wanted and he built his business around their
needs because he knew this would make him successful. He
didn't forget this simple premise when he turned his skills
to becoming one of the largest home builders in the United
States, helping thousands of families in need acquire their
dream of a simple, decent place to live.

Millard knew that the basic principles behind Habitat – that of working with, not for, people to help them build their own homes at no profit and with no interest – would appeal to people more than just another give-away programme. He knew that he was not only allowing the home-owners to retain their dignity, he was providing a method by which people who were capable of supporting the mission could also feel good about how their donations were being used.

Habitat is not an ordinary non-profit organisation. Habitat is not a charity. It describes itself as a Christian-based housing ministry.

Habitat does not give houses away. Instead, mortgage payments from home-owners go into a special 'fund for humanity' that, along with other funds raised, provides for continuous building of more homes with other families in need. Direct mail not only provides a way to raise the money to keep the programme growing, it is also the primary vehicle for explaining Habitat's principles and educating people about this unusual organisational structure.

No note goes unanswered

Sandi Byrd is very proud of one unusual piece of 'customer-friendliness'. 'It is not unusual for people to question, comment, or write encouraging, or discouraging notes, on their replies to non-profit direct mail. But it is very unusual for each and every note to receive a response. At Millard's insistence, that is exactly what has happened from the very first Habitat for Humanity International mailing.

'In the beginning there were just a handful of notes but the number grew as the programme grew. In 1995 more than 38,000 notes received a response. You might ask how this can happen. Are there 10 prewritten letters and the one that most closely resembles the questions is chosen? Does a donor get the same reply no matter what her or his request?

'The answer is simple, yet complex. In the beginning all

notes were set aside and Millard answered each of them personally. Even as Habitat grew and his workload increased proportionally, he still insisted that each and every note should get a reply. A special correspondence unit was established, led by a volunteer who had Millard's utmost confidence. The unit, then and now, has one primary concern – to answer every statement, note, criticism, comment, legible or illegible scrawl that comes in the mail. One memorable note was written on a piece of brown paper bag. It simply read: "I am requesting information packet. My address below...".

'The correspondence unit has created a new meaning to the term "form letter". Many of the enquiries are remarkably similar. Some ask why President Carter gave away the Panama Canal,[*] or want to know the difference between Habitat for Humanity and the Carter Center. Others are more sedate, they want to know if they can designate their gifts wherever they want, or how to start a Habitat for Humanity in their own communities. Then there are the "one of a kind" enquiries that require time and energy to answer. One of the thousands of such letters to be drafted was in response to the following.

> ...Today is Rosh Hashanah, the Jewish New Year day. I have chosen today as the time to renew my participation in Habitat for Humanity... Your letters to me did a great job of expressing what Habitat's all about. Thanks for the time and care that you put into them. I am delighted to hear about how the work of Habitat crosses religious and cultural lines and hope that will continue and grow in the future. Best Wishes...

'A staff of full-time volunteers, led by a paid staff member works daily to ensure that every single note is answered. Although Millard had to give up answering each one personally – there are now close to 40,000 a year – he remains in constant contact with the unit and visits it often during the course of the day when he is in the office. In this way he keeps a finger on the real pulse of our mail donors.'

*Former President Jimmy Carter is a very active supporter of Habitat for Humanity International.

All comments are welcome, and no note goes unanswered by Habitat's correspondence unit.

Here is an example of one of the many instances where donors have literally been turned around by the quick response they receive from the correspondence unit.

> Thank you for your very nice letter of 3-21! I have never had such a
> pleasant, detailed, full response from a development office. Mostly
> it's cold and greedy. You answered my specific case and I very
> much appreciate the time and trouble you took! I'll try to send
> extra because of it.

Some who have written that they would never give again to Habitat for either some real or perceived reason have given again and again, because their concerns were addressed in a timely and sensitive manner by the correspondence unit. One angry response that was addressed brought the following by return mail.

> Thank you for your letter dated December 7 1995... When I wrote
> the note on the response piece of 'acquisition' mail I really thought
> no one would look at it. Much to my surprise it was not only
> looked at, but responded to – with a neat, concise explanation.
> Thank you and thanks for all you do.

Although this special unit deals primarily with donors
through the mail, staff also make thousands of telephone
calls to donors during the course of the year, either to
reinforce the letter that is being sent or to clarify a concern or
perceived problem with the donor. This grassroots approach
to making sure the donor understands HFHI's mission and
the way it is pursued has made a tremendous difference to
its donors. The following report by a staff member in the
unit shows one such turn-round.

> [Donor's name] received a mailing that was one mailing too many.
> She wrote saying 'Take me off your mailing list. I gave once
> several months back because I felt you were worthy – it appears
> you are a scam. Get lost!'
>
> I called and spoke to her husband who, at first, was ready to
> put the phone down on me. However, once some cold water had
> been poured on the fire and he was given the option of choosing
> how many mailings he would receive, he was a happy man again.

Being responsive

As with any direct mail programme, the number of times
donors receive mail can be an issue. If a donor says he is
receiving too much, Habitat for Humanity asks him how
many times he wishes to receive mail. This information is
then added to the donor's record. Or if a donor has a
preference about what time of the year she wishes to receive
mail, that too is recorded and honoured.

Sometimes it means taking a donor off the solicitation list
altogether for reasons of age or diminished income. For
example, donors are always asked if they would like to

continue to receive the bi-monthly newsletter, *Habitat World*. This allows the organisation to keep in close contact with donors, without directly asking for support. It also creates amazing planned-giving opportunities for Habitat for Humanity and gives donors the opportunity to give again if their financial situation changes.

This sensitivity pays off by creating goodwill and a sense of partnership between Habitat for Humanity and its donors. The following is a good example of many letters received by Habitat from older donors.

> Thank you for your nice letter in response to my note explaining my inability to help financially. I will be very pleased to receive your complimentary bi-monthly publication *Habitat World*. I will most surely keep you and your work in my daily prayers. Thank you and God bless you.

Using sensitivity in telemarketing

The opportunity to opt out also exists in Habitat for Humanity International's telemarketing programme. Sandi Byrd explains, 'Although a young programme for Habitat, it first started in 1993, it is growing rapidly. Testing portions of our donor base for telemarketing is helping us to target those people on our list who prefer being called rather than receiving mail. Operators are trained to honour any requests regarding future phone calls by recording any specific requests on the donor's record.

'If a donor does not wish to receive phone calls from Habitat, he or she is excluded from future telemarketing efforts. Alternatively, if a donor voices a desire to be called rather than mailed this request can be honoured as well. The more we can accommodate our donors by soliciting them as they wish, the healthier our donor base will be, with far less likelihood of list fatigue.'

We just called to say thank you

'Of course, telemarketing for gifts is not the only way we use the telephone to cultivate our donors. Millard has always insisted on making the phone calls whenever possible to thank donors. With time, the number of calls he can make efficiently has diminished, but he still makes time to call a donor of any gift of $5,000 or more. Most are long-time donors and Millard has a personal relationship with many of them because of previous contacts during building events or speaking engagements. Many new donors are astonished to receive a call from Habitat's president, but enjoy that closeness and special treatment that only the top person can provide.

'A new major donor campaign was started in 1995 and donors making a gift of $1,000 to $4,999 are now called by the head of the major donor programme. This allows staff to get to know donors and helps target those who are capable of making larger capital gifts at some time in the future.

'This special treatment also helps uncover small problems that could become big problems, ie an incorrect address, a special interest, or a desire to be solicited in another way. When this happens these problems are turned into opportunities and the donors feel good about associating with an organisation that wants to know how they feel.'

These two phone processes only reach those donors of $1,000 or more. Yet more than 90 per cent of all gifts to Habitat for Humanity International are under $50. Will donors continue to give at their present level with only mail or an occasional telephone solicitation? Should donors expect that every time you contact them you are asking for more money? Is there an economical way to let donors know how important they are and ask for their input without asking for money?

These questions led HFHI to set up a 'thank you' centre, in late 1996. Phones are staffed exclusively by volunteers, who call a targeted group of current donors within a specific time after their most recent gift to Habitat.

Sandi says, 'Thank you calls are in addition to the written thank you letter and receipt that donors normally receive after a gift. And although these calls are used primarily to say thank you, the donors receiving them will have an opportunity to ask questions or request additional information about specific programmes.'

Giving is natural – being donor-sensitive should be too

Sandi Byrd sums up the Habitat for Humanity approach. 'Giving is a natural and rejuvenating act. It should be treated with respect and sensitivity. By allowing donors to respond, we are satisfying a normal, natural human emotion. Not only do people like to be thanked, they like to be asked their opinion, they like to know you want to know what they are thinking. We cannot afford to be afraid to listen to our donors. Our future depends upon two-way communication. The more we can do to shore up our communications with our donors, the more support we will be able to garner for our organisation. Being donor-sensitive should be treated as a matter of life and death by all organisations – because it is!'

A simple, decent place to live

Habitat for Humanity International has a simple, yet seemingly impossible mission – to make sure that everyone, everywhere, has at least a simple, decent place to live.

When the very first Habitat house was built in 1969 for Bo and Emma Johnson, nearly half of the citizens of the United States lived in substandard housing. In many other parts of the world the need was as great, or greater. An estimated 25 per cent of the world's population, some 1.38 billion people, live in substandard housing, or have no home at all.

Habitat for Humanity International has already built more than 50,000 homes. Through Habitat affiliates and offices in every US state and in 47 countries around the world, new homes are now being built with ever-increasing momentum.

When you combine that vision and achievement with the commitment and contributions of a growing band of donors, Habitat for Humanity International's mission doesn't seem so impossible after all.

Millard Fuller's latest book, appropriately titled *A Simple, Decent Place to Live*, ends on an upbeat, optimistic note, inspired by Habitat's remarkable record of achievement. He says,

> Make no small plans. Can we build houses for a million people? Why not? Why not a million houses for five million people? Why not even more?

Why not indeed?

Habitat for Humanity International
322 W Lamar Street
Americus
Georgia 31709-3498
USA

Tel: +1 912 924 6935
Fax: +1 912 924 6541

Greenpeace UK

Harnessing the power in suburbia

Politicians take note. There is a power out there in suburbia, so far harnessed only to charity drives, campaigns and parent–teacher associations which, if ever properly brought to bear on the great problems of the day, will have an impact so great the result of its being detonated (like the Amchitka A-bomb test) cannot be predicted.

Robert Hunter, writing in the Vancouver *Sun*, 2 October 1969

In Vancouver, Canada on 15 September 1970 an ageing 80-foot chartered halibut seiner set sail crewed by an odd assortment of just 12 people. They were united by a common objective – concern for their planet and the environment in which they live and a desire to stop the imminent testing of an atom bomb on Amchitka Island, just a hundred miles away in the icy waters off the west coast of Alaska.

The name they chose for their unusual enterprise was Green Peace. It seemed appropriate because their protest gave them a chance to affirm their right to live in a green and peaceful environment. And they were determined to pursue their aims by peaceful and environmentally acceptable means.

No one on board that old fishing boat on that cold September morning could have realised then that they were starting out on the very first action of what was soon to become the world's most dynamic and successful environmental pressure group – Greenpeace.

We are not radicals. We are conservatives who insist upon
conserving the environment for our children and future
generations of man.

The Greenpeace Story (Dorling Kindersley, London, 1989)

By the early 1990s, Greenpeace had grown into a truly
multinational organisation with a string of achievements to
its name. While it has been instrumental in virtually
bringing to an end commercial whaling and seal culling, in
bringing about the treaty that ensures the preservation of the
Antarctic continent, through influencing a range of
legislation on subjects such as the dumping of toxic waste at
sea and many other lasting victories, Greenpeace's greatest
achievement has been to lead a vast change in public
awareness and attitudes throughout the world on a wide
range of environmental concerns and issues. Much of
Greenpeace's work has been symbolic, but it has always
been significant.

Greenpeace is...

Greenpeace makes waves. It is symbolised by those fearless
folk in fragile inflatable boats who put themselves between
the greedy and cruel whaler and his helpless but mystical
prey, the whale. Greenpeace is also the carefully trained and
superbly equipped scientists who roam the seas in the front
line of planetary protection, a real-life international rescue
prepared to take direct, but always peaceful, action
anywhere in the world, with little thought to the risk, to
make a point or to prevent an abuse.

Greenpeace is the campaigners and researchers with facts
and figures at their fingertips ready to challenge all
commercial and political interests who would put profits
and convenience before the need to sustain life on earth.
Greenpeace is also the well-dressed specialists and experts
prepared to take on the captains of commerce and industry
on their own turf – the boardroom – and, increasingly,

The birth of Greenpeace: the original crew of the *Phyllis Cormack*.

prepared to propose and negotiate alternative, viable, but environmentally sound strategies, practices and solutions.

Greenpeace is the campaigning fundraisers who have established their organisation in 32 countries throughout the world from the USA to the Ukraine, from Austria to Australia, who have built public support up from scratch to staggeringly high levels, who have raised the money necessary to finance their high-cost, high-profile campaigns and who have never failed to keep Greenpeace and its causes prominently in the public eye.

Greenpeace is the millions and millions of ordinary people from every corner of the world who have paid money to join as supporters of Greenpeace, who believe with Robert Hunter that *they* are the power in suburbia, that if they unite under an effective campaign and show common purpose there is literally nothing that they cannot do.

They are Greenpeace and their mission is nothing less than to change the world – for good.

Greenpeace UK

Greenpeace UK started in 1982. In its early years there was no formal fundraising as such but the Greenpeace wave was rolling and people joined seemingly from nowhere. The first formal attempt at donor recruitment came when a sympathetic supporter donated some seed money specifically to test off-the-page press advertising. It worked enormously well, and with only the barest minimum and most basic of systems Greenpeace began quite rapidly to acquire a broad supporter base.

> I wouldn't be interested in briefings. I'm happy to support Greenpeace financially. I get dozens of letters from charities thanking me, and I think 'what a waste'. I can't remember whether Greenpeace are any worse than the rest of them.
>
> Mrs J De H Bell, Hertfordshire

Some interesting but rather inconclusive attempts at list building by direct mail soon led Greenpeace to re-evaluate its direct marketing potential. As so often happens, the great step forward came through an accidental but fortuitous chain of events, this time the one that led Charlotte Grimshaw to Greenpeace's doorstep in 1986.

Prior to joining Greenpeace, Charlotte had been actively involved in developing a new donor and membership system for the then hopeful – and now defunct – Social Democratic Party. Whatever else the SDP was, it was certainly a thorough and fast-moving education in donor and member recruitment and communication. Charlotte could hardly have had a better grounding for her new job.

On arrival at Greenpeace Charlotte found computerised records for about 40,000 assorted supporters. She immediately set about organising a regular communications programme with them, particularly with a view to sending regular special appeals and establishing a system for subscription renewals.

At this time Charlotte was *the* fundraiser. There was only her. But green issues were gaining status and generating

The classic Greenpeace image; making waves.

anxiety across the country. Concern for the environment had caught the conscience of the nation and the most vocal, most tangible demonstration against environmental abuse that most people could find was Greenpeace.

Greenpeace recruited its second professional fundraiser, Annie Moreton, in 1988.

An amazing time

The environment was then rapidly becoming *the* hot topic of the moment in most Western societies. The 'green wave', the huge swell of interest and concern for all things green, was just about beginning and Greenpeace was slap-bang in its path.

'I came in at an amazing time', explains Annie Moreton, describing the extraordinary fundraising environment that Greenpeace found itself in then, 'when really Greenpeace could do no wrong. We used to say then that everything we touched turned to green. It was a kind of environmental Midas touch. But the fundraising foundations had been well laid so we could take full advantage of the opportunity that presented itself.'

Thanks to the timely arrival of Charlotte Grimshaw and Annie Moreton, Greenpeace UK was able to grow rapidly and in a largely controlled manner. Through the late eighties and into the early nineties, the two-woman fundraising team expanded to nearly 20 people. Greenpeace UK's income soared. It became the fifth largest Greenpeace office worldwide, after Germany, Holland, Sweden and the USA.

Although they had established press advertising, direct mail and insert programmes to recruit new supporters, managing this extraordinary growth was far from easy. Annie says, 'It was a bit like driving at 200 miles an hour down a straight road, it takes all your efforts and energy just to keep looking ahead and you can't do anything else. There was no time to look at such things as creative testing, segmentation, varying propositions to different parts of our list. Looking back now I wish we had done so many things then when we were working with such huge volumes. We could have learned such a lot. But we didn't have the resources and it was all we could do then just to cope with organic growth.'

Just how extraordinary this growth was can be seen from the organisation's targets at the time. 'Normally, new memberships would come in each week in the low hundreds and that was considered to be doing well. When the green wave hit we could see quite quickly that new membership would rise past 1,000 a week. We had a bottle of champagne in the office to celebrate that milestone. Someone had given it to us in the distant past and we kept it for ages for just such an occasion, when we hit the magic

1,000. Five weeks later new membership broke through the 3,000 per week barrier...'.

Greenpeace in the UK was well and truly taking off and as a result Charlotte and Annie were struggling to stay afloat. Coping with growth became a full-time obsession. During this period Greenpeace had little contact with any other fundraisers or fundraising organisations.

In the UK Greenpeace is not a registered charity. For a campaigning organisation the fiscal benefits of charitable status have to be weighed against the restrictions, particularly in terms of explicitly setting out to influence the party political system, which is generally out of bounds for charities. The distinction is ridiculous, of course, as most major charities employ political lobbyists and few campaigners for any social change can avoid being political with both large and small Ps. The majority of charities work around the system at its muddy edges. Some, such as Oxfam and War on Want, have fallen foul of the restrictions and faced attempts to curb their campaigns. Rather than risk possible compromise, Greenpeace has decided not to seek charitable status, keeping for itself the right to campaign as it sees best.

Purity has its place

This imperative has implications for fundraising. Another difference from other charities is that Greenpeace has no mission statement. Instead each of the 32 Greenpeace national offices has to abide by a set of clear rules. Included in these are several fundraising restrictions. Greenpeace doesn't take money from governments, it doesn't take money from political parties, it doesn't solicit gifts from corporate entities. Only by sticking purely to these exclusions does Greenpeace believe it can stay free to pursue its other golden rule – that non-violent direct action is the cornerstone of all its campaigns. So all the many types and shades of corporate fundraising are completely closed doors to Greenpeace.

This means that Greenpeace is totally reliant on fundraising from individuals.

In turn this points to a singular dependency on direct marketing. Greenpeace originally perceived itself as a young organisation with, so it believed, mainly youngish supporters. As yet there is negligible legacy income. It can't take company or trust money. Greenpeace quickly realised that it had to make a success of individual direct fundraising or it would have to depend almost entirely on the vagaries of special events and public collections.

Greenpeace's success has mirrored the growth and development of direct marketing. Without a dynamic, successful direct marketing industry Greenpeace wouldn't have got so far. Direct marketing produces by far the largest part of the organisation's income and Greenpeace depends on direct marketing for its day-to-day survival. Just 20 per cent of Greenpeace's income comes from local fundraising (groups, collections, local events, walks, etc).

If much of Greenpeace's success is owed to the development of direct marketing, one of its more persistent dilemmas can be traced to the voluntary sector's traditional low subscription rates and confused, if non-existent, pricing policy. When Greenpeace UK was set up it simply looked around at the membership rates of similar organisations (Amnesty International and the Campaign for Nuclear Disarmament for example) and set its prices at similar levels.

This probably would have been a deliberate political decision. Greenpeace has always aimed for as large and as wide a supporter base worldwide as possible, so would not have wished to price itself out of anyone's reach. Part of the organisation's muscle depends on its ability to quote an impressive worldwide membership figure – now just short of 3 million. When you depend on lobbying, not only of governments but also of consumer organisations and the people who consume their products, size counts.

So Greenpeace would never wish to see a situation where there was no cheap, or generally affordable, subscription rate.

Annie Moreton explains, 'The people who do come in at the very lowest end – our current unwaged subscription is £7 a year – are often very active in campaigns, particularly in letter writing and lobbying. Often they are retired people, or students, or not in paid employment. But they'll be active in other ways, in giving their time and energy. So there is no way we would want to do other than encourage their involvement.'

The dilemma, of course, arises when pricing at the low end affects all the other entry levels and the average income from membership is too low to do little more than cover the cost of servicing. In fundraising pyramid terms, the base is too flat and the high point is too low.

During its growth years Greenpeace was enormously successful at bringing people in, but the new challenge it faced once this broad supporter base had settled down was twofold – first, to renew and retain those supporters for a reasonable 'lifetime' and to develop their giving so that those who could afford more than the basic minimum could be offered optimum opportunities to upgrade.

Belonging to Greenpeace (the term membership is not used in the UK as it is felt to imply voting rights and formal ownership that does not exist; annual subscribers are referred to as 'supporters') is essentially a very simple relationship. In return for their basic subscriptions, supporters are promised sufficient information to ensure they know what's going on. So inevitably the cost of maintaining basic communications is high. But it took some time for Greenpeace UK to recognise that its giving pattern was too uniform and too low and that steps would have to

> Sometimes I skim it when I get it, the newsletter is a lot of print. I think it depends on your level of interest in the nitty-gritty of environmental issues: I'm after the general picture.
>
> It's a more personal buzz than needing to feel my status in an organisation. It's self-interest here – I want the planet looked after. I'm doing it for me, not for Greenpeace. They are quite big issues Greenpeace deals with, it's not like some club.
>
> Miss D Quinn, Hampshire

be taken to raise giving levels. The necessity for this first became apparent in the early 1990s as many of the 'green-wave' supporters failed to renew, the flood of new supporters had begun to ebb and the green wave had slowed to little more than a ripple.

The concept of different giving levels or 'from each according to his or her means' is rather difficult for a culture such as Greenpeace's.

Annie Moreton has a lot of sympathy with this dilemma. 'Inevitably some people believe passionately that everybody should be able to join Greenpeace and that everybody should be able to get all the benefits. Some people also believe it is immoral to ask supporters to pay a larger sum and then give them special, privileged information that an unwaged supporter – particularly those who work really hard at campaigning – could not have. It smacks of élitism and the privileged rich – concepts quite foreign to Greenpeace.

'In the marketing department, we realised that the low-cost proposition was being taken up by many people who could afford to give more. So, for example, in our press advertising, where the cost of space and the value of response is critical, we didn't mention the low-cost proposition at all in our coupon copy. As a result we would get a stream of letters from local group supporters pointing out that we seemed to have made a mistake in our ads and that the unwaged rate had somehow fallen off. I would then have to stand up at local group seminars and explain the rather unpalatable truth that it was left out on purpose because we couldn't afford to recruit that way through the press – although it was explained in all the follow-up leaflets.'

The even more unpalatable truth, however, was that, deprived of the impetus of the green wave, press advertising responses had fallen steeply and even at the full subscription rate (in 1995 the single subscription rate was £14.50 a year with an annual family/household rate of

£19.50) press advertising had ceased to be viable.

Other forms of recruitment, including direct mail, were showing similar signs of sliding towards the uneconomic. The Greenpeace fundraising product was simply priced too low. Either every Greenpeace supporter would have to face a steep, and for many presumably unacceptable, increase or a range of products would need to be devised to allow supporters to find their own natural 'comfort level'.

Like many organisations before it, Greenpeace was coming to realise that financial necessity is the only effective way to get round the natural tension that exists between the 'movement' side of the organisation and the fundraising side.

Annie Moreton believes this tension is part of the fundraiser's lot. 'A lot of energy can be expended on circuitous, philosophical discussions about socialism versus capitalism, but ultimately wherever you go in the world you find that the more people pay the more they get. We have to live with that and accept it, as long as everyone is given the chance. We need to be able to give our supporters *choices*. If they want additional information and additional benefits then they can have them, if they pay. Many people simply don't want more information, or to be closer. They're not interested in the subject. Some even choose to pay more but don't want the extra information. That's fine. Now they have the choice.

'What we need to be sure of is that we can raise enough money, not just to service our supporters but also to campaign. As it's becoming harder and more expensive to find new donors, new supporters, then logically we must find ways to maximise the involvement and support potential of the supporters we have already got.

'That is why Greenpeace is committed to relationship fundraising.'

Fair-weather friends

The golden years for new supporter recruitment at
Greenpeace were 1989 and 1990. During 1989, 60,000 people
joined, with almost a further 50,000 the following year. By
the end of 1992, when the euphoria was clearly dying down,
the active supporter list stood at around 300,000 people. The
new people were not coming in with higher than average
gifts, nor were they giving more to the by now regular
appeals that were being sent out on specific campaign
issues. This was indeed a very flat file.

Greenpeace staff were well aware that very many of this
new intake were fair-weather supporters. Having joined as a
knee-jerk reaction to the spirit of the times, renewing a high
proportion of these people was always going to be difficult,
if not impossible. But the task of identifying real supporters
within the mass was compounded by another, sadly all too
familiar, fundraising problem – inappropriate database.

Annie Moreton explains, 'I spent much of 1990/92 trying
to lever out of our rigid database some information that
would point to which recruitment methods were bringing in
those supporters most, and least, likely to renew. Eventually
we did see that method of recruitment wasn't a particularly
significant factor, but it became clear that green-wave
supporters were more likely to leave at the end of their first
year – or perhaps more accurately, having given us one gift
many of those people had no real relationship with
Greenpeace so simply didn't renew. Probably not for any
conscious reason but because they weren't sufficiently
involved to get round to doing it.'

This predicted potential difficulty with current and future
renewals coincided with another realisation that, while
obvious in hindsight, usually only becomes apparent to
membership-based organisations after they have been in
business for a few years. The early years of most
membership organisations are characterised by steep
growth. Not surprisingly, there are few withdrawals or

cancellations. Then, as the natural supporter life cycle begins to be felt, members begin to drop out of the bottom at roughly the same rate at which they were recruited a few years earlier. How many years varies from organisation to organisation and is the average life cycle of its supporters. So it stands to reason that if your charity recruited 10,000 supporters five years ago and, over time, you have established that the average life span of a donor is five years, then some time around now you are going to lose approximately 10,000 of your existing supporters.

It's called built-in obsolescence and, whatever schemes or products your charity devises, it is something you need to understand, to plan for and to budget for.

A further difficulty, again exaggerated by an inflexible database, arises if your organisation's administrative systems are not sharp enough to pick up when a supporter stops being a supporter in the tangible, paid-up sense. This is tragic because lapsed donors who might be renewed can quickly go cold, but it is so common among charities that whenever sizes of database are quoted it is prudent to deduct mentally as much as 20 to 40 per cent to allow for what might be called 'silent withdrawals'.

In Greenpeace UK both problems combined simultaneously: the green-wave renewals difficulty coincided with the realisation that many of those who had joined in the organisation's early stages were leaving anyway.

Once again Greenpeace was in the fortunate position of being prepared for change. The fundraising department had expanded during the good years, so Charlotte and Annie now led an experienced team. With recruitment easing off, resources could be put into donor retention and into maximising renewals. Once again, the emphasis was on developing and extending relationships.

Evolution, not revolution

It is an over-simplification to say that Greenpeace moved from an 'oh it's time to renew, we assume you will' kind of approach to an all-bells and whistles donor-friendly renewal and reactivation programme. But it is not an inaccurate characterisation. The change didn't happen overnight and was as much evolutionary as revolutionary. Nor was its effect too startling, but nobody in Greenpeace's marketing department is unaware that if the changes hadn't happened Greenpeace's renewal rate would have declined massively and the consequences for Greenpeace UK would have been dire.

Every practical technique has been employed to encourage more supporters to rejoin, from additional reminders to pre-renewal invitations, from extensively personalised letters to telephone calls, from mild threats and insults to incentives. The renewal sequence is carefully and continuously tested at every stage and the result is that, taken over the years, Greenpeace's average renewal rates have more or less stayed the same. But without this degree of careful and consistent testing and innovation it would certainly have declined.

Each year since its records began, Greenpeace UK has renewed between 65 and 70 per cent of those supporters who pay by cheque, credit card, or similar one-off payments. Not surprisingly, those who pay their subscriptions by standing order renew almost without exception.

During 1991 and 1992, members of the Greenpeace team 'worked their socks off' – Annie's words – exploring and exploiting every possible means of renewal. The telephone was deployed particularly successfully as the final renewal request, to convert supporters to standing orders, and to upgrade supporters to regular committed giving.

In 1992 Greenpeace's renewal rate increased to 72 per cent, a mere two-point improvement but remarkable none the less in view of the difficult circumstances, which could

Protesting against nuclear testing in China.

only have been aggravated by a deepening UK recession. (The renewal rate declined somewhat from this point with the introduction of *Frontline* and other forms of committed giving, which have siphoned off many of Greenpeace's most automatic renewers.)

Who supports Greenpeace?

The Greenpeace image has always had a special kind of appeal, perhaps to a wider audience than many Greenpeace people realise. Greenpeace's USP, it believes, is that it takes non-violent direct action. Maybe that sounds rather worthy, but to Greenpeace supporters it means something that's delightfully cavalier, very David and Goliath-ish, characterised by a somewhat bolshy youth but with right on his side – a bit like Robin the Boy Wonder, but without the naff uniform.

The attractiveness of this image is *not* limited to the young, trendy, radical (and impoverished) individuals that most people associate with Greenpeace. Yet even inside the organisation that narrow view of the typical supporter still holds some sway. One of the reasons for this is that Greenpeace local groups, while not necessarily conforming to the classic image of open-toed sandals and John Lennon glasses, do tend to be comprised of the more committed environmentalists – possibly with strongly held pacifist views and very likely to be vegetarian. But local group activists are not typical of the Greenpeace supporter at large.

Research has shown that there is no stereotypic Greenpeace supporter. In fact it's a pretty broad church. There are some former hippies and some ex-yuppies gone green at the edges. There are also lawyers, teachers, bankers and a surprisingly large number of people who run their own businesses. There are quite a few retired people, some of them even downright elderly, and there are not a few schoolchildren and youth groups.

But if a researcher from Mars were to be forced to create a profile from this melting pot, the typical Greenpeace supporter would probably come out as aged 30–55, professional, AB1 (from the top social classification), comfortably off, with two cars (one in the garage) and several credit cards, politically neutral, generally concerned (but not particularly worried) about environmental issues – generally rather than specifically because the majority of Greenpeace supporters either say 'whaling' or can't name a single current campaign.

And if this profile troubles the conscience of the Greenpeace purist perhaps he or she can take comfort from the fact that at least these supporters have shown *some* interest and concern. From time to time, these people will listen. The rest of the public, if they can be touched at all by environmental issues, have still got that experience to come. And it will take some new moves by Greenpeace, or some environmental catastrophe, or a new organisation as yet undreamed of, to reach them.

One myth that time and extensive research is proving unfounded is the natural assumption many campaigners seem to make that Greenpeace supporters are issue-led. Few supporters join because they have an abiding interest in toxic waste, coastal pollution, drift netting, the nuclear industry – or even whales. Even if they had the interest, few Greenpeace supporters have the time to study these issues in depth, they tend (not surprisingly) to be busy people. This underlines the constant need to understand your donors and to talk to them where they are at, rather than where you want them to be. I never tire of reiterating this oft-quoted but rarely heeded advice because it is so apposite and important for fundraisers. Greenpeace's campaigners, of course, are issue-specific. They spend all their working days on their specialist subject – toxics, whales, nuclear power, chlorine, ozone, or whatever. Given the chance they'd love to unload their unique depth and breadth of knowledge on eager and enthusiastic supporters. That's not surprising and could be very valuable.

> I'd like to give more, but I've got to get the mortgage down and the kids educated. I'd like to give £100–200 a month and then have some say, be consulted. Discussion and interaction, a chance to influence what happens, that's what I'd really like.
>
> Mr J Barnes, Kent

Some supporters *are* that interested. They could, and perhaps should, have access to all the Greenpeace information and expertise. But the majority would not welcome that kind of involvement and Greenpeace has to live with that.

Annie Moreton has her own picture of the typical supporter. 'I see our donors as people who see us on *News at Ten* [the popular nightly television news programme in Britain] and say, "Way to go! That's good, isn't it? I gave them a tenner a couple of months ago. Did you see that on the telly?" And that's it. They'll watch a few documentaries, exclaim with genuine disgust, "God, doesn't it make you sick?" And they'll feel rather good that through Greenpeace they're doing something about it.

'Greenpeace is definitely providing something for them. It's not bad value for money.'

Annie is also aware, however, of the danger of stereotypes. 'Everybody who works in a charity seems to have a picture of their typical donor and they are generally wrong. I could be just as wrong too.

'Certainly many of our donors are much more involved, they know much more – often more than we do – and care every bit as passionately. Curiously enough, we get the best evidence of this from our most élite scheme, *Frontline*.' (*See* page 387.)

The other realisation that surprised many inside Greenpeace was that such a large number of their supporters, particularly the older ones, were actively supporting several other charities and worthwhile causes.

The demographic time bomb

Another phenomenon looms over fundraising organisations, foreshadowing social and cultural change that, despite its slow build-up, will hit the fundraising fraternity with the force and vigour of an environmental catastrophe. But the effects of the demographic time bomb will most likely be benign for the likes of Greenpeace.

Many older-established charities are worrying now about how the demographic time bomb will affect their supporter base. They see their traditional donors dying off in increasing numbers and while this bodes well for current and future legacy income in the short to medium term, these traditional donors are not automatically being replaced by new supporters, so the long-term prospects for these charities look bleak. Consider, for example, the future prognosis of a welfare charity set up to cater for wounded ex-servicemen and women and their families.

All the signs are that the ageing of the population will work in Greenpeace's favour. They have a strong following among the generation who were teenagers in the sixties, the flower children who ushered in the dawning of the age of Aquarius. Their coming of age as donors promises benefits for all fundraisers because of their numbers and affluence alone. But this is also the generation most in tune with the principles, attitudes and campaign values of Greenpeace, so Greenpeace should be well placed to move rapidly up the league table of favourite causes.

Greenpeace may have a larger than expected penetration among the current generation of donors, but it has had to reconcile itself to sharing their affections and often found itself way down on their 'most-favoured' list. Things should be different when the children of today's donors move to donor status themselves. Not only will there be more of them, but Greenpeace should be well placed to move to front of mind, to the top of these new donors' preferences, the fashionable cause of the age. (This may not last forever. The next but one generation may not be so benign for Greenpeace.)

But for now it is from the new generation of social causes, led by Greenpeace, Amnesty and the like, that the challenge to the established charities will come. And it will not come from the younger generation, or from any broadening of appeal to bring in new audiences. It will come when the current generation of donors is gradually replaced by another set of donors, seemingly identical, of the same age, interest and social background, but with a somewhat different set of attitudes.

These are the new-old. They already possess or control up to 90 per cent of their nation's disposable income. Their assets are predicted to treble in the next 20 years. They are the golden generation. Among them are almost all the real donors.

They could totally transform Greenpeace's financial situation and its potential in the next few years. How long that will last, and whether Greenpeace itself will in time be supplanted by a newer, more vigorous cause remains to be seen.

Service becomes acceptable

It is probably not revealing any secrets to say that in the very early days of Greenpeace UK the supporters were often regarded as little more than a pain in the butt. Membership appeared to offer a threat as well as a promise. Member control, internal insurrection and take-over from outside were vague and perhaps just imaginary dangers, but members or supporters may have been viewed as a distraction from the serious business of campaigning and therefore were, perhaps at best, a nuisance. (Greenpeace can be forgiven a slight tendency to paranoia. This is, after all, the organisation whose flagship was bombed and sunk by members of the French secret service and who saw, over the next decade, the public perception of history so manipulated that most French people believed Greenpeace sank a ship of the French navy.)

Postal supporters were certainly a lot less frightening than local groups, who in the early days frequently seemed to be asking for more support than the growing Greenpeace was able to give. Corresponding supporters at least were out of sight, and if dealt with by a few discreet individuals tucked away in a remote corner of the building then they could just as easily and quickly be out of mind.

Greenpeace was not alone in this attitude. Many charities regarded their mass of supporters as inconvenient, if not alarming. Some still do. But in the late eighties or early nineties that attitude began to change.

In 1988 Charlotte and Annie were on a roll, so effectively could get anything they asked for. With some foresight, they established a customer services unit – three people plus a supervisor – to open all mail and deal with the endless stream of practical questions now coming in from the growing band of supporters.

'We then set out to sell this service to our colleagues in the rest of the office. We had the idea that our supporters

MICHIGAN
F·U·GB
HAVE A NICE DAY!

Simons Palmer

Why does a Ford in Britain pump out 100% more toxic fumes than a Ford back home in America?

GREENPEACE

A gutsy and provocative challenge to Ford Great Britain gave Greenpeace UK supporters their first chance to campaign directly. Not only did they succeed in changing the law, this campaign also showed Greenpeace supporters that they could have a voice. Many campaigns later, Greenpeace supporters are still writing letters.

could be a campaigning resource, although they had never been used in that way before', explains Annie.

Turning donors into campaigners

The first time Greenpeace asked its supporters to get involved in a campaign was when Greenpeace was trying to persuade Ford in the UK to match the stringent emission standards necessary in the United States, and to fit catalytic converters to their small cars made and sold in Britain.

'We mailed 20,000 people and told them that it wasn't a fundraising mailing, but that we thought they could play an important part in the campaign. All they had to do was send a postcard to Ford.

'It was hugely successful. We had a 40 per cent response and people just seemed so thrilled to be able to do something themselves.'

The Ford campaign not only led to a change in the law, it also broke new ground in Greenpeace's relationship with its supporters. Suddenly, from being an alarming and irritating nuisance, this large and vague group – the donors – had become a highly effective and targetable campaign weapon.

'Suddenly the campaigners realised that we had 300,000 people out there', Annie says with some relish, 'and the only way to get to them was through the fundraising department. We've now got to the point where campaigners are beating down the doors of the marketing department and we can politely ask them to stand quietly in a queue!'

Now Greenpeace uses the campaigning power of its supporters with great care. Letter writers are asked if they wish to join Action Point, a special group for people who wish to campaign in this way. Having once taken part in an Action Point campaign Greenpeace can use that information to target the supporter by interest area in the future. 'But people are letter writers first', explains Annie Moreton. 'It's usually less important to them which campaign we ask them to write about, so selecting by interest area is of little use.'

Analysis of the database had shown that Greenpeace's donors too were not usually campaign-specific. If they were givers at all, they usually would give to everything, whatever the campaign subject. Effectively, they seem to give to the 'idea' of Greenpeace. So patterns of giving didn't give any clues as to which existing supporters would send cards in to which particular campaign.

Annie and her team got round this difficulty in a simple but very effective way, using that well-tried and tested device – the tick box. 'We simply added a new box to our reply forms and asked them to tick the box to let us know they had sent a card.'

Of course not all card senders would return the reply form as well, but many did and quite a few of those sent a donation too. When letters and cards were on occasion routed through the Greenpeace office it became clear that supporters under-reported the cards sent, by as much as 25 per cent.

Soon Greenpeace had 30,000 known letter-writers on its database, 10 per cent of the total file, all segmented by known areas of interest.

It's a good example of the simple but oft-neglected fact that if you want to know something about people you just ask them.

Greenpeace's fundraisers now took on a new role – as internal consultants to the campaigners on how to mobilise 'internal' support. This proved to be an invaluable tool in helping to overcome a perennial difficulty.

The relationship between campaigners and marketers is often not easy, with suspicion, cynicism and defensiveness being common features on both sides. But if fundraising is to be effective, the detailed and creative input of campaigners is essential. And effective fundraising is vital if the campaigners are to be paid each month. So both sides have much to gain from co-operation.

As Annie Moreton says happily, 'Now our campaigners come down to tell us, for example, that they'd like our supporters to write to the public inquiry on the siting of the NIREX deep nuclear waste dump. In our consultancy capacity we help them to design the pack and write the copy – without forgetting the tick box. And we can also advise on mailing times and even target the mailing specifically so it is sent to those supporters who, for example, live close to the dump and so will feel particularly strongly.

'There is only ever a very low-key, not specific, request for money in these mailings, usually as an option that allows them to say that they can't take part in the letter-writing campaign, but here's a donation to help cover costs. Nine times out of 10 this covers the cost of the mailing.'

Greenpeace makes sure that a reluctant retailer takes note of 'Greenfreeze', its ozone-friendly fridge.

Because it is so much more expensive, Greenpeace hasn't yet made much use of the telephone for campaigning purposes.

Annie explains, 'We did use the phone for a very specific reason a few years ago as part of a campaign to lobby the Department of Trade and Industry about the action they were – or were not – taking over ozone protection. We rang about 2,000 carefully selected people and asked them to call the top civil servants in the Department to ask them what they were going to do.

'It was very popular and quite effective. People liked being phoned and asked to do something. They didn't see it as a junk phone call at all. We did ask, very gently, for a donation to cover the cost of the campaign, and with a squeak we did – I think we even had £50 to spare.

'But it was all done very quickly and we didn't even have time to send a follow-up pack.'

One advantage of the telephone is speed, although Greenpeace has now so refined its direct mail strategy that quite complex mailings can be written, approved, produced and despatched within just a few days.

Some years before, when Annie worked at the Campaign for Nuclear Disarmament (CND) she had experience of a system called the telephone tree, which she thought might work for Greenpeace.

'The idea behind the telephone tree is that supporters are asked to volunteer to make five phone calls each to other supporters, to pass on the campaign message. Volunteers provide just their phone numbers – no addresses – and with their permission these are passed on to other supporters. To start the campaign all CND had to do was ring 10 people. They then rang their five people, who in turn rang their five, each time getting those five to agree also to do whatever the campaign required.

'When it worked, it spread like wildfire. But you had to make sure that no one broke the link. The other advantage, of course, is that it cost CND very little.'

This has now been used by Greenpeace local groups to recruit people to turn up and protest at the French embassy in London whenever the French were planning a nuclear test.

Picking up the phone

Greenpeace has for some time been acutely aware of the enormous potential that the telephone offers for fundraising and supporter involvement and development. Here it has a singular advantage over many other fundraisers – the Greenpeace supporter profile indicates that these are people who are very comfortable with the telephone.

Greenpeace UK started testing telephone fundraising in 1990 in the most obvious and lowest-risk area – the re-recruitment of lapsed donors. It worked very well.

One of the startling discoveries Greenpeace's research has

made over the years is that the majority of lapsed supporters had no real deliberate intention to lapse and many are quite unaware that they are no longer supporters, even if their last subscription was paid as long as five years ago.

Eventually use of the telephone was built into the renewal sequence, but only as a final – and most expensive – resort. The caller, when the call did come, could then adopt a genuinely concerned tone. 'We are a little worried because we have written to you several times recently about your membership...'. And so on. Most of the lapsed supporters would then renew on the spot simply because it was the easiest thing to do, whereas before they had avoided four or five postal requests to renew, for exactly the same reason.

The lumbering Greenpeace database remained a stumbling block for most sophisticated activity, and ability to make good use of the telephone suffered more than most.

Annie explains, 'Our database couldn't easily cope with small chunks of data on a weekly basis. Also, most telemarketing agencies were still working on pencil and paper systems, so getting any of their data back into the system was very, very cumbersome.'

Like all new systems, there had to be some compromises in the early stages. Telephone work was throwing up really important and useful information about donors, from those who really didn't want to be called at home through to those who clearly loved it, would really open up on the phone and who, if you let them, would happily have gone on for hours.

'We got the really important information', Annie says ruefully, 'like "don't ever call me again!" But we missed such a lot of useful information and eventually got ourselves into a bit of a tangle.

'It became apparent that we had to put every response back on to the database to know how people were responding. With our systems at the time that was very difficult. If we'd had an effective internal database and our telephone callers were on line – no problem. But we didn't.

'Still the telephone clearly worked, so we soldiered on.'

The telephone renewers, of course, only called those who had stubbornly resisted up to five increasingly insistent postal requests to renew.

But the telephone's very effectiveness brings with it additional worries.

As Annie says, 'Because the phone brings you so much closer to people, their expectations are automatically a lot higher. If you haven't done what they asked for on the phone they'll be twice as angry than they would be if, say, you'd not done what they asked through the tick box on a coupon.

'They actually *told* you. You can't say the paper got lost, or the instruction was somehow mislaid. They *spoke* to you.'

Annie Moreton is convinced that success or failure with the telephone is all down to how you manage it. If using a professional outside agency, fundraisers have to be clear about exactly what they want and have to supervise the process thoroughly. They have to be strong clients.

'Just agreeing the script and monitoring the first few nights' calls is not good enough. You have to sit in with the callers, to go there regularly and frequently and if you're not happy with something you have to say so. You have to make them change the script until they get it right and you have to insist on a high standard of caller.

'It takes a huge amount of time. You have to make it clear to the account manager at the telemarketing agency exactly what your priorities are and what your philosophy and attitude are towards your supporters. They must understand if you are prepared to take a lower income to ensure that supporters are not pressurised. They need to know when to stop asking and to just thank them for their support with good grace.

'It is definitely not telephone selling. Our approach is that when the caller senses resistance that's the time to break off and talk about something else.'

Like most fundraisers who have tested the telephone, Greenpeace quickly came face to face with its awesome power and its bewildering potential not only to raise lots of money, but also to upset lots of supporters.

This presents fundraisers with a dilemma and with a need for compromise that will lie at the heart of every fundraiser's definition of what is or isn't permitted in relationship fundraising. You can't run a direct mail campaign or a telephone fundraising campaign without some people complaining.

Annie Moreton believes that the telephone can quickly advance or just as quickly *damage* a relationship more easily that any other medium. 'We started using the telephone to reactivate a huge lapsed file. These people had no relationship with us: no expectations, no dialogue. So we would just call them and get straight to the point – yes or no?

'Once you start calling your existing supporters that's different. You do have a relationship with these people and they do have expectations. They're getting a very complex programme of communications – newsletters, catalogues, raffle tickets, campaign mailings. You get on the phone to them and before you know it they're saying that they really would rather just have the newsletter at Christmas. Or that we seem to be sending a lot of appeal mailings and maybe we could send just one a year, the one that we think is most important. Or that they don't want the catalogue, but would like two copies of *Campaign Reports* so that they can send one to a friend.

'Right now we can't answer these kinds of requests because our database isn't up to it. But it proves that necessity is the mother of invention. If fundraising is to progress, we need a better and more sophisticated type of database.

'Now I feel we have to hold off using this method of communication until we can live up to the expectations it creates.

'The more current supporters are, the more likely they are to make these demands. Lapsed people are easy because you are quite distant from them.'

To the logically minded outside observer it might seem clear that Greenpeace and other would-be relationship fundraisers will inevitably have to spend considerable sums investing in the kind of sophisticated database that will treat their members as individuals. Not so.

Greenpeace, Annie explains, shared its cumbersome database with many other membership organisations who, historically, got into the same kind of arrangement a decade or so back because, then, it seemed the best thing to do.

'It's a bit like the calculator. Initially they came in big boxes and were neither cheap nor flexible. We were running on very expensive hardware and very inflexible software that we adapted as best we could. It wasn't designed for membership marketing at all, it was designed for magazine subscriptions, to deal with routine transactions at given times of the year and to issue reminders. It was a transaction-based system meant for association memberships. Bulky, slow and expensive.'

Greenpeace has now moved to an in-house system, which is likely to halve its annual running costs once the capital investment is discounted. Based on PCs with a file server that 'fits in a cupboard under the stairs', as Annie puts it, Greenpeace has been partially operating in-house since April 1996 and the intention is that from March 1997 it will be completely in-house. Delays and bureau costs are already a thing of the past.

This is pretty important for a fast-response, campaigning organisation. No more five-week delays to get a label selection. No more will the database determine when Greenpeace mails its supporters, or even whether it mails them at all, or who it can write to, and so on. As Annie puts it, 'Admin is no longer determining who we write to, and when.'

Dying for a better planet? Greenpeace makes its point by littering Whitehall with volunteer 'corpses'.

The coming of *Frontline*

It has already been noted that a significant proportion of Greenpeace's supporters are very committed indeed and that within its database can be found doctors, lawyers, heads of advertising agencies and so on – in short, lots of people who could comfortably afford to give more. Greenpeace UK's committed giving scheme, *Frontline*, grew out of this perception – there were people out there who not only could, but who also would comfortably and willingly give more. But *Frontline* would probably never have happened if recruiting large numbers of new supporters at low cost hadn't become increasingly unlikely. So the story of *Frontline* is proof that out of adversity can come advantage.

It should be recognised that long before *Frontline* was conceived there were several successful monthly giving schemes already established in various corners of the Greenpeace world, particularly in Canada, Australia and the USA. *Frontline*, however, was somewhat different and more ambitious than most.

Although it didn't start life as such, *Frontline* is a classic monthly giving scheme priced at the top end of such schemes (£20 per month minimum, or $30 US, which adds up to at least £240, $360 US, per annum). Like other good monthly schemes, it has a very tangible purpose and function – to enable Greenpeace's campaigns to be quicker and more effective. Greenpeace had already identified a need to have much greater funding available for emergencies. *Frontline*'s purpose was to generate a reliable source of regular income to ensure Greenpeace was never short of the resources it might need to respond instantly when a drama becomes a crisis, when a campaign needs to be stepped up, or when a new initiative is called for.

Fixing the price was somewhat arbitrary but again typically Greenpeace. Charlotte Grimshaw realised that once the entry level for this top end scheme was fixed it would be difficult if not impossible to increase it further. But introducing a middle level scheme would always be an option at some future date. So she made the bold and then unprecedented decision, to go for an entry point of £20 each month.

In return for their increased financial support, the scheme provides *Frontline* supporters with several tangible benefits designed to bring them closer to the organisation. And it provides regular feedback. But it does all of these things in a particularly Greenpeace way.

Before the launch of *Frontline* even quick analysis of Greenpeace UK's sources of funds would reveal the absence of higher-value donors, committed giving and legacy income. So why didn't Greenpeace go down the conventional 'major donor development' road? The answer, as is so often the case, depended on the skills and experience that Greenpeace had within the organisation at that time.

The thinking behind *Frontline*

Originally *Frontline* (well before it was named) started life as a concept through which to attract major donors. It transpired from analysis that those who had given more than a few hundred pounds could easily and most effectively be dealt with on a personal basis, face to face. But there were very few of these apparently major donors, and finding many more seemed unlikely.

Charlotte Grimshaw, then head of fundraising for Greenpeace UK, explains. 'We could see the opportunity, we were well aware of the gaps. At that time we had received a lot of advice from outside about how to set up a high donor programme. I had even built a new post into my board proposal for the following year. But none of us had experience of really large donor work and anyway I wasn't convinced it was the right thing for Greenpeace. Our expertise was very heavily direct marketing. The thinking that led to *Frontline* grew out of that.

'But we also recognised that our new scheme couldn't be exclusively mail based. It had to give us the chance to communicate with supporters by phone and in person as well. In fact it would be an opportunity to practise relationship fundraising at all levels.'

What was missing was something in the middle, neither major donors nor mass donors, donors who didn't just say they were committed or turn up at an action on a rainy day, but donors who would show their commitment through increased and regular financial contributions. Not rich donors, but really committed donors.

The idea grew for a new and distinctive scheme to attract a substantial number of supporters capable of giving at a higher level. Charlotte and Annie knew this would lead to claims that they were fostering a new kind of donor élite, but they decided to tackle the problem in typical Greenpeace fashion – head on.

Leading up to the launch

Criticism of élitism was relatively simply and quite effectively answered. Greenpeace UK's stance was that any new benefits in terms of closeness to Greenpeace would have to be paid for by someone, and who better and more appropriate to pick up the bill than the supporter who received the benefits? From that point of view it was a commercial transaction just like any other.

Furthermore, Greenpeace needed to raise more money to do its job. As new supporters were proving to be more costly and difficult to find, it obviously had to ask existing supporters if they would be prepared to give more. As Greenpeace chooses not to raise funds from corporate or trust sources, there was no other way.

Other more practical considerations crowded in to confront Greenpeace in the all-important period leading up to the launch. What new administrative resources would be needed and what promotional materials? Precisely what new benefits should be specified? Could it develop as time went along, or would it have to be right from the start? What should the price structure be? How should the additional communications needs of these new scheme members be dealt with? Should they be removed completely from their existing communications programme, or should that be kept going too? Or should it be modified? Should members of the new scheme get regular mailings? And how, above all, would the database cope?

Greenpeace's inflexible database was already overstrained coping with the day-to-day volume, so this last question seemed almost insurmountable. But there were other basic anxieties. What on earth should it be called? Would it work? Would anyone respond? Would Greenpeace

> The way the whole *Frontline* project was initiated was well done. I do feel crucial and a part of it. I feel I've achieved things with my donation. The thanks isn't overdone either – there's no flannel, it's just 'we are out and about spending your money'. I want to feel money is going to the projects. I don't like to feel too much is being done in a flowery way.
> Mrs P Hafferty, West Yorkshire

375

Frontline was really about paying a bit more money. I don't feel any closer to Greenpeace as a result or any more special as a member. If they'd written to me and asked for more money I'd have considered it, but this 'you've given to us for years and now we're going to make you a special member' approach, which I've just had from Amnesty as well, makes me feel patronised. They can just be straightforward and write to me and say 'we need more money' and I'll see if I can respond.

Mr and Mrs J and D Ray and Temple, London

be left with an expensive promotional flop on its hands?

These same issues and anxieties confront any organisation attempting to start a monthly giving scheme and there are no easy answers because every organisation is different. But some are more different than others, and Greenpeace is more different than most. So even knowing how well monthly giving schemes had worked for other fundraisers was more of a challenge than a reassurance, at that time.

Greenpeace regularly writes to its supporters on a succession of colourful and compelling issues, so it quickly became clear that if supporters were to treat this new scheme as something different, something so important that they would increase their giving by a factor of 10 or more, then some very special new materials would have to be prepared.

Getting the message right

Greenpeace UK worked closely with its agency, Burnett Associates, to develop the proposition, find the right name and identity for the scheme and to devise a distinctive and compelling way to present it to supporters.

When the name *Frontline* was suggested there really wasn't much of a debate. All other candidate titles fell by the wayside for *Frontline* seemed more than a name, it embodied the concept Greenpeace was striving to define. A small, committed group of supporters at the very vanguard of Greenpeace actions, making the cutting edge of the organisation's progress possible and effective.

The name *Frontline* has all the cachet and implications that Greenpeace was searching for. The namestyle, or logo, devised to complement the title also speaks for itself. Reminiscent of the style of the famous UK illustrator Ralph

Steadman, it is very clearly a word in two halves. The capitals spell out boldness, the script indicates action and the final flourish ends in a wavy line synonymous with the element in which the most dramatic of Greenpeace actions take place – the sea.

The justification for *Frontline*, briefly described a few pages ago, had to be presented with equal clarity and power. Greenpeace UK was able to come up with a striking and very tangible reason to give. *Frontline*, it was decided, could be the means of providing Greenpeace with something it often desperately needed and which, at times, might dictate

the difference between success and failure for its most critical and most important campaigns.

By definition, Greenpeace operates in an uncertain world. With public attention its most potent campaign tool, Greenpeace has to move quickly to get behind the news stories as they break, to be in position with its banners, its blockades and its scientific reasonings so that when the world's press arrives Greenpeace is already there and prepared. Public attention being notoriously fickle, Greenpeace often has to scale its campaigns up or down at very short notice. More importantly, a continuing state of tightly stretched finances often means Greenpeace is faced with some invidious decisions as to which campaign priorities it can respond to immediately and which it has to raise funds for first.

The dilemma – and therefore the opportunity – was made

dramatically clear for potential members of *Frontline* in the introductory promotion. To ensure that Greenpeace would always be in a position to make a quick response to a sudden threat, or changing situation, or that it would immediately be able to move a campaign from low to high priority, a new source of regular income was needed. And who better to provide that than members of the new *Frontline*? What better use could there be for their enhanced contributions?

Benefits for all

This strong and very tangible reason to ask for higher-level support undoubtedly played a major part in *Frontline*'s success. Of equal importance (or so we thought at the outset) would be the range of practical benefits *Frontline* could offer supporters in return for their regular giving.

Central to all the benefits was the concept of allowing supporters to get closer to the organisation if they wished. (Greenpeace UK also intended to offer its supporters the ability to opt out of receiving more information and just give their money. Although this proved difficult in practice, it is an important option for a minority of people, one that further underlines the importance of a flexible database.) Closer to the organisation meant freely offering information that others might have to pay for and, more importantly, providing information such as internal memos and position documents that normally would not be made public. The idea of producing facsimiles or genuine reproductions took shape. Greenpeace wanted regular updates for *Frontline* members that would give them the feeling that Peter Melchett, Greenpeace's executive director, had gathered some important papers from his desk and stuffed them into an envelope to get them urgently to members of Greenpeace *Frontline*.

As part of their 'welcome to *Frontline*' pack new members would be sent a folder in which they could keep all this

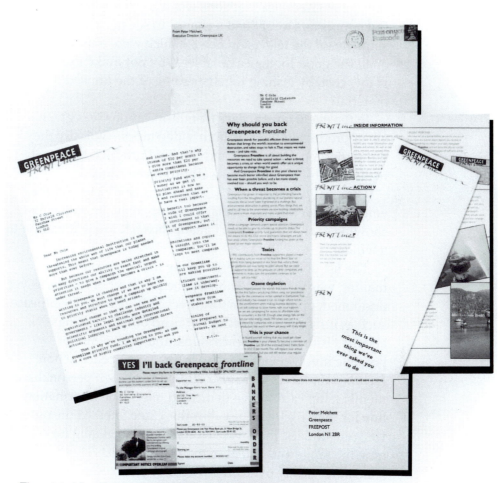

The original *Frontline* test pack looked important, inside and out.

information, thereby building, over time, a dossier of important Greenpeace news and background.

In addition, twice a year, *Frontline* members would be sent a rough-cut video magazine – compiled footage from a variety of Greenpeace actions around the world. This innovative and then rather revolutionary approach – for the UK – was built on the entirely reasonable view that Greenpeace worldwide was a prolific user of film, and footage of Greenpeace actions was a major campaign tool. But supporters rarely had a chance to see more than snippets on the television news, which were a tiny fraction of all the good footage available. Why not make use of this, at low cost, by lashing together some of the unused material?

In the event Greenpeace Communications was given the job of producing the half-hour video tapes. Typically they did rather too good a job and the final products were not really rough-cuts but very well-produced films.

The quality of material selected was first class and the emotive power of the message unstoppable. From the first showing of the first video, Greenpeace UK knew it was on to a winner.

The list of benefits offered in the first promotional mailing was then topped off by the prospect of future, as yet undefined, opportunities for direct contact with Greenpeace, such as information meetings at head office, briefings aboard visiting Greenpeace ships, and even a hint of possible involvement in some future Greenpeace action. *Frontline* members were also offered their own personalised membership card with a dedicated telephone information line for their exclusive use, but this came later. At the outset we were understandably hesitant about decreeing for all time the range and extent of member benefits. This problem was rather neatly overcome. The first pack contained the following announcement, 'This is just the beginning. We want you to get closer to Greenpeace if you wish, but we want these opportunities to reflect your interests. So we'll be asking for your opinions and suggestions on how we can develop this new initiative to match your expectations.' Not a bad way out of a dilemma!

The entire proposition was then put together in a mailing package designed to create maximum impact with selected Greenpeace supporters. Two further components distinguished the initial promotional package. The first was its very high degree of personalisation. Not only were supporters to be individually addressed with a laser-personalised letter, but the reply form was to be partially completed with bank details and supporter information, using information Greenpeace already held on each of its supporters. The result was a highly distinctive and personalised postal communication.

The second feature that distinguished this invitation was that it quite deliberately looked nothing whatsoever like any other piece of Greenpeace mail – or, for that matter, like any other fundraising appeal.

For a start its shape was like no other mail pack. The envelope was white and of very high quality. The name and address looked as if they were hand-typed (in later versions they were laser-printed in cunningly high quality; the first test *was* hand-typed). There was no window – and no string of computer numbers. Where the UK's distinctive 'MailSort' symbol (the logo of junk mail) was usually to be found, there was a *real* postage stamp. And in place of an envelope copy line was the simple phrase, 'from Peter Melchett, Executive Director, Greenpeace UK'.

When a package as impressive as this arrived, nobody would fail to open it. And when they did, inside they found a letter personally addressed to them, accompanied by a plain white, rather smart, up-market leaflet bearing the simple, but striking statement, 'This is the most important thing we have ever asked you to do'.

And so it was. But the question still remained uppermost in many Greenpeace minds. Would anyone respond?

> I have been invited to briefings. I might go – I'm a bit lazy and I'm not in London. One of these days maybe. I think meeting some of the staff would be the most interesting thing.
>
> I'd give *Frontline* eight out of 10. They're doing a reasonable job. I'm more interested in what's being done with the money, the progress they've made, or the lack of it. They should be candid about that. I've seen things they've done that haven't worked and that's good to know.
>
> Mr M P Hicks, Middlesex

Frontline goes public

Having been subjected to all the rigours and revisions of internal scrutiny and survived more or less intact, inevitably the day came when Greenpeace had to put the *Frontline* concept and materials to its ultimate critics, the supporters. The idea was to mail the best donors, all those who had given substantially above the basic Greenpeace subscription level either cumulatively or in one lump sum during the past 18 months. This gave a test mailing size of around 15,000 prospects, segmented into six bands according to their giving level. It was the cream of Greenpeace's list. If these people didn't buy *Frontline*, no one would.

I think it's really important to feel some sense of connection with the things I believe in and *Frontline* gives me that. Supporting assuages my guilt about not doing more if I can support people who are actively doing something. I'd love to be actively participating in Brazil, in Tibet, with the whales and I regret I can't be.
Ms P Griffin
West Yorkshire

There was no clear response target. We knew what was needed to break even but the objective was to do very much better than that. As a rule of thumb it was estimated that from a healthy donor file it was reasonable to expect between three and five per cent of donors to convert to a committed giving scheme.

So three to five per cent would seem a reasonable response. If they all came in at £240 per annum (£20 per month was the minimum entry point) then that level of response promised a very healthy return.

And if this first test on the cream worked well, we would then see just how far down the main list we could go before the return ceased to justify the investment.

The first test mailing also included two further, less important but nevertheless useful tests. One group was also given the option of making a donation if they were unable or unwilling to join *Frontline*. This noticeably increased response but at a very reduced value and with many fewer enrolments in *Frontline*. As expected, this test showed that when presenting an important and complex proposition such as *Frontline*, it is a mistake to allow supporters an easy, half-way option. A few extra gifts may be generated, but at the expense of considerably diluting the principal point of the request, the invitation to join the scheme.

The second test was the inclusion of an incentive offer, in this case a photographic print of Greenpeace in action. It may have been the wrong choice of incentive, but response was not significantly affected by this offer and subsequent contact with members of *Frontline* tends to confirm the belief that such an incentive would play a relatively unimportant part in anyone's decision to join.

But the main part of this select group of 15,000 received their invitation to join *Frontline* without these potential distractions. Unannounced and unexpected, our carefully prepared and produced package came through their letter-boxes with all the rest of that day's mail to land in a jumbled heap on the hallway floor, welcome or otherwise.

Would it stand out? Would it be taken seriously? Would anyone agree to take on such a commitment? Would anyone respond? These were an anxious few days for Greenpeace UK and its agency.

By now you probably can't stand the suspense any longer so I'll have to tell you – it worked. In fact it worked really rather surprisingly well. Responses did come back, and quite quickly. A few at first, then dozens, then hundreds. Then a reminder mailing was sent. Before long Greenpeace *Frontline* had more than 1,600 new supporters, and Greenpeace UK had a success on its hands.

The price of success

There is no denying that the success of *Frontline* was a considerable fillip for Greenpeace (not to say a considerable relief). Before long it was clear that all the original strategy had been correct, the research and testing had been vindicated. It was evident that a substantial group of supporters wanted both to get closer to and more involved with Greenpeace and had the financial wherewithal to back their interest with regular giving. *Frontline* looked set to grow. The results of the first test were good across all the segments/giving levels, so the indication was that substantial parts of the main supporter file would also be interested in *Frontline*.

Complaints were also minimal. The expected backlash of accusations of élitism proved to be tiny and easily answered.

But there were problems ahead, and for Greenpeace's small and highly stretched direct marketing department they were only just beginning.

Broadly the difficulties fell into two areas – staffing and database.

A decision had been made well before the launch to recruit at least one new staff member particularly to oversee *Frontline*, but with additional responsibility for legacy marketing (the two are, of course, not unconnected). In the event, it was to be nearly 18 months after the launch of *Frontline* before the right person could be found and put in place.

In the meantime existing staff took on additional responsibilities. Correspondence from *Frontline* members was sparse at first but it was clear that it would grow. Expectations had been raised and people paying at *Frontline* rates had a right to expect a higher than usual level of service.

The marketing director's assistant, used to dealing with complex and sometimes sensitive calls and correspondence, took on the role of *Frontline* membership secretary. This allowed Greenpeace to set up the telephone hotline, actually no more than an answerphone on her desk, and to ensure that all enquiries were dealt with personally and promptly.

But for a team used to dealing with large-scale direct mail communication, responding to the intricacies of *Frontline* members' preferences was novel and challenging. Some people did not want the video, some wanted only the video. Some wanted to pay the *Frontline* subscription, but not to receive special materials 'so as to save you going to extra trouble and expense'. Entirely reasonable, but requiring careful personal attention to get each one right.

The problems caused by an outdated database were harder to overcome and at times there was little Greenpeace staff could do but grin and bear it. It had been recognised from the start that Greenpeace's externally managed database was too inflexible to be able to provide the level of service *Frontline* members would need. Major changes in database were already being planned and a new system was long awaited and appeared imminent. Common sense had counselled from the outset that Greenpeace should postpone launching *Frontline* until it had the systems necessary to cope.

But an opportunity delayed could easily also have become an opportunity lost, and Greenpeace characteristically took its chance despite the risk. At the same time it was very well aware of the complications this would lead to in the future.

The problem wasn't of course with recruitment. New members were relatively easy to record and acknowledge. For the first recruits a thank you postcard was quickly dispatched acknowledging their commitment and trailing the imminent arrival of their membership pack. The finishing touches were even then being put to the membership pack, a substantial and attractive folder packed with a rich variety of materials culled from various Greenpeace sources (so the folder was the only item of print that had to be specially produced) and including the first video. Some materials, particularly the membership card, followed later.

Problems arose with the interruption of already-established systems for donor communications, taking one group of donors out of the system and introducing them to a new level of service.

The 15,000 selected for the first test were already part of an elaborate renewals and appeals system and were in different stages of it. The only thing to do was to take them out of it completely. This was fine for the small group who responded to *Frontline* for they then entered a new communications system. But what about those who didn't respond? How could they be returned to the old system? And at what point?

Ironically, this took some months to sort out, during

> I have a son and I want him to have a planet – that's why I joined Greenpeace. Joining *Frontline* was out of sheer laziness. The bank organises the money, it's a regular thing, it gets taken away and Greenpeace do useful things with it. I don't have to get my cheque book out and I feel I don't need to send extra money. I would give more but we're rebuilding the house at the moment.
>
> Mr J G Morgan, County Durham

which time a large part of the cream of Greenpeace's list was literally in limbo as far as appeals and other mailings were concerned.

More difficulties were caused by the sheer complexity of the *Frontline* communications strategy and particularly by the fact that relatively small numbers of people were joining at different times, so were each at different stages in the cycle of communications. There were many opportunities for getting into a tangle, and headaches and potential for confusion were numerous. But as *Frontline* grew it became clear that Greenpeace was dealing (albeit imperfectly) with a very special group of supporters indeed.

The best donors

One misconception that frequents the operators of monthly giving schemes is that regular donations preclude giving to special appeals and indeed that regular givers shouldn't be asked.

In fact the reverse is true and it proves the old truism that your best donor is the one who gives you most, most frequently and most recently.

Frontliners were immediately included in any special appeal. So far response to one-off appeals from the *Frontline* group has consistently exceeded all other segments.

When the moderately refined invitation mailing was rolled out to a larger audience a yes/no option was added, with space for comments. This brought in some fascinating responses. Now Greenpeace supporters who did not want to join *Frontline* could air their views. Remarkably, most of the huge number of comments received were overwhelmingly favourable. Many people liked the idea and wanted to join at a lower cost. This showed the way for a future development – the introduction of a special *Frontline* membership at a reduced monthly rate of just £10.

Know your donors

Not long after the launch of *Frontline* Greenpeace set about doing some basic research to find out a bit more about these wonderful people. A simple questionnaire was prepared and sent out. What came back was surprising.

Response to the questionnaire was high. Enthusiasm for *Frontline* and everything to do with it was evident. The materials were widely appreciated, although a significant group thought there was too much and were worried by the expense. (These supporters could easily be given the chance to choose their preferred level of communication – given a sufficiently flexible database!) The video was welcomed by the vast majority and many had shown it to their friends. And, most encouragingly, great enthusiasm was expressed for face-to-face meetings with Greenpeace staff, particularly campaigners.

> To me joining *Frontline* was giving money rather than having homework. A précis of actions and results would be better for me.
>
> Martin Dennis, London

The questionnaire also generated huge amounts of information in response to open-ended questions. This was clearly an informed and articulate group, with views on a wide range of subjects both central and peripheral to Greenpeace's interests. And 75 per cent of them volunteered their phone numbers and said they'd be happy to speak to Greenpeace over the phone.

It was also evident from the questionnaire that the traditional stereotypes of the major donor wouldn't fit most *Frontline* members. It was rather difficult to categorise them for they certainly weren't all rich. They seemed to be a cross-section of ordinary people distinguished by just two things – concern for their environment and profound belief in Greenpeace and its mission.

A wet Saturday in November

At that time, many people in Greenpeace and at its agency had had only remote contact with *Frontline* members. There there were still many assumptions and possible misconceptions about what *Frontline* was, who would join it and what it would mean to them.

All of this would be dispelled at the first *Frontline* open day. The format and timing of this event had been much discussed and much agonised over, even postponed mentally if not physically because it seemed such a huge hurdle and inconvenience.

The logistics of it alone were daunting. It made sense and made life easier to hold the first event at the London headquarters. But when? What should they be shown? Would they ask sensible questions? How would the campaigners feel about giving up an evening or weekend to meet these, perhaps, strange people? And, once again the age-old question, would anyone show up?

Invitations were sent out. Response yet again was staggeringly high. More than 10 per cent of the membership said they would like to come, and many others offered their apologies and said they'd try to make it next time. People from very far away said they'd come. Someone in Scotland promised to make a special trip.

Respondents were given the choice of an evening or weekend and response was so good it was decided to hold both. I went to the Saturday event and got rather wet getting there. It seemed the inclement weather would put many people off, but I was reckoning without *Frontliners*. About 170 visitors were expected, but well over 200 turned up, friends and family also jumping at the opportunity to see Greenpeace from the inside.

Let your donors caress your inflatables

Before the first *Frontline* members arrived, Greenpeace staff could be seen pacing nervously about the reception area, wondering what was about to happen. In the meeting room the huge table had disappeared beneath a mountain of sandwiches and plates of goodies for the buffet lunch. Cups and tumblers stood in ranks awaiting the assault. Vegetarian

Greenpeace takes on the mighty corporations – and wins!

and vegan stickers bristled amid the sliced cake.

Many were wondering what kind of people might brave the bad weather for this kind of occasion. More than one, I suspect, anticipated posh cars rolling up and disgorging elegant, elderly, rich people on to the Greenpeace doorstep who, before they'd mounted the third step, would turn to each other in dismay as they realised that they'd made a terrible mistake.

But, of course, it wasn't like that at all, even though the sheer number of visitors was somewhat overwhelming. On arrival they were randomly grouped in eights or tens, given a hastily conscripted guide and despatched on a tour of the building. So many conducted tours were simultaneously in progress that some bunching up occurred, but in fact Disneyland and Madame Tussaud's could probably learn from Greenpeace because it all went very smoothly.

The Greenpeace London office is quite a sight to see. An award winner for its environmentally sound design, it is also unusual and its open planning lends it well to the conducted tour. Furthermore, these privileged tourists were treated to a tour of the warehouse behind the office where resides all the paraphernalia of Greenpeace actions – engines, winches, banners, wet suits and, of course, inflatable rubber dinghies. The wide-eyed audiences were enthralled. Some were seen to reach out to touch the inflatables as if to confirm they were really there. This was indeed donors at the front line.

The conducted tour proved to be a good ice-breaker and lunch afterwards completed the job. Then came presentations from Peter Melchett and three of Greenpeace's campaigners, who were there to describe the campaign against THORP, a new nuclear waste reprocessing facility then about to be opened in the North of England, and Greenpeace's singular success in the campaign to stop the dumping of toxic waste at sea. The presentations were rounded off by Chris Williams, then Greenpeace UK's director of fundraising, whose task it was to outline the role of *Frontline* and to emphasise its potential and importance.

I do feel closer to Greenpeace through *Frontline*. I get information which the ordinary member doesn't get. I feel I'm doing a little bit more, I'll write letters and so on.

It's hard for Greenpeace to involve ordinary members. Unless you can go out in a rubber boat or sit in Whitehall in a mask, there's little you can do. So I thought *Frontline* might be a way of closing that distance.

I would like to know what *Frontline* itself has achieved. Is it a success? Has it made a difference, not just raising money?

Mrs M P Hobbs, Somerset

(Annie Moreton was promoted to marketing director at Greenpeace UK in February 1996.)

All the speakers rose to the task and to the enthusiasm and interest of their audience. I sat next to a nurse, the exact antithesis of the rich major donor, but someone who clearly believed that what Greenpeace does is more than just important and worth some sacrifice from her if she could be of use. Like the rest of the room, we were captivated and very moved by these unscripted but passionate presentations. The quality of questions from the floor was astounding. Here were real supporters, real donors, who believed in why they were there and what they were doing every bit as much as the staff. And the staff responded in kind. They got as much out of the encounter, I believe, as did the 200-plus *Frontline* members and their friends.

It was still raining when we left after five o'clock, but as all these donors and potential donors went happily home the remaining Greenpeace people were able to reflect on an extraordinarily effective and successful day that more than confirmed the durability and potential of the new *Frontline* scheme. Chris Williams predicted that within a year more than 20 per cent of Greenpeace UK's income would come from *Frontline*. It may well prove to be an underestimate. (Chris subsequently transferred to Greenpeace Sweden, where he was able to introduce a derivative of the *Frontline* concept and see it achieve just as much success there, if not more.)

Mistakes were made, but not many and not serious. The scheme now is working well. The future looks very bright, There was, however, one small oversight on that heart-warming November day – no enrolment materials were provided to sign up on the spot all the friends and family that *Frontline* members had brought with them, who will never again be in such a perfect place and frame of mind to commit themselves to *Frontline* – and to Greenpeace.

Oh well, we live and learn.

What's next?

The challenge for Greenpeace now is to sustain the interest and enthusiasm of a relatively small core of *Frontline* members who really want to be more involved. For a tightly stretched office like Greenpeace UK, it isn't easy.

The *Frontline* scheme has now proved to be popular and successful in many other Greenpeace offices around the world,* where it is not only raising substantial new funds, but is also proving to be an effective and relevant way to bind real donors to the organisation to the mutual benefit of both Greenpeace and its supporters.

Greenpeace UK
Canonbury Villas
London N1 2PN
United Kingdom

Tel: +44 (0) 171 865 8100
Fax: +44 (0) 171 865 8200

*At the time of writing, seven national Greenpeace offices had started *Frontline*-type schemes.

Greenpeace USA

Benefiting from a change of heart

This chapter is dedicated to the memory of David Lemos (1956–1995), formerly director of development at Greenpeace USA in Washington. I first met David in 1993 and took an immediate liking to him. He had recently joined Greenpeace and in doing so had inherited a pile of problems, including a very large and sophisticated direct marketing programme that was in substantial and increasingly rapid decline.

Greenpeace USA then had an unenviable reputation for practising the 'churn-and-burn' theory of direct mail fundraising. Its mailings were technically competent, but far too similar and too frequent. They often seemed to recipients no different from the many other communications that spewed forth from a host of indistinguishable organisations, all clamouring for more and more money. Greenpeace USA, at that time, was characterised for me as being very interested in the money coming in (everyone was anxious as there seemed to be less and less of it) but not at all interested in the people who were sending it.

David told me he had read my book *Relationship Fundraising*. That was sufficient to endear him to me, but he then went on (he was a great story-teller) to say that he had started reading it in his bath. Some time later, the water getting cold, he had risen, Archimedes-like from his tub, not quite crying 'eureka!', but confirmed in his conviction that Greenpeace USA had to change its approach, and fast. And

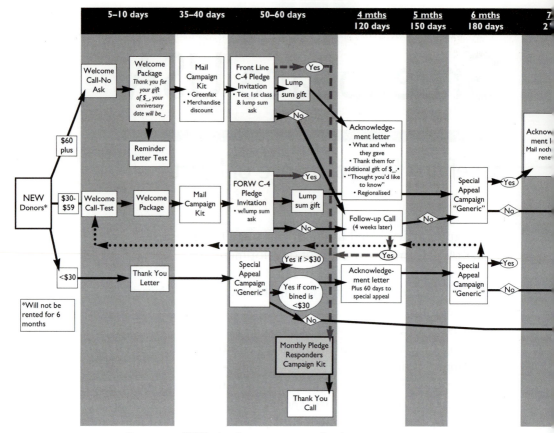

Greenpeace USA's development strategy for donors.

so a process was begun that David once described to me as like trying to change all the tyres on your car while driving along at 100 miles an hour.

David Lemos knew Greenpeace had to change, but that it had to keep raising money while doing it. Whatever else he did, nothing could be allowed to jeopardise current income because any disruption of fundraising income would put the whole enterprise at risk. This is a not-uncommon dilemma for anyone attempting to introduce a change-over from mass marketing to relationship fundraising.

David Lemos was able to see the implementation of much of his strategy before he became seriously ill and had to give up his position, and his mission. He died in the summer of

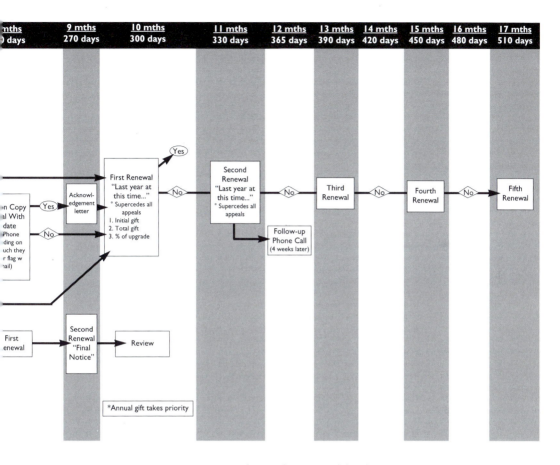

| nths | 9 mths | 10 mths | 11 mths | 12 mths | 13 mths | 14 mths | 15 mths | 16 mths | 17 mths |
| days | 270 days | 300 days | 330 days | 365 days | 390 days | 420 days | 450 days | 480 days | 510 days |

*Annual gift takes priority

1995. His successor, Tom McSorley, who David had originally appointed one year before as direct marketing manager and a key component of the radical new direction, then took over as director of development and communication with the commitment to put David Lemos's idea into action: to send Greenpeace's donors what they wanted to receive, rather than what the organisation thought they ought to have.

The year before Tom joined, I had visited the development department in Greenpeace's Washington office to help David and his colleagues draft a list of what needed to be done so they could begin to turn their mighty marketing machine around. Our list included recommendations for donor service and how the organisation should change its treatment of its supporters, right through to the need to project Greenpeace's unique personality and character in everything it produces.

Our list also took in personnel policy, time management, investment in donors and staff, developing new products, working better with suppliers, database issues and giving donors choices, as well as recommending that Greenpeace fundraising should develop a rapid-response capability to match that habitually offered by Greenpeace's campaigns staff, who react to an emergency within hours, not weeks.

It was a challenging agenda, but 18 months after he had started Tom McSorley was proudly able to go through that list with me, ticking off almost each and every area as either achieved or in progress. It was an amazing transformation.

The campaign to stop short-term thinking

'The key', explains Tom, 'was to move the organisation from its tradition of short-term thinking and planning to a long-range strategy of building donor relationships.

'Two years ago everybody in Greenpeace was treated in the same way. There was a monthly giving scheme that was quite successful but most of the communication was one-way traffic, us asking them for money. Supporters were never given any say in what they wanted to receive. The philosophy then was if we needed money we just wrote and asked for it. These strange beings called donors had responded in the past, but clearly fewer and fewer people now were prepared to give us that amount of trust. We had to change our behaviour and win them back.'

A glance at Greenpeace USA's strategy for communications with new donors (*see* pages 394 and 395) shows the scale of the organisation's change of heart. Prior to this structured plan, thank you and welcome letters were rarities. It was not unknown for donors to receive two further appeals *before* the acknowledgement of their last gift had arrived.

Now everything is designed to move new donors on, to give them options, and to respond appropriately to whatever donors decide they want. Most of Greenpeace USA's 'real' donors come from the top two bands of the strategy, but small donors are not neglected, or denied either appreciation or opportunities to upgrade.

The relentless cycle of special appeals every few weeks has been replaced by emergency appeals only at times of real need or opportunism borne of specific high media coverage. Greenpeace supporters love to see its campaigns capture the news. A colourful, newstand-quality magazine will soon be dropping through their letter-boxes, highlighting Greenpeace's most high-profile dramatic actions, as well as giving readers inside information on what their support is achieving.

YOU ARE THE ROOTS THAT MAKE GREENPEACE STRONG

"Never doubt that a small group of thoughtful, committed citizens can change the world: indeed it's the only thing that ever has."
— Margaret Mead

Welcome to GREENPEACE

A relentless cycle of appeals is replaced by a warm welcome.

The campaign kit shows Greenpeace in action.

Quality publications mean increased costs, but Tom McSorley is convinced it won't be long before Greenpeace sees the benefits of this donor-oriented approach.

A lot has happened in a short time and it's still early days, nevertheless Tom is confident that donors are responding positively to the new style of Greenpeace communication. 'Of course, some people will pick up on these changes more slowly than others, but we can see major benefits already. Donors are renewing [annual gifts] at a much higher rate. The correspondence we get is generally more positive, people are reacting well to the new materials, particularly the welcome pack.

'Recently we mailed 13,000 of our top supporters with a video package to illustrate the extraordinary year we've just had (the Brent Spar incident, French nuclear testing in the South Pacific and the seizing of the Greenpeace ships). The mailing cost just $3 per donor to produce and asked for $1,000 as a special gift. Response was 8.3 per cent with an average donation of $181 – much better than expected.

Greenpeace USA has also sensibly adapted the UK's *Frontline* concept. The 'Front Line' scheme was launched to American supporters as a top-end monthly giving scheme and has already proved to be their most effective

Our Green Guarantee

1. STOP ANY TIME! You're in control. Stop automatic deductions or charges simply by calling 1-800-701-3679.

2. If we ever make a mistake and charge you the wrong amount, we will correct it immediately. And, at your request, we will refund all money you have contributed for the past 12 months.

3. Green Giving will reduce the amount of fundraising mail you receive from Greenpeace dramatically.

THE BOTTOM LINE.
To become a Front Line member, make a minimum commitment of $25 a month. If you can afford more, we promise to put it to good use.

Fill out the membership application and return it in the enclosed envelope. Include your bank credit or debit card authorization. If you prefer to pay by check, enclose your first monthly payment.

And don't forget to select the Front Line services you want to receive.

MAKE A DECISION FOR THE FUTURE.
Becoming a Front Line Member is one of the most important things you can do to support Greenpeace and protect our future.

It brings us the base we need to respond quickly to each new threat to our environment.

It brings you a unique perspective and a chance to become part of the environmental movement in a challenging new way.

Enrich your Greenpeace experience. Help us act in defense of the planet whenever the need arises.

Join Front Line, today!
For information call 1-800-701-3679

...ted paper with no chlorine in the recycling process

GREENPEACE
1436 U Street N.W.
Washington, D.C. 20009

The Front Line logo and the Green Guarantee.

proposition for supporters old and new. There are other ambitious programmes currently in development, including an innovative scheme directed at older people, particularly grandparents. Greenpeace itself reached the grand old age of 25 in 1995, so there are more and more senior supporters who have been on the file for some time. And Greenpeace USA believes older donors will be a fertile area of new recruitment. Plans are already advanced for a legacy campaign.

Acquiring new supporters in the competitive and somewhat jaded market of North America is a problem for most fundraisers and one to which Greenpeace USA is not immune. Tom McSorley and his colleagues are reacting to this as a challenge and an opportunity for innovative new fundraising approaches.

'The churn-and-burn attitude', says Tom, 'that so recently held sway here is now a thing of the past. We intend to use our growing success in developing our current supporters to make possible a range of new initiatives that will bring in new friends and cement long-standing relationships. Never again will Greenpeace take its supporters for granted.'

At the end of 1995, for the first time in five years, Greenpeace USA saw a net increase in its fundraising income.

Greenpeace USA
1436 U Street, NW
Washington DC 20009
USA

Tel: +1 202 462 1177
Fax: +1 202 462 4507
Web address: http://www.greenpeace.org~usa

The Royal National Institute for the Blind

At the leading edge of legacy marketing

The Royal National Institute for the Blind depends on legacies. They are the charity's single most important source of funds, accounting for fully 68 per cent of its total voluntary income in 1994/95. Yet this massive contribution to one of Britain's top charities comes from approximately just 1,500 people each year.

The Royal National Institute for the Blind was founded in 1868. During its 128 years it has transformed public attitudes to blindness while achieving a revolution in the education, training, welfare and employment opportunities for blind and partially sighted people in Britain. RNIB has long been seen as a natural destination for charitable legacies, one of the most popular causes with donors who choose to give in this way.

Good eyesight – or the lack of it – is of interest to absolutely everyone. As people grow older it is natural that their appreciation of their eyesight will grow and so too that concern will grow, particularly if their eyesight begins to fail. One in five people over the age of 75 suffers from some sight loss, so RNIB's cause and mission automatically become more front of mind as people move towards their prime charitable legacy-leaving years.

This concept of self-interest has been commonly accepted as the reason why RNIB receives a greater share of legacy income than many other worthwhile appeals. But it doesn't explain why RNIB lags behind, for example, the Royal National Lifeboat Institution or the Royal Society for the Prevention of Cruelty to Animals.

Assumptions abound as to what it is that motivates the choice of charitable legacies. Donors who support a wide range of causes usually narrow the list down to just a few who will receive a charitable legacy. Most donors – even those who in life were regular and committed donors – *don't* choose to leave anything to a charity when they die, even their favourites. While clearly some public preferences can be seen from the ultimate destinations of legacies, research into the reasoning behind these choices is not easy because, not surprisingly, the customers in question are rather hard to contact.

Anything that might shed light on why donors choose their legacy destinations would be very valuable indeed.

The major reason surrounding the shortage of reliable information on Britain's largest, by far, source of voluntary income can be found within the charities themselves. For too long charities in Britain treated legacies as windfall income, the bounty of the gods, something to be gratefully accepted, but outside all possible reach or influence.

In the late 1980s all that changed. Perhaps this change was prompted by increased competition among fundraisers, perhaps it was the bursting of the direct mail bubble, perhaps it was the collapse of property prices after years of boom (the highest values in legacies often, but not always, come from the gift of property*). Perhaps it was a combination of all these things. But within the last few years Britain's leading fundraisers began to address the long-

---

*For RNIB the breakdown is 52 per cent cash, 25 per cent property, seven per cent gilts and 16 per cent securities.

neglected field of legacy promotion with vigour and enthusiasm. In the vanguard of this movement towards active promotion rather than passive acceptance was the Royal National Institute for the Blind.

RNIB's motivations were perhaps slightly different from many of the other charities jumping on the legacy marketing bandwagon. For some years the number of people leaving legacies to the charity had not increased, but legacy income had grown because of the escalation in house prices. Just when this growth faltered with the end of the property boom, RNIB found itself facing competition from other charities where previously there had been none, in a market that appeared static but where total income seemed likely to fall. As one of the biggest players in the legacy field, RNIB perhaps had more to lose than most. So the charity turned to legacy marketing, not just to generate new income but to protect its established position as one of the market leaders and its annual income from legacies, which even then was in excess of £10 million.

Confounding the sceptics

In the late 1980s there wasn't very much evidence to be found anywhere that could prove that legacy marketing of any sort actually worked. Many seriously doubted that it would. It is, indeed, a rather strange thing to sell.

RNIB's past experiences of legacy promotion were not auspicious. Responses to advertisements directly soliciting legacies had been sparse and disastrously expensive, both under its own initiative and as part of an ill-fated consortium of charities who briefly got together to promote legacies – a good idea but in this instance badly executed.

Measuring and attributing response will always be difficult in legacy marketing. Against this background, however necessary legacy promotion might be, it was inevitably going to be difficult to prove whether or not it would work. So, not surprisingly, many within RNIB had at best a wary scepticism towards the radical new proposals that were then beginning to emerge from the marketing functions within the charity.

In the early stages, the driving force behind a new approach to legacy marketing was Sanchi Heesom, a former marketing executive with British Telecom, who joined RNIB in 1987 as marketing manager.

Black Monday

Sanchi Heesom had joined RNIB at a rather traumatic time. 'My first day was Black Monday, the day the London stock market crashed in October 1987. On that one day RNIB lost a massive amount of its investment reserves – about £6 million. My boss – at that time Stephen Challacombe – was devastated and told me we would have to do something about the legacy market. At that time I hardly knew what a legacy was, but this dramatic start made a big impression on me.

'This was radical new thinking on Stephen's part because RNIB had never done anything about legacy income before then. Even now I'm not sure how serious he was – but clearly, at a time of need, we couldn't afford to ignore legacies.'

It's not quite correct to say that legacy marketing had been totally neglected. A few years earlier RNIB had produced a small leaflet called 'granny only left me the old armchair'. This was an enterprising piece of print, but it was not sufficient for an organisation with such a dependence upon what could only be described as a precarious and unpredictable source of income.

But the 'granny' leaflet should not be decried, because although there were many other legacy leaflets around from other charities this was perhaps the first to promote the benefits of making a will and how to go about it, rather than pushing the traditional message of 'leave your legacy to us'. The distinction between these two quite different marketing messages is fundamental to an understanding of legacy marketing in Britain at this time.

RNIB may have pioneered an important new strategy in the promotion of legacies, but the seeds of this initiative fell on stony ground because at that time there was no central fundraising at headquarters (RNIB has a strong branch network) and nobody was available to pick it up and make it work. It wasn't until the external relations division was set up in 1986, combining marketing and fundraising for the first time, that serious legacy marketing became a possibility.

> I have at last made a will with the help of the information you sent me…and the RNIB has been named as a beneficiary.
>
> RNIB pledger

One of the first tasks for RNIB's new marketing manager was to supervise the charity's input to a newly formed consortium consisting of RNIB and two other leading but quite dissimilar charities, Barnardo's and the Spastics Society (since 1994 known as Scope).

An above-the-line advertising agency had been commissioned to help these three jointly promote their interest in generating more legacy income. The assumption was that because they were not strictly speaking competitive they could advertise together without ill-effect. But the cultures and working practices of the three charities were totally different, and getting agreement or getting things done proved difficult.

Some large and expensive press advertisements appeared, but the response was poor to say the least. (What response there was was never followed up because one of the charities in the consortium didn't think it proper to keep the names and addresses.)

So another sortie into legacy promotion appeared to have been an expensive waste of time, further strengthening the resistance of the legacy marketing sceptics.

The promotion of a charitable legacy is quite different from any other kind of sales or marketing activity. Leaving money to a cause or charity through a will is obviously a charitable activity, so legacy marketing shares all those factors that distinguish fundraising from commercial selling.

405

But some additional facets have to be considered, most noticeably that legacies involve estate planning, so the charitable legacy is the pinnacle of planned giving.

Estate planning means contemplating one's own demise, which many find morbid and depressing, and others are extremely reluctant to do. Even those who accept the good sense of planning their exit consider it an irksome chore at best. So inevitably inertia plays an important role in legacy planning.

Preparing their estate is something most people will do out of necessity and only if it can be no longer put off. And in many societies there is another obstacle – the subject of death is, or has been, all but taboo. I have never quite understood this strange social convention of avoiding the subject of one's own final departure. Perhaps it arose because death has been such an oppressive part of the fabric of life over the last few war- and disease-ridden centuries. Perhaps it arose in the nineteenth century from Victorian England's morbid fascination with death and dying. Or perhaps it is a sign of everyone's innate belief that while we know all others must die we ourselves are immortal, yet we don't want to acknowledge this in discussion in case someone might find the idea a wee bit flawed.

Whatever the reasons, people's almost universal reluctance to contemplate the inevitable certainly makes life difficult for legacy marketers. Yet death is the last fact of life. No one is exempt. So legacy marketing is the one form of fundraising where *everyone* is a prospect.

Several social taboos were being dispelled around the early 1980s as newspapers dissected intimate sexual practices in the wake of the AIDS crisis and subjects such as child abuse and incest became acceptable breakfast-table topics. This relaxing of social taboos presented fundraisers with an opportunity to make the concept of wills and will making – and particularly charitable legacy making – much more acceptable than hitherto.

But in Britain in the mid-1980s the practice of legacy

marketing was not widely understood by fundraisers and, although most major charities had made gestures towards it, investment in legacy promotion was minimal and few regarded it as having much potential. For every far-sighted fundraiser who could see legacies as the pot of gold at the end of donor development, there were several others who persisted in the belief that legacy income was windfall income. Legacies might fluctuate in number with social whim or fluctuate in value with the property market, but there was little to be done to encourage them one way or the other.

A few enterprising charities – YMCA and the Worldwide Fund for Nature particularly – were not prepared to accept the *status quo* and began to lay strategies for some innovation. At around the same time, the concept of innovation in legacy marketing arrived at RNIB.

High stakes

There was a lot to play for. In a world where traditionally fortune favours the brave these front runners were after singularly glittering prizes. Each year in England and Wales* estates valued at more than £17 billion (no typo this, that really is 17 thousand million pounds) are left behind by people who have died.

A further £4 billion-plus is left by those who forgot, or neglected to, or were too late to make a will – the intestate. Death – nature's way of telling us to slow down – got to them all before they could shake off their inertia and make a will.

Taken together, this vast sum represents the unspent wealth of some 450,000 departed souls but, despite the fact that none of them could take any of it with them, only three per cent – only some 13,500 people – felt sufficiently committed in their support of a worthwhile cause to leave a legacy to charity so that after their death some good and worthwhile work could go on.

*Scotland has a separate system and the Scots characteristically are much more secretive about their bawbees and how they dispose of them.

And the truly most staggering statistic is that this small and highly praiseworthy band between them left some £700 million to British charities – more than one-third of all voluntary income.

What about the rest? Were the other 436,500 ever asked? Did all 436,500 of them consciously decide *against* including something for their favourite charity? Were they rotten meanies? Were they pressurised or cajoled by grasping families or acquisitive friends? Or did they simply not think about it because no one had made it desirable, no one had shown them that including a legacy to charity was something that they could easily do, that could mean a lot to them – that was *the* proper and decent thing to do?

Fundraising vision

This notion that people could be asked and that the proposition could be made attractive, even hard to resist, was soon to sweep the field of British fundraisers.

RNIB was slightly ahead of the game because the realisation of the importance of protecting its legacy base and developing new ways of promoting legacies had percolated right to the very top of the organisation. RNIB's fundraising strategy, however, had one even more important consideration. This was a strongly felt belief that too many of its eggs were in the legacy basket. The charity realised that if its fundraising was broader its overall security would be much greater. So simultaneously with its legacy marketing initiatives RNIB set about investing in, testing and developing a wider range of fundraising initiatives. Legacy marketing was still seen as the high-risk, slow-return end of this investment, so was very much the junior – in resources, commitment and expectations.

The early venture into advertising as part of a consortium may not have produced much in terms of tangible results for RNIB, but it did encourage a more positive approach within the organisation and it generated an awareness of legacy promotion, not just internally but also with many other charities who saw the ads and believed that if RNIB, the Spastics Society and Barnardo's were doing it then it must be all right.

Like most other sensible charities in the country, RNIB subscribed to the will-reading service of a remarkable little company called Smee & Ford Limited, which reads and reports on every will proved within England and Wales. When its heritable wealth research was introduced in 1988 RNIB was the first charity to subscribe. The statistical information this service gives RNIB is priceless, and its use of such statistics is increasingly sophisticated.

By overlaying a charity's legacy performance against the national picture, Smee & Ford can show the charity's areas of strengths and weaknesses in map form thus highlighting the geographical areas of most likely return. In conjunction with sophisticated techniques such as geodemographic analysis, Smee & Ford can produce a fairly accurate picture of the sort of people who have left the charity money and with this knowledge can predict the type of individual who might be likely to leave a legacy in the future and where they might live.

RNIB also took part in a major shared research project designed to look in detail at charitable legacies, who makes them and why. Several charities shared the costs and the information provided. The project was experimental and the information of limited value, but it was a step in the right direction.

I find it surprising, particularly given the sums of money involved, that there has been very little definitive research in Britain into public attitudes to legacies. Such as there has been has tended to show a public largely uninformed and uninspired by the subject. But not investing to find out what donors think may be a massive false economy.

Sanchi Heesom's next step was to write a plan to introduce a new approach to legacy marketing that included a recommendation to appoint a full-time legacy marketing manager, reporting through Sanchi to the director of external relations. There were others in the charity already working on legacies, but they were concerned with administering the legacies RNIB received and so came within RNIB's finance function. The split between the marketing and the administration of legacies is not unusual in British charities but it makes little logical sense and is often frustrating if not, at times, counter-productive.

The location of legacies is likely to be an issue for major charities for some time to come. It seems logical to me that the marketing and administration of legacies should be considered together. Marketing should drive the administration of legacies, not the other way around.

The traditional image of the legacies officer is also changing radically (as is, very often, the job title). Gone is the image of dusty old men in suits shuffling ledgers around a squalid and sunless office. Legacies advisers and managers are now likely to be well qualified and highly trained marketing professionals, and charities today are seeking the very best and most vigorous candidates for these jobs. In some cases they are even paying them appropriately.

The legacies officer Sanchi appointed was Hilary Partridge, who joined RNIB from a similar position with the NSPCC.

Not only did neither Hilary nor Sanchi look much like the typical image of the traditional legacies officer, the title for Hilary's new post didn't quite seem to match what they had in mind, so the position of RNIB's wills and legacies adviser came into being. There may not be much in a name but the change signified an important shift in emphasis, from collecting and processing wills as they came along to providing a genuinely helpful, proactive resource for those donors and others who might need help and encouragement as they came to plan their wills.

Goin' fishin'

If Sanchi and Hilary's objectives were frighteningly stark and simplistic – to protect and retain RNIB's existing share of legacy income and to open up new ways of attracting legacies from new sources – then the plan to achieve this was equally straightforward – they would go down the 'information service' route then being advocated by some of the more progressive charities. Only RNIB would do more of it, and better.

The essence of the information service approach was to set up a 'soft-sell' wills and legacies advisory service and to offer it as widely as possible to donors and other targets as a hook to attract a pool of potential supporters. Then, through developing a dialogue, those supporters might over time be encouraged to consider leaving a legacy to the charity that had been so friendly and helpful when assisting them in their will making. If it worked, this would be a perfect example of relationship fundraising in practice.

Easy to say, rather more complex to put into action.

Testing the water

RNIB had been something of a latecomer to fundraising direct marketing, having only just started to recruit and develop direct donors in 1989. So when the original legacy marketing plan was being prepared, just 18 months later, there was no established donor file and such donors as existed were already spoken for. There was also a reluctance to allow this new and questionable activity to approach RNIB's service-users – blind and partially sighted people.

So the fledgling legacy marketers were obliged to look outside for their prospects – to the general public.

RNIB was also well aware of the important role that image and identity play in attracting legacies. It could not just be coincidence that the largest number of legacies go to the most well-known charities. Although among the biggest,

RNIB was aware that its public recognition was limited. It was not one of the 'brand name' charities and, as part of its long-term strategy, this was something RNIB was committed to change.

But, as any fundraiser knows, creating a public profile for a service and welfare charity is no easy task. However effective it is in PR and advertising, most charities just haven't the resources to invest in achieving and maintaining high public recognition.

RNIB had frequently run information and fundraising campaigns in the national press and, like many charities, had found that while the cost was always both high and quantifiable the payback in direct response had been less than encouraging and the indirect results rather hard to measure. But clearly there were benefits in flag-waving, spreading information and generally increasing public recognition. While seemingly unquantifiable, there had to be some eventual benefit from advertising, in increased legacies.

In 1991, however, some cynicism prevailed in the charity around off-the-page fundraising advertising. All budgets were under pressure. All marketing functions had to demonstrate results. So press advertising had been sidelined for the time being.

Into this environment came the new approach to legacy marketing. Here was a strategy directed towards the general public, one that would present a very positive and helpful image of RNIB and that, by its very nature, had to generate direct response in volume.

Consequently, press advertising (particularly given Britain's wide choice of quality national daily and Sunday papers) became a natural option for the legacy marketers. Even the doubters of soft-sell legacy promotion had to admit that advertising the wills and legacies service would have at least as much chance of being effective in image and identity promotion as previous press advertising campaigns.

So Hilary Partridge and Sanchi Heesom put together a

strategy to test the new approach and were duly given appropriate resources (the total budget for the first year was £68,000, which grew to £200,000 a year later) and authority to appoint a publications and direct marketing agency with experience of this specialist area.

Initially the new legacy marketing campaign had four broad objectives.

■ To produce a high-quality package of appropriate wills and legacy information in a usable form and to offer that as widely as practical to selected audiences.

■ To test whether enquiries for the service could be generated cost-effectively against a target cost per enquiry of £10.

■ To develop a programme of communication with enquirers designed to lead either towards the pledge of a legacy or opting out of the programme.

The basis of the offer – free and accessible information telling you all you need to know.

■ To test whether or not the indirect approach would work better than directly asking for a legacy.

No advertising could be done, of course, without the relevant materials being available to fulfil any response. The charity already had a detailed and informative legacy booklet and in the interest of economy – and because it really wasn't bad – it was decided to redesign and update that rather than to invent something new. The booklet was to be the focal point of the new service and in keeping with the campaign's spirit of honest, no-nonsense, straight talking it was retitled *How to make or change your will*. (Later this became two books addressing two quite different audiences, *How to make your will* and *How to change your will*.)

Given RNIB's (and most other charities') history of indifferent responses to press advertising, it may have appeared a trifle over-optimistic of Sanchi and Hilary to imagine there would be much demand for this booklet. But when the legacy booklet was first revamped RNIB's press office had successfully generated mentions – in each case just a paragraph – in the *Radio Times* and the *Daily Mirror*, two mass-circulation nationals, the former a television and radio listings magazine, the latter a daily newspaper. These tiny snippets alone generated more than 2,500 requests for the new booklet. So clearly there was a demand for the service, ready and waiting. (Tragically, the department that fulfilled these requests failed to keep a record of the names and addresses, a classic lost opportunity that illustrates the need for marketing strategy to work with administration. And a quantifiable tragedy when one realises that a few months later RNIB would set itself a financial target of £10 that it would be prepared to pay for each such enquiry.)

The earlier booklet had been illustrated with light-hearted cartoons donated by the well-known cartoonist Ian Dicks. These were retained for the booklet and were to become a hallmark of the campaign and a feature of much of the material that was produced later. Ian Dicks' charming and amusing drawings helped give the campaign the friendly and informal style that Sanchi and Hilary wanted.

It was at this time that RNIB's newly appointed agency came up with the idea that would distinguish RNIB's legacy marketing campaign from all others – and at the same time provide a practical and highly visible service for visually impaired people everywhere.

The hook

The subject of accessible media for blind and partially sighted people was a hot topic within RNIB then. So why not produce the legacy information package in large print so older eyes could read it more easily?

This was good relationship fundraising in practice. And following on from large print, why not produce a taped version for those with reading difficulties and even a braille version for blind people who can only read braille?

The provision of legacy information in four formats – standard print, large print, tape and braille – could hardly have been more appropriate for RNIB, both because of its mission for blind and partially sighted people and because of its objective in promoting legacies. If the accepted wisdom is true and RNIB attracts legacies because people become more concerned as their own eyesight deteriorates through advancing years, then what could be more donor-oriented than making sure the people who need the information get it in the way they want it? And with over 1.7 million blind and partially sighted people in Britain, a shortage of demand for the special formats seemed unlikely.

Although this was the breakthrough, the factor that gave RNIB's legacy marketing its unique selling proposition, all is not unrestrained glee when multiple formats are mentioned around RNIB's HQ. Like most things in life, there is a price to pay for such an advance. With multiple formats it's not just a question of the cost, which is not inconsiderable, it is also a matter of complication. For having once been offered a special format, a supporter will expect all future communication in that format. In an already-complex communications programme, the offer of four different formats simply multiplied that complexity four times.

'It's not just that everything has to be produced in four different ways,' explains Hilary, 'there have to be changes to make the text suitable for each format. Text that is spoken and has no supporting illustrations, such as in the tape versions, is different in several ways from written text. Braille has to be formatted and can take a long time to produce. Then if a response comes back in braille I've really got problems. And, of course, each different format requires a different size and type of envelope, special stickers for articles for the blind, different accompanying material, and so on.

'It's a challenge, but you might also say it's a nightmare. However, we have to do it because we are committed to being at the forefront of accessible media. And we believe it will be worth it too.'

But clearly, having once embarked on this road, it requires real commitment and dedication to follow it through.

(Some time down the road RNIB also began to produce Welsh language versions of its materials, as well as editions particularly reflecting Scotland's separate legal system. Not just standard and large print but tape and braille too.)

There are many implications here for relationship fundraising. As a philosophy, relevant formats make sense. But the cost of implementation is a considerable price to pay for a hard-to-quantify increase in customer satisfaction. How many legacies will result from one or other of these formats that would otherwise not be received? It is almost impossible to say, so again, like relationship fundraising itself, the cost-effectiveness of multiple formats is really hard to prove. With time this should change and a clearer picture of their real value – or cost – will emerge. Visually impaired people have a right to receive information in appropriate

RNIB's unique choice of four
different formats – standard,
large print, tape and braille.

media, so perhaps RNIB – and other organisations – has to
offer the choice.

To my mind it *feels* right. If customer service really is
what will give fundraisers the edge in the future then, while
a choice of format may not be of much interest to the
majority of donors, it will be of great, if not paramount,
importance to a small but significant group for whom large
print, tape, or braille is the *only way* they can access
information. So how valuable do you think it will be, for
them?

Since the start of the legacy marketing campaign,
approximately 20 per cent – one in every five – of all the
requests RNIB has received have specified one or other of
the appropriate special formats. Of all the pledges received
by June 1995, 30 per cent had come from those who were
sent one or other of the special formats.

Makes you think, doesn't it?

At the launch of the campaign the problems and

complexities of multiple formats were a long way down the line and largely unforeseen. The campaign had a lot to prove, but it also had a clean sheet, a few lessons learned from past experience and some good role models in the one or two more adventurous charities who were then pioneering the soft-sell, information-led approach to legacy promotion. RNIB also had its USP of the four formats and was determined that, while perhaps not the very first, it would use all its resources and ingenuity to ensure it was the best. And in addition it had a rather significant piece of luck.

The bait

It was indeed lucky that Hilary Partridge's mother had a friend, Joan Hickson, who is a well-known actress.

At that time Miss Hickson happened to be enjoying her greatest fame playing Agatha Christie's Miss Marple in the popular television series of the same name. Of course it is lucky to have famous friends, but RNIB was particularly lucky that Hilary and her mother were able to ask for Joan Hickson's celebrity endorsement in the proposed new advertisements and the delightful Miss Hickson said yes.

With somewhat less charitable-mindedness the estate of the late Miss Christie refused to allow Joan Hickson to directly use Miss Marple in the ads. But, as you will see from the advertisements on page 421, the copywriter was able to get round this without much difficulty while mentioning neither Miss Marple nor Miss Christie by name.

Finding the fish

RNIB wasn't trying to attract just anybody on to its legacy database. While no reasonable request would be refused, there were clear if quite wide criteria for the kind of individuals it most wanted to find – middle-aged or older, mid- to up-market and, at that time, interested in making their first will (the emphasis on will-changers came later).

Most of the quality national newspapers were automatic choices, as were a wide range of specialist publications, although testing showed that many of these did not produce sufficiently large numbers of readers to meet the cost-per-reply requirement. From the outset, RNIB was aware that enquiries from some sources might well prove to be very much better prospects than others and consequently would be worth paying more for, but in the early days of the campaign the overriding requirement was to build volume at lowest possible cost and to prove that the concept worked as quickly as possible.

But no one really knew how quickly that might be.

It is generally accepted (thanks to some research from the wonderful Smee & Ford) that the time between including a charity in one's will and death is, on average, about four years. Some might argue in the interest of longevity that this is a good reason for not including a charity in your will, but the magic of averages is that they can be used to prove just about anything, including that on average you will live two years longer if you include a charity in your will than if you don't. So not including a charity in your will may be a quick road to sudden death. (This information has yet to be properly exploited by legacy marketers.)

By March 1991 the first advertisements were prepared, all the fulfilment materials were ready and waiting and appropriate spaces were booked at appropriate discounts in appropriate journals. All RNIB and its agency had to do was hold their breath until the incoming post would indicate that there was indeed a viable market for this most unusual of products, or alternatively that RNIB's first experience with two small PR announcements had been merely a fluke.

The catch

While waiting, Sanchi and Hilary may have been tempted to cast a speculative eye over the situations vacant columns in

Professional Fundraising, but if so they didn't tell me. But their foolhardiness, confidence, risk taking, foresight, intuition, skill – whatever you may call it – paid off substantially. Even if no one really knew what to expect, the initial responses to the advertising were much better than had been targeted and so the first part of the strategy – to generate enquiries cost-effectively – had been achieved. In the campaign's first year some 40,000 enquirers were recruited on to the specially established legacy marketing database, at an average advertising cost of less than £3.50 each.

This was a success, but very much a partial one. It would have soon become a useless success if the other criteria – that some of these would make pledges and that in time many of these pledges would turn into legacies – did not quickly follow.

Clearly, all candidate media had to be carefully tested and – despite normal charitable discounts, buying of distress space, skilful negotiation and tenacious haggling – some publications ruled themselves out because their cost per enquiry came in too high.

An early objective had been to test directly mentioning RNIB and legacies against a more service-oriented, 'this booklet is to help you', type of approach. The advertisements, A and B on the facing page, were split tested and, to no one's surprise, A outpulled B by a factor of 3:2.

Although this appeared to indicate that the more indirect the advertisement the more cost-effective the response, Sanchi and Hilary were aware that this could only be certain in terms of the cost of the initial enquiry. Only time would tell if that ratio was consistent when it came to the number of pledges and the number of actual legacies received.

A variety of other tests were done, and in time RNIB refined and improved its legacy information message, but Joan Hickson's 'solve the mystery...' ad has continued to be the star performer for RNIB.

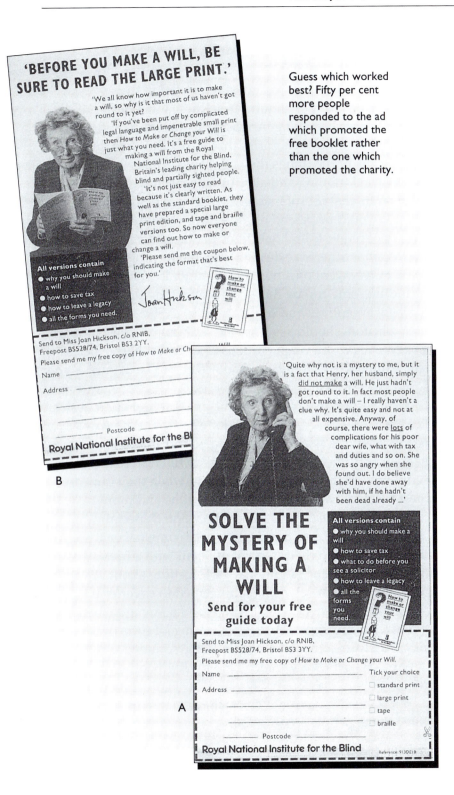

Guess which worked best? Fifty per cent more people responded to the ad which promoted the free booklet rather than the one which promoted the charity.

Coping with success

While Sanchi Heesom was most interested in the encouraging cost per enquiry from these initial tests, Hilary Partridge was becoming increasingly anxious, not just about the sheer volume of enquiries that were coming in, but about some of the things they might ask. Hilary had no formal legal training and although it was made clear to responders that if professional advice was required the request would be passed on, still there was anxiety as to the variety of requests and questions that might crop up, and how easy or otherwise dealing with them would be.

So Hilary went on a number of specialist courses, including some run by the Law Society and others designed for legal executives and trainee solicitors. She was anxious that solicitors should see RNIB not as a competitor but more as a source of well-prepared, possible clients. Nevertheless, she wanted to give only good advice and to be as sure as she could be of her field.

Most responders found the information contained in *How to make or change your will* to be quite sufficient for their needs. That was what it was designed for. The booklet even had a handy checklist questionnaire to fill in so readers could be sure they were well prepared when they came to meet their solicitor and so could save time and money.

But there were always some who wanted special information, whose circumstances were unusual or who simply wanted to check a point of detail with a friendly human voice. Before long Hilary was getting about 20 calls each week, which between them seemed to cover every conceivable aspect of will making – and a few more besides.

Hilary soon found she was answering all sorts of enquiries from all sorts of people. Some sounded like there might well be a legacy somewhere for RNIB, others not at all.

But there was no doubt about the demand, or about its value to the people who used it.

Commendable foresight

Several questions obviously occurred again and again. As the volume of enquirers was growing, a newsletter was clearly necessary, not just to keep people in touch but for donor development – to stimulate interest, encourage pledges and also to give those who had used the service but no longer had need of information the chance to 'opt out' of future mailings.

So the twice-yearly *Foresight* was conceived as a friendly, accessible, informative and topical newsletter concerned with legacy issues, a ready-made forum for the most commonly asked questions on this endlessly fascinating subject, which it covers through a regular 'questions and answers' feature. The editorial in *Foresight* is highly personalised and the first editions presented Hilary as an authoritative but attractive and very approachable source of information, someone the reader could trust.

It was a typical customer-oriented, service-oriented activity. Only in this case there was nothing to pay and service-users were not required to be current, or even past, supporters of RNIB. No doubt many freeloaders took advantage of this no-questions-asked, free service and, having had their way with it, left, perhaps impressed but without feeling any obligation to give anything to the charity. Others made just token gifts – *Foresight* generated worthwhile donations from its first issue. Perhaps a further group resolved to leave just a small financial titbit in their wills, so recently made with RNIB's help, in a kind of self-imposed *quid pro quo* arrangement. Yet another group, no doubt numerically the smallest, will have written their new wills to include RNIB in quite a substantial way, perhaps even leaving the charity the residue or a share in the residue of their entire estate.*

The process is rather like panning for gold. You have to

---

*In legacy marketing terms a specific gift is known as a pecuniary legacy, whereas what is left after all specific gifts of money and property is known as the residue. In charitable wills the residue is often shared among several organisations or individuals. In 1995, the average value of a pecuniary legacy was £3,200 and a residuary legacy £20,000 (data from Smee & Ford again).

sift an awful lot of sand, which is mucky, inconvenient and bloody hard work. And you do it in some strange, out of the way places. But it's all worthwhile when you find a few nuggets.

A few new friends

Press advertising, mainly in national newspapers and magazines, continued to build the list cost-effectively throughout the first two years of the campaign, when just over 50,000 names and addresses were added to the new legacy database. Regional newspapers were tested, as were several different radio advertisements, a natural development for a charity such as RNIB. Both media could sometimes offer appropriate editorial features around the RNIB ads and response, although patchy, was not bad. But cost of acquisition rose if the charity strayed too far from the small nucleus of large-circulation dailies that form the core of the British national press and deliver most readers at the lowest cost per thousand. Increased competition from other charities trying similar approaches also led RNIB towards cautious deployment of its limited advertising resources.

With the increasing trend in RNIB's legacy marketing department towards encouraging service-users to drop out of the legacy programme once they had finished with it, the size of the database settled down around 40,000, with limited new recruitment more or less just replacing those who opted to leave the scheme. RNIB didn't want the expense of sending newsletters and other materials to people who had no further use for them. As techniques for encouraging opt-outs improved, the legacy marketing department concentrated increasingly on improving the quality of its service and on building relationships with known prospects.

Just as gold diggers don't judge their successes by how big their pile of sand is, so legacy marketers can draw comfort from a declining list. Size isn't everything. It's quality not quantity that counts.

Demands on the service continued unabated in the form of letters and phone calls seeking personal consultancy. Dealing with the influx was a very time-consuming activity for someone working on her own, as Hilary was. Some of these requests were asking not just for letters or phone calls, but for personal visits. It seemed to Hilary that in some cases such one-to-one relationship building, however time-consuming, might be very worthwhile.

There's nowt so queer as folk

Some of the people who contacted Hilary in the early days (and since) were distinctly idiosyncratic and it soon became a challenge to sort out the serious enquirer from the time waster or, perhaps more appropriately, the lonely elderly person who just wanted a chat. But obviously lonely old people are just the kind who might wish to leave a legacy to a charity. The huge responsibility of her task and the grey areas of no man's land that inhabited it soon became apparent to Hilary.

There were quite a few characters among the contacts, providing more than a few opportunities for a good laugh. People had seen Hilary's photograph in *Foresight* and had received several of her friendly and helpful letters. Not surprisingly, when they wrote or called many felt they knew her quite well already (*see* panel, pages 445–448).

'One woman phoned me recently', explains Hilary, 'and came through saying, "It's Mrs Robson, Hilary. Can you send me a Christmas catalogue? I'm going on holiday so can you send it to me before so and so?" I was left wondering who on earth Mrs Robson was. I then discovered that she had sent in the pledge card indicating she had already made a legacy to RNIB.'

Perhaps someone so important will expect Hilary to know her straightaway. Perhaps that's the price to be paid for maintaining many simultaneous relationships at a distance. Hilary has many such anecdotes.

'A woman from Sussex informed me that her husband had left us a legacy to pay for one of our talking books (taped books for blind people). Ironically the title we allocated to him was *Dead Man's Ransom*. It was purely unintentional and she didn't seem to mind. She often calls me for a chat, often on a fairly slender pretext.'

The woman in Sussex is visited personally by Hilary at roughly six-monthly intervals. Although it is very hard to assess and not something that Hilary would ask, she thinks this degree of personal attention, while time-consuming, is definitely worthwhile.

So how do you decide whether somebody is worth spending time on, or not? In the end it must come down to purely personal judgement.

'A woman in Wales once phoned me to say she was most concerned about another national charity', Hilary recounts, 'who at that time was involved in a financial scandal that was in all the papers. She said she wanted to cut it out of her will. She had rung us because she was losing her sight and she wanted quite a lot of help. I arranged for one of our local appeals managers to find her a suitable solicitor. We were helpful to her at a time when she needed it and as a result, so she has told us, she is now leaving us rather a lot of money. We understand her estate is worth about half a million pounds.'

But this particular individual has clearly been a lot of trouble and may continue to be for some time. 'Every so often she rings me in a flap, worried about something or other, often trivial or imagined. And I try to be as helpful and reassuring as I can. Often all I do is just listen.'

Difficult and demanding customers are more the exception than the rule, but the service-oriented approach, particularly when run by nice people who can't say no, attracts more than its fair share of insufferables, and not all have large estates to make it worthwhile.

Hilary is also aware that her Welsh lady would probably

have come to RNIB, press advertising and legacies information advisory service or not. However, as Hilary asks, 'Would she have stayed with us if we hadn't given her the contact, the relationship building, that we have? And given the total numbers involved those requiring very special treatment seem few and far between.'

After three years of relationship building, Hilary calculates that there are only about 20 people that she really should visit on a regular basis. 'It is increasing slowly', she says, 'and I'm sure it's worth it.'

Sanchi Heesom is more tested by the management issues involved. How much time should Hilary spend servicing existing customers who already have established relationships and how much should she spend managing her growing department and developing and promoting new initiatives?

Delegation difficulties were apparent at an early stage. Perhaps because of the hype in *Foresight*, legacy prospects wanted to talk to and meet with Hilary and weren't happy being fobbed off on to anyone else.

This seems to be a familiar problem in donor development. Having once formed a relationship, donors are not keen to be passed on to another and to form the relationship anew. This begs the question: how much is relationship fundraising a relationship with the charity and how much is it a relationship with the individual fundraiser? This is not an unimportant issue when considering who a vulnerable elderly person might choose at the last minute to include in his or her will – the urgent cause or the nice young man or woman who presented it so caringly.

Before you can decide which side of the line you should be on you need to be able to find the line

This clearly is a remarkably sensitive and delicate area for would-be legacy marketers. Where is the line over which we should never go? At what point does good relationship fundraising end and cynical manipulation and exploitation begin? It may be a dilemma unique to the fundraising profession, but versions of the phenomenon can be found in other fields of commerce.

For example, when a really good salesperson changes job his or her customers frequently transfer their custom to the new employer, indicating greater loyalty to the person than to the product. This happens so regularly it is often a condition of the job offer that the salesperson brings some customers to the new job.

When advertising executives leave their agencies they often take some of their existing clients with them. These clients would rather take a risk and go with people they know even though they have no track record as a company.

As fundraising is such a 'people' business it is just as affected by this as other fields of work – but the moral issues and ethical questions are somewhat more involved for fundraisers. Everyone knows that commercial business is a dog-eat-dog world. But do such values – or the lack of them – fit as easily in the world of fundraising? And what would donors feel about it if they did?

A regional network

Hilary believes that pledgers (those who have returned the pledge card that comes with their legacy information pack to indicate that they intend to leave RNIB a legacy) should all be personally and individually dealt with from the centre, or by a regional legacy marketing specialist, who may be based a long way from head office but who nevertheless reports to the centre. It's not something that can be left to a regional fundraiser who, even if he or she has the necessary knowledge of wills and legacies, has 95 other competing things to do.

At the time of writing, RNIB has just one regional wills and legacies adviser, Sebastian Wilberforce (*see* pages 443–445). He is a solicitor who operates as an accessible resource for all RNIB fundraisers nationwide, a specialist who can be called in whenever legacies expertise is needed and who will develop his prospects by letter, phone and visits.

Clearly there are costs associated with this degree of personalisation. In practice there is something of a compromise and RNIB's task is to work out what is a reasonable if not an optimum level of service for each type of client. Inevitably it's not very precise and so judgement has to take over. But faced with the difficulty of choosing which clients to be nice to, most relationship fundraisers accept the impossibility of deciding and are nice to all of them, just to be sure. That's customer service.

The issue of database

RNIB's main donor database is currently held by an outside bureau. The service it gets is not unreasonable, but it is less than ideal as information is not instantly accessible and reports take time to produce and are costly. So, despite the obvious links and overlap between legacy prospects and donors, the charity decided early on not to piggyback on the main system but to set up a new database just for legacy marketing, as a temporary expedient.

'We know what we want the database to do', explains Hilary, 'but it is a complex data management task. Our strategy for enquirers means people have to get a variety of different things at different times, which is complex enough, but when you add the extra complication of four different formats it soon becomes mind blowing.'

A strategy for enquirers

What follows is a summary of RNIB's legacy enquirer development strategy.

Objectives:
(A) To develop a programme of planned communications with a view to converting the highest possible number of

enquirers of the legacies information service to pledgers and ultimately to legators.

(B) To use relationship fundraising to achieve this aim.

With a sizeable database (50,000-plus) and investment it is essential that each enquirer is communicated with in a planned, finite way and if the relationship does not result in a pledge it should be ended.

1. Recruitment

There are five main ways to recruit legacy enquirers.

(i)   Through direct mail from existing RNIB donors and supporters.

(ii) At grassroots level through meetings and other activities of regional members of RNIB's staff.

(iii) Through the PR activities of RNIB's head office.

(iv) Approaches to the general public through –
    (a) Press advertising.
    (b) Inserts.
    (c) Radio commercials.
    (d) Television advertising (possible future option).

(v)   Through referrals from solicitors.

2. Development from enquirer to pledger

All enquirers can be treated in the same way except group (ii) where some nominal link with the local staff member should be maintained. Donors and supporters who are also legacy enquirers need special treatment because of their existing commitment to RNIB.

With the help of a flexible database each enquirer can be communicated with in a given number of approaches.

Step 1: Welcoming letter together with legacy booklet and pledge card in response to the enquiry.

Step 2: Current issue of *Foresight* newsletter,* plus a letter

Foresight newsletter to contain a wide range of information subjects and involvement devices.

including promotion of the wills advisory service.

The issue closest to the budget should contain information relating to any changes proposed in that budget. Seasonal greetings at Christmas.

Step 3: Mailing of an incentive offer (a tape recording of the choir at RNIB New College Worcester*), plus a further copy of the pledge card, mailed between newsletters in September or February.

Step 4: Second newsletter mailing.
Special enclosure: request form for will-changers, insert/special publication; address verification invitation; offer to opt out of newsletter mailing.

Step 5: Third newsletter mailing.
Special enclosure: form to request future newsletter mailings.

Step 6: Fourth newsletter mailing.
Special enclosure: pledge card.

Step 7: Fifth newsletter mailing.
Special enclosure: donation request in order to be kept on newsletter mailing list.

Step 8: Transfer to donor file, but include a *Foresight* newsletter in future donation appeal mailings.

3. Enquirers who have opted in or out
Step 1: All non-converted enquirers can now be treated as a tepid file for a donation appeal mailing. This approach could take place nine to 12 months after the last newsletter mailing.

Step 2: Telephone research with a pre-call letter to establish –
   (a) How useful has the legacy service been?
   (b) Have the enquirers made or changed a will?
   (c) Has RNIB been considered in their wills?
   (d) Any feedback on RNIB and its service?

*RNIB New College Worcester is a school for blind children.

Non-responders will now be removed from the database on to a dormant file. This dormant file should be scanned once a year in future against RNIB legators who cannot be traced to the live enquirers list.

4. Pledgers
All pledgers will be sent the newsletter twice each year. Research has shown they want general RNIB information in preference to information about legacies or will changing.

In addition, different forms of involvement should be introduced, ranging from invitations to open days, special occasions, visits in their own homes, catalogues, etc.

5. Legators
When a legacy has matured RNIB should contact and thank known relatives as a final gesture. They themselves could be future legators.

What's it worth...?

Of the tens of thousands of people who use RNIB's legacies information service, only a few hundred need to actually leave a legacy to make the campaign a resounding financial success. Pledgers, of course, select themselves for special treatment and with such a small, discrete group it is really quite easy to be very nice indeed to them. But they are only the tip of the iceberg, so the relationship fundraiser needs to offer the same level of service to all the rest, so as not to risk offending or deterring anyone.

If you, the reader, are contemplating this kind of approach to legacy marketing for your organisation then you have to take a long view. You will, of course, do everything you can to encourage responders to opt out as soon as they have finished with your service. And if they choose *not* to leave you a legacy then too bad, you have to accept that and live with it until you can develop statistical models that can predict with reasonable accuracy that for every 1,000 people who request your legacy information you can expect X number of pledges and Y number of legacies within however many years. As all these figures will differ from organisation to organisation and will be influenced by competitive activity, audience familiarity, social trends and so forth, this particular type of legacy marketing seems likely to be quite difficult to quantify precisely for some time to come.

> Your booklet was extremely helpful and allowed us to make our wills quickly and easily… we have left a donation to the RNIB.
>
> RNIB pledger

But RNIB's early results were surprisingly concrete, and rather a lot earlier than expected. Not only were requests for the legacy information service package received in their tens of thousands and kept on coming, fairly soon after the first packs were despatched pledge cards began to trickle in. In ones and twos at first, but then several each week until if not a flood at least a flow of pledge cards arrived at Great Portland Street, to Hilary Partridge's office.

This was encouraging, particularly as the numbers grew. But what was a pledge worth? What did it mean? And, most importantly, how long might RNIB have to wait to get the money? Pledges may be tangible, but for results-oriented fundraisers they are not quite tangible enough.

The less savoury side of legacy marketing rears its unappealing head here. If not downright sinister, it is at least distasteful to find yourself wondering how soon your customers might die so that you can realise what good customers they were. Legacy marketing is, of course, the only source of fundraising not up for renewal.

Sadly it depends for its success on the demise of your donors. So it appears to be a once-only, non-renewable resource, rather like the front line in the trenches in the First World War. But no sooner is one group of legators laid to rest than a new generation of soon-to-be-departed prospects stumbles along to take their place. And this lot, like all those that have gone before, are just as rich if not richer than the last. And there'll be another batch next year, just like them, as sure as the sun rises. It's a remarkable business this legacy marketing.

...and how long will you wait?

The question of how long legacy marketers have to wait
before they can bank the fruits of their labour is rather like
the length of the proverbial piece of string. In some cases the
wait may be very long indeed, as in the instance of a young
couple seeking the help of the wills and legacies advisory
service as they sensibly consider the future when they plan
their family. The first will that is made following the
initiative may change several times in the anything up to 40
years that might elapse before any mention of a favoured
charity is converted into a real donation.

But it is equally possible that an elderly enquirer, already
feeling unwell as she cuts the coupon from the press
advertisement, is confined to bed by the time the package
arrives and barely has time to follow its advice and call in
the family solicitor before whatever affliction it was carries
her off with, despite the eleventh hour, all her affairs in
order.

It is possible.

For RNIB the first actual income from a legacy traceable
to the legacy marketing initiative was notified and received
within just eight months of the start of the campaign. At the
outset, no one had hoped for an income earlier than four
years after the start. This was encouraging.

Not surprisingly, notifications of directly attributable
legacies came in very slowly at first, but it wasn't long
before there were some indications that they were gathering
pace. Soon after that first notification RNIB learned of 43
legacies that were definitely coming its way, with a total
value in excess of £250,000. This was still a lot less than
RNIB had invested in mounting the campaign. More hard
facts were needed, particularly on the likely volume and
conversion rate of pledges, before the campaign could be
judged a success. With only one matched legacy in the first
year of the campaign there were eight in the second year, 14
in the third and 20 in the fourth.

Pledges, of course, were also coming in but rather more thick and fast than actual legacies. By the end of 1995 over 600 pledges had been received, with an estimated value over £3.5 million.

Only time, and a considerable amount of it, will tell what the non-completion rate of pledges will be. After perhaps 10 or 20 years have elapsed some kind of reasonable picture will emerge. Some aspects of legacy marketing really are long term. This could be short cut by audience research, although I'm not confident how reliable the outcome would be. But research in legacy marketing does have an important role and one of the most staggering statistics of all emerged when RNIB conducted postal research among its responders using that well-tried and tested old friend, the questionnaire.

Response to the postal questionnaire was encouraging. The majority of responders had found the legacy information package easy to use and of high quality. An astounding 30 per cent said they had used it to help them make a will and 24 per cent went on to say that they would consider including RNIB in their will. Six per cent said they already had. The number of people who said they would consider including RNIB in their will was very much higher than those who indicated that they had already returned, or would return, the pledge card.

> Thank you for the supplement on the making of wills. My wife and I found the tips very useful and we would like to inform you that we have made a legacy to the RNIB.
>
> RNIB pledger

The iceberg effect

This finding was of enormous significance, but perhaps should not have been surprising. Many donors don't like to talk about their giving, particularly in the field of legacies. Most people feel that any gifts they choose to make are a matter for themselves alone, a private and personal decision that they would not wish to share with others. So for every responder who, having decided to make a legacy to RNIB, did as he or she was asked and told the charity through the pledge form, there will be several others who preferred not to sign the pledge and kept quiet about it.

Unfortunately RNIB's research didn't provide a reliable way to quantify this difference. But it is safe to assume that, just as with icebergs, the bit RNIB could see was a lot smaller than the bit it couldn't. If so, then RNIB's investment in legacy marketing is likely to be repaid many times over in coming years.

But that money is not in the bank yet, far from it. While the signs look encouraging, the jury is still out on RNIB's particular brand of service-oriented, soft-sell direct marketing. Despite this result, some of the initial reservations about legacy marketing still remain. Sanchi Heesom explains, 'I think that we will have won that battle internally when we can say we've had 100 residuary notifications this month instead of the usual 60. Only then will people accept that marketing has made a difference.'

Experiments such as RNIB's are encouraging and exciting. They help to push forward the frontiers of what is and isn't thought possible in fundraising direct marketing. RNIB's experience has convinced many people that the legacy area is not only a legitimate area of marketing promotion but that, properly structured, legacy marketing could prove to be very profitable indeed.

Several charities have already copied or adapted the soft-sell, service-oriented approach to suit themselves. The potential in this market may be huge yet it seems likely that, as with most areas of direct marketing, in time the kind of system described in this chapter will begin to produce diminishing returns as more and more charities compete for the same audience, and the proposition becomes less appealing as more information becomes available.

Legacy marketing is a virgin field with possibilities far beyond the expectations of all but the most far-sighted and innovative of the current generation of fundraisers. Perhaps before this decade is out and a new century begins we will have seen not just one transformation of conventional thinking in legacy marketing, but several. There are more opportunities for creativity in fundraising than in almost any other sphere of direct marketing, and within fundraising more opportunities for creativity in approaches to legacy promotion than in any other area. This is just a beginning.

Doris from Romford

The extent of public demand for information on wills and will making was graphically demonstrated to Hilary Partridge when she was guest on a phone-in programme hosted by one of the UK's regional radio stations.

'It had been promoted all of the preceding week so everyone in the region knew it was going to happen. I remember that before I got to the studios I was wondering if anyone would phone. But calls were stacked up before we went on the air and they just kept coming and coming, with every conceivable type of question. And such enthusiasm and gratitude. They lapped it up, although it's difficult to say what RNIB got out of it, apart from a lot of mentions on the air.'

This kind of service is only marketing in the loosest possible sense. With its random coverage and the absence of any specific targeting, such activity would fall outside most academic definitions of marketing. But by its very nature legacy marketing is vastly different from other sorts. And just because something is hard to measure doesn't mean it doesn't get results.

Sceptics of the indirect method should perhaps try precisely targeting legacy prospects for a while with direct requests for a legacy. My experience is that the response is less than encouraging. In this delicate area offence is easily caused and often taken, which leads me to believe that legacy promotion has to be the softest sell of all.

Or, if you prefer, you can deny that it is possible at all.

Discussions over whether a broad-cast approach to legacy

marketing is better or worse than a narrowly focused, targeted approach will no doubt continue back and forth among fundraisers for some time. This debate is a thoroughly healthy thing, much better than when it was whether legacy marketing would work or not, and, before that, when the issue wasn't even considered, far less discussed.

Most fundraisers nowadays are aware that the promotion of giving by legacy is not only possible but is becoming increasingly essential. And many now agree that under ideal circumstances a legacy will be the ultimate and rightful reward for a lifetime of careful and considered relationship fundraising.

RNIB's approach, while clearly leaning towards the broad-cast method, is interesting in that it is very donor-led, was quite innovative and, most importantly, has already produced some quantifiable and not unimpressive results.

And of course, it is not RNIB's *only* approach to legacy marketing.

The move to integration

In mid-1995 two events coincided to influence the direction of RNIB's legacy marketing and indirectly led to a move to bring together all fundraising activities. This will ultimately result in legacy marketing being part of an integrated fundraising strategy rather than the quirky rather anachronistic activity that it has been hitherto.

The first was Sanchi Heesom's departure from RNIB (to become marketing services manager at Burnett Associates), followed closely by Hilary Partridge's promotion to corporate fundraising manager, a significant upward step. Legacy marketing, direct marketing, trading, trust and corporate fundraising are now incorporated into one new department – national fundraising – under head of national fundraising, Valerie Morton.

A living strategy

Valerie Morton believes that RNIB's strategy for legacy promotion is still evolving. 'We have had some early successes and many of the initiatives we started a few years ago are looking very promising, but of course our strategy is still evolving. We can't rest on our laurels in the belief that we have already got it right.

'Situations and people change, not just internally but externally too. Five years ago, when we started the campaign, the slowing of the property market had barely begun to be appreciated and few people were as interested as they are now in the rising cost of care as they grow older. Our strategy has to be adaptable enough to take account of such developments and to change appropriately.

> Yes, I want to make a will and and you have been so kind in helping me that I will leave you something.
> RNIB pledger

'But we have learned a lot and we are now applying those lessons to shape our legacy marketing strategy for the coming years. One thing we do know for sure is that the hard core of our legacy income comes to us from people who can directly relate to our cause – visually impaired people themselves. Even when we advertise to the broadest cross-section of the population, around 30 per cent of respondents request one or other of our special formats. So we now need to refine our targeting and focus our messages much more accurately on our best audience, visually impaired people.'

Another lesson RNIB has learned is that many of those who do intend to leave a legacy to the charity actually understand very little about it. Valerie explains, 'It seems that many of our pledgers only know about what we do in the very broadest of terms. Although that might at first seem rather serious, perhaps it isn't. They want to help a "blindness" charity. That's us, and that's enough for them. But it does mean we might want to rethink the amount and kind of information we are sending these people.'

Lessons from research

These insights into where the pledgers are and what they think come from recent qualitative and quantitative research RNIB has carried out among its pledgers, who by now number in the several hundreds.

Valerie says, 'Some of the messages from this research were very reassuring. Most importantly, some of us had expected a substantial number of pledgers to back out, deny ever having made a pledge. This didn't happen. The vast majority of those who said they would include us in their wills have done so, and are sticking to it. This is great news, because it clearly shows that legacy marketing works, particularly if you add in the iceberg effect.

'In the in-depth interviews two of the 16 people we talked to volunteered that they had included us in their wills simply because of the helpful advice they had received. That was very reassuring.

'But we also unearthed some confusion. Several claimed they were already helping RNIB through a home collection box, which we don't have. Many of our responders are elderly and so some confusion is perhaps understandable, but this kind of thing does show a worrying lack of closeness to the cause.

'Another source of misunderstanding derives from the language we use and this, I think, is our fault. We talk about pledging and pledgers, but the term is an Americanism and its use as we mean it is very recent, for example, in telethons and so forth. So most donors don't know the term. To them, the legacy itself is a pledge. Confusion, therefore, is rather easy.'

A perhaps unsurprising result from the research was the very strong identification most pledgers felt with RNIB's 'talking books' service. This brilliantly tangible and indispensable service is an ideal fundraising proposition. But, while the research results underlined its popularity, there was little indication that pledgers understand the connection between the 'talking books' service and RNIB who runs it.

First impressions count

Pledgers' responses underlined the importance of first impressions and the vital role staff and volunteers have as ambassadors of the organisation.

'Pledgers frequently referred to their contact with the organisation', explains Valerie, 'and it is obvious that perceptions of the charity and its work are strongly influenced by personal experience. Often apparently small things really matter.'

Such information should be gratifying for RNIB, which not only did quite well in the Myles Barnett tests but also has one of the more impressive charity reception areas – I speak as one who visits rather a lot of fundraising receptions and who is not generally impressed.

The visitor to RNIB headquarters in London is pleasantly surprised. Because so many of those who come are visually impaired, RNIB announces itself to passers-by audibly as well as visually through a well-designed frontage. Distinct but gentle bells lead the first-time visitor into a generous reception area that is well lit and professionally equipped with a display of the charity's work, a range of its many publications and a noticeboard boasting a welter of recent press coverage. There are plenty of comfortable seats and interesting materials to read while waiting.

Sometimes the receptionist may not be quite as quick at greeting the newcomer as he or she might be, but this is no problem as the receptionist is also visually impaired. This simply adds to the visitor's experience and underlines what RNIB is all about.

RNIB's corporate strategy lays heavy emphasis on the charity's need to reach out to more people, to bring in new audiences and expand its sources of support. Valerie Morton is determined that at the same time RNIB will become

> Please note, I have made a legacy to the RNIB in my will made last year after receiving your advice. As I would be interested to hear the tape, would you please forward.
>
> RNIB pledger

increasingly effective at 'closing the sale'.

'Rather than starting from cold, we need to get behind our increasingly high profile and capitalise on that improved environment and greater understanding to direct the people most likely to help us more quickly in the way they will find most appropriate to help.'

In RNIB's terms, press advertising that builds general awareness of the charity's work can also effectively promote its USP (special formats for visually impaired people) and generate legacy enquiries at a very cost-effective rate.

The 'double', or 'multiple function' becomes increasingly possible the more that fundraising activities are integrated. Now, prompted by the current mood of being donor-led, RNIB is creating a donor development department within the national fundraising division. All of a donor's needs or interests will be answered here and legacy promotion, important though it is, is just one of a range of products and propositions through which donors can support the charity's work. No more, for example, will the direct marketing section compete with legacy marketing over who can write to a particular donor about what and when.

Valerie thinks such internal competition often isn't in either the donors' or the charity's interests. 'It is increasingly common for potential legators to say that they were going to leave us a legacy but, for whatever reason, we can have it now. So instead of a legacy we get a major gift. The charity should be quite prepared to welcome that and not worry whether department A scores over department B.'

Integration will become very much easier when RNIB is able to operate just one donor database that will be managed in-house. The process will take time, but is under way.

Meanwhile RNIB is researching other specifics of legacy marketing, particularly what it is that most influences people to leave a legacy. Says Valerie, 'RNIB is interested in the part solicitors play – or don't play – in the influencing process.

'Solicitors may be a natural distribution network for our

materials, but there is little evidence of their role as influencers. Yet, like most charities, we spend quite a lot of our resources in trying to influence them. If this isn't cost-effective we could perhaps divert the resources towards another regional legacies adviser, where we do have evidence of some success.'

Sebastian Wilberforce, RNIB's regional legacies adviser, joined the charity in 1994 and has two advantages over others when face-to-face legacy fundraising for RNIB: before his current job he spent four years as a solicitor in private practice, advising people about making a will and administering estates, and he is visually impaired. He never uses this overtly when meeting legacy prospects, but it clearly helps as donors appreciate dealing with someone who can so directly relate to the difficulties they face. Sebastian is therefore well suited to his task and usually can start his meeting with a double quantity of assumed trust.

Solicitors – in Britain at least – are viewed with a degree of respect equalled only by doctors and nurses. This is strange, as most people's experience of the legal profession extends no further than the enormous bill they got from the firm who handled their house purchase and it's advocates, not solicitors, who usually enjoy glamorous portrayal on television. But there you are. The public trusts solicitors and in legacy marketing that is perhaps the most important thing.

It is perhaps an appropriate way to end this case history of innovation in legacy marketing by recounting a few anecdotes from Sebastian's treasure trove of interesting and amusing experiences while representing RNIB's legacy marketing strategy face to face.

One day at the sandwich counter of Boots, Sebastian met an elderly, rather well-to-do woman who was obviously having difficulty reading the labels on the range of displayed foodstuffs. Having introduced the bewildered woman to a chicken tikka on rye bread, Sebastian introduced himself and told her something about RNIB's services for visually impaired people. The woman, who told Sebastian she was 112 years old, nevertheless proved sprightly enough to later visit RNIB's resource centre, convincing RNIB's legacy adviser that even if she wasn't always quite truthful she at least possessed the mental acuity necessary to make a will.

Another legacy prospect intruded into Sebastian's life in the form of a company director who carelessly opened his car door without seeing that Sebastian was cycling by. Sebastian didn't get past the director's door, but neither did the director get past Sebastian. 'I wasn't sufficiently injured to sue', says Sebastian, 'but I will make a dent in his pocket for RNIB's benefit.'

Not all of Sebastian's experiences are so positive. Face-to-face fundraisers for RNIB sometimes have to bear the brunt of their prospects' frustration arising from their loss of sight. 'This is inevitable,' he explains, 'but can be uncomfortable.

'One pledger, who also has personal problems because she is the only member of her family to have survived the Holocaust, used to ring me almost every day. She not only involved me in making her will, but also in her dealings with her housing association and with the social services. She is a former painter and highly intelligent. At times she would get very angry, and at other times she would cry down the phone to me.'

Sebastian's repertoire of tales covers pledgers of every hue. The pledger who thinks fundraisers are social workers, the lonely pledger (usually of small value, but not always), even the pledger with a serious personality disorder, all are individual, many are demanding, some are delightful. They all merit the wills and legacies adviser's time, care and professional expertise.

Finally, the follow-up

Sebastian always seeks to establish why a pledger wishes to help RNIB. Before he leaves a meeting he knows what follow-up action might be expected of him and what will best suit his donor. 'I try to find out what relationship they would like with the charity in the future. What literature would they like to receive – if any? Would they benefit by visiting one of our centres? Would they like to learn more about any aspect of visual impairment?

'Then I ask if they will put the word out among their friends about the RNIB's wills and legacies advisory service. After that, when politeness permits, I edge towards the door, to my bicycle and the journey home.'

Cream cakes, long johns and luck

To acquire a flavour of what it's like to be a wills and legacies adviser it would be worth listening in on some of Hilary Partridge's conversations and visits with prospective legators.

Hilary enjoys face-to-face contact. She loves it. But it's also one of the most challenging aspects of the job of wills and legacies adviser. There are many issues for fundraisers who wish to embark on face-to-face legacy marketing – dealing with elderly donors, the long delay before payback, the potential for abuse, measuring success, personal safety, excessive involvement, and much else. In her time as wills and legacies adviser at RNIB Hilary came across all these issues.

Hilary Partridge.

Hilary frequently met RNIB's supporters. She visited a number of legacy pledgers on a regular basis and found that she constantly had to assess — sometimes from the most slender available clues — just who deserved a visit and who would be well meaning but a time waster.

'A woman in Macclesfield was leaving us her estate. I have never seen a house like it. Everything was immaculate, absolutely spotless, including the kitchen floor which she scrubbed with a nail brush every day — the boards looked like one of those butcher's wooden tables, bleached white. She showed me her cupboards, which had tins upon tins of carrots and rice pudding — nothing else — all lined up with the labels facing in the same direction.

'In her bedroom all the sheets and towels were folded or still in their packets. No bedclothes were left on the bed during the day, all were taken off and folded. The furniture and ornaments in her sitting-room were piled up in the middle to allow her to clean around them every day. I don't know where she ever sat.

'She also had a vast collection of teaspoons, which she was going to leave us.'

This woman spent most of her time knitting small squares for 'blind children'. When Hilary visited she was shown several dustbin liners full of them.

All very strange.

'I have regular conversations with another enthusiastic potential legator on the subject of his ulcerated legs. He is a battlefield buff and has the most tremendous knowledge of warfare history. Some time ago I made the fatal mistake of telling him that I had a history degree so a short telephone call from him averages 45 minutes to an hour. He has a perfect collection of model soldiers, the original hand-painted metal ones, which is so valuable that it is displayed at Sandhurst (The Royal Military Academy in Kent, England). They are buying it in two stages from him. He is fascinating, but very exhausting.

'Two talks I gave to a welfare association for people from Goa were very interesting, particularly when I was asked about dowries and whether the jewellery given to a Goan bride on her wedding belongs to her or her husband. Not an area I'm particularly strong on!'

Hilary was once invited to Yorkshire to discuss a potential legacy of £100,000. When she got there she was greeted with the words, 'I've always liked the Guide Dogs for the Blind'. After a friendly chat over a cup of tea the potential legator's confusion was sorted out. RNIB was notified that it would receive a 50 per cent share of the legacy – £50,000 it might otherwise not have had without that visit.

If that was embarrassing, the cake incident was even more so. Hilary went to visit a legacy pledger with a goodwill gift of a cream cake. It was a hot day and after a while it became clear the choice wasn't a good one. Not only were the cake's contents running all over the place, it wasn't well packed and got rather squashed. By the time she arrived Hilary had what amounted to a gooey mess in a box. Luckily the donor had laid on a perfect afternoon tea. Hilary was able to keep her box at her feet, and the donor didn't suspect anything.

One of Hilary's donors informed her that he and his wife had left RNIB £1.5 million in their wills. RNIB has power of attorney in this case so knows this is so. For such donors one would expect to go to some lengths, and would do so gladly. However, on one of her regular visits to the couple Hilary was rather taken aback to be asked if she would clear out their house prior to selling it. Not having anyone else to call on, Hilary had to do the job herself, including clearing cupboards full of the old lady's underwear and several hundred pairs of the husband's long johns.

Hilary's most alarming face-to-face fundraising experience involved a donor in his eighties living on his own in the North of England. Accompanied by the local regional manager, she visited him at home at his request. They were unable to avoid the subsequent invitation to dinner.

Dinner was a large, very greasy fish each, a mug of tea and a piece of bread. They were each given a fork and spoon, but no knife. The donor himself didn't eat, but removed his false teeth and stood watching the pair from the other side of the room. Dessert was an apple pie broken in half and served on the same plates as the fish. They had to eat it all.

The moral of these stories is that to succeed in face-to-face fundraising you have to be resourceful, good with people, dedicated, have a sense of humour – and a very strong stomach!

The Royal National Institute for the Blind
224 Great Portland Street
London WIN 6AA
United Kingdom

Tel: +44 (0) 171 388 1266
Fax: +44 (0) 171 388 2034

The Royal National Institute for Deaf People

Part 2 – turning pledges into income

This mini case history leads naturally from the last chapter and is somewhat detached in context from the first part of RNID's case history, which you will have found in chapter 8. So I have decided to treat it quite separately. It explains how the Royal National Institute for Deaf People (RNID) applies the principles of relationship fundraising to develop and cement a bond with a very special group of potential donors – those who have pledged to leave a legacy to the charity.

What is a legacy pledge?

A legacy pledge is either an indication of an intention to leave a legacy to a specific cause, or a confirmation that one has already been included in a valid will. It is neither legally binding nor enforceable and, like a last will and testament, it can be changed or rescinded. Anyone can complete and send in a pledge form at any time, so it is nothing more than an indication of income that may or may not come to the charity at some unspecified time.

Fundraisers vigorously try to generate as many legacy pledges as they can, for pledges are the only evidence they can present to show that the current vogue for legacy marketing has any impact whatsoever. Charities accept these promises from donors as an act of faith, confident that the vast majority will be honoured in the not-too-distant future and that when they are redeemed they will turn out to be worth more or less as much as any other legacy to their cause.

> The Institute was most helpful to my wife and during our visits from South Oxney we were given courtesy and helpful attention making our journey so encouraging and worthwhile.
>
> From RNID pledger letter

Some evidence supports this optimism, but the RNID believes that too much is at stake to leave legacy pledgers to their own devices and to rely on hope alone. Until the end of 1995, RNID's legacy officer was Vickie Kemp (she now advises clients of Burnett Associates on legacy marketing and development).

'Once a pledge has been received,' says Vickie, 'the pledger can too easily be forgotten. In reality, maintaining and developing a relationship with your pledgers is crucial, for several reasons.

'First, to maximise your donor's lifetime value. Because a legacy will almost inevitably be a supporter's largest-ever gift, charities have a responsibility to do all they can to ensure the pledge is honoured. The cost is small, but the rewards are high.

'Then, to get to know your pledgers. Understanding the interests and motivations of pledgers will inform your legacy marketing, particularly through improved targeting. It also strengthens personal relationships with your donors.

'Thirdly, to avoid becoming "out of sight, out of mind". Lifetime events, such as marriage, the arrival of grand-children, divorce, can all result in changes being made to a will. Unless you keep in touch you could easily be excluded and never know it.

'Finally, to protect your legacy base. Many charities are now experiencing a fall in legacy income. A programme to develop pledgers helps protect vulnerable promised income that will benefit your charity for years to come.'

Keeping in touch with pledgers can clearly be a long-term commitment. RNID has calculated that it can expect to be in touch with a pledger over 13 years before actually receiving a legacy. Of course, some will come in sooner, but just as many may take even longer to arrive.

Being convinced of the benefits of keeping in touch is one thing. Knowing how to go about it is another. Vickie Kemp has some useful advice. 'As always it helps if you can offer choices. Giving donors the choice of how they want to keep in contact enables them to define how they want the relationship to develop. They may wish to receive the charity's normal appeal letters, they may wish only to receive your special newsletter, they may prefer brief updates on your work, or they may wish to hear from you only at certain times of the year. If you find out what motivates your pledgers, you can keep them informed about the areas of work that most interest them.

'Pledgers like to hear how you are using legacy income and to see what a difference it makes. You can invite them to events, send them personal letters with, perhaps, special news of a project you know they are interested in. You might send a birthday or Christmas card. Certainly you'll want them to get your annual report and always you'll look for ways to involve them, so they can get in touch with you. And, of course, never forget to say thank you. That way your relationship will be genuinely two-way.'

Vickie Kemp had joined RNID in 1993, when the charity was reviewing its strategy for legacy pledgers. Until then, when a pledge arrived the donor-to-be would receive a personal letter of appreciation with a small gift, a shell in a basket (symbolic of hearing), which was sent whether the donor wanted it or not. Pledgers also had their names entered into a 'Book of Friends', which was kept at RNID's head office. But they were taken out of the main appeal programme and thereafter would receive no communication unless they contacted RNID themselves.

> Thank you so much for sending me the South Pacific shell – what a lovely surprise. It was especially nice, as my birthday (79) is today, and it was like receiving an extra present!
>
> From RNID pledger letter

Vickie explains, 'We had a number of issues to address when we reviewed our legacy marketing strategy. We did not know if our pledgers were at the same address, if they had changed their wills, or even if they were still alive. We had so little information about them that we were concerned about any impact our lack of contact may have had.

> I enjoy letter writing and my old friend in Cornwall writes every week, as I do, about 20 pages. We have been friends for 70 years.
>
> From RNID pledger letter

'We realised that we had to re-establish contact with pledgers. We had to develop a dialogue, to find out their interests and connections with deafness. We had to find out about their motivations for leaving a legacy to RNID and to ask them how they would like to keep in touch with the charity.'

RNID then had about 400 pledgers. Despite the potential value they represented, instituting a development programme for these donors could be done quite cheaply. Vickie's budget for direct costs was in the low thousands. She outlines what that investment enabled the programme to do.

'New pledgers continued to receive a personal thank you but were offered the option of receiving a presentation shell. A questionnaire was included with the thank you letter to encourage feedback.

'Pledgers who had not been contacted since they made their pledge received a personalised letter introducing me in my new job; this seemed like an opportunity to get back in touch without it appearing that they had been forgotten.

'The letter asked pledgers to let us know more about themselves and how they would like to stay in touch. It updated pledgers on RNID's news and activities since they had last heard from us. The questionnaire generated a 70 per cent response rate and the key findings were that pledgers were predominantly women, who were, on average, aged 76, and that 60 per cent had some affiliation with deafness. They liked going to church and hobbies included walking, knitting and music.

'Given the average age of a pledger and the average age

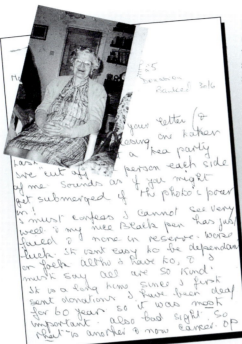

Far from being shy, many pledgers are only too happy to write about themselves and send photos too.

of its legators, RNID calculated the average length of a relationship with a pledger would be 13 years.

'Thirty per cent said that they wanted to start giving again during their lifetime and 70 per cent wanted to be kept in touch with RNID's activities.

'Pledgers were keen to give information and some continued the correspondence and wrote to me on a regular basis.

'As it developed, the programme included the option to receive one or two personal letters from me each year. These letters used different ways to generate feedback, for example asking pledgers to send photos, sending them our annual report, a Christmas and birthday card and the RNID newsletter. We offered a choice of appeal mailings, depending on their preferences for time of year, and an opportunity to visit regional centres and to come to special events.'

My big trouble is tinnitus. But I think it is less bad since eating bananas! I read of it in *Grace* magazine. I gave it a trial. I feel it does help and can recommend it!

From RNID pledger letter

453

People willingly send photographs of themselves when asked, which Vickie found not just involving, but useful. They were particularly helpful at receptions for pledgers, as Vickie would keep photographs attached to her clipboard and so recognise her potential donors as they came in. Nothing pleases the nervous arrivee so much as being recognised and welcomed by name.

> I have the *See, Hear* magazine every month, which I find very interesting, especially the letters – having suffered with tinnitus so many years, I am always interested to know how other people cope with it.
>
> From RNID pledger letter

The many letters the RNID receives from pledgers show that this approach works. The example shown is a genuine letter although for obvious reasons it has been disguised.

The future

To the casual observer this may seem a lot of trouble to go to just on the strength of a promise for the distant future. But RNID's supporters seem to appreciate it and Vickie Kemp has no doubt that in the long term it will help secure more legacy income.

'The programme also creates regular opportunities for pledgers to increase the value of a gift,' says Vickie, 'for example, to turn a pecuniary legacy into a residuary. It's low cost and low risk. It is helping RNID to make the most of what has to be seen as the last great fundraising opportunity.'

The Royal National Institute for Deaf People
19–23 Featherstone Street
London EC1Y 8SL
United Kingdom

Tel: +44 (0) 171 296 8000
Fax: +44 (0) 171 296 8199

16

WaterAid

Donors at the front line

> Flush the loo. Have a shower. Clean your teeth. Make a coffee. In
> our daily lives there is water, water everywhere. To drink, to wash
> in, to cook with, to provide sanitation. For most of us, it's always
> been this way. But one group of charity supporters will never
> again take for granted the ease with which this stuff gushes from
> the tap. For they, like me, made a two-week visit to Ethiopia
> where, as part of a group of WaterAid supporters, we visited a
> wide range of projects whose names had become familiar to me
> over the previous couple of years...

So began a report from one of my colleagues, Derek
Humphries, managing director at Burnett Associates. He
wrote that just days after returning from Ethiopia, where he
had the good fortune to see for himself the work of the UK
charity WaterAid, work that over the previous two years he
and others at Burnett Associates had striven to convey to
donors in direct mail appeals, press and radio
advertisements, education materials and other donor
communications.

Charities deliver their messages in many ways –
through postal appeals, newsletters, advertising, events,
radio and television. But how would it be if we could turn
the tables – if we could deliver donors to the cause rather
than vice versa? It sounds improbable, but it happens,
and when it does it can change people's lives, as Derek
found out.

A few words about WaterAid

Water is a powerful subject for fundraisers. Some years ago in the UK Oxfam produced a mailing pack with a classic envelope message. Now you probably know that copy on the outer envelope rarely improves response to appeal mailings. The addition of a promotional message seems to signal to many recipients that herein lies a fundraising message so many jettison it unopened.

But this Oxfam envelope message was different. It had all the ingredients of a perfect cover-line. It posed an intriguing question, was obviously important and you had to open the envelope to find the answer. The text ran, 'What gives life, but is a killer? And you can't live without it?'

The answer, of course, is water. Every four seconds a child somewhere dies from the effects of unsafe water. Only 13 million of Ethiopia's 52 million people have access to clean, safe water. Eighty per cent of all disease in Ethiopia is water related.

In Ethiopia, as in many countries, the task of collecting water – usually left to the women and children – is a formidable daily chore. In some countries it is not unusual for mothers and children to walk up to 15 kilometres a day over difficult, and sometimes dangerous, country to get water. The round trip can take up to eight hours. Water is heavy and awkward to carry. In high temperatures and barefoot on rough roads this endless daily grind must be almost unbearable. And when the meagre supply is safely home it is usually not water that you or I would care to drink. It's a murky brown colour and its brackish taste may disguise hidden perils that threaten the lives of malnourished under-fives.

Water and water projects make an ideal appeal subject. Everyone is familiar with water. Its importance requires little explanation. It is a highly visual theme and we can all imagine what life would be like without it. Thirst and the distastefulness of dirty water are easily imagined too. The

Water means life.

need for clean water requires minimal explanation.

This is the essence of WaterAid's appeal.

The charity was founded in 1981 as an appeal of Britain's regional water authorities. Originally it was aimed at people working in the water industry, but soon broadened to include the charitable general public. WaterAid now funds projects in 17 countries in Africa and Asia.

This is Derek Humphries' personal account of what happens when donors get the chance to see this kind of work for themselves.

Some union reps and plumbers

I first met the rest of the party a few months before the trip at a briefing day organised by WaterAid in London. This was an opportunity for the 20 or so participants to get to know each other, to hear about WaterAid's work with communities in Ethiopia and to sort out all of the important nuts and bolts of the trip – what jabs would we need, what would the accommodation be like, what should we pack?

In addition, a briefing from the PR department gave guidance on how to use the trip to gain valuable media coverage for WaterAid. This coverage would come through radio and TV interviews, as well as video news releases to be shot during the trip for use several months later on WaterAid Day (the UN's world day for water). The aim was to exploit the PR value of the trip while avoiding any exploitation of the people we met. The guidelines on positive-image photography we were given provided realistic help. Positive images don't mean just smiling faces. It's all right to show a situation warts and all, but only if there are warts in the first place.

It was clear that WaterAid had thought carefully about how to maximise the fundraising impact of the trip. My fellow travellers were a diverse range of volunteer fundraisers – water company employees, plumbers, union representatives and even a couple of donors unconnected with the water industry.

The charity had initially set up the trip at the request of Wessex Water, one of the UK's regional water companies, that contributes substantially to WaterAid directly and through the fundraising efforts of its staff. As well as these corporate supporters, the group included Bob and Harold from the Institute of Plumbing – an organisation with which

Water is heavy and difficult to carry – but it doesn't stop the women from smiling!

WaterAid was aiming to develop a fundraising relationship, regional fundraisers Clive and Stewart, Jackie from the National Rivers Authority, Richard from a church fundraising group and the intrepid Barbara, a personal supporter and at 74 the oldest on the trip. There could hardly have been a more varied group of supporters and potential supporters, all sharing a commitment to the work of WaterAid.

At the briefing it became clear that we all had our concerns about the trip, such as how effectively were donations being used and how would we cope with using pit latrines 'in the field' (a phrase whose literalness we came to appreciate more and more as the days passed).

I had one particular worry. Quite simply, I needed to reassure myself that we'd been telling the truth in all of those mail packs, advertisements and other promotions. We had portrayed WaterAid's in-country staff and local projects as minutely accountable, as delivering low-cost, appropriate-technology solutions that could be maintained by local communities without breeding dependency, and as involving local people – the women in particular – in finding the right solution. Above all, we had highlighted the profound, long-term changes that come about once a community has an assured supply of safe, clean water. I thought it was all true, but I had to see for myself.

It didn't take long. In a sprawling shanty suburb of Ethiopia's capital, Addis Ababa, we visited the Integrated Holistic Approach Urban Development Project. The name scarcely does justice to the vigour and vitality of a scheme that embraces all levels of this crushingly poor community.

Face to face with changed lives

Arriving by bus from a clean, if basic, hotel it was hard not to feel like a tourist. This didn't last long. It seemed as if we were collectively holding our breath. (Maybe it was the open sewers that ran down the sides or middle of every road, but there was something more.) I suspect we only really started to feel at ease after we'd visited the primary school and found ourselves mobbed by laughing children. Their lack of inhibition broke through the invisible barrier that had been separating us from our surroundings. The smiling faces of children that look to us from thousands of fundraising leaflets suddenly became real people with names, with families, homes, a school and, thanks to the work of the local community and WaterAid, a tap-stand in their playground. And of course they have lessons that embrace the vital issues of health education, without which any amount of clean water is worthless.

As we walked around the community workshops and education schemes the notion of 'helping people to help themselves' came to life. Soon I found myself thinking of the easy phrases that we use in our fundraising literature, 'Just £10 will provide a lasting supply of clean, safe water'. Here we were, face to face, with changed lives and with children who now stand a better than even chance of reaching their teenage years. Suddenly £10 seemed very little money indeed.

The regional fundraisers and water company employees went into overdrive as 'the need' and the ability to meet it came face to face. Soon calculations were being made as to how much it would cost to cover over the sewers. How much concrete would it take? How much would it cost per metre? Or per hundred metres? Could we get donors to sponsor 10-metre sections, or even a particular street? Having seen just how their support had already made a difference these donors were hugely motivated to do more, much more. For what they had found were low-cost, low-tech solutions bringing benefits to the whole community.

> Once you've been on a trip like this and really seen the work, you're involved for life.
>
> David Elliot, donor and member of a WaterAid regional fundraising committee

As we sat on low wooden benches in the project office to hear presentations on the work, the crucial role of the women became clear. These women, who had carried the burden of maintaining child care, washing and cooking without a safe water supply, were instrumental in forming a grassroots committee to identify the precise needs of families in the area. The impact is enormous. I'll never forget the woman who said, 'We used to live like animals. Now we live like human beings.'

The majority of our time was spent away from Addis, often in isolated rural communities where the need for a clean water supply is just as acute, but the solutions different.

One morning, after a hot, dusty journey, we left the bus and followed our guide towards the lip of a steep escarpment. As we approached, a panoramic rift valley came into view. Then we heard the singing, slow and rhythmic, of the 100 or more men and women working in the intense heat to dig a trench that would carry a water pipeline into the communities across the valley. Their song

© Alan Crofts

Brian Bowker, a retired water engineer, turns the tap that lets clean, safe water flow in Ethiopia.

was translated for us, 'We thank God that the safe, clean water is coming.'

The whole scene was awe inspiring for the volunteer fundraisers, who found themselves closer to the cause they support than ever before. Here was the industry of the local people, coupled with the efforts of WaterAid, its volunteer fundraisers and, of course, the thousands of donors, to transform the lives of isolated rural communities.

Clive Shelley, an engineer with North West Water and a volunteer fundraiser, saw how the money raised was meeting the need more clearly than ever before. 'You're seeing people pull themselves up. They're going to manage the system, they'll train people, create income. They've got a long-term interest here. And for just £10 a head, donated, this is here for lifetimes. It's tremendous!'

Clive for one was determined to return home to Lancaster to redouble his fundraising efforts.

Like all charity supporters, we wanted to be sure that WaterAid's money, the donors' money, was being well spent. Any worries about accountability were dispelled at the Hitosa project where we stood in blazing heat to be shown the ledger of the project's income and expenditure – line by line. How would charities react if donors turned up at finance offices in the UK and asked them to do the same thing?

Raising the money is the easy part

It has been said many times that fundraising is above all about people. And it is unlikely that anyone on the trip will forget the overwhelming warmth and hospitality of the people who turned out to garland us at every village. We were greeted with songs and flowers, with speeches and feasts (and, somehow, always a crate of Pepsi). Each of us was humbled, well aware that we didn't deserve this treatment. The only way to justify it to ourselves was to redefine our party, not as individuals but as ambassadors for the thousands of WaterAid supporters in the UK whose support maintains the programme of work.

Organising a visit like this isn't easy for WaterAid. A great deal of time and effort is invested. But it's an investment that certainly pays off in developing long-term relationships with key supporters. We all returned to England motivated in so many different ways. To give money ourselves. To organise events and talks. And to communicate the need with new insights and renewed vigour.

Certainly the problems of organising a multi-segmented appeal mailing, or talking to a small local group on a wet winter evening, or selling that final book of raffle tickets would somehow seem much less onerous in the future.

The hospitality and sheer hard work of everyone we met had more than overcome the apprehensions of those on the trip. The words of Colin Skellett, managing director of Wessex Water, summed up the feelings of many of us. 'When we came out here I thought it was going to be a depressing, miserable visit, but what we've seen is so much enthusiasm. It's incredible to see the number of people who turn out and what it means to them. And the work they do! We do the easy part raising the money. This is where all the hard work's going on.'

WaterAid
Prince Consort House
27–29 Albert Embankment
London SE1 7UB
United Kingdom

Tel: +44 (0) 171 793 4500
Fax: +44 (0) 171 793 4545

Southern Poverty Law Center

Making donors feel special

Recently I asked my friend Jennie Thompson who she thought was really in the forefront of donor development in the United States. Some 20 years ago Jennie was one of the founders of America's best-known campaigning and fundraising agency, Craver, Mathews, Smith and Company of Falls Church, Virginia. Over the past few years she has established a reputation all over the world as one of the leading specialists in direct marketing for not-for-profits. So she should know.

> As the rattle of automatic gunfire increases from their secret training bases, so will the bombings... unless we act... We must be able to go forward with the programs of the Southern Poverty Law Center.
>
> Leon Uris

Jennie hesitated for only a few moments, then said in that lovely Scarlett O'Hara drawl of hers that could only come from a genuine Southern belle,* 'Well, one of the best for sure is the Southern Poverty Law Center of Montgomery, Alabama. I just love the way it treats me. It seems really interested in its donors and has some great schemes for donor involvement.'

I had only vaguely heard of this organisation, but that didn't matter. I was prepared to take Jennie's word for it. She then introduced me to David Watson, SPLC's head of

*Vivien Leigh, who played Scarlett O'Hara in *Gone with the Wind*, came from Wales and was brought up in India. Her one-time husband, Lawrence Olivier, said the toughest test for an actor is to be able to fake sincerity – but once you can do that *anything* is possible. Jennie Thompson, however, is the real thing.

fundraising, and before I knew it I was looking at one of the most sophisticated donor communications programmes I have seen anywhere.

Anyone can dream...

When I was growing up in Scotland in the mid-1960s the name Montgomery, Alabama meant something to me and to thousands of others like me. Montgomery, Selma and other Southern towns were milestones on the long and painful journey towards civil rights in America. They featured large in those emotional 'freedom' marches that so powerfully symbolised the non-violent struggle for civil rights amid the mess of bigotry, race hatred and injustice that characterised those times in that country. Of course, I was safely insulated from such upheaval many thousands of miles away. But I was an idealistic adolescent then, and I had a dream too.

> One of my earliest and most vivid memories is of a Klan incident, the burning of a cross in front of a house rented by a black family in the small town of La Jolla, California... It must have been my first awareness that hate and violence existed in the world. The incident shocked me, and I suppose the concept of resisting and fighting racial injustice took root, and as I grew up became part of my character. The effort being waged by Klanwatch against the Klan deserves our vigorous support.
>
> Gregory Peck

The Southern Poverty Law Center is both a symbol and a product of that recent old South. It was founded in 1971 in a two-room office in Montgomery to help fight discrimination against the poor. Gradually, amid a stream of highly publicised successes, the Center considerably widened the scope of its activities to include a long-term commitment to solving the problems of hate, violence and intolerance. Now it is dedicated to seeking justice and fulfilling the promise of equality in America. Its joint founders, Morris Dees and Joseph Levin junior, are, respectively, chair of the Center's executive committee and chair of the Center.

Over the years the Southern Poverty Law Center has been involved in many historic legal battles, often against the odds and always on the side of the underdog. SPLC has taken on individual state governments to change unfair tax laws, has fought discrimination in the

Alabama State Militia and police forces and has, at times, carried its crusade for justice to the US Supreme Court, the highest court in the United States of America.

In 1981 the Center established the Klanwatch Project in response to growing activity by white supremacist groups. This project not only promotes hard-hitting lawsuits against those who violate the rights of others, it also monitors these groups and publishes its findings in an intelligence report that is distributed to 6,500 law enforcement agencies across the United States.

> You're doing a great job. As we move closer to a free and just society, the extremists try to stop history's progress with terror. We must resist their hatred and work instead for love for our fellow men and women.
>
> F Pierre, Washington

Then in April 1995 came the bombing in Oklahoma City, which shook the world into awareness of the hidden dangers of the white supremacist militias then flourishing across the USA. Anticipating this need, six months before, Klanwatch had begun its Militia Task Force to monitor the activities of America's private armies.

In 1991 the Center started its ambitious teaching tolerance project, its purpose being to reach the nation's young minds before they could be twisted by bigotry and racial hatred. The educational journal *Teaching Tolerance* is now published twice each year and sent free of charge to 200,000 teachers across America as a supplement and reinforcer to the Center's award-winning education kits

TEACHING
TOLERANCE

that help teachers to introduce students to concepts of tolerance, understanding and acceptance.

The Southern Poverty Law Center receives no state funding for its work, accepts no fees, nor does it take any part of any monetary award its legal work might win. It is entirely supported by the freely given contributions of friends and supporters across the United States – its donors.

Very important people

Clearly donors are very important to the Southern Poverty Law Center. Here is an organisation that shows its care in what it sends, that doesn't treat its donors as anything less than intelligent and discriminatory individuals who can make appropriate, rational choices, and who don't need to be constantly 'sold' the cause. The Center clearly believes in what it is doing and it obviously expects the same commitment and enthusiasm from its supporters. It isn't disappointed.

It doesn't always ask for money. In fact, quite often there is deliberately and rather obviously no ask. And sometimes it sends its donors a 'gift' – not just promotional videos and the likes (although it does that rather well), but publications such as its intelligence reports, which were originally produced only for law enforcement agencies but are now enthusiastically read by donors as well.

> I am a child psychologist who spends much time consulting in schools, primarily around multicultural issues. Last week in the teachers' room of one elementary school I saw a copy of the latest *Teaching Tolerance* magazine, with a teacher check off attached. When I asked if anyone had found it helpful, every single teacher said yes, each had found something in it to help in dealing with their students – living proof that my small contribution to the Friends of the Center has become part of something much larger.
>
> L Towler, Massachusetts

Distinctly unconventional

The key to the Southern Poverty Law Center's carefully planned and effective communications programme is the flow chart (*see* opposite). This shows at a glance where each piece of communication fits, from the donor's point of view. The programme is straightforward and in terms of American direct mail fundraising is essentially quite conventional, but a number of distinctive and unconventional components have been added, for sound donor development reasons.

As is normal for North America, the programme revolves around an annual gift-renewal cycle with frequent special appeals built in or added when appropriate, such as in an emergency. Prospecting (recruiting new donors) is a continuous process that, while competent and effective, is

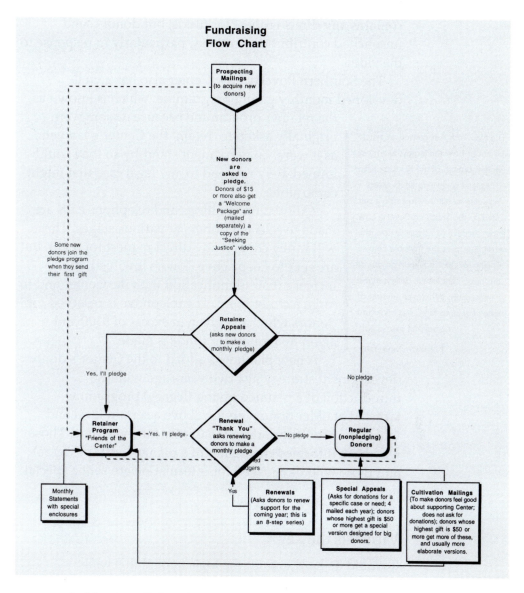

Fundraising Flow Chart

Prospecting Mailings (to acquire new donors)

New donors are asked to pledge. Donors of $15 or more also get a "Welcome Package" and (mailed separately) a copy of the "Seeking Justice" video.

Some new donors join the pledge program when they send their first gift

Retainer Appeals (asks new donors to make a monthly pledge)

Yes, I'll pledge

No pledge

Retainer Program "Friends of the Center"

Yes, I'll pledge

Renewal "Thank You" asks renewing donors to make a monthly pledge

No pledge

Regular (nonpledging) Donors

Monthly Statements with special enclosures

Yes

Renewals (Asks donors to renew support for the coming year; this is an 8-step series)

Special Appeals (Asks for donations for a specific case or need; 4 mailed each year); donors whose highest gift is $50 or more get a special version designed for big donors.

Cultivation Mailings (To make donors feel good about supporting Center; does not ask for donations); donors whose highest gift is $50 or more get more of these, and usually more elaborate versions.

unremarkable. A well-developed welcome programme is in place with two main components: the welcome package, sent to all new donors just after receipt of their first gift, and the 'seeking justice' video, a powerful and emotive piece of television that is sent only to larger donors with the request that they return it after viewing. Neither component contains any direct request for funds, but donors send unsolicited contributions anyway, particularly in response to the video.

The Southern Poverty Law Center also has a well-developed monthly giving programme, which is known as the retainer programme because donors were originally asked to 'retain' the Center's lawyers, as it were, on permanent stand-by so they could immediately respond to any legal case that might come along.

'Cultivation' mailings and telephone calls are made to selected donors at various stages. These will rarely contain any direct request for a gift, but are sent to keep active donors involved, to increase their identification with the Center and to forge a closer bond. The telephone is reserved for donors who have given in excess of $100 and again no request for funds is made.

A new plank was added to the Center's donor development strategy just two years ago with the introduction of a planned giving (legacy) programme targeted at older donors giving above a certain level and who have been supporting the Center for some time. Those who have informed the Center of a planned gift (pledgers) and those who have asked for information are sent a special newsletter.

> The *New York Post* carried an article today about how the largest and most violent branch of the Ku Klux Klan agreed to give up all its assets – including its name – to settle a suit filed by the Southern Poverty Law Center. According to that article, the settlement puts the Invisible Empire Knights of the Ku Klux Klan out of business. That article delighted me immensely. Whatever amount of money I gave to SPLC has benefited me beyond expression.
>
> J Dukes, New York

Variety is the key

It would be hard to fault the logic behind this well-structured and efficient donor development programme. Each component has been thought through with a clear understanding of the donor's point of view, yet the cultivation process is constant, no one is allowed to stand still. There is an almost total absence of pressure in any of the Center's materials, with no opportunity for donors to feel anything other than cared for and involved.

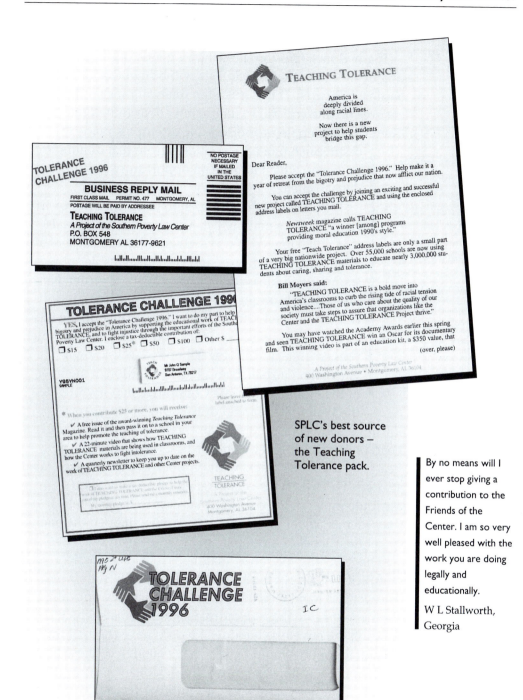

TEACHING TOLERANCE

America is
deeply divided
along racial lines.

Now there is a new
project to help students
bridge this gap.

Dear Reader,

Please accept the "Tolerance Challenge 1996." Help make it a
year of retreat from the bigotry and prejudice that now afflict our nation.

You can accept the challenge by joining an exciting and successful
new project called TEACHING TOLERANCE and using the enclosed
address labels on letters you mail.

Newsweek magazine calls TEACHING
TOLERANCE "a winner [among] programs
providing moral education 1990's style."

Your free "Teach Tolerance" address labels are only a small part
of a very big nationwide project. Over 55,000 schools are now using
TEACHING TOLERANCE materials to educate nearly 3,000,000 students about caring, sharing and tolerance.

Bill Moyers said:
"TEACHING TOLERANCE is a bold move into
America's classrooms to curb the rising tide of racial tension
and violence....Those of us who care about the quality of our
society must take steps to assure that organizations like the
Center and the TEACHING TOLERANCE Project thrive."

You may have watched the Academy Awards earlier this spring
and seen TEACHING TOLERANCE win an Oscar for its documentary
film. This winning video is part of an education kit, a $350 value, that

(over, please)

A Project of the Southern Poverty Law Center
400 Washington Avenue • Montgomery, AL 36104

TOLERANCE
CHALLENGE 1996

BUSINESS REPLY MAIL

FIRST CLASS MAIL   PERMIT NO. 477   MONTGOMERY, AL

POSTAGE WILL BE PAID BY ADDRESSEE

TEACHING TOLERANCE
A Project of the Southern Poverty Law Center
P.O. BOX 548
MONTGOMERY AL 36177-9621

NO POSTAGE
NECESSARY
IF MAILED
IN THE
UNITED STATES

TOLERANCE CHALLENGE 1996

YES, I accept the "Tolerance Challenge 1996." I want to do my part to help
bigotry and prejudice in America by supporting the important efforts of the Southern
TOLERANCE, and to fight injustice through the important efforts of the Southern
Poverty Law Center. I enclose a tax-deductible contribution of:

☐ $15 ☐ $20 ☐ $25* ☐ $50 ☐ $100 ☐ Other $

Y95VN001
SAMPLE

Mr John Q Sample
9707 Broadway
San Antonio, TX 78217

* When you contribute $25 or more, you will receive:

✔ A free issue of the award-winning *Teaching Tolerance*
Magazine. Read it and then pass it on to a school in your
area to help promote the teaching of tolerance.

✔ A 22-minute video that shows how TEACHING
TOLERANCE materials are being used in classrooms, and
how the Center works to fight intolerance.

✔ A quarterly newsletter to keep you up to date on the
work of TEACHING TOLERANCE and other Center projects.

Please leave this
label attached to form.

TEACHING
TOLERANCE

*A Project of the
Southern Poverty Law Center*
400 Washington Avenue
Montgomery, AL 36104

TOLERANCE
CHALLENGE
1996

IC

SPLC's best source
of new donors –
the Teaching
Tolerance pack.

By no means will I
ever stop giving a
contribution to the
Friends of the
Center. I am so very
well pleased with the
work you are doing
legally and
educationally.

W L Stallworth,
Georgia

If any donor fails to renew then a gentle but increasingly urgent series of renewal requests will bring back all but the hardest of hearts. This is a 12-step renewal process that ensures no one will fail to realise how determined the Center is to keep its supporters. No attempt is made to distinguish one-off responders from real donors, however, which may be an opportunity for future development.

It is well worth getting on to the Southern Poverty Law Center's mailing list. The variety of materials that will come your way will gladden the heart of any relationship fundraiser and provide a fertile source of training and ideas for any budding copywriter. New donors are brought in by direct appeals for support fronted by well-known signatories from outside the Center, including President Lyndon Johnson's former press secretary, Bill Moyers, now a well-known television journalist, and Barbara Jordan, a member of the House Watergate Committee that investigated the Watergate scandal during the Nixon years.

> I was born and raised in Bessemer, Alabama. When I was a young girl, we would sit on the front porch in the dark and watch the Klan pass our home in their white sheets. I experienced the back of the bus, attended segregated schools, etc. I have seen it all.
>
> I applaud the Southern Poverty Law Center and the fine work you are doing. I agree that teaching tolerance in schools is a good beginning.
>
> W Mitchell, Pennsylvania

However, according to David Watson, the Center's head of fundraising, the Center's best recruiter is the new 'teaching tolerance' pack, with its block of personalised label stickers. He says, 'This is not signed by an outsider. I attribute much of the package's success to these labels. It may seem a trivial gift, but most people will open the pack to get their labels. Once open, many must read the letter.'

The 'teaching tolerance' mailing is a gem of classic simplicity. Its bright multicoloured logo really stands out. The clasped hand-shaped symbol is sufficiently appealing for me to forgive those dreadful 'stick-on' labels which peer through the envelope window. I would have thought most potential donors would by now have enough of these to wallpaper their houses several times. However, Americans, it seems, are not yet tired of this gimmick for, as David says, the pack works rather well. Wishfully perhaps, I put its success down to its direct and simple proposition. It really

Facsimile press
cuttings add interest
and authenticity.

No soldiers have
ever been braver,
more honorable and
more patriotic than
the staff of the
Southern Poverty
Law Center.

Kurt Vonnegut

does challenge you to fight injustice by teaching tolerance. Anyone giving above $25 attracts a range of appealing benefits and there's even a subtly effective promotion for the monthly pledge scheme. Yet the whole pack is small, neat and economical.

I recently received the newspaper clipping and other related material concerning the bomb that was being developed to use against the Center. It seems the death and destruction caused in the Oklahoma bombing did little to quench the thirst of those who thrive on evil and violence. Unfortunately, very few people put themselves on the line as you do for what they truly believe in. Thank you for helping me to keep faith in the good of mankind.

M Radom, Kansas

Variety is the key to the appeal of the retainer proposition that goes out under the slightly more appealing name of 'Friends of the Center'. Monthly pledgers are sent a statement each month accompanied by an enclosure that tells them something about how their pledge is being used. 'We try to have as much variety as possible', explains David Watson, 'to keep the process interesting and involving. Sometimes we reproduce newspaper clippings that report our work. Sometimes we'll send a letter from someone who supports our work, or a sheet of good comments we have received from Center supporters. Without question the Friends of the Center are our most loyal and enthusiastic donors. Some have been supporters for nearly 20 years.'

The 'seeking justice' video and the frequent cultivation mailings all serve to encourage this enthusiasm, the same enthusiasm that I had found in Jennie Thompson when she first introduced me to the Southern Poverty Law Center. There could be few more valuable assets for a fundraising organisation.

The video was first used in 1983 to give new donors an inside look at the Center and the people who work there. One donor wrote about it, 'I have read everything you have ever sent me, but I didn't really understand what you were all about until I saw this video.'

Everyone is asked to return the video and about 50 per cent do. Many enclose an additional contribution. Without ever asking for a cent, the video has now generated more than $250,000 in extra gifts, paying for itself many times over. To encourage its return, a special rate shipping label is thoughtfully included.

The need to keep giving

Regular donors to the Southern Poverty Law Center will receive about five special appeals a year, each one focusing on a specific need.

November 1995's letter, for example, told the story of 13-year-old Henock Seraw from Ethiopia. His father had been murdered by a group of racist skinheads while he was attending college in Portland, Oregon. The Southern Poverty Law Center prosecuted the white supremacist group these skinheads followed, the White Aryan Resistance, and its leader, Tom Metzger. Although the White Aryan Resistance was found guilty of encouraging the killing of Henock's father and damages of $12.5 million were awarded, the process of collecting the money was also left to the Center. The racist group only had a fraction of this sum but the Center nevertheless managed to recover $100,000, enough money to make all the difference to a fatherless family struggling in Ethiopia.

This special appeal enclosed a facsimile photograph of Henock and a photocopy of his travel itinerary to go to America to help with the case. Such tangible and demonstrable results reassure supporters of the importance of their continued giving, which is all that keeps the Center going.

> As a member of the United States Air Force, I have pledged myself to defend our nation. And it is the work of organizations like yours that make me proud of our country today. As long as places like the SPLC fight hate organizations and strive to educate all Americans about tolerance for others, groups like the Klan can never succeed.
>
> B Stone, Virginia

Just a little bit different

Any supporter of the Southern Poverty Law Center can expect to receive communications on a fairly regular basis, particularly if his or her renewal is a bit slow. Two or three communications each month would certainly not be unusual. But the difference between junk mail and welcome

My family has lived in this area for over 9,000 years according to archaeologists, and as a native person armed confrontation is nothing new. We will be praying that your staff and offices are safe and hope that the Great Spirit protects the fine work that you are doing.

J Perkins, Washington

communication is just a degree of relevance, interest and appropriateness. I couldn't see anything in the Center's communications programme that was not very likely to be welcome, appreciated and also highly effective, both in building long-term relationships and in bringing in much-needed, immediate funds.

Jennie Thompson was right when she said that I'd love the way these people treat their donors as much as she does. And she speaks as a long-time donor. This is not just a worthwhile cause – it's a cause well worth watching.

The Southern Poverty Law Center
400 Washington Avenue
PO Box 548
Montgomery
Alabama 36101-0548
USA

Tel: +1 334 264 0286
Fax: +1 334 264 0629

The British Diabetic Association

The relationship audit

Hard on the heels of relationship fundraising came the concept of the relationship audit. The term will most likely have existed for years before, but for me it was a new idea and not a bad one at that. As everyone began to turn their fundraising attentions towards relationship building, why not formally evaluate all the complex and often inter-related relationships within one organisation to see the usual strengths, weaknesses, gaps and omissions?

It was the realisation of this phenomenon that encouraged me to include the following pages from Tony Manwaring of the British Diabetic Association. I first heard Tony expounding the BDA's relationship audit at a seminar I was chairing on relationship marketing for charities. The theme of the conference was a broad one and Tony's presentation was not only relevant, it held the audience in fascination.

The term audit, of course, may well be a misnomer. Fundraising audits often bear little resemblance to the precise and well-defined procedures that my accountants follow when they come in each year to check the books. As far as I am aware there is no equally well-defined series of checks and balances for auditing relationships and I have no intention of establishing one. There are probably as many ways of conducting a relationship audit as there are organisations thinking of carrying one out, but certainly the BDA's experience will be of interest and value to anyone who is.

This chapter was written by Tony Manwaring in the summer of 1995. I have made a small number of changes for editorial reasons but the style and content are his. Since writing it Tony has left the British Diabetic Association to take over as director of fundraising at one of Britain's oldest and most respected child-care organisations, NCH Action for Children.

A background to diabetes

It is estimated that there are around 1.4 million people in the UK who are diagnosed as having diabetes. Up to 300,000 people have insulin-dependent diabetes (IDDM) and over 1 million have non-insulin dependent diabetes (NIDDM). After asthma and cerebral palsy, diabetes is the most common chronic childhood condition. For every person diagnosed as having NIDDM, it is believed that there is another undiagnosed. When family members and carers are included, diabetes directly affects several million people in the UK.

Someone with diabetes is unable to convert food into the 'fuel' the body needs because of the inability to produce any, or sufficient, insulin. The symptoms include a lack of energy – feeling tired or drowsy – as well as high levels of blood sugar and frequently passing urine.

Insulin-dependent diabetes is usually diagnosed before the age of 40, often during childhood. The body stops producing insulin itself and regular injections are essential to give the insulin the body must have. Before the discovery of insulin, only 75 years ago, diagnosis was a death sentence.

Non-insulin dependent diabetes is normally diagnosed after the age of 40 and usually among those aged 50 or over. In this case the body ceases to produce sufficient insulin, or to be able to use the insulin it does produce. This is often related to people being overweight. Treatment takes the form of diet, tablets, insulin or a combination of these three.

Diabetes may result in several complications. It is the most common cause of blindness among the working-age population. Other 'micro-vascular' complications include the possibility of amputation of lower limbs, nerve and kidney damage and impotence. 'Macro-vascular' complications are blocked coronary arteries, heart attacks and stroke, particularly for those with NIDDM. These complications are much less likely to develop if those with diabetes can maintain good control of their blood sugar levels throughout their lifetime.

The causes are both genetic and environmental. Rapid progress in understanding the genetic basis of IDDM has been made possible through the mapping of the human 'genome', which identifies the specific genes possessed by those at risk of developing diabetes. While a cure remains a long way off, there is increasing confidence that prevention may soon be possible.

The British Diabetic Association

The British Diabetic Association is the only national charity representing the interests of all people with diabetes in the UK.

The BDA was set up in 1934 by Dr R D Lawrence and the author H G Wells, both of whom had diabetes. From the very beginning of the Association, those living with diabetes and those treating it were brought together. There are now around 150,000 members of the BDA. Two-thirds of the membership are known to have diabetes, divided almost equally between IDDM and NIDDM. Most donors are also members, although a further 20,000 individuals support the BDA as donors alone. Some of these donors will have diabetes, some not.

The majority of members tend to join soon after diagnosis, often as a result of referral by health care professionals. Most remain as members for around three years, so a large proportion of those with diabetes are, or have been, members of the BDA. Many people with diabetes serve on BDA committees as well as on its board of trustees.

Health care professionals, such as diabetes specialist nurses, dietitians and doctors, are also members and they too are represented on the board of trustees and committees.

BDA's annual budget of around £10 million is divided between funding research and care. The charity is one of the largest funders of diabetes research in the UK and spent nearly £4 million on research in 1995.

The BDA's Careline deals with around 100,000 enquiries each year from people with diabetes, their carers and from health professionals. Specialist staff give the latest information on a wide range of topics relating to the condition, and diet information staff advise on how to eat healthily. The Care Division organises activities such as educational holidays and weekends for young people with diabetes, family weekends, parents' meetings and a club for young children. It provides information packs for schools and a wide range of leaflets and booklets on all aspects of diabetes – even recipe books.

The BDA has regional offices in Scotland, Northern Ireland, the North West and the West Midlands, which reflects the increasing importance of local decision making in the UK's National Health Service. These offices work closely with the BDA's 450 local branches and groups, most of which meet to provide self-help but some are also active in fundraising. The eventual aim is to set up an office in every region in the country.

Beyond fundraising

The BDA is an interesting case study because at the BDA the principles of relationship fundraising have not only been applied to the fundraising strategy, they have also helped shape a review of the activities and services of the Association as a whole. It gives a perhaps still rare opportunity to consider the relevance of relationship building principles beyond fundraising and marketing, as well as the chance to assess the value, if not necessity, of being able to help shape the corporate development of the organisation as a whole using these principles.

To understand the context in which these developments have taken place, it helps to take a couple of steps back. The BDA is one of the country's major charities, but arguably is not one which has 'punched its weight'. It represents several million people whose lives are intimately touched by a condition that they have to manage and for which they must take responsibility. It provides services of real value and vital support at a traumatic time in people's lives – when they are diagnosed with diabetes. It is held in high regard by health care professionals. Nevertheless, in 1993 the BDA only had a total income of about £10 million and voluntary income of around £7 million, placing it at number 40 in the UK's league table of charity statistics. There was obviously great opportunity for growth.

There was also great need for growth. With more funds much more could be done to improve both the immediate care of people with diabetes and the prospects for the prevention and cure of the condition in the future. International developments in setting targets for care, which the BDA is helping to lead, new understandings in the long-term benefits of good care and the rapid progress being made in genetics, of which diabetes is at the forefront and in which the BDA is playing a pivotal role, all add to an exciting sense of opportunity and possibility for the BDA now.

But there were not just opportunity and need at the BDA. There was also organisational potential. In 1992, the BDA signalled its ambitions for the future by appointing a new director general, Michael Cooper. His initial focus was to ensure that the organisation could get things done and be an effective and dynamic vehicle for achieving its overall aims.

Key developments included:

■ A clear separation between the board of trustees' responsibility for setting the Association's aims and policy objectives and the staff's responsibility for implementing and achieving these aims, accountable to the board of trustees.

■ The setting up of a management board to bring together trustees and senior management to progress and monitor implementation of the strategy that would achieve these aims and objectives.

■ Clear authority for the director-general when making staff appointments.

■ Establishing a process for drawing up, on a rolling basis, a five-year plan. Drafted by staff in consultation with relevant BDA committees and the board of trustees, this plan provides a focus for setting clear policy aims that are periodically updated.

This potential is reinforced by a senior management team which is both supportive and wants change and has the expertise to make that change happen.

Some of the most important building blocks for a relationship approach were already there. A high-quality magazine, *Balance*, provided a basis for communication and establishing an expectation of membership involvement. A sophisticated database, with appropriate safeguards for confidentiality, recorded relevant details regarding members' diabetes, as well as up-to-date membership and donor records. And there was already a nationwide network of people living with the condition able to offer advice and support through BDA branches and groups.

The application of the principles of relationship fundraising did not, therefore, take place in a vacuum. The organisational potential, the need and the opportunity all existed, providing the foundation on which the newly appointed director of marketing and public affairs (Tony Manwaring) could build.

However, it was quickly apparent that these principles could not be applied in isolation if they were to have real impact. The content of fundraising appeals must touch the lives of those with diabetes – and must be acceptable to them.The nature of the condition is such that a crude appeal using simplistic fundraising images could be counter-productive. Any techniques used must be sensitive to the nature of the organisation. For example, telephone programmes are undertaken in the context of a developed and articulate branch structure, able to pick up swiftly on any bad experience and accurately report any complaint. For people with diabetes, fundraising has to be long term. It cannot be a series of one-off, emotional appeals. The BDA must develop an ongoing and dynamic relationship with people with diabetes if it is to be of real benefit to them. It cannot rely on a continuous turnover of new members and donors to grow.

There is also a more fundamental imperative for making relationship marketing central and for adopting an approach of 'whole organisation marketing'.

The BDA gets almost all its money from people living with diabetes. The condition is not understood well enough, or perhaps not seen as sufficiently serious or emotive to attract substantial funds from the general public, at least for the moment. So the BDA needs to build its membership/ supporter base to build income. Because of this, relevant and effective relationships are important at every level of the organisation, not just to deliver effective services and to build membership but also to ensure the funding that will be needed to pay for expanding research and care.

From inception to implementation: a comprehensive review of activities and services

The BDA's senior management group and management board agreed terms of reference for a wide-ranging review of how best to build membership and raise income. A programme of meetings was established during 1994 for the review, which focused on the needs of various 'key groups' of people with diabetes. At this stage, neither current provision nor budgetary/resource implications were considered.

Each meeting took the form of a 'brainstorm', explicitly adhering to rules of no criticism and the free exchange of ideas. Designated individuals introduced each session.

All staff were invited to these, and a process of natural self-selection quickly determined who attended. The meetings typically involved around 30 people. Minutes, pulling together ideas which arose, were sent by E-mail to all staff.

A drafting group prepared an initial summary report to bring together themes and recommendations for consideration by those who attended the review meetings and a presentation of the report was made to the senior management group (effectively the executive committee). A meeting of all heads of department and others invited for their particular expertise/experience was held to prioritise the major proposals and underlying themes, which were then integrated in annual budgets and a rolling five-year plan.

Cross-departmental, staff-based 'key group task forces' were established to oversee the implementation of recommendations. These task forces are able to call on focus groups of the people concerned to test and develop ideas with them.

A life cycle based approach

The foundation for the review has been the development of an analysis of the life cycles of people living with diabetes. The significance of this is that diabetes means different things to people with the condition at different stages of their lives, so the relationship that the BDA has with them also has to change to remain of value to them. Whether and how the BDA seeks income from them therefore also needs to be based on a much clearer understanding of these changes. The review was able to provide that understanding precisely.

The life cycle analysis begins with a better understanding of those who have diabetes. Making use of available data, we analysed people by whether they had insulin or non-insulin dependent diabetes, their age and gender and ethnicity. We then contrasted this picture with the BDA's current membership base to see where the Association was already most representative and where the opportunities for greatest growth exist.

The key conclusions were:

■ By condition. There is great potential for growth among those with non-insulin dependent diabetes. Indeed, if the proportion of IDDM to NIDDM within the BDA membership was the same as that of the population as a whole, the membership would treble to almost 500,000.

■ By age. While the age breakdown of the BDA membership broadly reflects that of the population as a whole, there is nevertheless a tremendous challenge to reach out to those aged 60 or more (especially those with NIDDM). In addition, the BDA needs to be more responsive to those aged 20–40, who will often no longer have a relationship with the BDA but who may be faced with the complications of diabetes as they grow older.

■ By length of time since diagnosis. Given that members tend to join soon after diagnosis and those who lapse tend to

Table I The diabetes life cycle – summary

Group	Age	Needs of person with diabetes	Needs of carer
	<5	Simple information.	Support.
	5–12	Praise/autonomy/speak to them as individuals.	Information/networks/trusting relationship with health care professional (HCP).
	12–16	Own organisation/pen-friend/relevant information in their own language.	Support/respect/reassurance and research information/materials to prepare teenager for future/local parents' groups.
IDDM	16–22	Adult information/research information/ OK to be fed up/rebel/teenage magazine/ insurance information.	As above and as teenager leaves home other forms of involvement. Redundant parent syndrome.
	22–40	Information on lifestyle, research and complications/be proactive, on an individual basis/help with HCP relationship/information on pregnancy.	New diabetes 'career': needs information and support network to deal with 'relationship crises'.
	40–60	Information on diet, complications, care to expect (NHS and HCP) and impotence.	As for person with diabetes, plus 'what does the future hold?'
NIDDM	60+	Targeted information/help the cause/ feel BDA is for them/diet – don't expect too much.	As above, plus support groups and publications for carers.

do so around three years after, the BDA has to re-establish its relevance to those who have lapsed.

Alongside these general conclusions, there is a need to recognise the needs of specific groups of people. For instance, women live longer than men so there will be more women with diabetes than men. And in their role as carers they have influence on matters such as the family diet and lifestyle. The high incidence of diabetes among the Asian and African-Caribbean communities within the UK also requires attention. Finally, the varying standards of diabetes care in different parts of the country also mean that where people live can be important in shaping their experience of diabetes.

The life cycle of particular groups of people living with diabetes was analysed by Kate Campbell, until recently head of the BDA's diabetes care and information services and a former diabetes specialist nurse. Her experience of working with people with the condition and those living with them uniquely qualified her to undertake this analysis, and the value of her efforts was reinforced by her forthright style and ability to confront 'awkward' issues.

Her analysis painted a picture which brought the review to life, giving it a depth of insight and integrity which shaped the more general discussions that followed. (The analysis is summarised in table 1, page 486.) Up until then, the needs and experiences of those living with diabetes, and how they change over time, had not been pulled together in so comprehensive or informed a way. Professional researchers using a variety of focus groups around the country would have cost a lot more, but would have been unlikely to come up with so sophisticated an understanding.

The full analysis cannot be reproduced here but the following extract gives a good understanding of the experiences and needs of people with IDDM and NIDDM at different ages, as well as for women with pregnancy-related diabetes. The section quoted here is for those with IDDM aged 16–22.

Life cycle analysis: an example

Adolescent, 16–22 years
■ Wants to be 'normal'.

■ May not feel fully confident to take complete control,

however, does not want interference from others.

- Has own agenda.

- May/may not want specific groups.

- Female wants to be thin, male may want to body build.

- Perhaps aware for the first time of prejudice, eg employment, driving.

- The BDA is often seen as a prudish, 'old age' organisation.

Requires
- Information in a teenage language that speaks to him/her as an adult.

- Information on research on diabetes.

- To be allowed to be 'fed up'/rebel as long as it is relatively safe.

- Development of teenage magazines to include advice on contraception, alcohol, drugs, etc.

- Information relating to employment/driving/insurance and the role of the BDA in lobbying on his/her behalf.

Parents of the adolescent
- No longer feel that they play an active role in their child's diabetes and therefore often need and want an alternative diabetes-related project to channel their energies. (Not uncommon to find parents of 20-year-olds, or more, still active in local parent groups.)

- Need to help others with their own experience.

Require
- New initiatives to involve the 'redundant' parent.

- To be part of an organisation that 'shows' they are still

concerned and have an interest.

■ May have more time to give to charitable organisations.

Implications and recommendations arising from the review

The impact of the review in developing ongoing relationships can best be understood by a brief summary of the principal recommendations.

1. To consider the requirements of each of the key groups, having first reviewed current and planned activities to see whether they were likely to be met.
This is a complex and detailed process which is continual. Some limited examples for each of the groups mentioned may, however, help to bring this to life.

One of the main proposals for IDDMs up to their early twenties is to develop a 'young person's passport' that would take very different forms at different ages, but would provide continuity and establish in their minds that the BDA will continue to be fresh and relevant as they grow older.

The significance of this proposal is rooted in the life cycle approach. It recognises that for their quality of care it is important to provide a continuous source of support and advice. At the same time, it is aware of the likelihood that rejecting the link with an organisation such as the BDA may be seen by young people as a source of rebellion, strength and identity. If the passport approach proves successful, the benefits in the longer term for membership and income are self-evident.

Having learned to live with diabetes, IDDMs in their thirties and forties may have pushed thoughts of complications to the backs of their minds. But they will not have forgotten them and complications will become increasingly relevant to them as they grow older.

The intention is to give these people the opportunity to

seek further information on the complications of diabetes as they either need it or feel they want it, perhaps by sophisticated use of the membership renewal programme, or by means of a 'voucher' system through the BDA's membership magazine, *Balance*.

This helps to resolve the problem that talking about complications can be a 'turn off', with the result that too little has been done for this important group. The fundraising and income benefits should be clear. The proportion of IDDMs in this age group who are members of the BDA is smaller than for any other group, yet these are precisely the people with discretionary income that many would expect to support committed giving and other initiatives and to become more involved in campaigning and lobbying activities.

A two-pronged approach is needed for NIDDMs to encourage those who have the symptoms of diabetes to be diagnosed and then to provide the support and advice they need to manage their condition.

A national poster advertising campaign, known as the 'symptoms campaign' (*see* facing page), aimed to achieve wider diagnosis and leaflets sent out to doctors' surgeries, alongside the poster and other media activity, have already recruited about 2,000 members over 12 months.

An 'after-diagnosis' care service is planned to provide support and advice with a phased programme of communication tailored to the length of time since diagnosis and the person's ability to take in the information given to them.

Again, this is vital in laying the foundations for future income growth. Perhaps a million people will, late in life and over time, have to come to terms with their diabetes. As the population lives longer, so the challenge and opportunity of developing and maintaining a relationship with those with NIDDM will also grow.

By adopting this more targeted and sophisticated approach, which aims to form continuing and changing

A leaflet and one of the posters from the 'symptoms' campaign.

relationships with people living with diabetes, the BDA is better able to provide activities and services that will be relevant to them at all stages of their lives. For this potential to be achieved, however, and relations actually to be established, those individuals need to be identified and an appropriate relationship developed. Hence the significance of the further principal recommendations.

2. By pulling together all the enquiries and other contacts the BDA has with individuals, to establish a common database and protocol for developing an ongoing relationship with each individual.

The BDA handles some 100,000 enquiries a year, of which around half are from non-members. A substantial number may, of course, be the same people writing or phoning more than once. Nevertheless, it is probable that the number of non-members who use the BDA is greater than the 20,000 who join every year. This not only suggests a significant potential for further growth but, just as important, it provides the means to enhance the quality of the service provided, for example by asking those who use the Careline what they thought of the information sent to them.

The value of this part of the review has been threefold. It has brought everybody together to identify the potential databases that they hold. A common understanding has been established of moving away from a one-off, random form of contact towards developing an ongoing relationship, for care as well as marketing purposes. And, finally, we have been able to identify and begin to resolve the complex issues of confidentiality and relationship development that will have to be overcome if an individual who receives a service is, over the years, to become more actively involved with the BDA.

3. The need for flexible and dynamic relationships to be built between the BDA and people with diabetes.

This includes the need for the maximum range of relationships so that people can choose the relationship that best suits them and can change that relationship over time. Underlying this approach are two dualities. The first is promotion of the BDA as a lifetime 'friend', providing a full 'after-diagnosis' care service yet, at the same time, empowering the individual to be as self-reliant as possible, to be active partners in getting the best possible care. The second is a change in the nature of the relationship away from one in which the BDA is there simply as a support towards one in which the BDA itself can receive support. This has important non-financial aspects, including supporters' involvement in campaigning and lobbying activities. It also sets the scene for asking people to contribute to the BDA's committed giving programme.

Examples of the form of relationship that is being developed include:

■ Membership, which entitles individuals to receive *Balance*, a discount on BDA publications and the opportunity to contribute to the BDA's voice as a campaigning body representing their interests. This is still very much the core relationship, which the BDA seeks to establish because it is the principal means by which the BDA can ensure a continuity of contact to provide ongoing advice and support.

Our review of the membership trends brought out a salutary lesson for practitioners of relationship fundraising. While it is important to acknowledge that the value of the membership relationship may diminish over time as an explanation of lapsing, the significance of members quite simply forgetting that they have failed to renew is perhaps even more important. Certainly a much more rigorous renewal programme, using mail and testing the telephone, is having substantial results – the number of people lapsing has been halved as a result. Renewal rates now stand at 90 per cent.

■ Diabetes 2001 is the BDA's committed giving programme to encourage monthly contribution by standing order and covenant. The launch mailing and insert in *Balance*, developed with the British direct marketing agency Brann, secured an additional £1 million over the next four years. After 18 months, the projected four-year income from Diabetes 2001 had increased to £2 million.

Diabetes 2001 offers members and supporters the opportunity to attend a programme of events, such as the

BDA's National Research Forum which brings together the most eminent diabetes scientists and supporters of the initiative. People giving over £5 a month receive a special ring binder containing regularly updated, custom-designed information sheets. The intention is not to give just a superficial incentive but to provide an 'open university' course in diabetes, so that people can develop the best possible understanding of their condition and of the advances in research and care that, through their money, they are helping to support.

■ BDA insurance services make available motor, travel, life and other insurance services to members and supporters. People with diabetes often experience discrimination in insurance, such as high loadings that drive up premiums and having to complete complicated, sometimes offensive, forms. The BDA has established arrangements to overcome these problems and give a sympathetic and high-quality service. This also allows a relationship to be maintained, especially with those whose membership may have lapsed. For example, the motor insurance scheme includes free membership, so when members renew their policies they also renew their membership of the BDA.

■ 'Lifetime supporter of the BDA' is the acknowledgement being given to those who pledge to leave a legacy to the BDA. Lifetime supporters receive a special medallion, regular information and an invitation to come to a special reception at the BDA's general meeting.

■ Having started from the position that people should be able to choose the relationship that best suits them, it is important to allow for the multiple relationships that they may want. It might be argued that this could be confusing and, in particular, would harm fundraising response. One

A range of striking materials from BDA's Diabetes 2001 committed giving scheme.

DIABETES
2001
where we are now

Thousands of people have now joined *Diabetes 2001*. Over 10,000 people have given donations, and the number of supporters giving monthly donations of over £2 has swelled from 2,000 to 7,000. Many are encouraging friends and family to join as well. And this support has meant that almost £2 million has been committed over the next four years through standing orders and covenants. So *Diabetes 2001* is providing regular income for research and care projects well into the future.

The BDA budgeted to spend over £4 million on research in 1995 - more than ever before and this is due to the success of *Diabetes 2001*. We believe in funding only the highest quality research that promises to make the maximum impact on diabetes. Scientists in a number of areas are at a critical stage of development and it is crucial that they receive the financial backing they need.

Dr Moira Murphy, BDA Research Director

Genetic wonders

In April this year, BDA members met one of the UK's leading diabetes researchers at the Science Museum in London. Dr John Todd brought to life the remarkable advances in the genetics of diabetes made by his team at the University of Oxford over the last few years.

He explained how his genetic research, partly funded by the BDA, has uncovered two new genes associated with causing insulin dependent diabetes. The team looks likely to discover further diabetes genes in the coming years.

I think that by 2001, we will know most of the genes that cause insulin dependent diabetes. This work is bringing us another step closer towards being able to prevent insulin dependent diabetes in the future.

Dr John Todd, Oxford University

Transplanting healthy insulin-producing cells into people with diabetes may be a solution for the future. Mr Nick London and his team at the University of Leicester were the first to carry out experimental islet cell transplants in Britain. "We have discovered a number of new techniques to make obtaining these cells from the pancreas more effective. With BDA support, we are also looking at how the cells could be encapsulated, to prevent rejection by the body."

Diabetes 2001 is not just about finding a cure and preventing diabetes, though these are both important aims. It is also about improving the lives of people like you, already living with diabetes.

DIABETES
2001
one year forward

In early 1994, the BDA wanted to bring diabetes...
...UK. We could see diabetes... ...momentum it needed...
...into the next century...

...designing a portable device for testing in the clinic environment.

Funding from the BDA has made our research and development work possible. Your support means that a broad range of diabetes related research throughout the UK is now up and running. This will bring real benefits for people with diabetes and for future generations.

Emily aged 10

answer is to have a programme of communications, each of
which is tailored to different aspects of those relationships.
In our use of the telephone to contact member and non-
member donors, however, we have used a script that falls
into three parts:

(1) Thanking them for being a member and asking them
what they think of the services they have received.
(2) Asking them to support the committed giving
programme, Diabetes 2001.
(3) Asking for their views on the BDA's campaigning
priorities.

The callers, from the UK's telephone marketing company
Pell & Bales, have been selected because they have a
knowledge of diabetes, direct or indirect. They are
encouraged to be both structured in their approach and to be
flexible in picking up on what the person is saying. Calls
often last for 15 minutes. The feedback indicates that the
calls are strengthening relationships and at the same time
achieving a good payback.

Taking a step back

To apply the principles of relationship fundraising to the
BDA it has been necessary to take a step back and look at the
organisation as a whole. The objective of meeting the needs
of all those living with diabetes has been facilitated by
identifying all those who *could* have a mutually supportive
relationship with the BDA and highlighting where the gaps
exist in current membership services. Filling these gaps
through a systematic review and the process of building
relationships broadens and strengthens the membership that
can both be supported by and in turn support the BDA.

The BDA's mission is the care of people living with
diabetes, which is a complex and changeable condition.
Asking for money or support cannot be seen in isolation, or
even as an end in itself. It must be understood within the
context of the overall pattern of relationships and the needs

and desires of people living with diabetes, of which the BDA is an important – but ultimately still only one – part. In other words, we need to start from where the person is and to have techniques and structures available that help us to identify this.

This approach of 'whole organisation marketing' is therefore helping to take the principles of developing ongoing relationships beyond fundraising into all aspects of the work of the Association. Applied within a vacuum, even the most sophisticated of relationship fundraising practices would fail. Integrally related to its strategic development as a whole they are essential to the achievement of the BDA's primary purpose.

The British Diabetic Association
10 Queen Anne Street
London W1M 0BD
United Kingdom

Tel: +44 (0) 171 323 1531
Fax: +44 (0) 171 637 3644

Tony Manwaring can be contacted at
NCH Action for Children
85 Highbury Park
London N5 1UD
United Kingdom

Tel: +44 (0) 171 226 2033
Fax: +44 (0) 171 226 2537

The Royal National Lifeboat Institution

Donor-friendly by instinct

> The mission of RNLI fundraising is to meet the financial needs of the RNLI, cost-effectively and sustainably, by developing high-quality relationships with our supporters.
>
> **From RNLI fundraising plans 1996**

The difference between Pamela McFarlane and Myles Barnett is that Pamela really exists (her name has been changed, for obvious reasons) and she is a lot more generous. But her motives when she wrote to a selection of the top charities a few years ago were exactly the same as Myles's. She wanted to put these organisations to the test to see if she could find one that would prove itself a worthy home for a really substantial donation. Pamela's test was successful and she chose one of Britain's longest-established and largest charities, the Royal National Lifeboat Institution.

Pamela's story really is evidence that it pays to provide an efficient response to all enquirers and to tailor that response to the particular donor and his or her wishes. Pamela had sent a number of charities, including RNLI, cheques for £500 and had asked for more information. The RNLI's response was to send round a senior member of staff.

This personal touch clearly found favour with Pamela, and stood out from the other responses she received. (I don't have any information on how Pamela felt about those who responded less well to her little test, which is a shame.) As a result of the RNLI's prompt and obvious concern she soon gave the charity a larger sum. By then the RNLI had established that Pamela, who is single, had inherited a large fortune from a relative who had owned a successful business. Her initial gift of £500 really had been small beer, intended to flush out those deserving of much more serious money.

Very gently and involving its most senior people, the RNLI offered more detailed involvement, which she welcomed enthusiastically. She was invited to see RNLI's work for herself, which led her to make, in a single gift, a donation large enough to buy a lifeboat – something in excess of half a million pounds. But her interest – and the RNLI's service – didn't end there. She decided to buy a cottage near where 'her' lifeboat was stationed and gained much satisfaction by involving herself with local fundraising. The lifeboat's crew got to know her well and welcomed her whenever she visited. A relationship of strong mutual benefit grew. Pamela then gave enough money to buy a second lifeboat (she regards both as hers, but in a nice way) and she even funded some major building work.

Pamela McFarlane is still a very close friend of the RNLI and is invited to all its major events. She supports other causes as well, but clearly 'the lifeboats' is special to her. It is highly likely that further gifts will follow, not to mention the strong possibility of a legacy. Whatever, Pamela won't find pressure. Even if she leaves everything to the local dogs home, Pamela is still a great friend of the RNLI. And all this because the RNLI values donors and potential donors at the highest level, as can be seen by its instinctive response in sending a senior person to visit the donor who gave just £500, but hinted at the possibility of more.

I call that exemplary relationship fundraising, although the events in this story took place long before the phrase had become common parlance among fundraisers.

Every prospective major donor is assigned a key person within RNLI, but it doesn't always have to be a senior member from headquarters. Sometimes a regional contact will be more appropriate, or the donor may have built up a relationship with a fundraiser, or even a crew member. The decision of key person is always influenced by the donor's wishes.

Sometimes the donor may not wish for a close relationship at all. One particular donor from the Channel Islands contacted the RNLI 10 years ago, but then insisted that although he had left the charity a gift in his will this was conditional on no publicity and no further contact. So for a decade the RNLI followed his wishes, until it received its biggest legacy ever – £6 million – from that unapproachable donor. There is nothing in the philosophy of relationship fundraising that says relationships have to be any closer than that. (Indeed many fundraisers might consider such a relationship ideal.)

For those in peril on the sea

The lesson here is to allow donors to choose the strength and style of relationship that most suits them. And then follow their wishes, even at the apparent expense of short-term donation income. This is a lesson that the Royal National Lifeboat Institution has learned well, from long experience.

Seafaring has always been a dangerous business and a risky pleasure. But in 1824 if sailors or travellers at sea got into heavy weather, or were knocked off course, or suffered any other kind of trouble then heaven help them, because no one else would. The sea isn't very forgiving and accidents, which were frequent, were usually fatal.

Just when hope was all but abandoned, the trapped seamen spot the
approaching lifeboat from the foretop of the *Indian Chief*.

One reason why few dared to risk their lives to save others was that if the dangerous task failed and the would-be life-savers lost their lives there was no Welfare State, or insurance, to take care of any dependants or family that were left behind.

The vision of Sir William Hillary, who founded RNLI in 1824, was not only to rescue seafarers, but to provide pensions for those who risked their lives saving others at sea. This fundamental philosophy has underpinned the RNLI's voluntary service ever since. If any lifeboat men, or women, were to lose their lives saving others then they have the assurance that their dependants will be looked after. This removes only one of the risks and the least immediate one, which means that those who volunteer to serve on the life-boats still have to bring considerable courage to their work.

Thanks to this philosophy the lifeboat service could get started. There are now 217 lifeboat stations dotted around the entire shoreline of the British Isles, with a total of 292 lifeboats – the largest private fleet in the world.

A local affair

A lifeboat station is still essentially a local affair run by volunteers and often based in a fishing community. Nowadays volunteers are less likely to be sailors or fishermen than they once were. Any competent, fit and brave person who will fit into the team can become a crew member.

Their task is to be ready and willing to go out at any time of day or night, often in the worst of possible conditions, to risk their lives to save others in danger at sea.

In return for this dedication and heroism, the RNLI's responsibility is to ensure that its crews have the very best training, equipment and backup possible to minimise the risks they have to take and to maximise their chances of saving lives.

Coxswain Charles Fish (bearded, centre) with the crew of the Ramsgate lifeboat
following the dramatic rescue of eleven seamen from the *Indian Chief* in 1881.

The Royal National Lifeboat Institution is Britain's third
largest fundraiser, behind only the National Trust and
Oxfam in terms of voluntary income. Of its total income of
£64.5 million in 1995, £35 million came from legacies, £12
million from regional fundraising, £6 million from various
gradings of membership and the remainder from major
donors and the corporate sector.

The RNLI's head of fundraising since 1990 is Ian
Ventham, who before taking this position was national
appeals manager at the NSPCC.

Principles and values

The reasons for the RNLI's success in fundraising are not as self-evident as they may at first seem. Although Britain is described as a nation of seafarers, quite a few RNLI supporters would not welcome the idea of taking a small boat out in rough seas themselves. Many live a long way from the sea and a large number would express little interest in it. And if it's not the appeal of seafaring and things nautical that attracts support neither is it the unquestionable achievement RNLI clocks up each year in actual lives saved. (Last year the figure was 1,624. In an average year it is between 1,000 and 2,000.)

Evidence from a variety of different sources now indicates that a reason stronger even than a love of the sea and a desire to save lives will be found to underpin the generosity of most of the RNLI's supporters.

Ian Ventham explains, 'It is an unusual example of money being given to the means rather than the end. Put simply, people give less for the saving of a life and more because they are moved by the heroism and self-sacrifice of the people who go and do it. The saving of life is important – the two go together – but it's the values shown in practical examples by the lifeboat men and women in the course of their duties that appeal so much to donors.'

So it seems that the RNLI and the lifeboat service it supports appeal most to a section of society that shares and admires those values of bravery and self-sacrifice.

'They see the RNLI', says Ian, 'as a bastion of heroic principles and values in an increasingly unheroic age. Not surprisingly, many of our most enthusiastic supporters fall into a certain age group.'

This is both a considerable asset – RNLI's income from legacies accounts for 60 per cent of its total – and a potential source of worry.

The changing donor

'People change as they get older,' says Ian, 'and their attitudes change too. The values the RNLI represents become more important and this will probably continue whatever else may change in society. But there is a fear that as we move further away from the Second World War subsequent generations will not appreciate these values in quite the same way.'

Ian isn't entirely convinced that changing demographics are a cause for major concern, but he is well aware that they could be. 'We can't be complacent. So to counter this possibility the RNLI is beginning to focus its attention on its natural audience, those who regularly go to sea either professionally or for pleasure. This way, it is hoped to maintain the support of those who share the values of the RNLI while developing more pragmatic support from those who might one day have to call upon its services.'

Through its huge and constantly enterprising network of regional and local activities, the RNLI probably reaches a high proportion of the population of the British Isles at least once in a year. But as much as three-quarters of its income comes each year from less than 3,000 people.

These are the legators. Such is the attraction of the RNLI and the tangibility – not to mention high price tag – of its very visible product or proposition that it clearly does very much better than most at attracting legacies.

But, for all the reasons that are now ringing alarm bells throughout the charitable sector, the RNLI again refuses to be complacent. Ian says, 'We've known for a long time that donors who give at a low level have the potential to give later – perhaps through a legacy – at a very much higher level. So our philosophy is to treat all our members and donors as if they were possible legators. We have done this intuitively and almost automatically, but it has paid off. When we research our legators, for example, we find that many have had some connection with the RNLI, usually going back many years.

'We also try hard to involve people. You don't have to give a lifeboat to enjoy some tangible identification with your gift. People give for all sorts of things we need, from special life-jackets, boots and hats, through to small boats and, of course, the very big and expensive – and now technically superb – lifeboats.'

When it can, the RNLI tries to link individual donors to a particular station, most often to the one nearest where they live. The link has many obvious advantages, but sometimes there can be drawbacks.

'The lifeboat men and women can sometimes get a little sensitive. Sometimes they feel that fundraising is a bit intrusive,' says Ian, 'and we have to be very careful about this. Of course, as volunteers themselves, they too are donors so they almost invariably understand the commercial realities of their situation. They recognise fully that they wouldn't have the excellent kit they have without fundraising.'

Recently a team from Central Television spent a year with the crew of the Salcombe lifeboat filming the highly acclaimed documentary series on the lifeboat service. There would have been no doubt in the viewing public's mind who were the heroes of that series, but the lifeboat crew themselves didn't like to see it that way at all.

Ian explains, 'I met recently with Frank Smith, coxswain of the boat, and he told me that they had *hated* the process of having a TV crew with them all year and had *loathed* the finished product – but nevertheless he recognised how much good the programme had done us.

'So, overall, the lifeboat men and women are very willing to get involved.'

Frequently it won't be the professional fundraiser who will go to give a talk to inspire local fundraisers, but one of the lifeboat crew. Donors and volunteers often visit stations and have done for years, so the RNLI must be one of the most experienced organisations at face-to-face fundraising.

Ian Ventham believes that this emphasis on face-to-face contact has underpinned the RNLI's success over the years. There is no culture here of fundraising from behind a desk. The mission statement from the charity's strategy clearly spells out the organisation's commitment to relationship fundraising.

The next two stories involve two very special and rather unusual donors, and illustrate the RNLI's natural instinct for donor development.

A very major donor

The loss of a lifeboat man or woman at sea is a national tragedy. When the Penlee lifeboat was lost with all its crew in December 1981 the news reverberated around the world and the whole of Britain was devastated.

A few days after the tragedy, among all the messages of sympathy and support, the RNLI received a phone call. The caller was an educated, well-spoken man who asked to speak to someone in authority. He was put through to John Atterton, the deputy director. His call, he explained, was to enquire about the charity's plans to replace the Penlee lifeboat. His various questions were politely answered by John Atterton, who was then in the process of handing over to his successor, Lieutenant Commander Brian Miles. The caller declined to say who he was and John Atterton didn't press him. He said he would call back later and specified a day and time.

At the appointed hour, the anonymous caller phoned again. He explained that he intended to fund a new lifeboat as an expression of his sympathy for the sacrifice made by the people of Penlee. Then the mystery deepened. The caller indicated that both John Atterton and Brian Miles should travel from London's Liverpool Street station to Cambridge on a particular day, when they would be met by a friend in a green Jaguar car. Again he declined to say who he was.

Both RNLI men believed the calls to be genuine. They

duly caught the stipulated train and were met in Cambridge by a Mr Evans who took them to a building on the outskirts of the city, which the visitors soon discovered was Cambridge University's Robinson College.

Eventually, as the adventurous but somewhat bewildered duo took coffee, their mysterious host, Mr, later Sir, David Robinson came in. Brian Miles recalls the encounter, 'He talked to us for about 20 minutes, asking numerous questions, and then he left. This was the only time I ever met him. But shortly after he did confirm that he would fund the new Penlee lifeboat.'

Thereafter Brian Miles was always Sir David's contact on the telephone and he called quite regularly to ask more questions, in a very direct way. Brian Miles was always relieved to have a ready answer. Sir David's personal secretary and lifelong friend, Miss Umney, was also quite often in touch and she proved to be an invaluable ally in informing the RNLI's director how best to deal with this generous, but idiosyncratic benefactor.

The new lifeboat at Penlee was named *Mabel Alice* in honour of Sir David's wife, who was then very ill. The new crew and the families of the original crew made arrangements for a painting of the new boat to be presented to Sir David. It hung in a place of honour in his living-room.

The RNLI's approach obviously found favour with Sir David. His secretary was able to report that he was very impressed indeed with the way the charity was dealing with him.

One day, out of the blue, Sir David rang Brian Miles and asked him where the RNLI wanted a boat in Scotland. 'I felt it was always important to give him a direct answer. He expected it. So without reference to anyone else I told him we needed an "Arun" lifeboat in Buckie on the north-east coast.' This was ideal as Sir David's great friend and former lawyer in Scotland, Charles Brown, had often fished with him on the nearby river Spey.

The appropriate lifeboat was allocated to Buckie and

Today's lifeboats are superbly equipped and very effective… and cost upwards of £1 million each.

named *Charles Brown*. His widow came to Buckie to name it.

Then Sir David rang asking Brian Miles to arrange for his body to be buried at sea when he died. 'He told me he trusted the RNLI to do the job properly. I suggested that he might like this to be arranged at Penlee or Buckie, where his lifeboats were serving, but he said that he didn't want the RNLI to waste money taking him so far. He would be perfectly happy, he assured me, with the lifeboat nearest to his home in Cambridge. Then he swore me to secrecy as he didn't want the media to be present at his funeral.

'Naturally, I said that while we would be honoured to carry out his request, I hoped it would be a very long time before we were called upon to do it. He told me that he was old and tired and would die in the near future. As it happened he died one week after our telephone conversation.'

The RNLI followed Sir David's wishes to the letter. On a bleak and windswept day, the Great Yarmouth and Gorleston lifeboat set out in rough seas to a spot some 35 miles from land where the Ministry of Agriculture, Fisheries and Food had given the RNLI permission to consign their extraordinary donor to the deep. The weather was so bad that the vicar who conducted the service had to do so ashore and then give the committal words to the RNLI inspector, Mr Dick Perks, so that he could say them at the actual point of burial.

But the hounds of the press had got wind of Sir David's intentions and sought to publicise his burial, whatever his wishes. Sir David, however, would have had the last laugh. Brian Miles explains, 'The press turned up in force at Penlee, some 300 miles away. I have no doubt that Sir David would have been delighted had he known that the media were outwitted at the end.'

In his will Sir David Robinson left the RNLI enough money to fund two more lifeboats, which were allocated to Lizard in Cornwall and Wicklow in Ireland. After consultation with his executors, the Lizard lifeboat was named *David Robinson*.

The story doesn't quite end there. It had been planned that Miss Umney would carry out the naming ceremony but unfortunately she died. Again after discussion, it was decided that Sir David's daughter should be asked. For family reasons, Sir David and his daughter had not maintained a close relationship during his final years. At the ceremony she spoke movingly of her gratitude to the RNLI for bringing her and her father together again and also for the fact that the boats bearing her parents' names were side by side at joint stations in Cornwall. After a long illness, Lady Robinson had died on the day before her husband's funeral. In her speech their daughter thanked the RNLI for bringing her parents together after their deaths as they had spent so long together in life.

Sir David and his family gave a great deal to the RNLI.

Clearly the lifeboat service gave them much in return.

An all-weather friend

Another wonderful friend of the RNLI is Miss Yolande Rampton. Her father had been in the Navy during the war and was involved with the Merchant Marines afterwards. So she has always had an affinity with the sea.

From the 1960s to 1985 the private trust of Miss Rampton's aunt had supported the RNLI with numerous donations totalling about £40,000. After her aunt's death, the trustees decided to wind up the trust and gave nearly half a million pounds for an all-weather lifeboat, which was brought into service in 1986. Miss Rampton was chosen by the family to name the new boat, perhaps because in 1984 she had become a life governor of the RNLI.

At the naming ceremony Miss Rampton was escorted and looked after by a senior member of RNLI staff.

Shortly afterwards she was in touch with her 'minder' to discuss the possibility of funding an inshore lifeboat, which she did in 1987 through a £10,000 deposited covenant. Meanwhile she had been giving the RNLI various small donations, mostly by deed of covenant.

Also in 1987, she paid for crew protective clothing for the boat her aunt's trust had funded. Then she funded the trailer for her own inshore lifeboat. Many gifts of shares and money followed from 1989 to 1995, totalling over £55,000. Each of these gifts was allocated to a particular project that she was interested in. Miss Rampton's current project is to provide funds for another D-class lifeboat, which is due into service in 1998.

Contact throughout has been maintained by one member of staff at the RNLI and the pace has been determined entirely by Miss Rampton's own needs and desires. She has received regular news about the RNLI in general, and her boats in particular.

Perhaps the most valuable service Miss Rampton has

provided to the RNLI, however, was when she agreed to take part in a film produced to promote legacies. As someone who has donated most generously to the RNLI, and because she has pledged a legacy to the RNLI, she was the ideal presenter. She readily agreed to participate and in the film gives eloquent testimony to the pleasures and satisfactions of being a donor and, in due course, a legator to the RNLI.

The Royal National Lifeboat Institution
West Quay Road
Poole
Dorset BH15 1HZ
United Kingdom

Tel: +44 (0) 1202 663000
Fax: +44 (0) 1202 669680

20

'Hello Mrs Donor...'

The telephone as relationship builder

Although I'd been a fundraiser for more than a dozen years, the first time I seriously considered the opportunities for using the telephone in fundraising was just seven years ago when I met an American evangelist for telephone fundraising who had come to Britain to convert the natives. His name was Rich Fox and he was then president of a company called Facter Fox International. He was clearly a man with a mission. When Fox introduced his concept for bringing telephone fundraising to the mass of British fundraisers in 1989, I was one of the people he came to see to discuss the potential. At the time it struck me as significant that he didn't try to sell me the idea on the phone.

An unfazed Fox responded, 'A face-to-face meeting is obviously better. But the reality is that you simply can't visit all your donors one to one. So the next best thing is to visit them by phone. Most fundraisers, of course, won't want to telephone their donors every time they've got something to say, nor should they. Communication by letter will often be more appropriate.'

This simple guidance still, I think, perfectly sums up the approach every fundraiser should have to communicating with his or her donors. Seen in this context, the role of the telephone is obvious.

I was immediately attracted by the idea of visiting donors by phone. It sounded some way away from the heavy, telephone-sales approach I had been expecting. It also made sense, and ever since then I have followed the progress of telephone fundraising with affection.

Nevertheless, I have mixed views about the telephone fundraising business and of how the phone is used by fundraisers. In the wrong hands, the telephone can lead to nightmare situations. That's why a properly structured and enforceable code of practice such as that produced by Britain's ICFM is so important, as is proper training, supervision, random testing, reputable vendors and all that. It is a tough market, certainly not a licence to print money. But as initial euphoria and over-optimism have worn away, it has become clear that in good hands the telephone really can be a great relationship builder. Sadly, the reverse is just as easily true.

The upgrading call

It may seem tedious to stress this but in fundraising the means of achieving a given end, such as upgrading, has to be distinguished from the medium through which you will make that upgrading proposition, ie by letter, over the phone or in person, face-to-face. Letters are not generally ideal for upgrading propositions because they don't allow for any interaction. Face-to-face would be best but it's time consuming and prohibitively expensive. So in many situations I prefer the telephone.

The telephone is a great medium for upgrading because you can use it to describe anything that requires individual explanation; the intricacies of a monthly giving scheme, the complexities of a direct debit form or a deed of covenant, the advantages and the ins and outs of making a will. Anything that is complex or potentially confusing will easily put donors off. The telephone is irreplaceable because it allows you to systematically make personal, one-to-one contact with lots of your donors quite quickly. Over the phone you can individually put them at their ease.

And that's the point. The telephone is a great medium for explanation but I believe as often as not you will come unstuck if you try to use the telephone to persuade. Remember comfort levels. Remember your donors' natural politeness and tendency to find it difficult to say no to you directly, over the phone.

Enhanced contributions from uncomfortable donors are not worth the increase. So use the phone to explain but not to sell.

The relationship telefundraiser

Telephone fundraising is one of those specialisations that with experience you can get better and better at. The daily flow of colourful success stories coming out of the telephone fundraising agencies points to ever-improving prospects for the phone in fundraising.

I've always been struck by how relationship-oriented the main telephone vendors are, in the UK at least. Mass marketing by telephone never really took off here. Those who have survived as specialist telephone fundraisers have had to adapt and work hard to prove their worth in an area where quality of call is what's considered important, rather than quantity and output. I personally advise those fundraisers who can to do as much of their telephone fundraising as is practical in-house. But the role of the agencies is indisputable. They are invaluable for special tasks for the big fundraisers and indispensable for the smaller charities who have got just as much to say but no resources or experience for in-house telephoning.

Here are just a few examples of the kind of triumphs being developed by professional telephone agencies. They come courtesy of the UK-based agency Personal Telephone Fundraising Limited.

■ Turning responders into real donors. Christian Aid's campaign to once-only, emergency givers was designed to convert their initial concern into long-term committed giving through standing order payments and covenants. The phone is the perfect medium for explaining a complex, high-value proposition such as monthly giving. Although fewer than 10 per cent of those called actually converted, the return on investment from this test was nearly 19:1.

■ Reactivating lapsed donors. Amnesty International had 10,000 past members who hadn't been in contact for two years or more and had resisted at least five written requests to renew. The telephone successfully reactivated 3,000 of them, more than half agreeing to pay by regular direct debit with an average annual gift of £71.

■ 'Please do something'. Cancer Relief Macmillan Fund wanted involvement from its donors and used the phone to put across a range of different opportunities from taking part in house-to-house collections to joining the world's largest coffee morning. Seventy-two per cent agreed to take part in some kind of voluntary activity, proving yet again that your best donors can be your best volunteers – and vice versa.

■ Giving donors choices. Greenpeace UK has been testing 'welcome' telephone calls to new supporters as an alternative to its innovative welcome mailing pack. Again the phone is ideal for explaining several complex and widely different options and new supporters are normally very receptive to being offered the early chance to help. They are usually bowled over when allowed to choose whatever most suits them. In Greenpeace UK's test 889 offers of help were received from just 340 calls to new supporters and a lot of additional information was also gathered. Most supporters offered to help in several ways.

But this is just the tip of an iceberg. Each success story leaves the charity fundraiser with fewer and fewer reasons not to get serious about using the phone to build and develop donor relationships. Certainly there are new, creative and effective uses for the telephone just waiting for fundraisers to plug in. The downside of this is that the telephone is very uneven and when it does go wrong lasting damage can be done.

Anyone who has listened in to fundraising calls made by professional telephone fundraisers as part of a structured campaign will have witnessed conversations that illustrate both extremes of this dilemma.

However good the caller is, there is a world of difference between a call to a keen supporter who is comfortable about being called at home and receptive to the charity's suggestions and the call that has come at a less than convenient time, is tolerated out of politeness and during which it becomes clear that the supporter is vague about his or her relationship with the charity and is less than enthusiastic about what's on offer, or even continuing the call. Experienced callers can deal with this by politely extricating themselves after some damage-limiting statements. The dilemma is that it

> I'm sorry if I sounded grumpy when you phoned – recently we have been plagued with calls from firms who 'happen to be in the neighbourhood'... I thought you were another one of those...
>
> However, as soon as I was clear that you were a Camphill/Botton lady, I was delighted to hear from you.
>
> Peter Jellinek, Buckinghamshire

is impossible to predict in advance how a fundraising call will be received – not to mention some of the other problems telephone fundraisers encounter, such as age and infirmity, deafness, confusion, bad timing, bad moods and so forth. If, for whatever reason, the call is not well received, engineering an appropriate and speedy call back can be difficult and risky. Direct mail may be more often wasted but it is much less likely to offend, or to leave a situation where restarting the relationship can be awkward.

Two sad stories

The following stories illustrate the point.

Ian Ventham's father (*see* chapter 19) is a typical English gentleman born some years before the generation that is comfortable with the phone. He supports several charities in a modest way including one that he habitually helped, not with his own gift but by organising a street collection that annually raised £30 or £40 – quite a bit more than he would have thought to give himself.

One evening Mr Ventham senior received a fundraising phone call at home from the organisation on whose behalf he collected each year. It was an unexpected and somewhat confusing experience because the caller was unaware of *how* the donor had made this contribution and simply wanted to persuade him to increase his gifts. So confused was Mr Ventham that he eventually agreed to give £50.

To people of Ian's dad's generation a commitment is a commitment. Whether he could afford it or not, or wanted to do it or not, he now had to pay up. But the bitterness he felt then at being misled and coerced has never subsided.

My second sad story concerns someone more able, or at least willing, to confront infamy in whatever form it may strike. My sister-in-law Lynne is a teacher and rather a formidable one at that, the kind that has terrified and quietened me since childhood. One day, moved by a particularly emotive television advertisement, she sent a donation to a major child-care charity.

Imagine her outrage when, some weeks later, that charity rang her at home to ask for another gift. Now Lynne is not a regular donor. She had responded emotionally to a single, specific need. There was no suggestion of an ongoing relationship and it had never occurred to her. Now here was someone apparently saying that she hadn't given enough. She sent this poor unfortunate caller off with a flea in his ear and was still heatedly going on about it at least six months later. Her words to me were, 'I'll certainly never send a donation to that lot again.'

With these cautionary tales in mind, let me tell you why I am a passionate advocate for the telephone in relationship fundraising.

The quiet and effective trailblazers

The pioneer of the telephone in UK fundraising is unquestionably the charity ActionAid. It had been quietly and effectively telephoning its own supporters and those of a few other enlightened charities at least five years before Rich Fox reached these shores and established telephone fundraising as a hot topic.

ActionAid is one of Britain's largest overseas development charities and raises over 50 per cent of its income through child sponsorship. Darren Instrall, head of ActionAid's subsidiary National Telephone Team, explains how they came to be the innovator in what may be the fastest-growing area of charity marketing.

'The department, now NTT, grew from our sponsor services division, out of a customer care programme rather than from fundraising itself. It was only after we'd had some considerable successes that we began to see real fundraising potential in the telephone. In the early days we used the phone to recruit volunteer fundraisers to do house-to-house collections and to take part in ActionAid Week. The phone was only one part of what was going on.'

The telephone already had two other important functions for ActionAid. Enquirers for child sponsorship were telephoned if, after a reasonable time, they had not completed their sponsorship form and asked to return the details of the child that they had been sent. Many 'converted' from this call (*see* page 523). The phone was also recognised as invaluable in explaining the covenant process (Britain's quirky but valuable procedure for allowing charities to reclaim tax already paid on a supporter's regular gift). Around 80 per cent of ActionAid sponsors sign covenants, allowing the charity to claim an additional 30 per cent of each donation as an unearmarked extra gift. Most will agree to do so following a letter of invitation. For those who don't, follow-up by phone is particularly effective.

ActionAid realised the importance of looking long term

at enhancing its relationship with existing regular supporters. Darren says, 'The average life of a sponsor is about nine years. These donors already support us substantially and regularly. We found that the phone helped us to cement that already-powerful relationship and then these people would go on to do even more.'

The telephone was also the avenue to ActionAid's most cost-effective method of sponsor recruitment, sponsor get sponsor. ActionAid's telephone team would ask donors (among other things) if they would introduce a friend. Fifteen per cent of all sponsors have now joined by this method.

Each year the NTT makes about 200,000 calls to ActionAid supporters, calling each donor twice on average. They first establish if a sponsor is happy with what the charity enables them to do. If they are, then encouraging further support is quite straightforward. If not, then any problems can usually be resolved then and there, over the phone.

ActionAid learned early that the key to successful telephone fundraising was happy donors. Ideally the donor's enthusiasm takes over, and no selling is necessary. Now many years later the number of people willing to recruit a friend has not diminished, but there are signs of falling returns. 'Many people have done it for a few years now', says Darren, 'and they simply seem to be running out of friends to ask.'

The National Telephone Team was formed in 1988. It now has a calling centre in Bristol and four home-based teams, with 32 staff and 150 part-time callers. It not only serves ActionAid and several other charity clients for outbound telephone fundraising but also provides an in-bound facility taking calls generated by direct-response television and radio advertising.

ActionAid first started to ask directly for donations by phone in 1991. Despite years of experience in house-to-house collections, this idea nevertheless prompted internal consternation from those who considered the telephone unduly intrusive. 'Knocking on doors, of course, is far more intrusive,' says Darren, 'but no-one seems bothered by that.'

The results speak for themselves, as the following examples show. But everyone at NTT ascribes at least part of their success to another factor: ActionAid is well known for both the quality and the consistency of its feedback to donors.

Darren explains, 'In the main we are talking to regular givers and good feedback is important to them and to us. It's not a big issue for one-off donors, perhaps for obvious reasons. And if someone doesn't want feedback they don't need to have it. It's their choice and it's part of our service to donors to ask these questions when we call. Donors always appreciate it.'

The 'make or break' story

In 1992 ActionAid had 80,000 names on its database about whom it knew very little. They had come from a variety of often not very promising sources – raffle ticket sales, catalogue buyers, general enquirers and so forth. Most had never donated and normal postal appeals to them were not cost-effective.

So the make or break initiative was born, its primary objective being to prove the potential of this list so that some new supporters would be generated and the rest, having been given all reasonable opportunity, could be discarded in clear conscience. The secondary, but none the less important objective, was to do this profitably, to raise much-needed income for ActionAid's underfunded programmes.

Make or break 1 was an emotive, hard-hitting direct mail appeal to all 80,000 names, focusing on ActionAid's work in Malawi and El Salvador. The appeal even included a 'would you like us to stay in touch' box. Four thousand people responded and £73,000 was raised, giving a return on investment of 3.5:1. The moral here is that you should never leave your lapsed names languishing.

Make or break 2 was also planned to be a postal appeal to the remaining 76,000. While it was in preparation the crisis in Somalia blew up. A special appeal for Somalia was sent that generated a 10 per cent response and raised £247,000, returning 8.5:1.

ActionAid was able to trace phone numbers for fewer than half of the remaining 68,000 names. However 24,000 were telephoned in what became make or break 3.

This group was considered very much the 'worst of the worst' by ActionAid. Clearly something really powerful was needed to persuade them to respond. ActionAid had raised the funds it then needed for Somalia but a new quite positive story was breaking in another part of troubled Africa, Mozambique. Until then, only emergency-type measures had been possible there. Now a ceasefire in the civil war persuaded ActionAid field workers that some longer-term development would be possible.

Mozambique was not sufficiently stable for a regular sponsorship programme, however, so funding had to be gained from other sources. Would the diehards of make or break see this as their turning point?

Twenty-five per cent of them did. Six thousand people immediately agreed over the phone to give regular support by direct debit; £185,000 was raised in first-year gifts alone, giving a return of 4.5:1.

But the remaining 60,000 plus were not excused yet. Nine months after that first appeal a further positive mailing on Mozambique arrived. Four per cent responded with £40,000.

By now NTT had experience that enabled it to target different types of donors based on past responses and to vary calls accordingly. Make or break 5 also produced a 25 per cent response with many committing to regular giving.

In all the make or break initiative activated 19,250 of the original 80,000 names and raised £1,077,000 while doing it. Thirty-five per cent of all individuals telephoned responded with a donation. Campaigns in the make or break style are now a regular feature at NTT.

Keeping your friends...

Darren Instrall attributes the low attrition of make-or-break donors – just two per cent a year – to the high quality of the original call. In fact, after nearly a decade of vigorous telephoning, ActionAid is convinced that, while a small number of sponsors clearly dislike calls, phoned donors, on average, stay longer.

'We now have evidence', says Darren, 'that there is no negative effect on sponsorship attrition rates from regular calling. Obviously that was initially a concern and it's something that is quite difficult to prove. But our complaints level also is very low, which is reassuring. In 1995 we received just one complaint for every 900 calls.'

...finding new ones

As previously explained, converting enquirers to sponsors was one of NTT's earliest and most fruitful functions.

Prior to this, enquirers who didn't sign up as sponsors from their 'welcome' materials were reminded and then chased through the post. ActionAid's NTT expected from the start that a telephone follow-up would be more effective, but just how much more is quite staggering. Nearly seven times as many 'tardy' people will agree to become sponsors over the phone than will by mail. Whether this is a sign of the telephone's undoubted ability to overcome inertia, or the donor's inability to resist a reasonable request is as yet unclear. It is probably a bit of both.

...and upgrading existing sponsors

NTT has also used the telephone to effectively follow up a request for sponsors to increase their contributions if they were paying below the normal sponsorship level. Thirty-eight per cent of ActionAid's sponsors can be expected to agree to such a request as soon as they are notified of it (by post). But the telephone encourages another 40 per cent to do it too.

The phone has also played an important part in upgrading non-sponsoring donors, of which ActionAid has quite a few.

Darren Instrall is confident of the growing importance of the telephone to ActionAid and optimistic about the opportunities facing NTT. 'Selective calling with carefully tailored scripts shows that we are thinking more about our supporters and their needs. This will make our calling more cost-effective, but it will also enhance our supporters' already-high impression of ActionAid and the important work it does.'

Simon Pell of the London-based telephone fundraising specialists Pell & Bales echoes Darren Instrall's positive experience of the telephone in fundraising and is no less enthusiastic about its future. His experience in working with a wide range of different types of fundraising client has given Simon a unique perception of how the phone is being used to build relationships and how it might be used in coming years.

'People like to talk', says Simon, 'and donors are no exception. Generally they are very willing to talk to you and that means they will tell you things, often whether you ask them or not. Telephone research, of course, is a well-developed practice and in-depth interviews of about 20–25 minutes by phone are not unusual and not difficult to organise.

'In these discussions people are often surprisingly candid about what they will tell you – the salary they earn, their religious affiliation, voting intentions and so on. They may be more guarded if they think you are leading up to asking for a donation, but if you are genuinely seeking opinions and attitudes they will talk.

'This willingness to talk makes a variety of calls possible to capture information that may have marketing relevance.'

Capture and use of information is a big issue among telephone fundraisers. Obviously information is worse than useless if it isn't properly stored and used. Many charities now are collecting vast amounts of information that is not being kept, mainly because the charities themselves don't know how to use it. Yet, as Greenpeace's Annie Moreton says, donors may well remember what they have told you and may be upset if you haven't acted on it.

Simon believes charities are currently losing useful information and he sees the potential for gathering such information as a huge opportunity. 'If you know someone's attitude to an issue then it's not too difficult to make a case that they can and should do something about it. For example, if you know how a donor feels about, say, the provision of information and facilities for deaf people then it wouldn't be too difficult for a charity such as the Royal National Institute for Deaf People to prepare a pretty compelling appeal letter to that person.

'Deaf people on the phone may sound unlikely, but a lot of people have hearing problems or know someone who has. If you can find out by phone that an individual is suffering from tinnitus – a ringing in the ears – then clearly funding a tinnitus helpline would be a strong proposition. Or people with a hearing aid will inevitably respond well to a proposal to fund hearing-aid research. And so on. Donors connected with a cause also are better prospects for a covenant proposal, or a committed giving proposition. By being able to identify people on the *scale* of their deafness, the RNID can actually direct different propositions to them in the mail.

'The more you know about someone, the more accurate, targeted and specific you can be. So the telephone clearly has an indispensable role in relationship fundraising, even without ever using it to raise money directly.

'It is critical that charities pool or cross-refer all their sources of information internally. It's just not good enough to have donors on one database and catalogue buyers on another, and so on, so that you can't identify whether you are talking to a mail order customer who has also made a donation. If for no other reason, it plays havoc with the poor telephone fundraiser when he or she calls. And that's how people get offended.

'Knowing about donors, yes it's been said before, is the key to segmentation. Members, particularly of activist organisations, are often armchair activists and sometimes feel guilty about being a "bad" member and not doing more. Others strongly believe that just being a member, ie paying their subscription, is enough. With such information to guide the fundraiser there can be less waste and more appropriate fundraising.'

There is no point in sending in lots of pieces of paper and other information into the charity if there is no one there to process it. Charities should decide which data they want to capture – what they can use. Then the caller should input them directly on to the database.

You have to know what to ask

Out of the thousands of things that could be asked of donors, how does a charity identify the few really important things that are practical and usable? Simon Pell believes that much of the excitement in fundraising comes from methodically figuring that out. And each organisation is different.

'Each call is expensive so must have a specific job to do. But it is often possible to drop in a question at the end, for example to find out if they are phone-friendly or not by asking how they would feel if we were to call again.

'We did this for the Worldwide Fund for Nature in the UK. Less than 15 per cent said no don't call back. Some said they'd like the charity to send fewer letters and to call instead. Most said they'd be quite happy to be called. The point is that at the end of the exercise the charity had a list of phone-friendly donors prepared to act very quickly. Combine that with another piece of information, such as ownership of a credit card, and the potential, say, in times of emergency is clear – you have automatically identified people you can go straight to.

'Obvious, perhaps, but if this is taken a little further, why not ask some of these self-confessed phone-friendly people to be part of an informal research panel for you, and ring them every three or six months to monitor their reactions to you? And why not have a panel of donors or members who you can call over the year to discuss issues that affect the charity?'

> I am really bothered by charities who telephone in an over-friendly manner to thank you for your previous support even when you have had no previous contact with their charity. The tactic is clearly designed to disarm, but in fact is devious and manipulative and shouldn't happen.
>
> Simon Duffy, London

At this point Simon accepts that a knowledge of social science or some formal research training might come in handy. Anecdotal evidence is one thing but quota-based sampling that is representative of the whole group is not territory for even the enthusiastic novice. Firms like Pell & Bales, however, are experienced at large-scale, structured research.

'For Oxfam Week we called 40,000 people over 15 weeks with about a dozen questions. Each week we asked 500 of them two different questions, some general, some specifically related to Oxfam. In this way we got a good picture of Oxfam's donors' habits and views on specific questions.'

A few years ago, the housing charity Shelter decided to try to rank its donors on a scale of attitude and activism. This split reflected the origins of Shelter, which was formed when two very different constituencies – housing rights activists and church groups – came together in the early 1960s.

This polarisation of people, the very religious and the very radical, was assumed to still permeate the database. Shelter was sending the same mailings to everyone, yet clearly different messages might be expected to find favour with one group, and not the other. An appeal that said, 'Housing in crisis, Government cuts funding' might appeal to one group, whereas a focus on forlorn-looking kids in a damp bedsit might have more effect on the remainder.

Of course, telephone research showed that Shelter's donors didn't just divide into two neat camps, there were at least five or six different types, with several shades in between. This information is priceless to charities prepared to really segment their communications.

A few years ago, fundraisers were being encouraged to write down and circulate a description of their typical donor. Now they'd have to describe five or six, or more.

Our flexible friend

The future for fundraising seems likely to be intimately concerned with issues surrounding the more intelligent use of data and strategic approaches to donors using the nuances within databases of class, gender, age and interests. This will affect our use of all media, but the telephone is uniquely geared to exploit immediately these factors because, within limits, you can have as many different creative approaches as you have phone calls, all within one fundraising campaign. Fundraisers talk of writing individually to their donors, sending each a different and tailored letter, but that isn't possible yet and won't be for some time. It is possible now with the phone.

Creativity in phone calls is perhaps dangerous – callers can't be allowed too much licence to say what they like – but it is nevertheless quite possible. You can underline on the phone and even add a postscript, just like in direct mail. Verbal imagery too can be just as persuasive as the printed image and even the use of pauses and silence (knowing when to listen) might just be as important as the creative use of white space.

Certainly the telephone has some hurdles to overcome. Many people really don't like it, but with demographic and social change that too might disappear. Better-trained, more relationship-oriented callers will help also. Then there's the expense, although that often falls by the wayside when cost is related to benefit.

But telephoning a donor, or potential donor, is an awkward and unnatural thing. Even if the donor doesn't object, the process often leads to anxiety, both for caller and the called.

Simon Pell is acutely aware of this issue and believes telefundraisers need to overcome it. 'Often donors are well aware of the purpose of the call, perhaps because of a pre-call letter. They know they are about to be asked for money and that leads to anxiety The caller senses this and becomes anxious too. It's an awkward thing to do even at the best of times and it's tricky, however good the message. Quick-fire, short calls on high-profile issues, such as disasters or elections, may be less stressful for both parties than a general fundraising call.

'I believe telefundraising is almost inevitably an anxiety-making process, but relationship fundraising by phone needn't be. For one thing, you can tell your callers there is no target rate of calls to make each night. That will hugely relieve their stress immediately.

'Calls then can become less structured, less relentlessly driven towards the ultimate demand for money. The caller can take her or his time and set the donor at ease by discussing the issue and asking opinions.

'So the best calls are not just about asking for money, but about customer care, information gathering, and servicing too. Donors are happier with that kind of call and callers are too. There's less anxiety all round.'

The argument about how long or how short a direct mail letter should be rages on, but Simon Pell is unequivocal. 'Longer calls produce a better response, not just in satisfaction but in funds raised. We can prove it. Longer calls will cost more, but the difference in response is quantifiable. And I believe that is not just because longer calls allow for a better discussion and more developed arguments, but because with a longer call we can structure the conversation specifically to take the pressure off both parties.'

There does seem to be an important lesson here for fundraisers. Donors, by and large, are polite people. If someone calls they'll listen, and talk. Their natural niceness may then become a barrier that prevents them telling the caller what they *really* think. Only after the caller has hung up, chalking up another hit, will the donor give vent to what she or he really feels, either to the phone itself or to a hapless partner sitting in the next room.

If fundraising calls are all about asking for money, that scenario will become increasingly common and telephone fundraising will become increasingly unacceptable.

But the telephone is a very versatile instrument. It has many more uses than the crude asking for money and is very much more effective if it can be deployed with skill, sensitivity and imagination, all backed by accurate donor records that point to what might turn the individual on the other end either on or off.

So once again the future is up to the fundraiser. I don't get many fundraising calls at home (perhaps I'm seldom in before the average fundraiser's bedtime) and I always enjoy them when I do, even though at least half are remarkably crass. Will that enjoyment, tinged as it is with professional interest, turn to disappointment and despair?

It'll be interesting to see.

No delegation

Simon Pell is also a man obsessed with quality control. Perhaps he has to be. After all, the average telephone caller is a low-paid, part-time, casual worker who may know very little about the charity on whose behalf he or she is calling. Without rigorous quality control the outcome is obvious.

Careful recruitment and large investment in training, both up front and on the job, are the only solutions. In-house teams may have the disadvantage that their staff lack the variety and, therefore, freshness of an agency caller, but they can more easily become knowledgeable about the cause and sensitive to the donor. The management and supervision of telephone teams is clearly a crucial issue: no fundraiser can afford to delegate it entirely.

'I have seen the future and it is one to one'

So said one of the enthusiastic reviewers of Don Peppers and Martha Rogers' runaway best seller, *The One-to-One Future* (UK edition by Piatkus Publishers, London, 1994) – which incidentally first appeared in print in the USA in 1993, a year after *Relationship Fundraising*. If the future really is one to one, then large-scale marketing will be increasingly dominated by the telephone.

Technological and social advances will help the trend. The new-old generation of telephone-friendly baby boomers will replace the older conservative 'civics', who were suspicious of the telephone and nervous whenever they used it. The new generation will be totally at ease with it, having several phones – at home, in the office, and even one in their handbag or top pocket.

Some of the new technology coming our way promises increased applications for the telephone in fundraising – and sound like fun too. To complete the circle, I went back to my friend Rich Fox, the man who brought commercial telephone fundraising to Britain all those years ago, and asked him what he thought the future might hold for us.

Rich, who is now back in the United States assisting not-for-profits by advising on all aspects of relationship fundraising, said, 'Some very exciting things that just a year or two ago would have seemed like science fiction are already happening in various parts of the world. There are several examples. One that has great potential for fundraisers is what is known as the "pass through call".

'A company called Share in Boston used it recently for

Greenpeace USA when calling donors to ask them to protest about Shell Oil's activities in Nigeria and their impact on the Ogoni tribespeople. If a donor responded enthusiastically the caller was able to say, "Well, would you like to register your protest at the highest level? I can pass your call through to the White House. Right now, if you wish." And boy, of course, many of those enthusiastic donors did. What an opportunity. Others will have respectfully declined, as not everyone is that "in your face". But it must have been nice to have the chance!'

In Argentina Greenpeace has been running a hugely successful direct response television campaign which features a number viewers can call for information. The advertisements tell responders that as they call $5.00 will automatically be charged directly to their phone bill. Suddenly, thanks to this technology, Greenpeace has a new cost-effective way of recruiting new supporters. In Brazil Unicef has used this same idea to raise $10 million.

Equally useful is the technology that recognises the caller's number as soon as he or she calls you and instantly displays the donor's record so the receptionist has it in front of him immediately when he answers the phone. This not only saves time and inconvenience, it impresses the hell out of the donor. This system is known as automatic number identification (ANI) and many corporations use it already. But most not-for-profits are as yet some way behind.

Donors in the United States are getting harder and harder to reach, partly because of the growth of answering machines and partly because of the low opinion many have of fundraising calls, bred from years of inappropriate telemarketing. So it makes sense for many organisations to have their own in-bound programme in-house and to use every possible device to encourage donors to call them. Automatic number identification, in combination with dialled number identification service (DINS), enables the in-bound receptionist to immediately recognise not just who is calling but what they are calling about, even if you have 10 different campaigns running simultaneously. That way the right script or prompts can appear before the receptionist as soon as the call comes in, again saving time and impressing with efficiency.

Of course, ANI machines are now being advertised for your home, so you can plug a tiny digital display into your phone and read who is calling you before you decide whether or not to answer.

While this may create problems for telephone fundraisers, Rich Fox believes the organisation that serves its donors carefully and well will benefit. 'There are some organisations donors love to hear from, but in the absence of this technology they just screen out all marketing calls. In future the relationship fundraiser may well get through.'

One recent technical innovation that finds little favour with Fox for fundraising is the predictive dialling machine. This is a gizmo that automatically pre-dials potential donors in advance, based upon a predictive algorithm (or formula) that determines when the caller is likely to be ready for the next call. If the predictive dialler is set too aggressively, the caller may find that he or she hardly has time to pause for breath between calls. When one call finishes, the next is right there waiting. It's a system designed to maximise the number of calls and rather cuts across Simon Pell's initiatives to overcome anxiety. (Wouldn't you be anxious, talking to your donors like that?)

The other major problem with predictive dialling is that it is immediately obvious to the donor as there is almost always a delay between the phone being answered and the caller's voice being heard from the other end. 'Donors in America are now beginning to recognise this', claims Fox, 'and use the pause to register their reaction to what they perceive as junk calls – they hang up.'

> I dislike being phoned by a charity and asked to do door-to-door collection. I have no objection to doing it sometimes, but I do not like to be pressurised on the phone which is how I feel because I do not like to say no. It is not possible to collect in the same road for about six charities without it becoming embarrassing.
>
> Anonymous NSPCC supporter, Croydon

The telephone at the crossroads

So changing telephone technology will ensure that this area of fundraising will not be standing still, even briefly. It strikes me that already, after what has been a colourful but very brief history, the telephone in fundraising is at a crossroads. Technology will allow us to make our phone calls to donors even more appropriate and more customer-friendly in the future. Or, alternatively, our unbridled collective enthusiasm for the cash we can raise from telephone fundraising could render us insensitive to the damage that inappropriate telephoning can do to our relationships with donors.

For many the damage has already been done, and a fundraising call from a charity at home in the evening will forever be seen as an unwelcome intrusion. This will be a difficult position to change. And it will require policies and procedures that are truly donor-led, not target-driven.

In time we fundraisers may come to agree on these, but can we make sure they are applied?

Rich Fox & Associates Inc
21476 Paseo Portola
Malibu, California 90265
USA

Tel: +1 310 317 9501
Fax: +1 310 317 9601
E-mail: foxrich@aol.com

ActionAid's NTT
Hamlyn House
Archway
London N19 5PG
United Kingdom

Tel: +44 (0) 171 281 4101
Fax: +44 (0) 171 272 0899

Personal Telephone Fundraising Ltd
Garden Suite, Blenheim House
119–120 Church Street
Brighton
East Sussex BN1 1WH
United Kingdom

Tel: +44 (0) 1273 698697
Fax: +44 (0) 1273 868006

Pell & Bales Ltd
91–93 Farringdon Road
London EC1M 3LB
United Kingdom

Tel: +44 (0) 171 404 3833
Fax: +44 (0) 171 404 8064

21

The British Home Office

Relationship consultation

Perhaps the most unusual example of relationship fundraising in practice comes not from a charity but from a government department.

In England and Wales responsibility for legislation relating to charities rested with the Home Secretary, advised by officials in the Home Office Voluntary Services Unit (VSU). Responsibility is now with the Secretary of State for National Heritage. To carry out that policy effectively, officials needed some understanding of practice issues and a good working relationship with practitioners.

In 1993, about a year after *Relationship Fundraising* was first published, VSU was occupied in extensive consultation on the shaping of the Charities Act 1992, which was to be the most wide-ranging legislation to affect Britain's voluntary sector in most people's memory. That summer, Frank Smith, head of charity law at VSU, attended a lecture at the Institute of Charity Fundraising Managers' (ICFM) National Fundraisers' Convention and he has written this chapter to explain what happened.

Relationships are for everyone

I recall Ken Burnett's presentation very well. Ken described with careful accuracy the exploits of his pseudonym Myles Barnett, who had sent £5 to each of Britain's top 50 charities, expressing admiration for their work and asking for information about their activities. He had then recorded what the charities had sent him.

This was fascinating, particularly woven into an exposition on the art and practice of relationship fundraising. But I felt uncomfortable. The more Ken outlined his theory and identified the mistakes some of the charities had made, the more I wondered how government consultation exercises would stand up to the same analysis – such as the consultation document I had written on Part II of the Charities Act 1992, then about to go into print.

Input from fundraisers was something I took very seriously, and I had already held a consultative workshop with several leading figures in the world of fundraising and charity law, including the director of ICFM, to find out what those with 'front line' experience thought was important. Their views had been a big influence on the draft regulations. I hoped that our efforts to get the design right would win support when the proposals were published. But I had not thought of the consultation document in terms that were similar to a fundraising direct mail appeal. For example, what reaction would the envelope evoke on arrival? Excitement, disinterest, or concern that it might be a demand for tax?

The more I reflected on Ken's lecture, the more I realised that much of the concept and detail of relationship fundraising was closely applicable to presenting government proposals for change, inviting comments and seeking to persuade those concerned that the proposals were right. Putting the theory into practice led to a number of useful initiatives and I am sure improved the reception the proposals achieved. I developed a checklist for information

mailings at that time that might be as useful for others as it
was for us.

Mail pack as the focus

What does the mail pack look like when it arrives? Is it clear
what it is? Is it attractively presented and interesting? Is
there a covering letter inside from a named individual
greeting the recipient and telling her or him very simply
what all of this is about?

Detail

Is it clear what the consultation document itself contains?
Are the issues set out clearly and in a way that is
appropriate to the expertise and interests of the audience?

Response

Is it clear what the recipient is invited to do? Has the
maximum been done to help the recipient understand the
issues and encourage her or him to comment constructively?

Two devices I adopted were the inclusion of a
questionnaire and freepost return address. In later
documents, I structured the questionnaire more fully to
mirror the structure of focus issues set out in the main
consultation document, so that completion of the
questionnaire reinforced the understanding of the main
document.

Product identity

From the outset I envisaged a series of consultation
documents on related topics, such as fundraising, charitable
collections and charity accounts. I therefore sought to give
the series an overall product identity through similar cover
design and the use of a logo, which could be slightly varied
each time, to give an eye-catching headline. Hopefully
confidence achieved through one exercise would then carry
forward to the next, to make the task a little easier each time.

Feedback

Anyone commenting on a consultation exercise probably accepts that there are a number of views and everyone can't get their way. But they do want some recognition that their views have been given a fair hearing. However, there are too many comments to reply to each in detail so, when respondents have given their name and address, the thing to do is to send a prompt thank you letter. At the conclusion of a consultation exercise it is only fair (and sensible from a relationship point of view) to publish feedback explaining the comments received and the decisions reached. Hence the detailed paper, *Talk Back*, we issued in relation to Part II: 'What you said... What we have done about it'.

Public speaking

Participating in seminars and workshops for fundraisers and charity people helps to get good coverage during a consultation exercise. It increases the dialogue (information giving *and* feedback). It can also give recipients more confidence about the good intent of the department publishing the proposals.

Publication of comments

A fundraiser telephoned me after the publication of the fourth consultation document on these principles. 'Well,' he said, 'it looks as if you mean this stuff about consultation, but how do I know you won't say the comments you received were one thing when they were really another?' The clearest evidence, surely, for the need for a relationship approach to consultation. It is true that after a consultation exercise ministers may judge that the best course of action on a particular issue differs from the majority view that has been expressed, and may say so. But it simply would not help to misrepresent the views received. If there is sufficient doubt to question the integrity of the person summarising the comments, why not offer copies of the full set of comments for sale as bound volumes after the end of the consultation period?

We did it ourselves

Information technology is developing rapidly these days and one effect is the improved ability to develop applications cost-effectively for operations on a smaller scale than the huge databases already used by leading charities for direct mail and relationship fundraising. Running Windows office software, we made effective use of database software to maintain lists of people with whom we consulted. We used spreadsheets to analyse the results of questionnaires and advanced graphical word processors to produce consultation documents and questionnaires to a good standard of layout. We produced the final copy to go to the printer on our own laser printer. We were impressed with the ease of adaptability, and the productivity, of the products now available.

My experience has not been without its mistakes, such as entering Myles Barnett on the mailing list as Esq Miles Barnett. But a certain amount of well-judged risk-taking and innovation is necessary if opportunity is to be exploited. I am sure that the advantages of trying to adopt positive relationship principles have outweighed the cost and the errors I have made along the way.

The bottom line is that the view I formed listening to Ken's lecture in 1993 has worked well. Relationship fundraising ideas do apply, and do work, in the context of consultation. Setting out to build an effective working relationship with the community interested in the issues can help to put over a message well – though, as with relationship fundraising, success also depends on having a good story to tell and on the genuine interest and bona fides of those putting out the material.

Godfrey Jackson, when commenting on small consultative workshops (but the comment would apply equally to relationship building with the larger, general audience) in an article in *Charity News* in November 1994, said, 'If the end result is better law, we have all won'. I agree.

Voluntary and Community Division
Department of National Heritage
2–4 Cockspur Street
London SW1Y 5DH
United Kingdom

Tel: +44 (0) 171 211 2820
Fax: +44 (0) 171 211 2807

Part III:
What's next?

All change

> In 1883 it was finally agreed to introduce time zones and synchronise clocks. The date was set for November 18 of that year. For two weeks beforehand people everywhere fretted and fussed as if the country were about to be struck by an outsize meteor. Farmers worried that their hens would stop laying or that their cows would go dry. Workers in Chicago, suspecting they were to be compelled to work an extra nine minutes on the big day, threatened to strike. By the dawn of the appointed day, the nation was in a fever of uncertainty. Just before noon people everywhere began silently gathering by town halls and courthouses to watch the clocks change.
>
> Although the time change had no legal authority – it was done solely at the behest of the railways – it was introduced almost everywhere, and almost everywhere the event proved to be disappointingly anticlimactic. Millions watched as the hands on their courthouse clock were summarily advanced or moved back a few notches, then pursed their lips and returned to business as it dawned on them that that was as exciting as it was going to get.
>
> **Bill Bryson**
> *Made in America*

Most of us dislike and distrust change but accept it is inevitable. And it's not all bad. Although change can be destructive and disorientating, it can equally be positive and revitalising. The closing years of the twentieth century have underlined what most of us are instinctively aware of: change is a constant feature of our modern lives and its pace is accelerating. This applies to fundraising as much as anything. While the fundamentals remain, we have to get used to living in a state of constant change.

The pace of change in the future will probably be far, far greater than it has been up until now. If you were working in a fundraising office 25 years ago and an alien had whisked you off into outer space and then returned you to that fundraising office today you would see some changes, but basically it would be more or less the same.

However, if you left your fundraising office now, with the same alien and the same knowledge you have now, and were to come back to it in 25 years and still know where you are, I suspect you'll be in a museum.

Reasonable people, it is said, accept things the way they are, consequently all change is in the hands of the unreasonable. Fundraisers, therefore, have to be very unreasonable people. We exist to resolve the world's imperfections, not to accept its compromises.

It's up to the likes of us, surely, to keep alive the spirit of protest, for without it the human condition seems unlikely to progress. It's not that there's anything less to protest about nowadays, but the drive for change seems to be rather dormant now in most developed societies.

If people are apathetic it's up to us to change that. In many ways, I regret that my children are growing up without a sense of outrage. They won't be marching from Montgomery to Selma in Alabama. They won't be there in London's Grosvenor Square demanding an end to the Vietnam War, or chorusing 'smash the National Front' in Lincoln's Inn Fields.

And I think that's a shame. We fundraisers must want to do more than raise money. We've got to demand and encourage change. Not small change. Real change.

For fundraisers, the really important aspects of change can be divided into two parts – social change and technological change. I don't want to go into these in any great depth, but just to try to identify what changes are already happening, or are likely to happen and to flag up some of the consequences for fundraisers.

Our changing society

We have already noted that people are living longer (*see* page 116) and that this will bring significant change for fundraisers. In her book *Global Demographics: Fundraising for a New World* (Bonus Books, Chicago, 1995) Dr Judith Nichols points out that it is not only the age paradigm that is changing, but also that people are (collectively) becoming increasingly diverse. No longer, she says, will our best prospects be similar to one another, we will deal increasingly with diversity between age groups, lifestyles, interests and even ethnic/racial backgrounds.

Traditional donor groups are being outdistanced numerically by ethnic and social groups as yet unproven as a source of potential donors. The current generation of mature donors brought up before the Second World War is dying out, being rapidly replaced by a new breed of older donors with a quite different set of moral and spiritual values and much less rigid attitudes to social and political issues.

These changes are not negotiable. They are happening – now. I think they add up to a major opportunity, and a potentially rewarding challenge.

Our changing donor

It seems likely that we would be rash in the extreme to make the kind of assumptions we used to about our donors. The caricature of the little old lady of Tunbridge Wells, or wherever, will only represent one kind of future donor, perhaps one of diminishing importance. And even within our stereotypes, important differences will continue to emerge.

So the opportunity is to get closer to our donors, to get to know them better and to understand them more as individuals. The challenge will be to make our organisations much more appealing, relevant and accessible to this fresh, diverse and non-traditional donor universe.

We have to broaden our appeal as much as we can. If we don't, we face the prospect of decline, talking to fewer and fewer people. Even if we can persuade this smaller audience to part with more and more money, the end will be postponed but still inevitable. Voluntary action is not an exclusive store just for the rich. Its uniqueness is its universality, its variety, and its power is that it is action of the people. Not all the people, but a substantial chunk.

All producers have to be prepared to react to change in their markets and customers. The penalty for failure to change is obvious. But equally obvious are the rewards for those who can anticipate change.

Remember Mr Daimler the pioneering car maker. When planning for the then fledgling, but growing automobile market, Daimler estimated that the maximum size it might reach would be about 1 million, because he believed that was the maximum number of chauffeurs that society could produce. It never occurred to him that people would drive themselves, or that other than the very wealthy would ever own a car.

There are now more than 450 million automobiles in the world, and rising.

Technological change

It is well beyond my powers to attempt to understand, far less analyse, the implications and effects of all the technological change that has swept over us in recent years. I am a baby boomer, so not only was I raised before the invention of the electronic calculator, I also spent my early years in publishing in such arcane pursuits as 'casting off' copy, scaling photographs and correcting text manually by writing between lines and along margins. In this I was aided by liberal applications of liquid Tipp-Ex correcting fluid. Such was our dependence on this magic stuff that I reckon our postage bill must have halved when word processors came along, simply because the weight of tipp-exed (it even created a verb) corrections was no longer included. Somehow Tipp-Ex survived the changing world and seems to be flourishing. Perhaps Tipp-Ex has a telling case history about adapting to technological change? In Britain, despite the prevalence of word processors and spell check, each year the retail chain W H Smith sells enough correcting fluid to paint 1,700 London buses.

It's no secret that computers and desktop publishing have revolutionised business activity since then and have had a powerful effect on our social lives too. Add to that the invention of the fax machine, mobile phones, E-mail and the Internet and, perhaps, it's a misconception to say that the office of today would be recognisable to the time traveller of 25 years ago.

In 1899 Charles Duell, then head of the US Patent Office, resigned because he believed that everything that could be invented had been. Almost inevitably he was proved totally wrong the very next day.

So I subscribe to the belief that technological change is the norm. It's here to stay. In the future change may be the only certainty.

But what will our future be like?

As I've done enough crystal-ball gazing I thought I'd turn to a specialist for some insights into the likely shape of the fundraising office of the future.

So here is computer wizard John Rodd and a brief insight into a day in the life of a future fundraiser.

Abel's day – the shape of things to come

John Rodd is a specialist in information technology for charities. He is a former fundraiser (for Save the Children in the UK) and is evangelistic in championing the role of the computer in fundraising. But he believes that current practice is lagging far behind what is practically possible, particularly in terms of managing data to equip and enable the relationship fundraiser.

'Most of us are aware that technology doesn't just progress', says John, 'it rockets forward. We already live in the global information age but many people seem as yet unaware of it. The management of information, seen and unseen, permeates everything we do.'

John Rodd believes he has an answer for those who question the practicality of building a relationship simultaneously with thousands and thousands of individuals. 'The underlying technology for mass solicitation to individual donors is already around. What's missing is an expert system that will make it happen and that is constrained only by the imagination of the people in the voluntary sector and its IT suppliers.'

To illustrate his point, John has created an imaginary fundraiser and dropped him into a possible sequence of events that could happen now, or in the not too distant future, in any fundraising office anywhere in the world. With his permission, I'd like to introduce you to Abel Newman, fundraising director of the fictitious environmental charity AirWatch.

Abel is well trained, an IT-literate professional. Like most fundraisers of his day, he has become an everyday user of IT services that to him are as normal as breathing.

Let's drop in on Abel now at his home base in a leafy English country village, miles from the hurly burly of the city. (In the future no one will commute unless absolutely necessary.)

Just another day

It will be a quick planning meeting. As he waits for the video conference to begin, Abel reflects on how much things have changed in his career. Planning meetings are no longer a huge drain on time and resources – the eight regional organisers avoid travelling by each dialling into ConferenceNet for the AirWatch slot. Now Abel only has to go to London once a fortnight. Everyone at the old HQ has been out-posted, barring a few older souls and the chief executive. The fundraising department is now a virtual community. Even meetings with the advertising agency are performed three-quarters by videocon and electronic data interchange. Good on productivity, but Abel does miss those agency lunches.

In the meeting Abel and the regional organisers review forecasts and performance against targets using the financial planning and modelling tools provided by AirWatch's central computer. Figures and charts appear alongside each organiser's face on the videocon and they can all share in the general view of the team's performance.

Recently, a reorganisation of the western region used the computer's integrated geographic information system. It took just a few clicks to establish the wealth potential of the territory. Gradations of wealth, social class and other economic indicators appeared, colour coded. AirWatch's supporter base, shops and key corporate donors were overlaid on to the maps. The location of the new regional organiser, replacing one who had recently resigned, had meant revising the territory. Using the drive-time program, Abel had seen at a glance that the regional organiser could not possibly cover east Devon if she were to retain optimum performance. But, even as he thought about it, the software looked for spare resources and indicated by screen message that there was some unused capacity in the adjacent region.

In Abel's optimum performance age, regional organiser targets are based on the giving potential of the territory, not the arbitrary county divisions that charities have been using for decades. The software used, adapted from commercial field sales territory systems, allows for economic indicators such as unemployment and the demography of the region. It even compensates for known competitor activity – the opening of yet another Save the Planet shop can substantially alter the forecast income for a local branch of AirWatch.

As the video conference closes, Abel reflects on how woolly regional planning used to be. In the old days, the difficulty of obtaining timely and relevant information made it impossible to keep tabs on the activities of the people in the field. Now the computer reports each organiser's performance against target, with variances shown in detail and with projections updated – daily if necessary – to the end of the financial year. 'Flashing-red-light' reports (the screen really does flash too) have made taking corrective action easy.

A pinging from the screen alerts him to an incoming call.

'Hello, Jane here.' Jane Forward is Abel's manager of central fundraising. 'Can you look at some new ideas I want to program into AutoPers? I'd like your approval before I commit – you know how sticky the trustees can be.'

AutoPers is the latest tool from SyberSoft – a 'cybernetic', self-steering communications planner. The principle is simple – let the charity decide what to send to supporters and make the software do the work. If a supporter expresses a preference – 'only mail me at Christmas' – this is planned in. If a supporter has a known predisposition to certain work, this too is built in to the planning. The most commonly used tool, however, is the 'propensity' to respond software, which uses the supporter's previous contact and giving histories as 'drivers' (determinants) of what is sent, what it is about and when it is released.

Key to the process is the Logic Manager, which plans the communication 'tracks' and sets the crucial 'jumps'. The jump comes into plan when a supporter has responded, in which case a new track is made that takes account of that response. However, if a supporter has not responded after a defined communication sequence or time period then, by using a combined measure of time lapse, previous giving history and cause-support profile, the supporter is moved to another track.

AutoPers has changed Jane Forward's life, freeing her

from 'pulling all the selection and segmentation levers manually', as she described things under the old system. It has released time for her to do more creative fundraising.

When AutoPers is coupled to the charity's in-line, colour laser-printing and mail-finishing equipment, AirWatch can deliver perfectly individualised communications.

The delivery to supporters is determined from the system's optimised timing functions, which control the release of each supporter's letters or phone calls on a small batch basis.

But it was a hard battle to get it accepted. One trustee, a self-confessed Luddite, reacted passionately calling it, 'the software from hell – relentless, like *Reader's Digest*, logical, like a gas bill, and too damned smart, like Skynet!* '

The decision to try AutoPers had gone through only with the understanding that it would remain top secret, especially from the supporters, who quaintly believe that the personalised communications dialogue set up by AirWatch is handcrafted for them, one at a time. As the chief executive commented, 'If they ever get wind that silicon, statistical modelling and fundraising software are determining what we send them, we could be in deep trouble.'

As Abel settles to his E-mail the voice synth on his PC chimes in, 'Abel, KPIs now available. Do you want me to display now?' Key performance indicators are Abel's way of keeping control of the overall fundraising programme – his own executive information system. A bar chart appears showing campaign income. 'Not bad', he thinks, 'but I want to see if it is shops or legacy income that has caused that blip. Computer! Enhance 35 to 46 and drill down.'

The chart duly explodes, decomposing the data. 'Computer! Project all shops' income to end quarter four.' 'OK Abel, but I anticipate a 5.5 minute delay for the updates – I will call when ready.'

'Great,' mused Abel, 'it does what I say, doesn't go sick and never takes a holiday. Pity it can't make coffee too.'

Another call is coming in.

*Skynet: a reference to the self-aware computer that caused global war in the Terminator films of the 1980s.

'Abel, it's Lucinda here. I've got some people for you to call.' Lucinda Peel is AirWatch's VIP and high-level donor manager, and she doesn't let you forget it. She continues in her Knightsbridge tones, 'The interface to the gold database has traced some new donations back to some very well-placed people indeed. I think you and the chief exec should call them, say thanks and invite them to the next cultivation session. You know the form. All the data is on the E-mail file attached.'

The gold database is known internally as 'fat cats'. A wag in the IT department has created a picture of a corpulent Siamese with a diamond collar as the program icon. The gold database is the country's definitive listing of the rich. It offers sophisticated name and address matching, recognises aliases and holding companies and can cross-link the wealthy so that one door can open another. It was costly to set up but has repaid itself a thousand times over. 'OK Lucinda, I'll take the top 20 per cent and give the CEO the rest. I'll ensure that our telecons are recorded so you can have them for your follow-ups. Bye.'

The future is now

The staggering thing about Abel's day is that while it seems like science fiction all the technology described in it is already available or at least technically feasible right now. Most of it is affordable as well.

Or is this all charming but harmless fantasy? Are you preparing for the future by saying 'it will never happen to me'?

Of course some version of it will happen, and soon. But there is a need for great caution. In John Rodd's fantasy, Abel's chief executive confesses that if donors knew what they were doing with all this technology they'd be appalled.

I don't believe this need be so. Donors too want to be communicated with effectively and well. Tomorrow's donors will be much more comfortable with this technology and even some of the more conservative can be encouraged to accept the good side of technology when they can see the advantages in it for them.

But if we allow technology to come *between* us and the donor then its benefits will be temporary and superficial.

Equally, if we are insensitive or inappropriate in introducing new developments, donors will be alarmed and will seek to surround themselves and the new technology with protective legislation. And we don't want that.

Sod's Law and the machine

Sod's Law is more politely known as Murphy's Law and it states that if something can go wrong, it will. That's where the scenario so vividly promoted in Abel's day breaks down. Yes, something like it could happen, but quite possibly it won't because of Sod's Law and the fundamental flaw with machines.

Think about it for a moment from a different angle. You know and I know that machines are fundamentally straightforward. Garbage in and garbage out. Most of the problems occur when the unpredictable factor is added – the human ingredient. Machines are made by humans so can, and do, go wrong. The fundamental law of the machine is that it will break down, usually when you need it most.

You and I also know how simple and straightforward all this technology really is, yet we have to admit that it is almost impossible to run off a set of labels without something or other going wrong. There's always some bored clerk in some dusty accounts department who'll cock it up either deliberately or by accident, or simply because the glistening, highly expensive machine and the less than glamorous and underpaid operative are just not going in the same direction. And every piece of progress increases the cock-up potential. This is Sod's Law, and because of it Abel's day may never dawn.

Maybe it's just as well. Call me old-fashioned but I worry

sometimes about machines not just being cleverer than me but being cleverer than the donors too. I worry about machines coming between me and the donor. If donors might be upset by how we are using technology then things are going sadly wrong.

The future, of course, as always, is up to us – proof perhaps that you can't take the individual out of fundraising, it will always be the ultimate 'people' business.

It will be interesting to see what we make of it.

Doing without

The wonder of modern gadgetry and gimmickry is how good you feel when you do without it. This reminds me of the story of the rabbi and the poor man who lived in one small room with his wife and three children.

'I can't stand it!' wailed the man. 'What can I do?' The rabbi told him to get a dog. The dog barked at the children and messed up the floor. Then the rabbi suggested he get some hens. The dog chased the hens, which frightened the baby. 'Get a goat,' insisted the rabbi. And so on, until the rabbi added a horse and the whole thing became completely impossible. 'Now, get rid of them all,' said the rabbi, 'and tell me how you feel.' 'It's wonderful!' cried the man in gratitude. 'There's just me and the wife and the children, and we have the whole room to ourselves.'

Possibly the gadget we really need is the one that we can program to get rid of all the others.

All progress may indeed be in the hands of unreasonable people, but it seems to me that the rest of us should reserve a healthy scepticism for all changes and, supposed, advances. To underline this point in a book that starts each chapter with a pithy quote, I'll end with one.

> Advances – what advances? The number of hours women devote
> to housework has not changed since 1930, despite all the vacuum
> cleaners, washer/dryers, trash compactors, garbage disposals,

wash-and-wear fabrics. Why does it still take as long to clean the house as it did in 1930?

It's because there haven't been any advances. Yet 30,000 years ago when men were doing cave paintings at Lascaux, they worked just 20 hours a week and the rest of the time they could play, or sleep, or do whatever they wanted.

Ian Malcolm, the mathematician in Michael Crichton's *Jurassic Park*

Evidence perhaps that we have made no progress whatsoever. But I suspect that 30,000 years ago, while the men had all that time to play, sleep, or whatever, the women still had to spend just as long doing the housework. *Plus ça change.*

Future bright?

Some challenges, predictions and requests

 Everything has been said. But as no one listens, everything has to be said again.

André Gide, French philosopher

The final chapter of *Relationship Fundraising* is called 'The future'. In it I outlined some of the major problems facing fundraising and rather hesitantly attempted some crystal-ball gazing.

Most of the things I predicted have not yet come to pass and after such a short time it would be unreasonable to expect them to. However, during the past four years I have perhaps become a little more cynical and even more reluctant to try to second-guess the future. Although I'm confident that the predictions that I made then for the world of fundraising will, in time, come true.

So I've amended my plans for this final chapter of the one and only sequel from focusing on predictions to making requests. And I want to build up to these requests by outlining a number of the major challenges facing fundraisers today. These challenges are important because, as I said in the opening chapter, fundraising is a business undergoing rapid change. How we respond to these challenges will shape the future of our business and, I believe, largely determine how successful or otherwise we are as we enter the next millennium.

Millennia don't come round very often. The last time we entered a new millennium King Ethelred the Unready was sitting rather precariously on the throne of England. King Ethelred was known as the 'Unready' because he was singularly unprepared to react to the apparently rapidly changing times in which he lived.

There's a lesson for us in this, as well as a distinct sense of *déja vu*. Unready though he was, Ethelred was in fact a thousand years ahead of many present-day fundraisers who, despite the lessons of the last decade, are nowhere near ready for the changes that are coming and the staggering potential they herald.

What follows is almost certainly not comprehensive, but it includes what I believe to be the major challenges that confront fundraisers in almost every developed economy at the closing years of the twentieth century.

Challenges also inevitably represent opportunities. What we make of them is up to us.

■ We need to establish usable, comprehensive donor histories.

This means database, the keystone of relationship fundraising. The technology we need to store and access this information is already here. But fundraisers need to be quite clear about what information they absolutely need (as opposed to what might be quite nice but isn't essential and that which isn't worth the cost of inputting and storage).

The challenge here is to record the right information in the right way at the right price.

■ We need to identify the real donors.

Most people who respond to fundraising appeals are not real donors. If you analyse your supporters you'll find that up to half of those who give a single gift never give again. Of those who do make that all-important second gift fewer than half have even the potential to become committed, regular donors – real donors. We need to develop systems that will identify the real donors, the real supporters, and treat them appropriately.

At any one time up to 65 per cent of your supporter database will be out of relationship with your organisation. Many of these will be what I call responders, and not real donors. You can expend a lot of energy trying to till this infertile ground. Fundraisers need to find the real donors and devote the best of their energies to them. (When I find myself using a phrase like 'out of relationship' I think I really am spending too much time in the United States. I mean, of course, that they are either going through the renewal process, or are lapsed, or haven't given for some time. Actually, out of relationship is a pretty good description.)

Collecting the information to identify the real donors will not be difficult because donors will see it as in their own interests to provide it. Some donors are worth more than others, but all real donors are worth a lot of effort. So we're going to treat them so well they'll feel really special.

◼ We need to switch from monologue to dialogue with our real donors.

Most fundraising communication is one way. That's not what many donors want. Instead of bombarding our supporters, we need to find ways to open dialogue with them.

◼ Then we need to find practical ways of forming lasting relationships with these donors.

Not all donors will want lasting or very deep relationships with us.

Some may prefer casual and infrequent contact, and that's fine. Quite probably most will not want the same intensity that we do. That's to be expected. Our challenge will be to create the kind of environment that will make donors much more than customers, much more than passing trade. We need to find ways to encourage our donors to become friends for life.

Marketers and customers don't usually like each other. So we have to stop thinking of ourselves in this way – and change the way others see us too.

■ We also need to find practical ways to evaluate supporters over the long term – to measure and predict lifetime values.

This will not only be an invaluable guide for donor recruitment, it will also be a first step towards eliminating the blight of short-term thinking and planning in fundraising. Yet, according to research by Dr Alan Tapp of Greenwich University in the UK ('Relationship fundraising techniques in charities: are they used and do they work?' *The Journal of Database Marketing*, vol 2, no. 4 1995), only 31 per cent of the top 500 British charities attempt to keep estimates of donor lifetime values.

Sophisticated scoring systems will need to be devised to monitor donors' progress and to enable us to include predictions of future giving as well as recency, frequency and monetary value.

If suitable models can be found (they are possible now), then perhaps it won't be long before fundraising success (and fundraisers themselves) will be recognised and rewarded, not just for this month's, this quarter's, or this year's achievements, but for success in long-term development, the building of assets for the future.

■ We have to acquire new donors at acceptable cost, or find new ways to attract them.

Donors, increasingly resistant to our marketing techniques, are becoming harder and more costly to find. Most fundraisers are spending far too much on acquisition and so spend far too little on donor development. If we cannot respond to this challenge then our modern system of fundraising will, in time, become untenable.

■ We must develop an integrated approach to donor

communication by post, phone and in person.

The direct marketing ghettos – fostered mainly by direct marketing agencies – have to be destroyed. By this I mean the convention that separates postal donors from telephone donors, donors we can visit from those we can't. And different departments of the same organisation contacting donors independently for different reasons.

The challenge, of course, is to see our communications from the supporter's point of view. If we do that, inevitably, that means integration of all contact.

■ We need to identify the real competitors clamouring for our donors' attention and develop strategies to beat them.

Our competitors are not primarily other charities, universities, or schools. Nor are they trusts, companies, or museums. Instead (*see* pages 54–59), they are distrust, uncertainty, lack of comfort, inertia, fear of criticism, boredom and confusion.

■ Most crucially, we need to segment our databases effectively.

Supporters are different. They have different interests and different needs. Therefore, they should not be communicated with in the same way. The challenge is to divide our supporters into manageable groups or segments so they all receive the most appropriate communication.

■ We need to find suitable ways to use the new technology.

Not just our ever more sophisticated databases, but the flood of new media and methods for communicating with donors. Faxes, the Internet, touchtone technology, voice mail, interactive television and radio, local broadcast media: the possibilities are endless. But we mustn't overlook the basic distinction between medium and message.

■ Our donors must be given choices – so they'll tell us what they want, rather than us telling them.

Which do you think will most likely appeal to donors: if you send them what you think they want, or if you ask them first and then do what they say?

■ We have to encourage donors to give more, and more regularly.

It's as simple as that. Donors now just don't give enough. Real donors can and will give more. The challenge is to show them how.

■ We need to encourage donors away from prompted giving and on to planned giving.

That means automated banking – direct debits, bankers' orders, electronic funds transfer, autogiro, or pre-authorised checking. And it means monthly giving and legacies. It means that donors have to understand the new methods of payment and feel positive and comfortable about using them.

■ Donors should find giving by legacy irresistible.

This is the bonanza – the gift to a favourite institution or charity from the donor's estate, after the donor's death. What better way could there be to support an organisation or an ideal that you have believed in all your life?

In Britain one-third of all donated income comes from legacies, from bequests, but from a tiny, very special group of people. Less than three per cent of the population, just 13,500 people each year, leave in excess of £700 million.

Why so few?

Until very recently this income was treated by British charities as windfall income. Now fundraisers have woken up to the fact that legacies can be, and are being, directly influenced and usually by individuals who are very good at customer care.

In North America, Europe and just about everywhere, giving by legacy has not yet come close to achieving its fabulous potential.

■ We have to rewrite the typical fundraising organisation chart.

Better still, the challenge is to throw out traditional

concepts of organisation structure and come up with our own. This means moving people away from responsibility for functions such as direct marketing, or field fundraising, or trading and getting them to accept total responsibility for a group of donors. They must be donor service managers.

The idea is not new nor is it confined to charities. American Express has done it by shifting from a product management system to a customer management system. As a result, AmEx customers in future won't need to be troubled by different product managers promoting different lines, often conflictingly. Instead they'll have one point of contact looking after their entire interests.

How will fundraisers do the same? Perhaps by allocating a service manager to all donors of a certain age group, or geographical location, or area of interest, or giving level. One donor service manager may be responsible for all donors above retirement age. Another may be responsible for all lapsed and archived donors. Different structures will be appropriate to different organisations, but the key thing is to be donor-led.

Enthusiastic donor service managers then will want to show their donors how hard they are prepared to work to keep their interest and support – why not? If United Airlines can encourage their management employees to 'adopt a premium' (their top segment of customers) so they call these people at home and even arrange to meet them at the airport next time they're flying, why can't we? (Don't worry, you won't have to meet anyone at the airport.)

■ We have to give donor service managers authority and scope. And donors should know they have it.

The challenge is to give these key staff a real say in what kind of work your charity is doing and in how your programmes are run.

Finally, there is the challenge to:

■ Adapt to the requirements of new legislation.

In Britain, and I think in America, Canada, Australia and elsewhere, our legislators have their beady, critical eyes on fundraisers and fundraising. The challenge for fundraisers will be to keep as much control of the legislative process as we can. In Britain, the ICFM is very effective in defining the worst excesses of government control and other professional bodies are springing up, or have sprung up, in countries in Europe, Australasia and elsewhere where voluntary action is increasingly seen as important. But we also have to adapt our practices, to turn new legislation to our advantage.

Now for the six requests

■ Can we start now on the segmentation revolution?

It's about time. Fundraisers have always tended to treat everyone the same, and it's an expensive mistake. In 19 years of writing fundraising copy it was only recently that someone asked me to write a different letter for the men and the women – yet men and women are totally different when it comes to giving. In fact some believe that while men conservatively give to preserve the *status quo*, women give to effect change.

Yet most fundraisers write to men and women in exactly the same way.

Again, until recently no one had ever asked me to write differently for older donors, or younger donors, even though we all know that older donors are motivated by quite different beliefs and values than younger donors. Also, many donors give as a couple. Yet how many fundraisers recognise this when they write to their donors?

So please can we segment far more in the near future – by sex, by age, by couples, but most of all by choice? Let's ask donors how they want to hear from us, when they want to hear and what they want to hear about. It will mean major change.

We will have to move on from the two principal methods

of segmentation we rather imperfectly employ now. Not-for-profit marketers will have to move on to level three.

Of course, this depends on having a very flexible and accessible database and the detailed institutional memory to put in it. Database is the major preoccupation for fundraisers everywhere right now, even if few have got it right yet.

Fundraisers represent an important market opportunity for database suppliers. Please can we make sure that the power of our collective voice proves that necessity is indeed the mother of invention?

■ Let's make individual donor development strategies the norm, not the exception.

The days of the conveyor belt, where every supporter gets the same message, are over for good.

So let's make sure that in the near future individual supporters, donors, or groups of donors have their own communications strategies charting all postal, phone and face-to-face contact throughout the year and its effect on relationship development.

Let's treat supporters with specific interests or enthusiasms to an annual cycle of communications that will reflect and develop those interests and enthusiasms.

Catalogue purchasers, magazine subscribers, monthly donors, bequest pledgers, donors who want a close relationship, donors who wish to hear just once a year, donors who specify interest in a particular part or parts of your work, supporters who have recently visited your facilities – all these special groups, and more, demand and deserve their own tailor-made schedule of communications. So let's give it to them.

Then perhaps real segmentation will not be a case of 19, or 25, or however many, tiny adjustments to the same letter. Let's put real care into what we say to donors and how we say it – in 19, or 25, or however many, separate, individual letters.

■ Please, let's get much better at customer service.

I suspect Myles Barnett, Agnes Holliday, Rebecca Brown, Dora Smith and Camilla Cole would all have something to say about supporter service. Most major not-for-profits are clearly not very good at customer service. But there are signs that they are getting better.

I hope we'll all get much better. Customer helplines, specially trained staff equipped to deal with supporters' needs and desires, policies for thanking and welcoming people, friendly reception areas, strategies for encouraging complaints and for responding to them effectively – these will be bread and butter to fundraisers in the near future.

We'll develop a new culture of customer service so that dealing with us will be a real pleasure. Why should profit-oriented companies such as Marks & Spencer and the Co-operative Bank have better developed cultures of customer service than we do?

My plea is that providing ever more efficient customer service should become a preoccupation, if not an obsession, for fundraisers.

■ Please, can we be sure we always believe in what we say?

In the heyday of direct marketing, fundraising copy suffered through the direct-response imperative overriding everything else. We were told that the most important component of fundraising direct mail was the list. Then came the offer. Then after these two, a long way behind, came the format. Last of all came what we said – the copy – way down the list in terms of its importance and its effect on results.

Now I believe that copy (ie in its widest sense – the words and images we use to convey our message) can come out of the closet and regain its rightful place.

The messages we present in words and pictures really matter to donors.

Copy, I predict, will regain its glory.

And I hope that as a result fundraisers will be a little more careful about some of the things they say to donors.

■ Please let's come up with a flood of creative responses to the challenge of providing a range of products and propositions for the new-old – the grey market.

This has been described as the biggest marketing opportunity of this or the next decade, the growth of the 50-plus market, our best donors.

– There will be many more of them.

– They'll have far more money

– They'll have much more time on their hands.

Increasingly, this group will be joined by the baby boomers. The flowers of the sixties, now getting on a bit. I should know, I'm one of them.

How will this once idealistic but later materialistic and morally ambiguous generation behave as they reach prime donating age?

That's the challenge of the new-old. Success will come to those who can coincide with this group's interest – and fundraisers can, at many levels.

■ Please, let's co-operate, we fundraisers, on areas of mutual interest, not just in our own countries, but internationally.

It is crazy for fundraisers not to work together in areas where individually they can never have the impact necessary to bring about real change. These include the centralised promotion of tangible giving methods, fundraising propositions such as monthly giving and legacies, and the status and achievements of fundraising.

Unity is strength. For too long fundraisers have been divided, and divided they have had very little voice.

So let's co-operate on subjects concerning legislation, on campaigning issues such as the status of fundraising, on recruitment into the fundraising profession, and on the centralised promotion not of intangibles such as charitable giving but of tangible propositions such as the monthly giving concept. And, as I said in chapter 5, and probably several times elsewhere, most importantly the charitable legacy, the bequest.

Centralised legacy promotion could open up the biggest potential bonanza in fundraising of all time.

These issues are hugely important for fundraisers and are central to any meaningful concept of relationship fundraising.

Bloopers

Now to close this chapter and this book, I am going to leave you with a final plea.

I lecture at many seminars and workshops for fundraisers around the world and I'm always grateful for the fact that English has become the universal language of fundraising, for I am fairly restricted in anything else. And I am always hugely impressed at the ability of other people to listen to and to contribute in English when it is not their native language.

But, not surprisingly, they will sometimes have difficulty, as all who are brave enough to use a foreign language will inevitably have found. This difficulty has given rise to what are known as 'bloopers' – phrases or sayings that arise from an innocent misuse of the English language. Bloopers can often be funny, sometimes are a little risqué perhaps, and sometimes can be quite profound.

An example of a blooper is the sign on the wall in a hotel in Athens, which informed guests that,

> Visitors are expected to complain at the office between the hours of 9 and 11 am daily.

Or the notice in the rooms of a Japanese hotel that said,

> You are invited to take advantage of the chambermaid.

Laundries and dry-cleaners suffer from the problem of bloopers particularly. For example, the rather ambiguous sign in a Bangkok dry-cleaners that invited patrons to,

> Drop your trousers here for best results.

And similarly in a Rome laundry a notice informed patrons,

> Ladies. Leave your clothes here and spend the afternoon having a good time.

But I was particularly struck by the appropriateness of one blooper that appeared on the wall in the reception of a hotel in Paris. The sign simply said,

> Please leave your values at the front desk.

I believe we have a tremendous responsibility as fundraisers and direct marketers in this rapidly changing world. Of course, we must take advantage of all that modern technology and marketing methodology have to offer. But please, let's not forget that our supporters are people, that we are a service industry and we will not prosper if we cannot firmly put our customers needs and interests first. That's what relationship fundraising means.

Donors are only donors because they care. Supporters only support you because they care. They need to believe you care too. They need to see not just your passion but also your values coming shining through in everything you say, write and do.

The work we do in our various organisations in our various countries around the world is important. The work we do as direct contacts with our supporters, our public, is important.

We should set an example. We should have a moral role. We should be crusaders, not bureaucrats, or flashy sales people. Let's change the world. Someone should. Let's change the world, even if it's just in the way we write to, and talk to and think about people.

Because if we all treated each other just a bit better maybe that really would change the world. After all, that's what fundraisers are here to do.

So, as you embark on your very, very important mission, please don't leave your values at the front desk.

Appendices

Introduction to the questionnaires

I have used the three questionaires that follow in various seminars and workshops to involve participants and encourage them to think about their own approach to donor development. And that's why they are included here.

Some people take these questionnaires terribly seriously and get worked up if they think they have not answered as they should. Please don't worry. I hope you will find them useful and thought-provoking but really they are just a bit of fun.

As with so many things in life there are few absolutely right or wrong answers. At the end I have given what I think is a reasonably fair scoring system so that if you wish you can add up your score and see how well or otherwise you have done. No answers or scores are given for questionnaire 2 because it is based on your interpretation of what a typical donor would choose – and all donors are different.

Good luck!

Appendix I

Questionnaire – how donor-friendly are you?

1. How often do you write to your donors?

   (a) Every month.
   (b) Four times each year.
   (c) Three times each year.
   (d) Twice each year.
   (e) Whenever you have a good reason to write.

   Answer..........   Score..........

2. Do you thank donors...

   (a) For every gift?
   (b) For gifts over a certain value?
   (c) Only when asked?
   (d) Never?

   Answer..........   Score..........

3. Do you give your donors the chance to increase or reduce the number of letters they receive from you...

   (a) With every communication?
   (b) At regular intervals?
   (c) Never?

   Answer..........   Score..........

4. When did you last meet with some of your donors?

   (a) Last month.
   (b) Last year.
   (c) Never.

   Answer..........   Score..........

5. How often do you organise donor receptions, open days, or meetings?

   (a) Monthly.
   (b) Quarterly.

(c) Annually.

(d) Never.

Answer..........   Score..........

6. When do you consider a donor to be a lapsed donor?

(a) Eighteen months after the last gift.

(b) Two years after the last gift.

(c) Three years after the last gift.

(d) When the Post Office tells you (gone-aways).

Answer..........   Score..........

7. How do you welcome new donors?

(a) By special letter/welcome pack.

(b) With a special programme of communications during their first year.

(c) By letter, but with a phone call to major donors.

(d) With just a preprinted receipt.

(e) No specific welcome or acknowledgement.

Answer..........   Score..........

8. Do you encourage donors to complain?

(a) Yes.

(b) No.

Answer..........   Score..........

9. On average, how quickly does your organisation respond to a donor's request or gift?

(a) Within one to three days.

(b) Within two weeks.

(c) Within a month.

(d) Longer.

Answer..........   Score..........

10. If a donor requested information from you in large print would you...

    (a) Send it?
    (b) Ignore the request and send your normal material?
    (c) Apologise and send nothing?

    Answer...........   Score..........

11. How do you react when you receive a £250 gift from a donor?

    (a) Write a personal thank you letter?
    (b) Telephone immediately, or that evening.
    (c) Offer to visit.
    (d) Nothing special.

    Answer..........   Score..........

12. Do you personalise your letters to donors...

    (a) Every time?
    (b) From time to time?
    (c) When tests show that it pays?
    (d) Never?
    (e) Only to high-value donors?

    Answer..........   Score..........

13. Different people respond to different things. Do you...

    (a) Segment your file by size of recent gift only?
    (b) Write individual tailor-made letters to each donor?
    (c) Send the same letter to all your donors?
    (d) Send a different letter to each group or type of donor?

    Answer..........   Score..........

14. Some supporters cannot afford to give as much, or as regularly as others. Do you...

    (a) Position the cost of, say, scheme membership low enough so as not to exclude anyone?
    (b) Offer different levels and frequency to different groups?

(c) Leave it to donors to decide?

(d) Have no pricing policy?

Answer.......... Score..........

15. What proportion of your donors have only given once?

(a) 20 per cent.

(b) 50 per cent.

(c) 80 per cent.

(d) Don't know exactly.

Answer.......... Score..........

16. Reception, switchboard, legacy administration and the postroom are...

(a) Not part of fundraising's responsibility.

(b) Key parts of fundraising.

Answer.......... Score..........

17. What research have you done among your donors?

(a) Qualitative only.

(b) Quantitative only.

(c) Both qualitative and quantitative.

(d) None (what do qualitative and quantitative mean?)

Answer.......... Score..........

TOTAL SCORE..........

Suggested scores

How donor-friendly are you?

Question 1: (a) 2, (b) 2, (c) 2, (d) 2, (e) 4. Question 2: (a) 4, (b) 2, (c) 1, (d) −2. Question 3: (a) 4, (b) 3, (c) 0. Question 4: (a) 4, (b) 3, (c) 0. Question 5: (a) 3, (b) 3, (c) 3, (d) 0. Question 6: (a) 3, (b) 2, (c) 1, (d) 0. Question 7: (a) 3, (b) 4, (c) 3, (d) 0, (e) 0. Question 8: (a) 2, (b) 0. Question 9: (a) 4, (b) 3, (c) 2, (d) 1. Question 10: (a) 4, (b) −2, (c) 0. Question 11: (a) 2, (b) 3, (c) 3, (d) 0. Question 12: (a) 3, (b) 3, (c) 2, (d) 1, (e) 2. Question 13: (a) 2, (b) 4, (c) 0, (d) 3. Question 14: (a) 1, (b) 3, (c) 1, (d) 0. Question 15: (a) 2, (b) 2, (c) 2, (d) 0. Question 16: (a) 0, (b) 3. Question 17: (a) 2, (b) 2, (c) 3, (d) 0.

Maximum score 57

Appendix 2

Questionnaire: a donor's view of your communications

We all know the importance of research. So if you want to find out how good, or otherwise, your publications and other communications are what better way than to ask your donors?

How good are you at putting yourself in your donors' shoes? Imagine you have now made the 90-degree shift in perspective. 'The Organisation' referred to is *your* organisation. So please answer the following questions as if *you* were the donor.

1. You support a number of national and local charities. How often would you *wish* to hear from The Organisation?

   (a) More than once each month.
   (b) Every month.
   (c) Four times each year.
   (d) Three times each year.
   (e) Twice each year.
   (f) Whenever The Organisation has a good reason to write.

2. Do you receive material from The Organisation...

   (a) Much too often?
   (b) Too often?
   (c) About right?
   (d) Not often enough?
   (e) Far too rarely?

3. You would like to *choose* how often you hear from the charities you support. Does The Organisation...

   (a) Always give you this option?
   (b) Sometimes give you this option?
   (c) Never give you any choice?

4. You dislike being treated like a number. How would you evaluate the individuality of the communications you receive from The Organisation?

(a) Obviously computer-driven.
(b) Reassuringly personal.
(c) Something in between.
(d) Always covered with strings of computer numbers.

5. Which of the following statements best describes your relationship with The Organisation?

(a) Close.
(b) Superficial.
(c) One-sided.
(d) Involving.
(e) Purely financial.

6. You prefer not to be constantly asked for money. Evaluate The Organisation's communications in terms of balance.

(a) Always asking for money.
(b) Usually asking for money.
(c) Well-balanced communications.
(d) 'If I get another appeal from them I'll scream!'

7. How welcome were you made to feel as a new donor?

(a) A lovely special letter and welcome pack.
(b) Just a preprinted receipt.
(c) A special phone call from the director.
(d) Immediately asked for more money.

8. How do you think The Organisation would react if you were to complain?

(a) Do everything possible to answer my query.
(b) Make me feel a nuisance.

9. Your eyesight is getting bad. How easy to read are The Organisation's letters?

(a) Very easy.
(b) Sometimes easy, sometimes not.
(c) Very difficult.

10. How easy is it to complete The Organisation's reply forms?

(a) Very easy.

(b) Sometimes easy, sometimes not.

(c) Very difficult.

11. You appreciate and respond to exciting and readable materials. How do you rate The Organisation's productions?

(a) Terrific, an inspiration.

(b) I really can't remember.

(c) Insipid and boring.

(d) Always asking for money.

(e) Other...

12. You have telephoned The Organisation asking for two more lots of raffle tickets, but no more mailings on Cambodia and to be sure not to send your Christmas catalogue before July. Your reception was...

(a) Friendly and helpful?

(b) Frankly confusing?

(c) Uninterested and unhelpful?

(d) So pleasant you feel really good about The Organisation?

Appendix 3

Questionnaire – how reader-friendly are your publications?

1. Who in your organisation is responsible for publications?

   (a) The chief executive.
   (b) The chief executive's secretary.
   (c) The head of fundraising.
   (d) A publications sub-committee.
   (e) The editor.
   (f) No one.
   (g) Someone else..

   Answer..........   *Score*..........

2. Is there a clear copy approval system?

   (a) Yes.
   (b) No.

   Answer..........   *Score*..........

3. The contents are decided by...

   (a) The board?
   (b) The chief executive?
   (c) An editorial panel?
   (d) The editor?
   (e) The readers?
   (f) Whoever sends anything in?

   Answer..........   *Score*..........

4. You circulate the proposed contents and structure...

   (a) More than two months before publication?
   (b) One to two months before?
   (c) The week before publication?
   (d) Never?

   Answer..........   *Score*..........

5. Your regular publication comes out...

   (a) Always on time?

(b)   Occasionally a little late?
(c)   Sometimes very late?
(d)   Always late?

      Answer..........   *Score*..........

6.   Your publications are...

(a)   Just the right length?
(b)   Too long and wordy?
(c)   Too short and cramped?
(d)   Inconsistent?

      Answer..........   *Score*..........

7.   You research your readers' opinions and attitudes...

(a)   Regularly and well?
(b)   Occasionally?
(c)   Never?
(d)   Badly?

      Answer..........   *Score*..........

8.   The publication is designed by...

(a)   An in-house graphic designer?
(b)   An outside graphic designer?
(c)   The chief executive?
(d)   The chief executive's secretary?
(e)   The editor?
(f)   The printer?
(g)   No one in particular?

      Answer..........   *Score*..........

9.   Applicants to join your organisation are...

(a)   Proudly sent your publications?
(b)   Sent the annual report with some embarrassment?
(c)   Sent nothing – 'We don't want to put anyone off!'

      Answer..........   *Score*..........

10. Your board's view of your organisation's publications is...

    (a) A necessary evil?
    (b) A complete waste of money?
    (c) A vital part of your organisation's public image?
    (d) They don't know they exist?

    Answer..........   Score..........

11. Your budget for photography is...

    (a) Just adequate?
    (b) More than 25 per cent of all costs?
    (c) Less than 10 per cent of all costs?
    (d) 'What budget?'

    Answer..........   Score..........

12. Which of the following are trained in how to use your publications?

    (a) All relevant staff, including switchboard and the regions.
    (b) Head office staff only.
    (c) Just those who produce the publications.
    (d) 'What training?'

    Answer..........   Score..........

TOTAL SCORE..........

Suggested scores
How reader-friendly are your publications?
Question 1: (a) 1, (b) 1, (c) 3, (d) 2, (e) 3, (f) 0, (g) 1. *Question 2:* (a) 3, (b) 0. *Question 3:* (a) 0, (b) 0, (c) 2, (d) 3, (e) 4, (f) 1. *Question 4:* (a) 3, (b) 3, (c) −1, (d) −1. *Question 5:* (a) 3, (b) 2, (c) 1, (d) 0. *Question 6:* (a) 3, (b) 1, (c) 1, (d) 1. *Question 7:* (a) 3, (b) 1, (c) 0, (d) 0. *Question 8:* (a) 3, (b) 3, (c) 0, (d) 0, (e) 0, (f) 0, (g) 0. *Question 9:* (a) 3, (b) 1, (c) 0. *Question 10:* (a) 0, (b) 0, (c) 3, (d) 0. *Question 11:* (a) 1, (b) 3, (c) 2, (d) 0. *Question 12:* (a) 3, (b) 2, (c) 1, (d) 0.
Maximum score 37

Appendix 4
The International Fund Raising Group
Fundraising for a better world

The International Fund Raising Group is an independent
non-profit organisation promoting fundraising worldwide.
It was founded in 1981 to establish a forum for fundraisers
from various countries to come together, exchange ideas and
learn from each other. The result was the first ever gathering
of fundraisers in Europe for the first International Fund
Raising Workshop held at Noordwijkerhout in the
Netherlands in October 1981. Some 50 delegates participated
from Europe and the USA. The 1980s saw a constant growth
of this event with more delegates attending from more
countries each year.

The first workshop in a developing country took place in
India in 1989. The success of that event as well as the quick
growth globally of the voluntary sector led to the launching
of IFRG's worldwide programme in 1993, bringing annual
workshops on fundraising to Africa, Asia, Latin America
and Eastern Europe. The financial support of 10 major
international donor agencies made this programme possible.
In 1996 11 workshops were scheduled, one each in Central
America, South America, West Africa, East Africa, Southern
Africa, the Middle East, South Asia, South East Asia, East
Asia, Central and Eastern Europe and, of course, the 16th
International Fund Raising Workshop, in Holland. In
addition a detailed handbook on fundraising has been
produced, written particularly for the needs of fundraisers
in developing countries. And to complement the workshops
a series of in-depth training courses in specific aspects of
fundraising has been prepared, which can be run jointly by
IFRG and local trainers almost anywhere in the world.

For 10 years IFRG functioned on a purely voluntary basis.
The growth of its work meant the establishment in 1991 of a
permanent secretariat in London, which now consists of five

staff headed by chief executive Per Stenbeck, formerly head of fundraising at Radda Barnen, Sweden's Save the Children. IFRG's voluntary board of directors is elected on a three-year basis. Currently there are seven members of this board from five different countries. They and the staff are assisted in programme formulation and promotion by an advisory board, which includes representatives from Austria, Belgium, Canada, Denmark, France, Germany, the Netherlands, Sweden, Switzerland and the USA.

The International Fund Raising Group
295 Kennington Road
London SE11 4QE
United Kingdom

Tel: +44 (0) 171 587 0287
Fax: +44 (0) 171 582 4335
E-mail for the International Fund Raising Workshop: gen.ifrg@dial.pipex.com
E-mail for the worldwide programme: wwp.ifrg@dial.pipex.com

Index

A promise from
The White Lion Press

You will have gathered from this book that the author is committed to many of the most important principles in fundraising: mutual benefit, honesty, openness, accountability and the value of a long-term relationship. The White Lion Press is equally committed to these principles. We would like to start our relationship with you on the best possible basis to ensure that it will develop into a long and mutually beneficial association. So here is our promise to you, and our offer.

Books by The White Lion Press will repay your investment many times over – and you'll enjoy reading them too. But if your purchase is damaged in any way or if you feel any of our products do not live up to your expectations simply return them to us and we will issue you with a full refund, including any reasonable associated costs. We'll ask you to tell us why, so we can put right anything that might be wrong, but we won't quibble. Unfortunately we can only offer this if you bought the book directly from us or from one of our recognised distributors, but even if you didn't, please let us know your problem and we'll do all we can to ensure your supplier matches our commitment to you. After all, you are our ultimate customer.

This guarantee applies to any books or videos you may purchase from us. We further promise to handle your orders with speed, efficiency and impressive politeness.

If you wish to make an order, please detach or photocopy the following order form. We endeavour to despatch faxed orders within 24 hours, so fax is fastest.

If you have any query at all regarding any books published by The White Lion Press please telephone Fay Buller or Mike Kerry on +44 (0)171 490 4939 or fax us on +44 (0)171 490 3126.

YOU CAN ORDER THESE WHITE LION TITLES TODAY

Asking Properly: the Art of Creative Fundraising. By George Smith.
ISBN 0-9518971-1-X

You will never read a book quite like this. George Smith tears open the conventional wisdom of fundraising creativity and so changes the rules for an entire trade. This book is irreverent, funny, savagely critical and genuinely inspiring, often on the same page.

Asking Properly is almost certainly the most authoritative book ever written about the creative aspects of fundraising. It is likely to remain a key text for years to come.

The author offers a profound analysis of donor motivation and is critical of the extent to which charities take their supporters for granted. But this book is no mere commentary on current practice – it offers a comprehensive checklist on how to optimise the creative presentation of the fundraising message. How to write, design, use direct mail, press advertising, broadcast media and the telephone, how to think in terms of fundraising products… the whole gallery of creativity and media is surveyed and assessed, with hundreds of examples of fundraising campaigns from around the world illustrating the need to 'ask properly'.

This book will prove invaluable to anyone involved in the fundraising process. It is provocative, entertaining and, above all, highly instructive. Read it, apply its lessons and it must enable you raise more money.

Relationship Fundraising: a Donor-based Approach to the Business of Raising Money.
By Ken Burnett.
ISBN 0-9518971-0-1

The voluntary organisations that depend on fundraising represent a vigorous, fast-growing and surprisingly substantial business sector. In recent years the often counter-productive amateurism of the past has given way to professionalism in strategy, materials and approach from fundraisers.

But dangers and pitfalls lurk among the benefits of modern marketing methods. *Relationship Fundraising* identifies and defines these risks and describes a donor-based approach that is not only more appropriate but is more likely to be successful for both the fundraiser and the donor.

First published in 1992, this is the classic textbook of donor development. Now an international best seller *Relationship Fundraising* has been sold in more than 35 countries worldwide. The comments opposite give just a taste of the enthusiastic praise this seminal book has received.

'Culturally revolutionary...'
John Rodd, ICFM's *Computers in Fundraising*, UK

'...a different mood has swept through the fundraising world.'
Tom Smith, *Teach Yourself Fundraising*, UK

'Burnett... has provided a new framework for thinking about fundraising strategy.'
Rob Paton, Open University, in *The Journal of Nonprofit and Voluntary Sector Marketing*, vol 1 no 1, UK

'This book is the fundraiser's bible.'
Conrad Lauritsen, Stroëde AB, Sweden

'I have bought many, many books about fundraising. This is the best.'
Michael Roelen, International Physicians for the Prevention of Nuclear War, Germany

'...it will revolutionise the way in which development officers treat their donors and prospects.'
Dr Judith E Nichols, CFRE, author and consultant, USA

'...every page I turn leaves me wanting more and, hey presto, I always find it.'
Stewart Crocker, fundraising director, Children's Aid Direct, UK

Friends for Life video series

A series of half-hour videos from the *Friends for Life* sessions featuring Ken Burnett in Vancouver, Canada in July 1996. Filmed by Canada's Knowledge Network and produced jointly by Harvey McKinnon & Associates and The White Lion Press, the series will be available early in 1997. Please tick the box on the order form overleaf if you would like to receive further information.

Please send me the following titles:

No of copies	Title	Price*	Post & packing†	Total
_____	*Relationship Fundraising*	£21.00	£_____	£_____
_____	*Friends for Life*	£28.50	£_____	£_____
_____	*Asking Properly*	£28.50	£_____	£_____
			Total remittance £_____	

Please send me information on the *Friends for Life* video series, featuring Ken Burnett ☐

*If you order any two titles from this list you will be entitled to a 10 per cent discount on the retail price of each book. Orders of three copies or more will entitle you to a 20 per cent discount. (NB these offers only apply to orders placed directly with the publisher.) †For postage and packing **UK mainland** please add £3.00 per copy. **All other countries** please add £3.50 per copy. Books will be despatched by first class post (UK mainland) or surface mail (overseas). Please contact us for overseas airmail costs.

I enclose a cheque for £_____ payable to The White Lion Press Ltd

Please bill my organisation at the address below ☐

Please debit my Visa/AmEx/Mastercard

Number ☐☐☐☐☐☐☐☐☐☐☐☐☐☐☐☐   Expiry date _____

Signature _____

Your name _____

Organisation _____

Your position _____

Address _____

_____

_____

Postcode _____   Telephone _____

Fax _____   E-mail _____

Please return to The White Lion Press Limited, White Lion Court, 7 Garrett Street, London EC1Y 0TY. Tel: +44 (0) 171 490 4939 Fax: +44 (0) 171 490 3126.